Lecture Notes of the Institute for Computer Sciences, Social Informatics and Telecommunications Engineering 474

The LNICST series publishes ICST's conferences, symposia and workshops.

LNICST reports state-of-the-art results in areas related to the scope of the Institute. The type of material published includes

- Proceedings (published in time for the respective event)
- Other edited monographs (such as project reports or invited volumes)

LNICST topics span the following areas:

- General Computer Science
- E-Economy
- E-Medicine
- Knowledge Management
- Multimedia
- Operations, Management and Policy
- Social Informatics
- Systems

Yuanlong Cao · Xun Shao
Editors

Mobile Networks and Management

12th EAI International Conference, MONAMI 2022
Virtual Event, October 29–31, 2022
Proceedings

 Springer

Editors
Yuanlong Cao (iD)
Jiangxi Normal University
Nanchang, China

Xun Shao (iD)
Toyohashi University of Technology
Toyohashi, Japan

ISSN 1867-8211 ISSN 1867-822X (electronic)
Lecture Notes of the Institute for Computer Sciences, Social Informatics
and Telecommunications Engineering
ISBN 978-3-031-32442-0 ISBN 978-3-031-32443-7 (eBook)
https://doi.org/10.1007/978-3-031-32443-7

This Springer imprint is published by the registered company Springer Nature Switzerland AG
The registered company address is: Gewerbestrasse 11, 6330 Cham, Switzerland

Preface

We are delighted to introduce the proceedings of the twelfth edition of the 2022 European Alliance for Innovation (EAI) International Conference on Mobile Networks and Management (MONAMI). This conference brought together researchers, industry professionals and practitioners from around the world to share recent advances and research results on mobile networks and management technologies. The theme of MONAMI 2022 was *"Emerging Mobile Network and Management Technologies for Future Sustainable and Intelligent Internet Ecosystems"*.

The technical program of MONAMI 2022 consisted of 31 full papers. The conference tracks were: Track 1 – Innovative Artificial Intelligence Applications for Smart Cities; Track 2 - The New Era of Computer Networks using Machine Learning; Track 3 - Advanced Technologies in Edge and Fog Computing; Track 4 - Emerging Technologies in Mobile Networks and Management; and Track 5 - Recent advances in Communications and Computing. Aside from the high quality technical paper presentations, the technical program also featured three keynote speeches and one technical workshop. The three keynote speakers were Shuiguang Deng from Zhejiang University (China), Celimuge Wu from University of Electro-Communications (Japan), and Xin Luo from Chongqing Institute of Green and Intelligent Technology, Chinese Academy of Sciences.

The workshop organized was the Innovative Defense Technologies in 5G and Beyond Wireless Networks Using Machine Learning (IDT5GML). This workshop aimed to provide a platform for researchers, academics and industry professionals to present their research work on machine learning in 5G and beyond network security, with the goal of addressing network threats using novel machine learning-based technology.

Coordination with the steering chairs, Imrich Chlamtac and Jiankun Hu, was essential for the success of the conference. We sincerely appreciate their constant support and guidance. It was also a great pleasure to work with such an excellent organizing committee team, we thank them for their hard work in organizing and supporting the conference. In particular, the Technical Program Committee, led by our TPC Co-chairs, Wei Quan, Qiang Guan, Soufiene Djahel, Cunhua Pan and Jinshan Zeng, who completed the peer-review of the technical papers and made a high-quality technical program. We are also grateful to Conference Manager, Ivana Bujdakova, for her support, and all the authors who submitted their papers to the MONAMI 2022 conference and workshop.

We strongly believe that the MONAMI conference provides provide an interdisciplinary platform for all researchers, developers and practitioners to discuss and disseminate the latest innovative mobile network solutions. We also expect that future MONAMI conferences will be as successful and stimulating, as indicated by the contributions presented in this volume.

Yuanlong Cao
Xun Shao

Organization

Steering Committee

Imrich Chlamtac	Bruno Kessler Professor, University of Trento, Italy
Xun Shao	Kitami Institute of Technology, Japan
Jiankun Hu	University of New South Wales at Australian Defense Force Academy, Australia
Yuanlong Cao	Jiangxi Normal University, China

Organizing Committee

General Chair

Zhiyong Feng	Tianjin University, China

General Co-chairs

Xun Shao	Kitami Institute of Technology, Japan
Yuanlong Cao	Jiangxi Normal University, China

TPC Chairs

Yuanlong Cao	Jiangxi Normal University, China
Xun Shao	Kitami Institute of Technology, Japan

TPC Co-chairs

Wei Quan	Beijing Jiaotong University, China
Qiang Guan	Kent State University, USA
Soufiene Djahel	Manchester Metropolitan University, UK
Cunhua Pan	Southeast University, China
Jinshan Zeng	Jiangxi Normal University, China

Sponsorship and Exhibits Chair

Linghong Zhu   China Unicom, China

Local Chairs

Gang Lei   Jiangxi Normal University, China
Su Yao   Tsinghua University, China

Workshops Chair

Shuai Zhao   University of York, UK

Publicity and Social Media Chairs

Gaurav Dhiman   Bikram College of Commerce, India
Yeonseung Ryu   Myongji University, Korea
Taras Maksymyuk   Lviv Polytechnic National University, Ukraine
Yuping Lai   Beijing University of Posts and
                                      Telecommunications, China

Publications Chair

Yulei Wu   University of Exeter, UK

Web Chair

Jianmao Xiao   Jiangxi Normal University, China

Posters and PhD Track Chair

Longzhe Han   Nanchang Institute of Technology, China

Panels Chair

Lei Liu   Xidian University, China

Demos Chair

Dan Tang   Hunan University, China

Tutorials Chair

Yugen Yi   Jiangxi Normal University, China

Technical Program Committee

Jiyan Wu   Advanced Digital Sciences Center, Singapore
Meifang Shen   Talend Inc., USA
Chenxi Huang   Ximen University, China
Shujie Yang   Beijing University of Posts and
                                  Telecommunications, China
Yingjie Wang   Yantai University, China
Runze Hu   Tsinghua University, China
Mu Wang   Tsinghua University, China
Zhenzhen Luo   Jiangxi Normal University, China
Tiehua Zhang   Ant Group, China
Hongyue Wu   Tianjin University, China
Hao Hao   Shandong Academy of Sciences, China
Xiaoling Gui   Jiangxi Normal University, China
Xingyan Chen   Southwestern University of Finance and
                                  Economics, China
Kai Peng   Huaqiao University, China
Binbin Huang   Hangzhou Dianzi University, China
Dong Qin   Nanchang University, China
Xinping Rao   Xidian University, China
Xin Huang   Tongji University, China
Yongbin Liu   University of South China, China
Chenjun Xu   Wuhan University, China
Libo Feng   Yunnan University, China
Wei Yang   Jiangxi Normal University, China
Wei Zhou   Shenyang Aerospace University, China
Jianzhong Wang   Northeast Normal University, China

Contents

Edge Computing and Fog Computing

Mobile Networks and Management

Network Communications and Computing

Artificial Intelligence Applications for Smart Cities

Research of Electronic Medical Record System Based on Blockchain

Lizhou Deng[1], Teng Long[1], Yuan Wang[1(✉)], Jianmao Xiao[1], and Li Fang[2]

[1] School of Software, Jiangxi Normal University, Nanchang 330022, Jiangxi, China
jxnuss@jxnu.edu.cn
[2] Ji'an Central Hospital, Ji'an 343000, Jiangxi, China

Abstract. The traditional medical record system is stored in the hospital side, which is not convenient for data sharing and transmission between hospitals; Patients can see the medical records data, therefore it is challenging to maintain patient privacy. Based on this, a disaster-tolerant Alliance blockchain is used to construct a distributed electronic medical record system that includes a peer-to-peer (P2P) network with mutually lengthy links and improved Practical Byzantine Fault Tolerance (I-PBFT). The system encourages medical data exchange and sharing, makes the flow of medical data transparent to patients, and transfers ownership of medical records back to patients, turning medical data into a valuable data asset for patients.

Keywords: Alliance Blockchain · P2P · Consensus Plugin · Medical Records Systems

1 Introduction

The amount of medical data has significantly increased with the growth of the medical business, particularly under the effect of COVID-19, making administration and preservation of medical data particularly crucial. Due to the importance of medical records as a source of data, several hospitals have developed electronic health records (EHR) for administration. The large volume and variety of medical record data are of great value to the diagnosis of patients' conditions and to the analysis and research of hospitals [1].

On the one hand, the disparate standards and file formats used by each hospital's electronic medical record system, along with the centralized storage approach, make it challenging to efficiently transmit medical record data between hospitals in today's Internet of Everything. In contrast, patients as users are fully unaware of how their personal medical information is used, which makes it challenging to protect its privacy and increases the danger of data shipping. Therefore, it is required to research a medical record system with secure storage, simple distributed storage sharing, and privacy protection in order to overcome these issues.

The blockchain technology can meet all these requirements at the same time. It was proposed in 2008 with features such as distributed storage and tamper-proof protection

Y. Cao and X. Shao (Eds.): MONAMI 2022, LNICST 474, pp. 3–17, 2023.
https://doi.org/10.1007/978-3-031-32443-7_1

[2], and has received a lot of attention and application worldwide for more than 10 years [3, 4]. Moreover, The state has given blockchain a lot of attention, and it is now part of the national information development plan [5], which has caused extensive research. Blockchain can be broken down into three main types based on application scenarios: public blockchain, private blockchain, and alliance chain.

The public blockchain is the most decentralized, and its typical applications are represented by bitcoin and Ethereum. Free from the control of any third party, each participant on the Internet (i.e., the nodes involved in consensus) is free to join as well as exit the blockchain network and to read the data records on the chain and participate in transactions as they wish. The fact that its operation is not controlled by a third party affects its use in the entity's organization. A small number of entities or people, whose access to data is constrained by organizational rules, govern and initiate consensus on private blockchains. Private chains are better suited for internal institutional use because of their rigorous access restrictions, despite the fact that transactions and consensus take less time. A stakeholder alliance can be formed in an alliance chain, which is a structure between public and private chains. The vetted nodes in the alliance have the power to fight for consensus ideas. Each participant in the chain is authorized to join the network. Obviously, the alliance chain is more suitable for transactions between different entities [6, 7]. Blockchain-based electronic medical record systems provide distributed storage to facilitate the sharing of shared medical record data, and their consensus mechanisms protect data privacy [8]. The electronic medical record system is designed with an Alliance chain structure and requires regulated data access, node addition and deletion, and other actions between patients and other hospitals.

A storage structure combining Merkle trees and directed acyclic graphs (DAG) is used to ensure the security of medical record storage, and a consensus mechanism using blockchain is used to protect the privacy of patient medical data. We have built a distributed medical record system using the Alliance chain to facilitate sharing among hospitals.

Building a disaster-tolerant de-primary node Alliance chain, building a peer-to-peer (P2P) network based on the T-io framework, designing distributed storage based on Merkle and DAG, and improving the Practical Byzantine Fault Tolerance (PBFT) consensus plugin are some of the main contributions made in this paper.

Organization. The remainder of the paper is organized as follows. Section 1 is an overview of this paper, and the related work is described in Sect. 2. Section 3 describes the paper's overall framework and main contribution. Section 4 briefly introduced a distributed storage design based on Merkle and DAG. We introduced P2P network based on the T-io framework in Sect. 5. Section 6 we propose I-PBFT consensus algorithm based on PBFT. The simulation experiment setup and results are presented in Sect. 7. Finally, in Sect. 8, we summarize the conclusion and future work.

2   Related Work

2.1   Blockchain Electronic Medical Records

The main goal of medical data platforms is to make it easier for doctors and patients to use and share data, including querying data on patients' symptoms, tests, and medications.

However, each platform currently has its own set of standards for collecting data, which are mostly fragmented, heterogeneous, and semi-structured, and these imperfect data add to the burden of integrators [7].

As blockchain technology advances, its study and use in the healthcare industry are gradually growing. Yang et al. [8] designed a blockchain-based EHR system to prevent data tampering and misuse by tracking all events that occur in the database. Dagher et al. [9] proposed a medical record system framework that gives ownership and control of the EHR to the data owner and uses multiple smart contracts to protect data privacy, and provide a secure and reliable medical record access process for patients and institutions. Wang et al. [10] proposed a blockchain-based EHR sharing approach with searchable symmetric encryption to improve privacy leakage and control issues during medical record sharing. Zhang et al. [1] implemented a dual-chain form of storage for medical record data, using a combination of attribute encryption and multi-keyword encryption to achieve accurate retrieval of data, to anonymously implement data sharing between different groups and achieve traceability. In May 2020, XENIRO on a mobile web edge server [11] will be released. It is based on the development of SnapScale, a platform for medical image data interaction with patient-centric access control and trusted storage for data sharing, the use of AI algorithms to perform auxiliary diagnosis on image data, and the encryption of the diagnosis results on the chain.

2.2 Consensus Plugin

The well researched consensus technique is employed in distributed environments to ensure that nodes concur to confirm the system state. Bitcoin system adopts the whole network consensus method based on proofs of work (referred to as POW [12]), which can resist the double spend attack under a certain probability.

However, POW algorithm has some problems such as low throughput and high resource consumption. A series of advanced protocols have emerged, such as proof of stack (referred to as POS [13]), which improves throughput and reduces resource consumption. So, resource concentration will affect fairness.

In addition, pease et al. Consider the fault tolerance of the system. The famous Byzantine fault tolerance (BFT) algorithm is proposed, but it has the problems of excessive network overhead and high resource occupation. Castro et al. [14, 15] first proposed PBFT algorithm can meet the tolerance of no more than 1/3 of Byzantine nodes and is adopted by fabric 0.6 project under Linux foundation. The PBFT method does, however, have a performance issue. A number of enhanced algorithms have been put forth by researchers to decrease communication costs and increase election security.

In the alliance blockchain, it is necessary to consider the existence of Byzantine nodes and the number of nodes is controllable, PBFT consensus algorithm is more appropriate. In PBFT algorithm, the block proposal node is always the main node. If the main node is not updated for a long time, other nodes cannot get the opportunity to be elected as the main node to obtain system incentive, which has a certain centralization risk and is not conducive to the long-term operation of the alliance system. Moreover, with the increase of the number of nodes, the PBFT communication overhead increases Huge [16].

To sum up, the PBFT method has to be improved to increase the reliability of master node selection, optimize the consensus procedure, decrease communication cost, and decrease the algorithm's temporal complexity. In this study, a distributed electronic medical record system has been constructed based on a disaster-tolerant alliance chain.

3 Overall Framework

The data layer, persistence layer, network layer, and consensus layer are the four primary divisions of the distributed electronic medical record system based on blockchain. The data center, business service layer, data access layer, and business model layer are the divisions that can be made from the standpoint of system development, and Fig. 1 depicts the entire system architectural diagram.

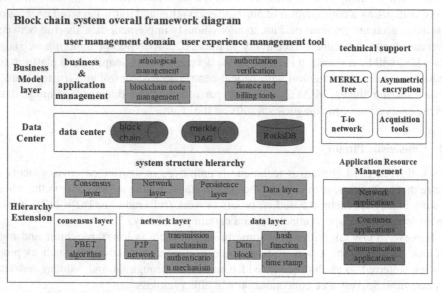

Fig. 1. Overall system architecture of the electronic medical record system

As shown in Fig. 1, the blockchain perspective includes the data layer, the persistence layer, the network layer, and the consensus layer.

- **Data Layer.** Consists of Data Blocks, Chained Structures, Hash Functions, Merkle Trees, Asymmetric Encryption, and Timestamps.
- **Persistence Layer.** The data for the project is primarily stored in this layer. The hospital node server information and log information of this project are primarily stored in the relational database MySQL since MySQL is lightweight and open source, making it easier to handle the node server information by utilizing MySQL. Among the additional essential data held on RocksDB are blockchain and medical record data, with the latter having been segmented and hashed for security.
- **Network Layer.** T-io network framework serves as the foundation for the network layer. T-io uses a network infrastructure called Asynchronous Blocking IO (AIO),

which has good translation performance. T-io is thought to utilize system resources more effectively in a network with many long connections and also includes grouping features, making it ideal for federated chains.
- **Consensus Layer.** The PBFT consensus plugin, a more effective consensus algorithm that is well suited for the establishment of the Alliance chain, was selected as the consensus layer. And in this project, we have improved this algorithm.

In addition, from a system architecture perspective, the specific layers of the system correspond to the following.

(1) **Business Model Layer:** Corresponds to the entity of each table in the database.
(2) **Data Access Layer:** It is used to access the database, operate the database and realize the persistence of data.
(3) **Business Service Layer:** The business service layer references the corresponding DAO database operations, encapsulates the requests of the representation layer, and each request is encapsulated as a method of the Service class; and the layer provides the corresponding interface for the Rest (Controller) layer to call.
(4) **Data Center:** Refers to the database and file system.

4 Distributed Storage Design Based on Merkle and Dag

This paper uses distributed storage technology in conjunction with blockchain to store data because of the importance and privacy of medical data. More specifically, Merkle and DAG are paired to swiftly delete duplicate data by the same hash value in order to reduce storage space, utilize hash ID to uniquely identify the content of a data block against tampering, and slice a whole data into numerous blocks. Assembling data can be done using the Kademlia (KAD) method, while downloading data can be done concurrently with the aid of hash addressing and downloading.

4.1 Storage Structure of Merkle and DAG

- **Storage method.** The file is divided into several pieces, and the hashing of each piece produces a distinct ID that can be quickly recognized and de-duplicated in the storage network. In order to maximize transmission efficiency, a block is typically kept in several copies on various network nodes.
- **Content Addressing Method.** Because each block has a distinct ID, you only need the node's ID to find the corresponding block. The Data Block holds the hash values of the files, while the Merkle Tree, also known as a Hash Tree, is a hash-based data structure in which the hash values are mostly kept. A concatenated Hash string of a node's associated children makes up a non-child node.

4.2   KAD Addressing Algorithm

The Kademlia (KAD) algorithm, which provides a decentralized file query system, is primarily a distributed hash table (DHT) based on an XOR distance algorithm. KAD uses both node hash and object hash addressing and uses XOR to determine the distance between hashes. The XOR (specificity or operation by ratio) technique is used to determine how far apart the keys are from one another.

The P2P node is the leaf node at the end of the 160-level binary tree created by KAD, and each node's location in the tree is determined by its 160-bit node hash. Whether a node is in the left or right sub tree of the tree is determined by the two potential values of each bit (0 or 1).

The KAD algorithm in our medical record system distributes data blocks with various hashes to nearby network nodes determined by XOR for the purpose of distributed storage. We just need to download the block data from the associated network node when requesting the file using the KAD technique, which is based on Merkle and DAG as well as the Hash value of each block. Finally, just verify that the data is complete and finish stitching. The blockchain data structure, Block, is designed as Table 1.

Table 1. Blockchain data structure

type or value	name
blockHeader	BlockHeader
blockBody	BlockBody
hash	String
calculateHash()	blockHeader.toString() + blockBody.toString()

4.3   Storage Design Implementation

The creation of the blockchain's most fundamental data structure serves as the foundation for implementing the data layer storage function. After unifying the data structure, by building the SpringBoot development framework, we construct the medical data storage function based on three technologies: the blockchain, relational databases, Merkle and DAG. Block, the blockchain's data structure, is created as follows.

5 The P2P Network Based on T-io Framework

We will use P2P network architecture to construct the blockchain network layer based on the data privacy and node correlation of the blockchain electronic medical record system presented in this study. We suggest that while choosing nodes for a P2P network, hospitals and medical research facilities should be considered. According to the alliance chain conceptual design, the P2P network system will chose or choose a trusted node as a manager to create an alliance chain, and this trusted node will be responsible for doing a lot of management tasks. To maintain the integrity of the entire P2P network, new nodes may be added and existing nodes may be removed. The trusted node connects to each configuration node it finds in the database when the P2P network is launched. A node officially enters the P2P network and begins connecting other nodes once it has been successfully joined by a trusted node. The trustworthy node will determine if a node is invalid and restrict it from connecting to the P2P network if it is unable to connect. After that, until the failed node is linked to the trusted node, the trusted node frequently makes connection requests to the failed node.

5.1 P2P Network Characteristics of Applicable Alliance Chain Based on T-io Architecture

The P2P network uses the T-io framework, which is based on the AIO design, to accommodate the prolonged connection and separation times between each node in this medical record system. The performance is excellent, resource consumption is modest, and group function is maintained when maintaining a high number of heartbeat packets across long connections. SaaS platforms with several alliance chains are therefore especially well suited for it. In this project, each node serves as both a client and a server. It will link to additional $N-1$ nodes if it serves as a server. If the server is a client, it is connected to other $N-1$ nodes. Every time you wish to send a message, create a Group in the same federation chain and call the send Group method directly.

The Fig. 2 shows the flow of the application layer enabling the kernel process to the kernel and returning a response. When there are many lengthy connections, the performance is good, the server's total resource usage is very low, and the grouping function is there. This makes it ideal for P2P network alliance chains. When the assigned resources are used up, any process in the network can use the AIO technique to directly request resources from other processes without the use of an event pool or resource monitoring. As a result, sustaining heartbeat packets with a lot of lengthy connections has good performance and a tiny resource footprint.

5.2 P2P Network Nodes Distributed Storage——KAD Algorithm

Based on KAD algorithm, we set a 160bit ID identifier for network nodes. In the algorithm, each node joining the network will be assigned a 160bit node ID (node ID), which is randomly generated. The key/value pair data is simultaneously stored on the nodes whose ID value is closest to the key value.

In light of this, XOR processing can be used to calculate the logical distance between Kademlia-based network nodes. An ID's key is associated with a data structure that

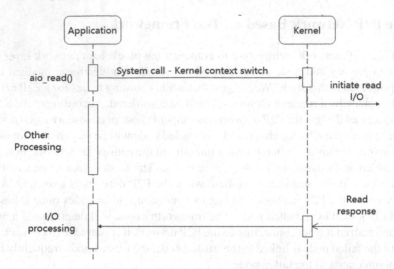

Fig. 2. AIO asynchronous non-blocking I/O mode adopted by T-io

resembles a binary tree. The n level of the binary tree corresponds to the NTH bit. A 1 or a 0 is processed for this bit, with the left subtree receiving the result. In the end, an ID binary tree is created.

Every item has a distinct binary ID, and the ID XOR operation reflects the bit differences in the ID. The ultimate difference outcome is more heavily influenced by the bits the higher they are. A binary tree is created if all of these IDs are stacked, with the highest bits on top and the lowest bits at the bottom, with the lower bits all on the same branch. The difference between the leaves (the ends of the branches) of the tree is represented by the difference between the IDs.

When dealing with 160bit network node ID, the storage space can reach 21 60. Therefore, binary tree splitting is carried out. For route queries, the tree is broken up into numerous smaller trees that are stored on each node. For each 0 5 i 5 160, each node stores some node information within the range [2i, 2i + 1), which is composed of some data lists. The information in each of these lists is kept in chronological order according to the most recent time it was seen, with the most recent information at the head and the latest information at the tail of each K-bucket. There are no more than K data items in each bucket.

When you initially start, the entire ID digital region is often contained in just one K-bucket. When detected a node, we calculate the distance from ourselves and add it to the existing corresponding K-bucket:

Algorithm 1: K bucket.

Input: a new node $node_i$;

    K - bucket;

Output: K *-bucket;*

1.   **if** K *- bucket is not full* **then**
2.   Add $node_i$ to the end of K — *bucket;*
3.   **else if** *K-bucket is full and the K — bucket contains* $node_i$ then
4.   the *K-bucket* splits downward *node branch direction* until it is no longer
        separable (i.e., i=0);
5.   **else**
6.   take out the earliest inserted node and start Ping Node again;
7.   **if** *there is no response* **then**
8.   delete the node and add $node_i$ to the end of K *-bucket;*
9.   **end**
10. **end**

In order to guarantee that searches eventually converge, KAD tries to store as many "nodes closer to it" routing designs as it can. The P2P network is successfully completed without the involvement of the central node to finish the address search as a result of our innovative usage of binary tree ID storage in the absence of a central server in the address operation after splitting into k-buckets.

6   De -Masternode Federation Chain Technology Based on I-PBFT Algorithm

6.1   I-PBFT Algorithm Without Elections

Because the federation chain itself exists in a trusted environment, any node can generate blocks and broadcast over the entire network, so the standard PBFT technique is enhanced without picking the leader in this study. Other nodes enter the preparation state after receiving a Block request and check the format, hash, and signature. They move into the prepare state and full network broadcast state after the verification is successful. When the accumulated number of Prepare for each node is greater than $2f + 1$ (f is the tolerable number of Byzantine nodes), the system enters the COMMIT state and broadcasts the status throughout the network. Each node believes it has reached consensus and adds the Block to the Block chain before executing the SQL statement in the Block when the Commit number it has accumulated is more than $2f + 1$ (f is the number of tolerable Byzantine nodes). The Leader is eliminated, resulting in a speedier and less resource demanding algorithm overall. For the I-PBFT algorithm, the process is as follows:

1   A node 1 in the network broadcasts the transaction requested by the client to the whole network. All nodes except node 1 hash and broadcast across the network.
2   Each node performs a hash calculation and broadcasts to the entire network.

3 Assuming that a node receives $2f$ (f is the tolerable number of Byzantine nodes) hash equal to itself sent by other nodes, commit to the whole network.

4 If a node receives $2f + 1$ (f is the tolerable number of Byzantine nodes) commit messages (including itself), it can submit a new block to the local blockchain and state database.

Every node is equivalent and performs better. Three phases make up the I-PBFT consensus algorithm without elections: the voting queue, the submission queue, and the consensus algorithm. The following diagram illustrates how each stage is implemented in pseudo-code. Naturally, the method will save the hash set of the node's confirmed status during the voting phase, i.e., whether the node broadcast a commit permit or deny message.

After each node in the commit queue algorithm receives more than $2f + 1$ commit messages from different nodes (including itself), the block is considered to have reached a committed state and persisted to the blockchain database. The algorithms of voting, submitting and consensus are described as algorithm 2, 3 and 4 respectively.

Algorithm 2: voting algorithm

Input: *voteMsg* : voting queue;

      hash : hash value of confirmed state (possibly null);

      VoteMsgtemp : 1;

      key : key value in *voteMsg* ;

      number : the block number of the vote that has been received;

1.   *voteMsg.get(hash)* ;

2.   **if** *voteMsg is null* **then**

3.   *voteMsg.put(hash, voteMsg)* ;

4.   **else**

5.   **for** *VoteMsgtemp* : *voteMsg* **do**

6.   **if** *VoteMsgtemp.IP* $=$ *voteMsg.IP* **then**

7.   return;

8.   end

9.   **end**

10. **for** key : VoteMsg, keySet(1) **do**

11.   **if** hash $=$ key **then**

12.   continue;

13.   **end**

14.   **if** voteMsg.get(key).getNumber() < number **then**

15.   continue;

16.   **end**

17. **end**

Algorithm 3: submitting algorithm

      preMsgQueue : submitting queue;

          voteMsg : voting queue;

          hash : hash value of confirmed state (possibly null);

          VoteMsgtemp : 1;

          key : key value in *voteMsg* ;

          number : the block number of the vote that has been received;

1.   *preMsgQueue* arrive;
2.   *voteMsg* arrive;
3.   *hash* = *voteMsg* .getHash();
4.   **if** *voteMsg is null* **then**
5.   *voteMsg.put*(*hash, voteMsg*) ;
6.   **else**
7.   **for** *VoteMsgtemp* : *voteMsg* **do**
8.   **if** *VoteMsgtemp.IP* == *voteMsg.IP* **then**
9.   return;
10.   **end**
11.   **end**
12.   **for** key : VoteMsg, keySet **do**
13.   **if** *hash* == *key* then
14.   continue;
15.   **end**
16.   **if** *voteMsg.get*(*key*).*getNumber*() < *number* **then**
17.   continue;
18.   **end**
19. **end**

Algorithm 4: consensus algorithm

Input: *key* : key value in *voteMsg* ;

Output: *blockHashes* ;

1. List <BlockHash> *blockHashes* = get(*key*);
2. Map <String, Integer> map=new HashMap<>();
3. **for** BlockHash blockHash: *blockHashes* **do**
4.   String hash= *blockHashes.getHash*() ;
5.   map.merge(hash,1,(a,b)->a+b);
6. **end**
7. String hash=getMaxKey(map);
8. Return *blockHashes* ;

7 Experimental Performance and Simulation Analysis

This article evaluated the system, rapid link, and LAN Fabric in the local LAN environment. The following diagram illustrates the precise evaluation environment and configuration: Three nodes, a CPU with four 2.0 GHz cores, eight gigabytes of RAM, and CentOS 7.2 make up the configuration.

The transaction throughput of the Blockchain network serves as the performance efficiency evaluation index for Blockchain. The maximum number of transactions that may be performed in a given amount of time is known as transaction throughput:

1) Suppose N_t is the number of transactions sent in the statistical time and N_b is the number of transactions recorded on the block in the statistical time, and the transactions are randomly generated by a transaction generator with adjustable frequency to satisfy N_t controllability.
2) When measuring the transaction throughput, random transactions are concurrently generated at a certain rate. The transaction generation rate is continuously increased until N_t is greater than N_b, and the configuration parameters of the piezometric system at this time are recorded, which are the optimal piezometric parameters.
3) According to the optimal pressure testing parameters, the blockchain system is stress tested for several times, and the number of transactions recorded on the block per unit time is recorded and averaged, which is the transaction throughput. Transaction throughput is mainly tested on one metric: invoking contract TPS, TPS can be expressed as Eq. (1).

$$TPS = transactions/\Delta t \tag{1}$$

where transactions is the number included in the blockchain over a period of time. And Δ_t is the recording time, which is generally an integer multiple of the block generation time. The TPS comparison is shown as Table 2 (Fig. 3).

Table 2. TPS Comparison

	chain	Fabric	I-PBFT
TPS (pen/sec)	*388*	1368.7	1599.6

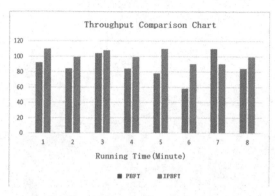

Fig. 3. Throughput Comparison Chart

Using the transaction confirmation rate as the evaluation metric, we compare the operational efficacy of the PBFT consensus mechanism and the I-PBFT consensus mechanism proposed in this paper. We also test the performance differences between the two algorithms under various ratios of false nodes to total nodes and under various running times. The outline is depicted in Fig. 4.

Figure 5 shows the change of transaction confirmation rate of PBFT and I-PBFT over a long period of time.

With PBFT and its derivate consensus processes, there is a communication barrier between nodes that must be overcome. In the new PBFT, the check-pointing protocol does not call for additional communication because the Leader election mechanism has been eliminated, and the system starts up quickly or has fewer error nodes. On the other hand, this decreases the volume of data while also reducing the view switching protocol

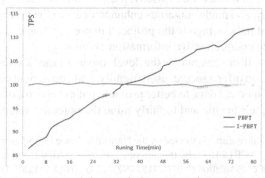

Fig. 4. Comparison of changes in Long-term throughput rate Chart

calls in scenarios where there are more error nodes. The graph compares the volume of data sent between nodes. The system duration is plotted on the horizontal axis, while the number of P2P communications with complexity O(n2) needed to construct a block is plotted on the vertical axis.

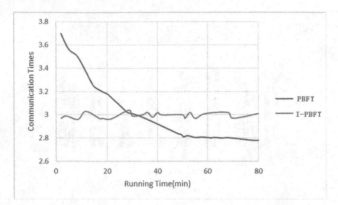

Fig. 5. Comparison of changes in Construct block per unit time rate Chart

8   Conclusion

Electronic medical record systems have demonstrated a tendency toward patient-centeredness in recent years with the promotion and deployment of cloud computing and big data technologies, where patients have more authority over their own medical records. In accordance with this paradigm, people maintain their medical records on cloud servers and selectively share medical information through controlled access with physicians or other third-party providers.

The development of blockchain technology has made decentralized data storage possible. Referring to various well-known blockchain systems including Bitcoin, IPFS, and Ethereum, this system has taken a year. At the same time, we customized the blockchain system for the storing of medical data, discovered more blockchain applications through exploration and study, and made numerous enhancements to the system as it stood at the time. The distributed data storage is the project's major challenge, and few papers and Internet sites provide comprehensive information about it.

In the future, we will concentrate on the development of medical data and transaction security mechanisms to offer a secure, user-friendly, and convenient environment for the value co-creation of medical data, to better promote patient control of their medical data and to promote people's health, and to fairly mine the potential value of medical data.

Acknowledgment. This research is funded by the Natural Science Foundation of Jiangxi Province under Grant No. 20192ACBL21031, by the Science and Technology Research Project of Jiangxi Provincial Department of Education (No. GJJ181492), by the Higher Education Research Project on Educational Reform in Jiangxi Province (No. JXJG19221).

Data Availability. The data, including block and performance indicators in the experiments, used to support the findings of this study are available from the corresponding author upon request.

Conflicts of Interest. The authors declare that they have no conflicts of interest.

References

1. Zhang, L., Zheng, Z.Y., Yuan, Y.: A controllable sharing model for electronic health records based on blockchain. Acta Automatica Sinica **47**(9), 2143–2153 (2021)
2. Nakamoto, S.: Bitcoin: A Peer-to-Peer Electronic Cash System. http://www.bitcoin.org/bitcoin.pdf (2008)
3. Kang, J., Xiong, Z., Niyato, D., Ye, D., Kim, D.I., Zhao, J.: Toward secure blockchain-enabled internet of vehicles: optimizing consensus management using reputation and contract theory. IEEE Trans. Veh. Technol. **68**(3), 2906–2920 (2019)
4. Dinh, T.T.A., Liu, R., Zhang, M., Chen, G., Ooi, B.C., Wang, J.: Untangling blockchain: a data processing view of blockchain systems. IEEE Trans. Knowl. Data Eng. **30**(7), 1366–1385 (2018)
5. Wu, M., Wang, K., Cai, X., Guo, S., Guo, M., Rong, C.: A comprehensive survey of blockchain: from theory to IoT applications and beyond. IEEE Internet Things **6**(5), 8114–8154 (2019)
6. Mao, H.-Y., Nie, T.-Z., Shen, D.-R., Yu, G., Xu, S.-C., He, G.-Y.: Survey on key techniques and development of blockchain as a service platform. Comput. Sci. **48**(11), 4–11 (2021)
7. Jacob, F., Mittag, J., Hartenstein, H.: A security analysis of theemerging p2p-based personal cloud platform Maidsafe. In: 2015 IEEE Trustcom/BigDataSE/ISPA, Helsinki, pp. 1403–1410 (2015)
8. Liu, J., Li, X., Ye, L., et al.: BPDS: a blockchain based privacy-preserving data sharing for electronic medical records. In: GLOBE-COM 2018 IEEE Global Communications Conference. IEEE (2018)
9. Dagher, G.G., Mohler, J., Milojkovic, M., et al.: Ancile: Privacy-preserving framework for access control and interoperability of electronic health records using blockchain technology. Sustain. Cities Soc. **39**, 283–297 (2018)
10. Wang, S., Zhang, D., Zhang, Y.: Blockchain-based personal health records sharing scheme with data integrity verifiable. IEEE Access **07**, 102887–102901 (2019)
11. Chuang, I.H., Chiang, S.H., Chao, W.C., et al.: A hierarchical blockchain-based data service platform in MEC environments. In: ACM 2nd International Conference on Blockchain Technology, 12–13 Mar 2020, pp. 95–99. Association for Computing Machinery, Hilo, USA (2020)
12. Jakobsson, M., Juels, A.: Proofs of work and bread puddingprotocols. In: Ifip Tc6/tc11 Joint Working Conference on Secure Information Networks: Communications & Multimedia Security Kluwer, B.V. (1999)
13. King, S., Nadal, S.: PPCoin: Peer-to-Peer Crypto-Currency with Proof-of-Stake (2012)
14. Castro, M., Liskov, B.: Practical byzantine fault tolerance and proactive recovery. ACM Trans. Comput. Syst. **20**(4), 398–461 (2002)
15. Xu, G., Liu, Y., Khan, P.W.: Improvement of the DPoS consensus mechanism in blockchain based on vague sets. IEEE Trans. Industr. Inf. **16**(06), 4252–4259 (2019)
16. Qian, W.N., Shao, Q.F., Zhu, Y.C., Jin, C.Q., Zhou, A.Y.: Research problems and methods in blockchain and trusted data management. J. Softw. **29**(1), 150–159 (2018). (in Chinese)

Consortium Blockchain-Based Student Status Management Framework

Jinxi Yang, Jianmao Xiao(✉), Jiangyu Wang, Yujie Liu, Wei Yang,
Zuoyi Liao, and Qiangqiang Zhou

School of Software, Jiangxi Normal University, Nanchang 330027, China
{jm_xiao,yw,qiang}@jxnu.edu.cn

Abstract. Student status management has always been an indispensable part of the education system, but due to the insufficient application of information technology, there are still a series of pain points in the traditional student status management system, such as easy to falsify student status, serious information islanding, and complex management. Blockchain 3.0 is a consortium blockchain model that uses protocols and consensus mechanisms for property rights confirmation, measurement and storage, with the characteristics of decentralization, immutability, traceability, collective maintenance, security and reliability, etc., which puts forward excellent solutions for student status management. This paper uses the thinking mode and framework of the blockchain to improve the logic and storage mode of the previous student status management system, and uses the Fabric consortium blockchain framework to design and realize a student status management system that can be initially put into use. Test results show that the throughput of the student status chain system can be stabilized at 200tps, which can basically meet the actual application needs of the student status management system.

Keywords: Blockchain · Student status management · Smart contract · Education · Consortium Blockchain

1 Introduction

Student status is a symbol of determining the identity of students, which is closely related to students' right to education, and is also used as an important basis for the certification of social talents, which continues to receive widespread attention from all walks of life [1,2]. Within colleges and universities, student status management needs efficient, convenient and safe management system support. At the social level, student status certification is an important evaluation criterion for employers to evaluate talents, which needs true, reliable and rich talent education background data information. As an integral part of the operation of society, the student registration system still has a lot of room for demand and the need to build a solid foundation.

Y. Cao and X. Shao (Eds.): MONAMI 2022, LNICST 474, pp. 18–31, 2023.
https://doi.org/10.1007/978-3-031-32443-7_2

At the level of student status management, most schools in China currently rely on the student information network, and some schools use their own independent student status management system. In this management model, many problems have cropped up, such as mading irreparable mistakes in student status because of the management negligence, which eventually leads to students being unable to graduate normally, been compromised and attacked on account of database intrusions, resulting in the collapse of the student status management system and malicious tampering of data, and high load on the student status management system during the opening and graduation seasons give rise to system congestion. These problems have hindered the functioning of society and need to be addressed urgently [2].

When conducting academic certification, in addition to referring to CHSI, most companies often spend a lot of money and time to entrust back-adjustment companies to find out the authenticity of personal information, which reflects the current problem that the academic certification body is still not enough to win enough trust. Therefore, it is also important to create a student certification platform that can build a high level of trust in society. As an emerging data management method with decentralization, transparency, security and strong confidentiality, blockchain technology has pointed out a new path for student status management [3] Zhong-Zhen Li et al. [4] have already proposed the idea of using blockchain technology for student status management in 2019, this work mainly uses the consortium blockchain smart contract technology and blockchain storage method to manage and store the student status, this paper improves on this basis, deepens the advantages of the smart contract using the blockchain, improves the closedness of the student status management, and introduces and designs a student status management depository framework based on the consortium blockchain, which can be used to help solve a series of problems such as poor sharing of student status information between universities, excessive reliance on third-party authoritative institutions for information credibility, excessive data storage, inconsistent award recognition, and low information security. The main features of the framework are as follows: by linking universities within the alliance chain, the problem of information islands between multiple universities is solved, and the migration of student registrations between schools is facilitated. In addition, the using of the blockchains mart contract scheme can quickly generates the student status early warning scheme, and in the form of deploying smart contracts within the organizational nodes established by each university, uses the consensus mechanism [5] to reach an award consensus among the universities. The contributions of this paper are as follows:

- We proposed the student status management and storage model under the framework of blockchain, providing a brand new solution for the pain point of the traditional student status information management and storage.
- We deepened the application scope and thinking of smart contract, analyzes the network and storage architecture of Fabric, and broadens the application approach of blockchain.

– We tested the performance of the system under normal running state and analyzed the change of system throughput with nodes.

2 Related Work

2.1 Blockchain

Blockchain technology is a collection of distributed ledgers, cryptography, consensus algorithms and a series of technologies [6], first has been known as the core technology of the Bitcoin system, although mining and speculation and other behaviors violate the core values of society, resulting in a large waste of resources, but the blockchain technology has entered the 3.0 era as a great innovation, and successfully "out of the circle" [7]. It has put forward new challenges and opportunities for all walks of life, and China has also proposed a large number of incentives for the development of blockchain. At present, many domestic and foreign research has made great progress in the application of blockchain, for example, Abeyratne et al. [8] proposes to use blockchain to provide a highly trusted, transparent, collectively maintained ledger for the supply chain information platform, and provide traceability for it. Christidis K et al. [9] combines blockchain with the Internet of Things to achieve service sharing through the core concept of P2P. Hou H et al. [10] proposed that blockchain combines e-government to increase information sharing and transparency. Moreover, many ideas and researches have emerged on the cross-application of blockchain transactions, blockchain currency, blockchain insurance, blockchain news verification and other fields [11].

2.2 Blockchain Education

The transparency of the blockchain system and the immutable data are fully applicable to the credit management of students, further education and employment, academics, qualification certificates, industry-university cooperation, etc., and have important value for the healthy development of education and employment. The application of blockchain education has been carried out in many countries for a long time: Kazakhstan built a blockchain kindergarten platform to reduce the opacity of kindergarten information and provide more objective choices for parents. South Korea's Pohang University of Science and Technology led the development of blockchain knowledge sharing platform to break down communication barriers between schools. MIT MediaLLab issued blockchain certificates to more than 100 students, ensuring that the pilot student's student status was immutable [12]. On the basis of foreign research results, a series of studies on blockchain student status have been carried out in China [13]. The current domestic existing a lot of research about student status block chain, By indexing CNKI with student status and blockchain as keywords, we found that there were 21 related papers published in the past 18 to 22 years, but most of the research stayed at the level of feasibility analysis and theoretical research, and most of the research only focused on the decentralization and security of the blockchain, and did not use the blockchain system to make landmark innovations in the logic and form of student status management, nor did it actually consider the development details and specific needs. Therefore, this paper uses the technology of the consortium blockchain, builded a blockchain platform for the union of universities, through the adjustment of the consensus mechanism and the use mode of smart contracts, establish a consensus on awards and mutual recognition of student status among universities [14].

3   Overall Architecture and System Implementation

This paper is based on Fabric's school registration system framework logic as shown in the Fig. 1.

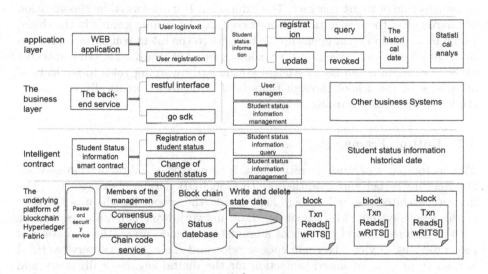

Fig. 1. system framework

The overall system architecture can be divided into surface layer and bottom layer according to the depth. The surface layer is composed of application layer, service layer and smart contract, and the bottom layer is supported by fabric network and storage technology.

3.1   Surface Frame

Application Layer. The application layer mainly includes the user's registration login, the tracing query of the student's educational background information, the administrator's query and management of the student's information, which is edited by the JavaScript and Vue framework to realize the interactive page, deployed on the server by using the Nginx technology, and provides the operating interface of the information in the chain to the vast nodes.

Business Layer. As the front-end and back-end interaction service, the service layer transfers the parameters to the web end by calling the Restful interface, realizes the interaction with the blockchain bottom layer including the smart contract through Fabric-Go-SDK, and calls the invoke function in the smart contract to operate the data. When the system is in operation, the front end will pass in parameters and request to call the smart contract. When the rules of the smart contract are effective, the data will be transmitted to the bottom layer for processing.

Contract Layer. The smart contract layer is the key technology of the alliance chain and the core innovation of the blockchain student status system [15]. The smart contract layer has two functions: award mutual recognition and student status early warning. The principle of award mutual recognition is based on the consensus rule of smart contract. The Education Bureau forms the classification of awards after the recognition of smart contract by issuing awards in the chain, which to a certain extent opens up the barriers to the talent comparison between different schools and prevents some malicious fraud of awards. The student status early warning function issues student status early warning rules to students of all grades of the school through the school node to automatically realize the student status early warning judgment.

3.2   Bottom Frame

The bottom layer of student status chain is composed of Fabric bottom network architecture kernel and blockchain with CouchDB database storage [16]. The network architecture and storage logic inside the school log chain is the core of the whole system. The school log chain network layer is mainly responsible for the endorsement of the school administrator node users, the operation of the consensus service, the chain code service and the encryption service. HSM is used to provide advanced protection for the digital key. Node discovery and data broadcasting are realized through Gossip, node communication is realized through channel, and the application function is realized through the interaction between the service layer and the application layer. At the same time, the CouchDB database directly supported by Fabric is connected inside and outside the student status chain to store huge student data, and the student data contained in the ledger is saved to the database with faster speed in a similar way to the merkle tree storage. Meanwhile, the high support of CouchDB for rich query is utilized to efficiently use the database storage space and enhance the query efficiency of data.

Network Architecture. The network architecture of the student status chain mainly includes a client node for interaction between the school node user and the student status chain, a CA node for verifying identity information, a Peer node for processing smart contracts, maintaining student information, and processing student requests and responses, and an Orederer node for receiving, packaging, sorting and generating student status information blocks and broadcasting [17]. Nodes communicate with each other through channels to ensure data security. The network architecture model of student status chain node as shown in the Fig. 2.

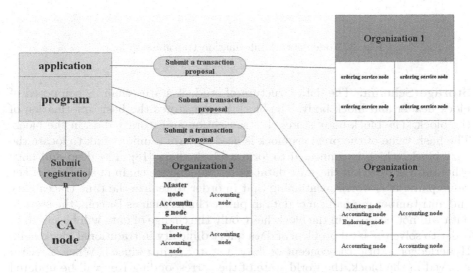

Fig. 2. Network architect

As the division of labor of nodes is clear, so it is different from the public chain. The alliance chain is a weak centralization rather than a decentralized framework, which is a double-edged sword for the application of blockchain, but it has a good coupling with the school status management. The student status chain uses the Kafka protocol to build a conventional fabric network architecture [16]. After the user sends a change or query request to the student status information at the front end, the user sends the modification action to the CA node through the client node for authorization. After the CA node authorizes and issues the self-signed root certificate of the node, the Endors endorsement node stores the operation in the node in the form of "transaction information". Only the endorsed student status information can be submitted and added to the alliance chain. After the endorsement is completed, the Orderer node sorts the endorsed information by consensus, packages the block and broadcasts. The student status information is recorded by each peer node through Gossip protocol, and each node updates the world status tree and node information. The Node network information transmission logic as shown in the Fig. 3.

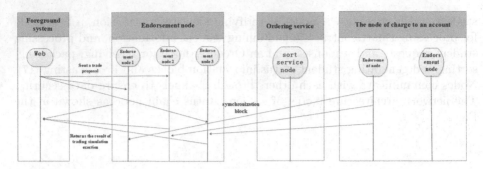

Fig. 3. Node network information transmission logic

Storage Schema. The data structure of student status chain is composed of block header and block body. The block header stores the basic information of the block. The block body stores the transaction and storage data in the block. The hash value of the previous block is used to form a unique link to locate the next block, which is connected to form a block chain [18]. The deep and huge other data is stored in the state database of the alliance chain in the form of key value pairs. It is worth mentioning that in order to realize the time traceability and anti-tamper mechanism of data in public chains such as Bitcoin, the state of data will not be saved in the blockchain, only the change of data will be saved. In order to solve the fatal problem of data query difficulty in traditional blockchain, Hyperledger Fabric the concept of "world state" is introduced. When a record is saved in the block, the world state of the corresponding Key will be updated synchronously. When a key value needs to be queried, you only need to query the corresponding world state without full-chain traversal [19]. The concept of world state greatly reduces the query overhead of blockchain, makes a revolutionary contribution to blockchain enterprise, and also plays an important role in this work.

The data stored in the blockchain includes "ledger" number, "ledger" data, block index, world tree status and historical data. The "ledger" is used to store student information and the modification of student information, so as to organically combine the blockchain and student status storage. In the blockchain application of the system, we use the classic hierarchical storage mode, and the data is stored in the blockchain and CouchDB database hierarchically by type. On the blockchain, the saved work is completed by the Peer node, which maintains four databases, i.e. IdStore, StateDB, HistoryDB and BlockIndex, which are indispensable key information in the chain. The vast student database is stored in the built-in database CouchDB. The storage system architecture as shown in the Fig. 4.

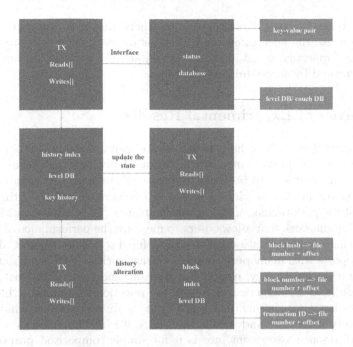

Fig. 4. storage system architecture

The "ledger" is used to store students' information and the modification of students' information. It is stored in the CouchDB database together with the historical status index and the block index. As for these data, it inevitably involves students' personal privacy. Therefore, this paper proposes to use SHA256 encryption algorithm [20] to encrypt students' data in one direction. Overall, SHA256 is similar to the operation flow of hash functions such as MD4, MD5, and HSA-1. Before the message to be hashed continues the hash calculation, the following two steps shall be performed:

- Complements the private information of students so that the final length is a multiple of 512 bits.
- Block messages in 512-bit units.

$$M_1, M_2, M_3, M_4, \cdots, M_n \qquad (1)$$

The student private information blocks will be processed one by one: starting with a fixed initial hash H_0, the following sequence is calculated.

$$H_i = H_{i-1} + c^{M_i}(H_{i-1}) \qquad (2)$$

where C is the compression function of SHA256, the plus sign is mod 2^{32}'s addition. By using the flexibility of SHA256 algorithm's input length and using SHA256 one-way encryption to protect the students' partial information, the privacy of partial information is strengthened. When the students need to verify this part of information to others, they need to input Plaintext, and then use the encryption algorithm for one-way encryption to compare with the Ciphertext saved in the database, and the information authenticity can be proved by successful comparison.

4 Analysis of Experimental Results

Performance Test. Blockchain technology is gaining attention, but it is not possible to test the performance of the various blockchain platforms available before creating solutions to business problems. To address this pain point, the Hyperledger community provides a tool called Hyperledger Caliper that can be used to test the performance of blockchain platforms [21]. Caliper is a blockchain benchmark framework that allows users to measure the performance of a particular blockchain implementation using a predefined set of use cases. Caliper will generate reports with many performance metrics, such as TPS (transactions per second), transaction latency, resource utilization, and so on. The goal is to use Caliper results as a reference to support the selection of a suitable blockchain implementation. User-specific use cases. Given the diversity of blockchain configurations, network setups, and specific use cases, it is not intended as an authoritative performance assessment, nor is it for simple comparison purposes. The caliper's running logic as shown in the Fig. 5.

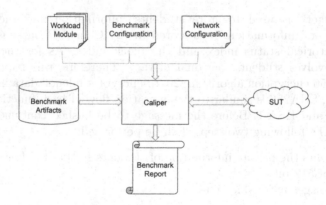

Fig. 5. Caliper's running logic

4.1   System Test Environment

In order to test system performance by ciliper, the author of this article set up the test environment and began rigorous testing. The test environment as shown in Table 1.

Table 1. Test Environment

node deploym	Versi
Operating system	Ubantu 20.04.3
CPU	Interl code i7
Memory	16G DDR4
Hard disk	1T HDD
Hyperledger Fabric	2.2.0
Docker	20.03

4.2   System Test Cases and Results

System Test. For different types of universities and degrees, the test case collected the information of 50 students from 10 universities. Due to space reasons, here to Jiangxi Normal University students as an example to operate.The test example as shown in Fig. 6.

```
'use strict';

const { WorkloadModuleBase } = require('@hyperledger/caliper-core');
class MarblesInitWorkload extends WorkloadModuleBase {
    constructor() {
        super();
        this.txIndex = -1;
        this.entityID=['360202020202020200','360202020202020201','360202020202020202','360202020202020203','360202020202020204'];
        this.name = ['Xiaolin Cheng','Yuyu liu','Liwei  Liu','Qiqi Hua','ZengHao'];
        this.birthday = ['2002-11-7','2002-10-3','2001-1-7','2000-9-7','2002-7-7'];
        this.age = ['19','20','21'];
        this.place = ['JiuJiang','JDZ','NC','JiuJiang','ShangRao'];
        this.nation = ['The han nationality','The han nationality','miao'];
        this.address = ['JDZ','NC','JDZ'];
        this.sex = ['male','male','female'];
        this.id = ['20202610','20202611','20202612'];
        this.states = ['1','1','1'];
        this.schoolName = ['Jiangxi Normal University','Jiangxi Normal University','Jiangxi Normal University'];
        this.enterTime = ['2020-9-12','2020-9-12','2020-9-12'];
        this.graduateTime = ['2024-6-24','2024-6-24','2024-6-24'];
        this.major = ['Computer Science and Technology','Computer Science and Technology','Computer Science and Technology'];
        this.grade = ['1','2','1'];
        this.credit = ['20','40','60'];
        this.averageScore = ['79','79','79'];
        this.poorsubsid = ['0','0','0'];
        this.aSW = ['0','0','0'];
        this.level = ['Undergraduate course','Undergraduate course','Undergraduate course'];
    }
```

Fig. 6. Test case

Test Results. This paper mainly tested open, Query, transfer and other methods. From the figure, we can clearly see the success rate of the project, transaction throughput, transaction delay (minimum, maximum, average, percentage), resource consumption (CPU, memory, network IO, etc.), and open, The success rate of query method is almost 100%, and the highest success rate of Test test is 32.90 TPS. Detailed test results as shown in Table 2.

Table 2. Test results about throughput

Test	Name	Succ	Fail	Send Rate	Max latency	Min latency	Avg latency	Throughput
1	open	100	0	48.8tps	4.88s	3.65s	4.11s	17.4tps
2	query	100	0	56.8tps	1.99s	0.12s	1.44s	32.9tps
3	transfer	33	66	50.8tps	5.42s	2.41s	5.02s	5.11tps

This article is mainly on the docker environment, in this environment, there are two groups: each group contains a peer node(Peer0.org1.example.com and Peer0.org2.example.com), a special deposit certificate of the ca nodes, There are CouchDB nodes to enhance security for compliance and data protection in the blockchain, as well as an organization node. It is not difficult to find the memory occupied by nodes in the figure. Peer nodes account for most of the memory, so the CPU utilization is also very high. Blockchain network consists of peer nodes, each of which can save a copy of ledger and a copy of smart contract. Therefore, the input and output of transactions are mainly dominated by peer nodes. Detailed test results as shown in Table 3.

Table 3. Test results about the use of organization

NAME	Memory	CPU	Traffic in	Traffic Out	Disc Out	Disc write
Peer0.org1.example.com	264.4MB	9.54%	717.6KB	468.7KB	536.0KB	704.0KB
Peer0.org2.example.com	266.4MB	9.73%	719.1KB	512.2KB	860.0KB	704.0KB
Ca.org1.example.com	15.5MB	0.00%	0KB	0KB	0KB	0KB
Couchdb.org1.example.com	90.5MB	8.49%	181.5KB	297.7KB	296.0KB	260.0KB
Ca.org2.example.com	7.9MB	0.00%	0KB	0KB	0KB	0KB
Couchdb.org2.example.com	92.9MB	7.00%	301.7KB	301.7KB	156.0KB	272.0KB
Order.example.com	31.9MB	2.35%	819.1KB	819.1KB	548.0KB	508.0KB

System throughput refers to the number of transactions that a system can process per unit time, which is an important indicator used to measure system performance. For online trading systems, system throughput refers to the number of transaction requests successfully processed and responded to per unit of time. Calculation of average number of concurrent users:

$$C = nL/T \tag{3}$$

where C is the average number of concurrent users, N is the average number of daily access users, L is the average time between login and logout (average operation time) in a day, and T is the length of time. When there is no performance bottleneck, there is a certain correlation between throughput and virtual users, which can be calculated by the following formula:

$$F = VU * R/T \tag{4}$$

F is throughput, VU is the number of virtual users, R is the number of requests sent by each virtual user, and T is the time taken for the performance test. In the case of RAFT algorithm, the throughput of the student roll chain system can be stable at 200tps and it has the commercial function of carrying the student roll storage system. It can be seen that the read throughput decreases while the write throughput increases with the increase of the number of nodes. The read throughput and the write throughput as shown in Fig. 7.

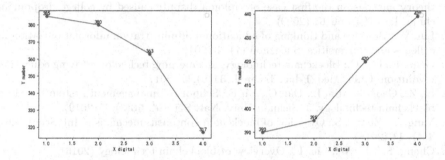

Fig. 7. Experimental results of the authors

5   Conclusion

The use of blockchain technology has slowly shifted from the traditional financial industry to all walks of life in society, this paper combines blockchain technology, in view of the traditional student registration management certificate system information islands, management complexity, user security, storage transience and other pain points, proposes a new type of multi-organization joint student status chain management and registration system, which effectively combines schools, academic affairs offices, and employers, and develops a Hyperledger Fabric consortium blockchain system [22] with basic functions. The test analysis shows that the system has higher throughput compared with other similar blockchain systems, and has stronger security and sharing compared with the traditional student status management system. However, the system proposed in this paper still has throughput and other aspects' problems to be improved in system security. With the further solution of the problems, blockchain will play a greater role in the field of education. In the future, enterprises can be continuously introduced into the Consortium blockchain, and external certification of academic qualifications can be completed in the system through the cooperation of schools, enterprises and the Ministry of Education, so as to further expand the application of this framework.

Acknowledgements. This work is supported by the No. 62067003, 62262030, National Natural Science Foundation of China (NSFC) under Grant No. 61962026, the National Natural Science Key Foundation of China grant No. 61832014 and No. 62032016, the National Natural Science Foundation of China under Grant No.62002143, the Natural Science Foundation of Jiangxi Province under Grant No. 20192ACBL21031 and the Foundation of Jiangxi Educational Committee under Grant No. GJJ210338.

References

1. Cheng, Y.: Legal theory discussion on several issues of college dropout right - legal theory analysis on the first case of diploma dispute caused by college dropout in china. Law (04), 56–61 (2000)
2. Lin, W.: Practice and thinking of educational administration informationization in colleges and universities. Shenzhou (1), 1 (2018)
3. Geng, F., Lin, C.: Blockchain technology: an emerging technology driving education revolution. Chin. Med. Educ. Technol. **31**(6), 5 (2017)
4. Li, Z., Gao, C., Min, L., Dai, C., Yi, F.: School roll management system based on blockchain technology. J. Sichuan Univ. Nat. Sci. Ed. **56**(3), 7 (2019)
5. Yang, Y., Zhang, S.: Overview of blockchain consensus mechanism. Inf. Secur. Res. **4**(4), 11 (2018)
6. Cheng, S., Shi, W., Liu, L.: Overview of blockchain technology (2016)
7. Yong, Y., Wang, F.Y.: Development status and prospect of blockchain technology. Zidonghua Xuebao/Acta Automatica Sinica **42**(4), 481–494 (2016)
8. Abeyratne, S.A., Monfared, R.: Blockchain ready manufacturing supply chain using distributed ledger (2016)
9. Christidis, K., Devetsikiotis, M.: Blockchains and smart contracts for the internet of things. IEEE Access **4**, 2292–2303 (2016)
10. Hou, H., Pan, Q.: Research of it outsourcing strategy and evaluation systems in China. In: 2011 International Conference on Computer Science and Service System (CSSS) (2011)
11. Marc, P.: Blockchain technology: Principles and applications. Post-Print (2016)
12. Wu, Y., Cheng, G., Chen, Y., Wang, X., Ma, X.: Research status, hot spot analysis and development thinking of "blockchain + education" at home and abroad. Distance Educ. J. **38**(1), 12 (2020)
13. Li, Q., Zhang, X.: Blockchain: using technology to promote openness and credibility in education. Distance Educ. J. **35**(1), 9 (2017)
14. Huang, S.L., Shen, D.Q., Liang, W., Huang, R.J.: Study on the adaptability of college student status management and information management system. China Manag. Informationization **19**(10), 173–174 (2016)
15. Lauslahti, K., Mattila, J., Seppl, T.: Smart contracts - how will blockchain technology affect contractual practices? ETLA Reports (57) (2017)
16. Nguyen, M.Q., Loghin, D., Dinh, T.: Understanding the scalability of hyperledger fabric. arXiv preprint arXiv:2107.09886 (2021)

17. Leng, J., Lu, X., Jiang, Y., Li, G.: A survey of research on consortium chain consensus mechanism. Data Anal. Knowl. Discov. **5**(1), 10 (2021)
18. Dinh, T., Liu, R., Zhang, M., Chen, G., Ooi, B.C., Wang, J.: Untangling blockchain: a data processing view of blockchain systems. IEEE Trans. Knowl. Data Eng. **30**(7), 1366–1385 (2017)
19. Chen, Y., Chen, S., Liang, J., Feagan, L.W., Han, W., Huang, S., Wang, X.S.: Decentralized data access control over consortium blockchains. Inf. Syst. **94**, 101590 (2020)
20. Appel, A.W.: Verification of a cryptographic primitive: SHA-256. ACM SIGPLAN Notices **50**(6), 153–164 (2015)
21. Mazzoni, M., Corradi, A., Nicola, V.D.: Performance evaluation of permissioned blockchains for financial applications: the consensys quorum case study. Blockchain Res. Appl. **3**(1), 12 (2022)
22. Androulaki, E., Manevich, Y., Muralidharan, S., Murthy, C., Laventman, G.: Hyperledger fabric: a distributed operating system for permissioned blockchains (2018)

A New Home-Based Pension Mutual Aid Framework Based on Blockchain

Ridong Huang, Jianmao Xiao[✉], Siqi Cheng, Ronglin Zhang, Hao Zeng, Xin Huang, and Zuoyi Liao

School of Software, Jiangxi Normal University, Nanchang 330027, China
{jm_xiao,xinhuang}@jxnu.edu.cn

Abstract. In the context of the public's response to home-based care, the "Time Bank" care model has attracted more and more attention as an effective supplement to home-based care. Although there are cases of Time Bank implementation in China, it still has many problems such as extreme centralization, lack of credibility, and opaque and imperfect circulation of time currency. In response to this, this paper integrates blockchain technology based on the traditional time banking model and proposes a new home-based care mutual assistance framework driven by blockchain technology, which utilizes the distributed decentralization, collective maintenance, and data immutability of the blockchain. The characteristics of the blockchain provide credit guarantees by combining the community-based management agency and the channelization of the service network. Time-based transaction process service matching, smart currency scoring module. And use their respective financing agreements and other technologies to safely circulate, jointly establish a chain-wheel interoperability chain, and cooperate with various contract models to jointly establish various on-chain contracts. Experimental analysis shows that the new framework involved can realize secure encrypted storage and transmission of information, solve the problem of cross-regional storage and exchange, and provide a new feasible solution for home care.

Keywords: Blockchain · Smart contract · Decentralization digital signature · Shared ledger · Time bank

1 Introduction

According to the data of the seventh national census, the population aged 60 and above reached 263 million, accounting for nearly 18.70%, and it is expected to reach 487 million in 2050, accounting for 34.9% of the total population. The degree of aging in China continues to deepen. Combined with changes in population structure, urban and rural labor flow, and demand for elderly care services, the pressure on elderly care has intensified, the function of family elderly care is lacking, and the problem of elderly care is serious. Based on the promulgation of a series of support policies by the country, various socialized elderly care institutions have emerged in the context of expanding market opportunities, and

© ICST Institute for Computer Sciences, Social Informatics and Telecommunications Engineering 2023
Published by Springer Nature Switzerland AG 2023. All Rights Reserved
Y. Cao and X. Shao (Eds.): MONAMI 2022, LNICST 474, pp. 32–47, 2023.
https://doi.org/10.1007/978-3-031-32443-7_3

elderly care has increasingly become a "sunrise industry" in which capital is chasing after each other. Problems such as uneven distribution of pension resources, shortage of professional nursing staff, and insufficient pensions between large cities and small and medium-sized cities have gradually become acute [1]. The elderly service is in a difficult situation and urgently needs new feasible solutions.

Compared with the traditional old-age care model, the community is used as a link for the acquisition of old-age care services, and the platform helps intelligent home-based care for the elderly. Realizing the multi-directional interaction between the elderly, children, service centers, and the government, active monitoring and other functions of the new home-based care model. In the context of the public's response to home-based care, the "Time Bank" care model has attracted more and more attention as an effective supplement to home-based care. Time Bank motivates volunteers in a "paid" way. Short-term volunteer time coins can be exchanged for daily necessities and long-term exchange for equivalent services, to solve the problem of volunteer needs and alleviate the insufficient supply of elderly care services. Although there are many examples of time bank development in some areas of China, such as the "Bu Lao Time Bank" in New Taipei, Taiwan in 2013, and the "Time Bank of Shanghai Hong Kou Changning elderly care service" in 2019, the current pension model in China is still dominated by family pensions, and there are extreme risks. The traditional pension model has pain points such as centralization, lack of credibility, opaque circulation of time currency, and imperfect operation model [2]. The development of practice is slow and it is difficult to implement.

Blockchain is a distributed database system and a distributed technology system in that multiple parties jointly maintain public ledgers. It is characterized by decentralization, openness and transparency, traceability, security, and information encryption. The chain nodes constitute a distributed ledger, and the completion of the transaction conveys the confirmation of each point, and the result is collected together. The decentralization feature enables Time Bank to transmit service requirements point-to-point, we use algorithms to intelligently generate keys, accurately match service requirements, and ensure data security. The above advantages prove that the effective use of blockchain can provide strong technical support for time banking issues.

This paper designs and implements a blockchain-based time chain model by analyzing the pension dilemma, and the time bank process, and combining blockchain technology and fabric institutions. The experimental analysis is feasible to carry out tests in terms of transaction throughput response time to ensure the implementation.

The contribution of this paper is:

- A time banking system solution based on blockchain technology is proposed. By analyzing the current problems of time banking, according to the actual business needs of the time banking system, combined with the blockchain, it analyzes and proposes solutions.
- Designed a blockchain-based time banking system framework.

– Through a series of experimental tests, the performance of the system is analyzed, and it is shown that the new framework can realize the secure encrypted storage and transmission of information.

2   Related Work

2.1   Blockchain

With the increasing popularity and development of virtual digital currencies such as Bitcoin, the underlying blockchain technology has received widespread attention [3]. The blockchain is essentially a decentralized, tamper-proof, and trustworthy new distributed database, which is integrated and innovated by existing technologies. It integrates distributed data storage, p2p data transmission, consensus mechanism, and technologies such as encryption algorithms and smart contracts. Each data block contains the data information of transactions on the network for a certain period to verify whether the information is valid and generate the next block. A block consists of a block header and a block body. The block body contains a certain number of transaction sets. The association with the previous block is maintained by PrevHash to form a chain structure. So that every transaction in the block is traceable and well-documented. At the same time, the integrity of the block transaction set is quickly verified through the root hash (Root hash) generated by MKT (MerkleTree) [4].

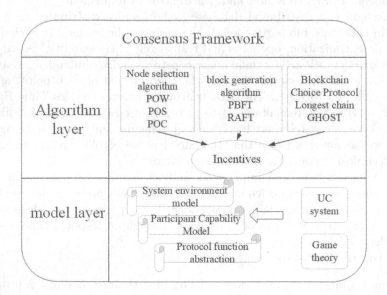

Fig. 1. Blockchain Consensus Framework

The blockchain consensus framework diagram as shown in the Fig. 1. Decentralization is the most significant feature and core idea of the blockchain, which adopts the P2P network structure. So - called decentralization means that it does not rely on the central node for accounting, and all nodes in the network have equal status and jointly manage the data in the system. This kind of data management is based on the blockchain structure to verify and store data, use consensus algorithm to generate and update data, use cryptography to transmit and protect data, and jointly supervise each node on the network, so as to achieve no need for a third-party trust agency. Endorsement [5]. Every node participating in the blockchain network are both a client and a server. When a node on the chain initiates a transaction, other nodes in the network will conduct consistency verification of its accuracy and validity to achieve transactions after consensus is added to the blockchain. In the blockchain, in a distributed trust less environment [6], the consensus mechanism is used to achieve consensus among nodes.

Due to the two characteristics of process credibility and decentralization, blockchain can build a trust base in a low-cost way in the scenario of multistakeholder participation, aiming at reshaping the social credit system. In the past two years, the blockchain has developed rapidly, and people have begun to try to apply it in the fields of finance, education, medical care, and logistics.

2.2 Time Chain Research for Time Bank

Operating Mechanism Model. The time bank mutual assistance pension model is a mutual aid pension model in which people with self-care ability and social behavior ability provide services for the elderly, to save time, and withdraw time to obtain services when needed. The specific operation mechanism is: the user registers as a member of the time bank and establishes a time account. Elderly care service demanders publish their elderly care needs through the Time Bank, and participants contact the demanders through this intermediary platform to provide services. After the end of the service transaction, the demander of the old-age service deducts the corresponding time collateral, and the supplier gets the time collateral. The converted time collateral is chained to TBC (time chain Time Block Chain), that is, by generating new transactions (the owner of the time collateral recorded in the transaction is the elderly care service provider) and send transaction information to the TBC [7]. In the future, the suppliers of old-age services will be transformed into demanders of old-age services, and the above process will form a complete closed loop [8]. The system operation process is shown in Fig. 2.

Theoretically speaking, the timing chain designed in this paper is a brand new blockchain, and it does not belong to the public chain, private chain, or consortium blockchain. Compared with the public chain, users using the timing chain need to be authenticated, but it can also realize complete anonymity between users. Compared with the consortium blockchain and private chain, all users on the timing chain can participate in the consensus process of the system and can obtain all the data on the chain.

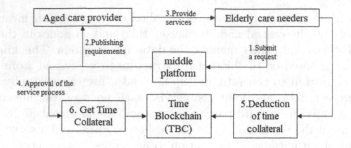

Fig. 2. Operating Mechanism Model

3   Blockchain-Based Time Banking Framework Model

3.1   System Architecture

The time bank system based on blockchain technology designed in this paper adopts the Hyperledger Fabric consortium chain architecture. The Hyperledger Fabric consortium chain is a distributed system that ensures the security and reliability of transaction data. Different servers are configured as different nodes and play different roles during actual operation, to realize the functions of each module in the system architecture. The system is divided into four levels: data layer, transaction business layer, security layer, and user layer as shown in Fig. 3 [9].

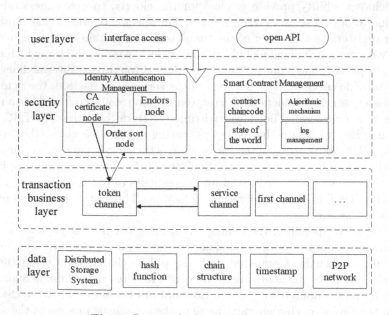

Fig. 3. System Architecture Diagram.

3.2   System Data Layer

The data storage structure and data organization method of the system are based on the fabric consortium blockchain architecture. The system data layer organizes data records into blocks and organizes the blocks into a chain structure by recording the hash value of the previous block in the block header of each block. Since the Time Bank network itself is a decentralized network, the participating nodes are completely autonomous, and there is no unified node responsible for management and maintenance. For this reason, each user of the network needs to use P2P technology. The P2P network [10,11] is used in the blockchain, which can establish a trust-enhanced blockchain P2P topology through fast and reliable broadcasting [12]. The correct information is broadcast to the entire blockchain network through a series of encoding sequences formed by specific hash functions [13,14] and encoding functions such as base58 and base64, and timestamps are added to realize data broadcasting and update node state information and ledger information as shown in Fig. 4.

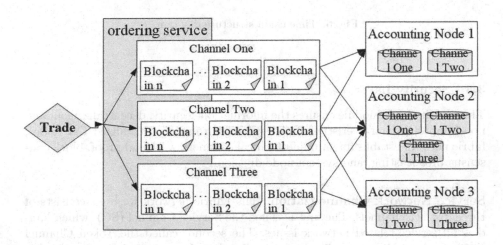

Fig. 4. Time Banking System Data Layer.

Once wrong information or network virus invades the entire blockchain network, in the process of blockchain P2P topology transmission, each node must determine whether all the information is correct. The character sequence formed by the hash function calculation and the encoding function will be greatly changed. The node compares the original correct encoding sequence with the public and private keys of the digital signature. If the sequence does not match, the node will refuse to accept the information. At the same time, the consensus mechanism in the time chain ensures the consistency of node information in the entire Time Bank network [15]. If the user is hacked and modified, the Time Bank network will trace the timestamp of the information to find the wrong information, delete the wrong information through the information rollback mechanism, and Re-update the node's state information and ledger information through the consensus mechanism. In the face of irresistible damage, as long as there is one node in the entire time chain network, all nodes can restore the data information in the entire time bank network as shown in Fig. 5.

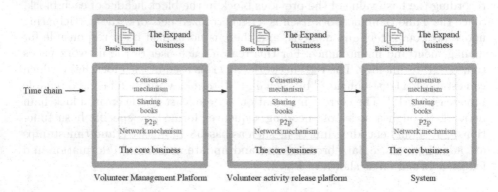

Fig. 5. Time chain structure diagram

3.3   Security Layer

The security layer module ensures the information security, decentralization, and non-tampering characteristics of the system through decentralized CA nodes, fabric network establishment of hierarchical channels, workload proof, block consensus broadcasting, and system node division.

Service Network Channelization. The Fabric network we built consists of three distinct channels. The first is called the Service Channel (SC), which handles all service-related network issues. The second, called the Token Channel (TC), is responsible for collecting all wallet data from the ledger. The third is called the grading channel (GC), which allows registered members to rank each other. Each channel is attached with Chaincode running on peers and provides a platform for program execution to transmit transactions. In the Fabric framework, all transactions are evaluated and agreed upon at the ordering stage. Finally, all transactions are sent to a special entity called the "orderer". The orderer puts all transactions in order of execution and updates them on the ledger, the same for the original channel for endorsing and non-endorsing peers.

Proof of Work. After the time bank system has been running for a while, the local settlement point will integrate all the valid data collected during this period to make it a collection of transaction data, and then use the Merkle Tree algorithm to achieve Merkle Root Hash (assuming this hash value is MRash) is generated, and then assembled with the random number Nonce and other related fields, and finally, it becomes the data of the blockchain header, we assume that the header data is Headdata, and then continuously adjust the value of Nonce, so that Hash (Headdata is always less than Difficulty, where Difficulty refers to the correct value of the speed of the Nonce random number obtained by the system during the adjustment process of the end node. In this process, With the help of the first calculated Nonce random number specific settlement node, the acquisition of the settlement power in this round is realized, to realize the generation of new blocks and broadcast them.

3.4 Transaction Business Layer

The transaction business layer mainly provides technical support for the time currency transaction, and the timing chain provides the core business of the time bank system by implementing the underlying mechanism of the fabric blockchain, such as time currency settlement, transfer, query, etc. The full-service nodes in the entire time banking system run the timing chain, provide channels for the circulation of time coins in the entire system, and provide blockchain services for the audit platform and third-party business systems through the restful service interface.

Time Currency Transaction. In the time bank chain, the most important part of the whole service process of volunteers and the elderly being served and the process of time currency transfer, inheritance, and lending between users is the module involving time currency transactions.

The entire time currency transaction process is divided into three steps. First, the time currency sender (A) fills in the transaction information and sends the transaction information to the time currency receiver (B); The information is digitally signed; finally, the entire transaction information is encrypted and broadcast to the entire time bank system through the P2P network. All members of the system can use the public keys provided by A and B to verify the transaction information after receiving the broadcast information as shown in Fig. 6.

The digital signature [16] and encryption algorithm [17] adopted by the time chain ensures that the data transmission [18–20] between nodes is safe and shared. The system adopts elliptic curve encryption algorithm [21] and elliptic curve digital signature [22, 23]. The digital signature should meet the following requirements:

1) The signature cannot be forged.
2) The signature is non-repudiation.
3) The identification and application of the signature is relatively easy, and anyone can verify the validity of the signature.
4) The signature cannot be copied, and the signature and the original text are an inseparable whole.
5) The signed message cannot be tampered with. Any bit data is tampered with, and its signature changes with it. Anyone can verify and refuse to accept the signature.

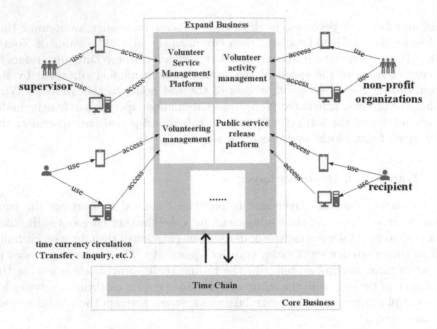

Fig. 6. Time Coin Circulation Chart

Elliptic curve digital signature core code: A function to generate a digital signature for a tx object as shown in Fig. 7.

```
func SignTx(tx *Transaction, s Signer, privatekey *ecdsa.PrivateKey) (*Transaction, error){
    h := s.Hash(tx)
    sign, err := crypto.Sign(h[:], privatekey)
    if err != nil {
        return nil, err
    }
    return tx.WithSignature(s, sign)
}
```

Fig. 7. Digital signature function

It can be seen from the body of the SignTx() function after the Signer. The Hash() method provides the content to be signed (that is, the hash of some members of the Transaction object after RLP encoding), and the main work of generating the signature is handed over to the Sign() function to complete.

Elliptic curve digital signature verification principle [24,25]:

$$\frac{hG}{s} + \frac{xK}{s} = \frac{hG}{s} + \frac{x(kG)}{s} = \frac{r(h+xk)G}{h+kx} = rG \tag{1}$$

Elliptic curve encryption algorithm:

1) Select an elliptic curve Ep(a, b) and take a point on the elliptic curve as the base point P.
2) Select a large number k as the private key and generate the public key $Q = kP$.
3) Pass Ep(a, b) and points Q and P to the user.
4) After receiving the message, the user will encode the plaintext to be transmitted to the point M on Ep(a, B) and generate a random integer R.
5) Public key encryption (ciphertext C is a point pair):

$$C = \{rP, M + rQ\} \tag{2}$$

6) Private key decryption (M + rQ − k(rP), the decryption result is point M)

$$M + rQ - k(rP) = M + r(kP) - k(rP) = M \tag{3}$$

7) Decode the point M to get the plaintext.

Assuming that in the encryption process, there is a third party H, H can only know the elliptic curve Ep(a, b), the public key Q, the base point P, the ciphertext point C, and the private key k is obtained through the public key Q and the base point P Or it is very difficult to obtain the random number r through the ciphertext point C and the base point P, so the security of data transmission can be guaranteed.

Encryption:

$$Ecc\_points\_mul\,(\&c2x, \&c2y, px, py, \&r, a, p) \tag{4}$$

$$Ecc\_points\_mul\,(\&tempx, \&tempy, qx, qy, \&r, a, p) \tag{5}$$

$$Two\_points\_add\,(\&mx, \&my, \&tempx, \&tempy, \&c1x, \&c1y, a, zero, p) \tag{6}$$

Timecoin transaction is the core of the entire time chain and provides security for the entire transaction process through digital signatures and encryption algorithms. Digital signature and encryption algorithms greatly improve the security of data in the process of writing, transmitting, and reading, and the data association method between blocks through the concatenation of hash values and the data writing mechanism based on the consensus algorithm [26] to confirm the block It also makes the data on the blockchain extremely difficult to tamper with.

Transaction Process. Based on the Fabric architecture, the system proposes an overall framework combining six modules. The transaction process is divided into three major processes: service matching, token transfer, and scoring system as shown in Fig. 8.

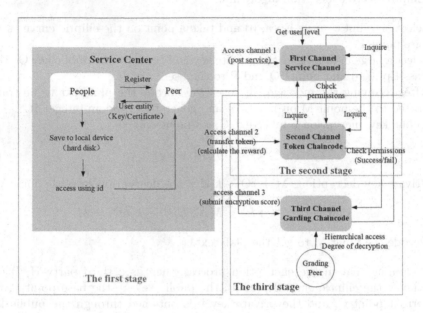

Fig. 8. Service Match

Before talking about service matching, services need to be released first, and registered members on the chain publish their service-related data (i.e. proposals) on the blockchain. They can use their key pair to access peers, upload their service proposal, and call the PostService function on the service Chaincode in SC. Users have access to different peers, which means they can travel to different timebank centers as long as those peers belong to the same channel. On this basis, after a member's service proposal is published on SC, the proposal system tries to find a match as much as possible. Without loss of generality, this paper only uses a simple (intuitive) matching scheme to find matches, while the adoption of other complex matching algorithms will improve the matching performance [27,28]. Either SP or SR needs to compare all attributes (except location-related attributes) to find a matching service. In addition, there is an important factor to consider when looking for a match by considering various attributes, which is the level of service involved in our matching process. Those low-ranking members should be punished systematically in order to preserve the core values of the Time Bank. One possible solution is to make it harder for those lower-ranked members to get matched. In other words, a lower rank indicates a lower priority and probability that he or she can be matched with others.

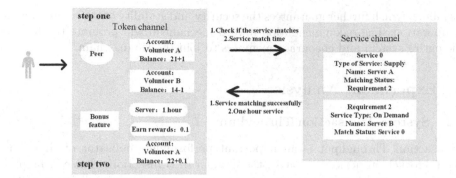

Fig. 9. Token conversion

The next stage is the token transfer as shown in Fig. 9. The token transfer between SR and SP in TC after service exchange. The whole process (taking volunteers A and B as an example). First, the user executes the application to access the TC and calls the token transfer function to embed the token Chain-code. In this case, after the SR and SP have exchanged their services, the SP wants to receive time credits for the services he or she provides. Due to the passive nature of the blockchain, tokens are only transferred when users access it and invoke smart contracts on it. Since only SPs have an incentive to obtain time coins, the transfer of tokens must be activated by SPs. He or she can call the token transfer function in TC directly through the app and get time credits in return.

3.5 User Layer

The user layer interacts with the underlying timeline through the restful service interface. In this time bank system, all users need to be authenticated by the CA (Electronic Authentication Service) system, and only after passing the authentication can they become a legal user in the time bank chain, and at the same time obtain a certificate and key that can encrypt data.

New members are added to the timeline. If a new member joins by himself and there is no recommender, his new member information will be reviewed by all members in the system. If the new member fills in the recommender information, the recommender will review the user information of the new member. Audit information includes personal information, digital signatures, and more. After all, information is reviewed and approved, new members will have a limited publicity period. If any members object to joining, or malicious behavior is detected, the system will automatically remove new members. If the new member successfully joins the Time Bank Chain, the recommender will be rewarded with corresponding work points, that is, the recommendation reward mechanism of higher-level recommender: recommender: me = 5:3:2. The entire registration review process is open and transparent, and all members jointly certify new members, which further guarantees the security and stability of the entire system in operation. The recommendation reward mechanism will promote the flow of the entire system and encourage members to join the timing chain.

4 Experiment Analysis

4.1 System Transaction Throughput

Transaction Throughput is an important performance indicator of the Time Bank blockchain network, that is, the number of transactions that can be processed per second, which represents the business processing efficiency of the Time Bank blockchain system. This paper uses the Fabric blockchain network performance test tool Hyperledger Caliper to test the transaction throughput. The specific operations are divided into two types: time bank ledger write operation (invoke) and ledger query (query) operation, each of which initiates 10,000 transactions The request is divided into multiple rounds, and a different transaction sending frequency (Send Rate) is set for each round to test the transaction throughput. The specific test data of transaction throughput are shown in Table 1.

Table 1. Time Bank System Transaction Throughput Record Table.

Test round	Transaction Type	Number of transactions	Sending frequency(tps)	Transaction throughput(tps)
1	invoke	10000	25	25
2	invoke	10000	50	43
3	invoke	10000	75	55
4	invoke	10000	100	59
5	invoke	10000	125	52
6	invoke	10000	150	48
7	query	10000	50	50
8	query	10000	100	81
9	query	10000	150	134
10	query	10000	200	181
11	query	10000	250	202
12	query	10000	300	193

Figure 10 and Fig. 11 show the write throughput versus sending frequency and the query throughput versus sending frequency. Analysis of the transaction throughput chart data shows that for the ledger write throughput, when the sending frequency is below 100tps, the ledger write throughput increases with the increase of the sending frequency. When the sending frequency reaches

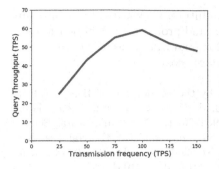

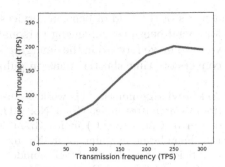

Fig. 10. Write throughput varies with send frequency

Fig. 11. Query throughput varies with sending frequency

100tps, the ledger write throughput reaches 100 tips. The peak value is 60tps, and when the sending frequency exceeds 100tps and continues to increase, the ledger writes throughput decreases slowly and fluctuates around 50tps; for the ledger query throughput, when the sending frequency is below 250tps, the ledger query throughput increases with the increase of the sending frequency. It keeps increasing. When the sending frequency reaches 250tps, the ledger write throughput reaches a peak value of 198tps. When the sending frequency exceeds 250tps and continues to increase, the ledger query throughput decreases slowly. Ledger writing requires multi-organization endorsement consensus, but the ledger query does not. Therefore, the ledger writing operation takes extra time, making the ledger query throughput higher than the ledger writing throughput, which is consistent with the test results. Based on the above analysis results, it can be concluded that the transaction throughput of the Time Bank blockchain network meets the system performance requirements.

5 Conclusion

Given the extreme centralization, insufficient credibility, opaque circulation of time coins, and imperfect operating models in the service of pension services, this paper proposes an innovative model of blockchain + time bank for mutual assistance in-home care. The time bank is used as a blockchain distributed ledger, collectively maintained, removing the centralization of the traditional time bank, and using the blockchain to integrate the work point and point system, while ensuring transparency and security, and improving credibility. In the orderly advancement of the time bank project, at the current stage, the application of core technologies and the construction of the basic platform have been completed, and the follow-up will expand the application of the system and improve the functions of the platform, and in the next stage, further research will be carried out according to practical investigation and experimental analysis. The timing chain of "blockchain + time bank" innovation will be widely used in all aspects of the field of pension services in the future, alleviating major pressure for social pensions, enhancing personal value, and promoting social pension services to move forward in the emerging direction, and will eventually form a "time conversion, time shuttle" pension public welfare ecosystem.

Acknowledgements. This work is supported by the Foundation of Jiangxi Educational Committee under Grant No. GJJ210338, the National Natural Science Foundation of China (NSFC) under Grant No. 61962026, the National Natural Science Key Foundation of China grant No. 62262030 and No. 62067003, the National Natural Science Foundation of China under Grant No.62002143 and the Natural Science Foundation of Jiangxi Province under Grant No. 20192ACBL21031.

References

1. Jiang, Q.: Current situation and future development of institutional pensions in my country. Coop. Econ. Technol. (16), 3 (2021)
2. Boc's "time bank" public welfare mutual aid platform to explore the development of time bank with Chinese characteristics. Chin. Civil Aff. (2), 1 (2022)
3. Chuangchuang, Luan, H., Yang, X., Guo, X., Lu, Z., Niu, B.: Overview of blockchain technology research. Comput. Sci. **48**(S02), 9 (2021)
4. Cai, X., et al.: The principle of blockchain and its core technology. Chin. J. Comput. **44**(1), 48 (2021)
5. Shen, M., Zhang, H.: Overview of blockchain technology research. Wirel. Internet Technol. **17**(10), 3 (2020)
6. Liu, F., Chen, Y.: A review of blockchain technology research. J. Shandong Normal Univ. Nat. Sci. Ed. **35**(3), 13 (2020)
7. Xiao, K., Wang, M., Tang, X., Jiang, T.: Public welfare time banking system based on blockchain technology. J. Comput. Appl. **39**(7), 6 (2019)
8. Tao, S., Zhang, Y.: The mechanism and path of "time bank" mutual aid for the elderly: from the perspective of time and money, (2), 7 (2022)
9. Xia, Q., Dou, W., Dou, W., Liang, G., Zuo, C., Zhang, F.: Overview of blockchain consensus protocols (2021)
10. Zhou, Y., Fang, J., Jia, Y., Jia, L., Shi, W.: Consortium chain consensus algorithm based on PBFT. Comput. Sci. **48**(11), 9 (2021)
11. Sun, Z., Zhang, X., Xiang, F., Chen, L.: Research progress of blockchain storage scalability. J. Softw. **32**(1), 20 (2021)
12. Tetarave, S.K., Tripathy, S.: PJ-sec: secure node joining in mobile p2p networks. CCF Trans. Pervasive Comput. Interact. (4) (2020)
13. Wu, Y., Li, J.: The evolution process of blockchain P2P network protocol. Appl. Res. Comput. **36**(10), 7 (2019)
14. Deng, Y., Ji-Tao, M.A., Hai-Hong, W.U., Liu, W., Zhang, R.B.: Analyse operation mechanism and management styles for the public service network of science and technology which is built under the principle of "innovation-driven"-take the joint construction and application of scientific instruments and equipments. China Soft Science (2011)
15. Liu, F., et al.: Blockchain cross-chain asset interaction protocol based on improved hash time lock. Comput. Sci. **49**(1), 9 (2022)
16. Baccara, M., Lee, S.M., Yariv, L.: Optimal dynamic matching. CEPR Discussion Papers (2018)

17. Carrara, G.R., Burle, L.M., Medeiros, D.S.V., de Albuquerque, C.V.N., Mattos, D.M.F.: Consistency, availability, and partition tolerance in blockchain: a survey on the consensus mechanism over peer-to-peer networking. Ann. Telecommun. **75**(2) (2020)

18. Liu, F., Yang, J., Qi, J.: Research on two-party elliptic curve digital signature algorithm of blockchain based on hash proof system. Inf. Netw. Secur

19. Wang, R., Tang, Y., Pei, X., Guo, S., Zhang, F.: Blockchain privacy protection scheme based on lightweight homomorphic encryption and zero-knowledge proof. Comput. Sci. **48**(S02), 5 (2021)

20. Qian, W., Shao, Q., Zhu, Y., Kim, C.-C., Zhou, A.: Blockchain and trusted data management: problems and methods brief. J. Softw. **29**(1), 10 (2018)

21. Liu, S., Liao, S., Yang, C., Fan, J.: Research on real world data sharing system based on blockchain. Inf. Secur. Res. **8**(1), 6 (2022)

22. Wang, G., Ding, H.: Blockchain-based business collaboration data security sharing scheme. Inf. Secur. Res. **7**(7), 9 (2021)

23. Liu, Y., Lang, X., Pei, S.: Encryption algorithm based on ECC and homomorphic encryption. Comput. Eng. Des. **41**(5), 5 (2020)

24. Zhang, P., Li, Y.: A forward-secure elliptic curve digital signature scheme. Comput. Eng. Appl. **56**(1), 6 (2020)

25. Xiao, S., Wang, X., Pan, F.: An elliptic curve digital signature algorithm based on modular inverse operation. Comput. Eng. Appl. (2020)

26. Zhang, X., Li, Q., Fu, F.: Confidentiality verification method of blockchain transaction amount based on digital commitment. Comput. Sci. **48**(9), 6 (2021)

27. Chen, C., Long, X., Jiang, Z., Liu, Z., Meng, Q., Long, L.: Research progress on the application of time banking model in the field of elderly care. J. Nurs. Training **36**(12), 4 (2021)

28. Li, C., Jiang, M.: Research on the optimization strategy of blockchain embedded "time bank". Changbai Acad. J. (4), 7 (2021)

Blockchain-Based Cross-Border Supply Chain Model

Jianyu Zou, Jianmao Xiao$^{(\boxtimes)}$, Xuanying Long, Xin Yang, Yu Xiao,
Yuanlong Cao, and Yong Luo

School of Software, Jiangxi Normal University, Nanchang 330027, China
{jm_xiao,ylcao,luoyong1020}@jxnu.edu.cn

Abstract. With the rapid development of cross-border e-commerce in
China, cross-border transactions are becoming more and more frequent,
and the problems of centralized and easy tampering, information siloing,
difficulty in traceability, and cumbersome recourse mechanism of traditional cross-border import and export systems are becoming more and
more serious. Blockchain technology has the characteristics of decentralization, distributed storage, openness and transparency, security, information encryption, and anonymity, which provides an important way to
solve the problems of cross-border transactions. In this paper, by analyzing the business logic of cross-border products, the parties related
to cross-border products are set as organizations to participate in the
Consortium Blockchain Hyperledger Fabric, followed by combining the
business logic of each participant, configuring the network environment,
proposing the dual-chain architecture, designing the corresponding smart
contracts, and finally conducting performance tests in terms of throughput and response time through Caliper. The results show that compared
with the traditional inventory management system, the system throughput can be stabilized above 300 TPS while ensuring data security and
safety, which meets the current inventory business requirements.

Keywords: Blockchain · Cross-border transactions · Supply chain ·
Information security · Smart contracts

1 Introduction

Nowadays, China's economic environment is developing steadily, residents can
continue to expand consumption, cross-border transactions are frequent, enterprises are beginning to look at cooperation with multiple institutions to reach
alliances to enhance market competitiveness, and the scale of the supply chain
industry is expanding, and the scale of the cross-border e-commerce industry
has almost maintained a growth rate of more than 20% since 2016, and the scale
of China's cross-border e-commerce transactions will reach 12.5 trillion yuan in

© ICST Institute for Computer Sciences, Social Informatics and Telecommunications Engineering 2023
Published by Springer Nature Switzerland AG 2023. All Rights Reserved
Y. Cao and X. Shao (Eds.): MONAMI 2022, LNICST 474, pp. 48–62, 2023.
https://doi.org/10.1007/978-3-031-32443-7_4

2022 [1]. Blockchain is an important part of the new generation of information technology and a new database software integrated with various technologies, which is expected to solve the trust and security problems in cyberspace and reconstruct the information industry system. Combining blockchain with cross-border import and export inventory is of great significance to the development of cross-border trade.

The growing scale of cross-border transactions has generated a series of issues, To ensure the accuracy of the information, the traditional technical solution will generate many intermediate links, which is tedious and inefficient and consumes a lot of resources, and at the same time, the authenticity and reliability of the information of each enterprise are not guaranteed, so the merchants change the labels and counterfeit the national products, the manufacturers tamper with the shipping places, and the goods information is not updated in time, which leads to the accumulation of inventory, and other problems occur frequently. The IoT system for collecting information is set up in different participants' systems, and the actual data of the supply chain which seems to be connected through the Internet is relatively independent, with centralized data storage and serious information siloing.

In this paper, by analyzing the current situation of cross-border inventory, analyzing the supply chain business process, and combining it with blockchain technology, we design and implement a model of a cross-border inventory system based on blockchain, and also compare the changes in the system throughput under different number of nodes and transaction volume. Blockchain is a distributed database system, a distributed technology system in which multiple parties work together to maintain a public ledger. Its features include decentralization, immutability, traceability, Enhanced Security, information encryption, anonymity, and so on. Once the transaction information is uploaded to the chain through the nodes, no one can change it. This feature of being difficult to forge comes from the blockchain mechanism itself rather than through the operation of developers, and the features of being open, transparent, and traceable can quickly locate and pursue responsibility in the case of product problems. The above excellent features make blockchain technology an effective solution to the trust problem and provide important technical support to solve the cross-border transaction problem. The main contributions of this paper are as follows:

- The new model of combining blockchain and cross-entry supply chain is proposed to provide a feasible solution to the traditional cross-border cross-entry supply chain pain points.
- It proposes a dual-chain model for product transaction separation, which solves the problem of traditional blockchain supply chain information ecological silo.
- The changes in throughput with different numbers of nodes and transaction volume are tested, and effective module matching is proposed to support the business.

2   Related Work

2.1   Blockchain

After Satoshi Nakamoto proposed the concept of Bitcoin in 2008 and made it publicly available, blockchain technology also gradually entered people's view. The blockchain 1.0 period is represented by the decentralized concept of Bitcoin, which plays more of a distributed bookkeeping role; the 2.0 period is represented by the smart contracts of Ether, and in the upcoming blockchain 3.0 era, it is an era of comprehensive application of blockchain technology. Blockchain is essentially a decentralized distributed database, relying on peer-to-peer transmission, cryptography, algorithms, and other technological fusion to jointly secure the distributed ledger.

Weili Chen et al. [2] stand for the data type and environment to divide the blockchain into three horizontal and one vertical structures. As shown in Fig. 1, the three horizontals represent both the three key stages of blockchain development from1.0 to 3.0, and also divide the underlying technology. The one vertical represents the distributed environment throughout the blockchain architecture, which summarizes the blockchain as a distributed database with decentralization, immutability, traceability, and multi-party maintenance, which can establish trust without the need for a third-party centralized system.

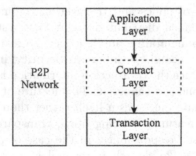

Fig. 1. Three horizontal and one vertical structures.

A block in blockchain is a storage unit. Blocks containing transaction information are connected in chronological order by pointers to form a blockchain, and blocks are composed of a block header and a block body. The block header includes parent hash, version number, mining difficulty, Merkle root hash, timestamp, and mining difficulty.

Meanwhile, blockchain is divided into three categories according to the access mechanism: public chain, Consortium chain and private chain. The public chain is open and transparent, and anyone has read and write access; the Consortium chain is open to specific organizations and groups, and read and write access is developed only to alliance members; the private chain read and write access is limited to a certain node.

2.2   Supply Chain Model

The traditional supply chain is a network of companies and departments that acquire and process materials into intermediate or finished products, and then deliver the finished products to users [3]. Ma Shihua et al. [4] proposed a supply chain cooperation method based on Shapley value for solving the revenue distribution problem among supply chain partners [5]. The supply chain management is a network consisting of suppliers, manufacturing and assembly plants, distribution centers, retailers, and end customers in the supply chain. Since the concept was introduced in the early 80s, the supply chain has developed greatly and can be divided into four levels according to the scope of coverage [6]: The Internal supply chain, Supply management, Chain structured supply chain and Mesh supply chain.

In recent years, with the popular application of blockchain technology, barcode technology and electronic fund transfer technology, blockchain technology provides technical support for new ideas in supply chain management. Naif Alzahrani et al. [7] proposed Block-Supply chain, which uses blockchain and near-field communication (NFC) technology to detect counterfeit attacks, replacing centralized supply chain design and balancing efficiency and security. Meanwhile, Thomas Bocek et al. [8] Abeyratne et al. [9] build a conceptual model of manufacturing supply chain management using blockchain technology, which guarantees the transparency and traceability of information and reduces supply chain management costs and operational risks. Srinivas Jangirall [10] et al. designed a blockchain and RFID-based authentication protocol for supply chains in 5G mobile edge computing environments to better trade-off the overhead of supply chain communication between security and computational cost, and improve the security of supply chain information transmission.

Supply chains exist in all service and manufacturing industries, but they differ greatly in structure and complexity [11]. However, compared with other fields, the research on the application of blockchain technology in the field of supply chain is not abundant. Most of the existing literature discusses the application of blockchain technology from a single perspective of supply chain finance or supply chain products, and the supply chain conceptual model or supply chain collaboration process model constructed in this way is rather thin, without exploring the specific application of blockchain consensus mechanism and smart contract in the field of the supply chain in depth [12]. The supply chain concept model or supply chain collaborative process model is thin, and does not explore the specific application of blockchain consensus mechanism and smart contract in the supply chain field.

This paper aims to use blockchain technology to build a dual -chain model of cross-border supply chain, to involve cross-border product-related parties as organizations in the alliance chain Hyperledger Fabric, to form an industrial environment of multi-party collaboration and win-win cooperation, and to adjust the inherent mode of blockchain consensus mechanism and smart contracts, so as to provide new ideas for the application of blockchain technology in supply chain information systems.

3   Blockchain-Based Supply Chain Framework

3.1   Model Overview

The cross-border supply chain system designed in this paper is an alliance chain Hyperledger Fabric platform with multiple participants and multiple maintenance, featuring decentralization, low deployment cost, and high scalability. Each organization node participating in the cross-border inventory system must first accept CA authorization from a third-party authority to read and write blockchain information, which raises the access threshold and reduces maintenance costs. In this system, each alliance chain node backs up an identical ledger, i.e., the public ledger, which makes the quality information and flow direction of each product in the supply chain transparent and cannot be modified. At the same time, the built-in multi-channel structure of Hyperledger Fabric can realize the data independence of different businesses, and each channel corresponds to a public ledger, which is maintained by the members in the channel, and the setting of the channel is also the basis for building a dual-chain model. Channel information is shown in Table 1.

Table 1. Blockchain information on the chain schematic.

Symbol definitions	Description
P = {P,P,P,P}	Channel node members
C = {C,C,C,C}	Channel
B = {B,B,B,B}	Block
T = {T,T,T,T}	Transaction
N	Blockchain network
O	Orderer nodes

. The basic architecture of the blockchain-based cross-border supply chain dual-chain model is shown in Fig. 2. The dual-chain system is divided into five layers: application layer, contract layer, consensus layer, network layer, and data layer. The cross-border supply chain industry focuses on the win-win cooperation of organizations and the ability of the system to handle business. Value transfer and profitability are the common goals of organizations, so the cross-border supply chain dual-chain model eliminates the incentive layer and adds the contract layer for business processing compared with the traditional blockchain system. In the data layer, the cross-border supply chain is different from the traditional blockchain system in that it uses IoT collection devices to automate the information processing on the chain, which eliminates data loss and modification in the process of information collection and transmission, and at the same time, the dual-chain structure built to cooperate with the import, export and inventory business separates product information from transaction information to solve the problem of blockchain supply chain information ecological silo. The network layer encapsulates the networking method, information dissemination protocol, data validation mechanism, and other elements of the dual-chain system of inventory and sales, which is the basis for data tamper-evident. The contract layer serves as a data interaction medium with the application layer, logically processes requests sent by the application layer data, and returns the corresponding results. The application layer calls the chaincode to query and verify the data on the chain by calling the SDK to realize functions such as product traceability, logistics tracking and privacy protection, and is the interface between the system and the outside world. There are many kinds of cross-border supply chain business information, and in order to facilitate classification and verification, this paper divides them into the following two categories and defines them.

Definition 1 Cross-border supply chain information data mainly includes Cross-border Product Information (CPI) and Financial Transaction Information (FTI), CPI includes information on the attributes of the products themselves, including production time, quality grade, yield, quality period, etc., FTI includes information on contracts, invoices, financing, credit, and other related transactions. CPI includes product attributes, including production time, quality level, yield, shelf life, etc. FTI includes contracts, invoices, financing, credit and other related transaction information.

Definition 2 CPI is stored in the Cross-border Product Information Chain (CPIC); FTIC is stored in the Financial Transaction Information Chain (FTIC).

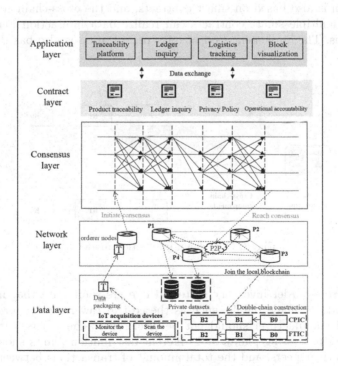

Fig. 2. Basic architecture of blockchain-based model for supply chain traceability.

3.2   Data Layer Module

Blockchain is a new software architecture to ensure the authenticity of data can only work in the blockchain network, and any step of product information from collection to transmission to the blockchain system may be modified. The data generated without relying on the support of hardware cannot ensure its original data authenticity. The model expands the scope of authenticity through the form of blockchain + IoT, so that the data is real and verifiable from generation to the whole chain, and after the external IoT node authorizes the read and write right, the product automatically records the data in the local network through the detection and scanning devices, and transmits it to the network layer through the local server, which receives the information After the package will be packaged into blocks and passed to other nodes in the channel to save.

In order to solve the problems such as confusion of books and difficulties in checking accounts, the model uses the dual-chain model of product information and transaction information, and the dual-chain model of blockchain-based inventory system can effectively isolate product information and transaction information and solve the problem of information silos in different chains. To solve the problem of information island on the chain, the system uses the cross-chain interoperability model and adds a relay organization to act as the medium of information interaction to achieve information separation without losing the internal connection of data, as shown in Fig. 3, the implementation of the relay organization is also based on smart contracts, and the cross-chain components formed by multiple smart contracts can realize data interaction between different chains. The implementation of relay organization is also based on smart contracts.

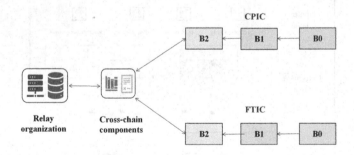

Fig. 3. Dual chain interaction model.

In the cross-border inventory system, there are some data that need to be recorded and not made public, such as the cost of raw materials produced by the original manufacturer should not be disclosed to consumers, the cooperation between processing plants and different distribution plants should not be disclosed to their peers, and the total amount of transactions between different organizations should not be disclosed, which need to be stored in the privacy data set in the network. For privacy data, the relevant participants will set up hardware sending routes in advance, and the information will not be sent to all nodes after collection by Orderer nodes but directly stored in the privacy database by privacy data authorizers and through Gossip protocol [13] It is sent to all authorized nodes, and only the privacy data hash value is provided to the public, as shown in Fig. 4, Organization 1 and Organization 3, where the authorized nodes are located, share a private dataset, while the unauthorized organization nodes only have the channel public ledger.

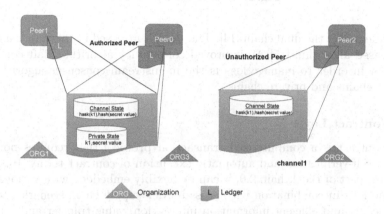

Fig. 4. Dual chain interaction model.

3.3 Network Layer

The network layer module contains the organization of node communication to synchronize the information uploaded from the IoT collection devices. All the nodes deployed by the supply chain participants need to communicate in a P2P network. As shown in Fig. 5, the relevant participants as nodes in the blockchain network upload the product information through the chaincode, and the Orderer node equipped with each channel sorts and packs the uploaded information submitted by the supply chain participants and then generates blocks and broadcasts them, and all nodes in the network receive the transaction blocks and verify the rationality, and after successful verification, they will connect with the local blockchain, and the block height increases and the uploading operation is completed.

3.4 Consensus Layer Module

Each node in the blockchain network can individually provide services for the application, preventing a single point of failure from affecting the normal operation of the entire supply chain system, and the consensus mechanism also ensures

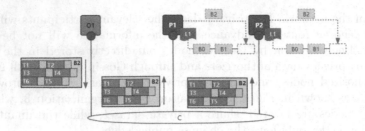

Fig. 5. Network layer module.

the uniqueness of the dual chain [14]. The model proposed in this paper uses the Paxos-based algorithm [15] An improved consistency algorithm Raft consensus algorithm in order to manage logs is the mainstream consensus algorithm for coalition chains and private chains.

3.5 Contract Layer

Smart contract is a computerized transaction protocol that requires no intermediary, self-verification and automatic execution of contract terms [16] As an important part of Blockchain 2.0, it can be flexibly embedded with various business functions in combination with cross-border supply chain scenarios to help realize secure and efficient information interaction, value transfer and information protection. As a middleware for business processing, the contract layer processes the requests issued by the application layer and data layer, which include product traceability, ledger query, privacy data inspection, logistics tracking, etc. The execution processing of the contract is embedded in the nodes of the blockchain bookkeeping function, and the requests arriving at the contract layer will be processed by the corresponding smart contracts and return the corresponding data, and the overall flow of contract invocation is shown in Fig. 6.

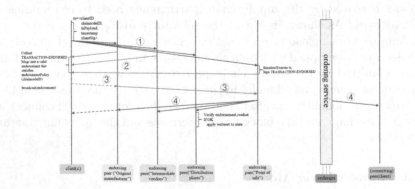

Fig. 6. Contract execution process.

1. The client initiates the transaction proposal, the backing node executes it and produces the signature. The transaction initiated by the client contains ¡ clientID, chaincodeID, txPayLoad, timestamp, clientSig¿ and other information sent to the endorser node in the organization node that has deployed the corresponding smart contract, and the endorser node simulates the proposal execution and produces its own signature.
2. The endorsement node returns the execution result with signature to the client. The endorsement node executes the proposal and packages it and returns the result to the client, which receives a certain number of returned results and executes the next step.
3. The client submits the transaction. The client receives enough endorsement results to combine the proposal, the results, and its own signature into one transaction to send to the Orederer node, which sorts and packages the submissions.
4. Commit. the sort node broadcasts the sorted packed blocks to all nodes in the organization.

There are more entities involved in the cross-border inventory system, and the business needs of different entities are different. In this paper, the participants are divided into five categories by analyzing the cross-border inventory process, and the process and the functions of each participant are shown in Fig. 7.

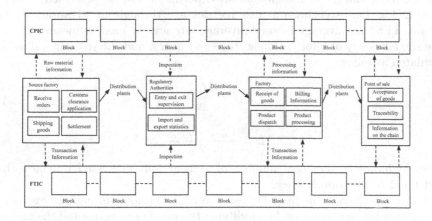

Fig. 7. System flow and each organization function diagram.

3.6 Application Layer

The application layer mainly realizes the interaction function between the terminal and the user, converts the interfaces provided by the outside world, such as traceability interface and book checking, into requests to the server side, and the server side returns the corresponding results. For example, if a consumer receives a product and wants to verify whether its origin is shown in the logo, the user only needs to input the product traceability code in the import and export platform, and the underlying business will return all information of the product after processing.

By Postman simulating the application layer to accept the request and return the query supply chain system product block information, the following information can be returned by selecting the product traceability code as DF-001 json values: "date": ["Key": "DF-100", "Record": "Date": "2022-06-04 20:19:42", "Id": "DF-100", "Name": "Jiangxi Nanchang", "ObjectType": "proObj", "ProdutName": "Pure Milk", "Quality": "Excellent", "State": "1", "Transaction Hash": "a9e8f73a477004cbc57654bf5ef28a03d88ec26cb62774a45c6954ed5d1fbdea"], the transaction ID indicates the summary of the transaction that enables the traceability of this product.

4   Analysis of Experimental Results

4.1   Test Indicators

In order to test the effectiveness of the blockchain-based dual-chain model proposed in this paper, the information storage and query of this system under the supply chain scenario is tested using Caliper, a performance testing plug-in, and the methodology of the simulation experiment will be described in detail in Sect. 4.3. The experimental test metrics are throughput (Transaction Per Second, TPS) and average latency (average latency. AL) as the metrics to evaluate the efficiency of information storage and query, and the relevant values are calculated as follows.

$$T_{\Delta t} = \frac{M_{\Delta t}}{\Delta t} \tag{1}$$

$$AL = \frac{T_{\max} + T_{\min}}{2} \tag{2}$$

where M indicates the total number of transactions processed by the t time model and transaction latency.

This chapter tests the model's resource consumption, throughput variation, and average latency variation by modifying the number of nodes and the amount of data in the test dataset.

4.2   Test Environment

This paper builds a supply chain based on blockchain model based on the Hyperledger Fabric federated chain framework, writes smart contracts using Golang programming language and integrat, es them into chaincode, and the chaincode containing multiple smart contracts is deployed in the blockchain network in the following experimental environment: virtual machine Ubuntu 20.04 64-bit, Fabric 2.2, Docker 20.10. 16, Golang 1.17.5, Caliper 0.42, a 1.10 GHz Intel Core i7-10710U CPU computer. The Fabric network is simulated to run through Docker containers, and the Docker containers launched during the experiment are shown in Table 2. The cross-border import and export system consists of multiple organizations, and for the convenience of simulation, each organization consists of a Peer node, an Orderer node, CouchDB as the database to store transaction information, and Caliper as the tool to test the performance.

Table 2. Docker containers started during the experiment.

Docker Container name	Quantity	Function
Fabric-Peer	4	Client to initiate a trade request
Fabric-Orderer	4	Transaction orderer nodes
Fabric-CouchDB	4	Transaction storage database
Caliper	1	Blockchain performance testing

4.3 Efficiency Testing

In order to test the write throughput and average latency of the model under the condition of different alliance chain nodes, two sets of test datasets were created, and 2000, 4000, 6000, 8000, 10000, and 12000 transactions were initiated by Caliper to an organization node with a guaranteed write success rate of 100%, and in order to avoid experimental accidents, each experiment was repeated 5 times to obtain the average. Avoid experimental chance, the results are shown in Fig. 8a), it can be seen that when the number of nodes is 2, the transaction TPS is stable above 300 transactions/s. The throughput decreases more significantly, when the throughput in each data volume case is less than 2 nodes, but still can maintain above 300 transactions/s. As shown in Fig. 8b), the response time of system writes increases with the number of nodes, and the system latency can reach below the second level.

The resource consumption when recording the maximum throughput is shown in Table 3. The hardware consumption of the components in the model is not high, which can meet the deployment requirements in the actual cross-border supply chain scenario.

Table 3. Resource consumption at maximum throughput.

Node type	Cup% (avg)	Memory (avg)
Peer	31.05	82.2
Orderer	5.25	20.5

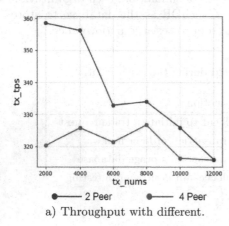

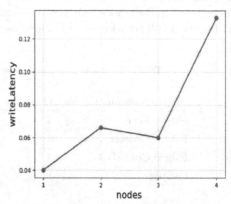

a) Throughput with different.   b) Write latency with different nodes.

Fig. 8. Performance chart

Table 4. Model Comparison.

System model	Article [17]	Article [18]	Article [19]	Article [20]	Model of this article
Decentralization	No	Yes	Yes	Yes	Yes
Control access	No	Yes	Yes	Yes	Yes
Privacy Protection	No	No	Yes	Yes	Yes
Gas consumption	No	No	Yes	No	Yes
IoT devices	No	Yes	No	No	Yes

Different information storage methods have a greater impact on the query efficiency, the system query is achieved by key-value pairs efficiency graph shown in 10, from the graph it can be seen that the number of nodes has a greater impact on the query throughput, when the number of nodes is 4, the query throughput is 40TPS (Table 4).

Article [19] is a traditional inventory management model where control access does not exist at the system level and requires manual processing arrangements based on actual business, Article [20] equipped with IoT collection devices but not equipped with private datasets for supply chain information, private data cannot be handled, Article [21] The blockchain framework used is Ether, and transaction fees need to be submitted for each Article [22]. The literature is equipped with privacy protection module, but the source of information cannot be guaranteed to be true and accurate.

5 Conclusion

Blockchain technology is in the development stage, and how to realize industrial combination is the focus of the industry. In this paper, we propose a blockchain-based inventory dual-chain model for cross-border inventory problem, which solves the problems of easy data tampering, opaque information and confusing books of the traditional inventory system, promotes the cooperation among global enterprises and improves business efficiency. Experiments show that the blockchain-based inventory dual-chain model has the ability to carry current inventory commercial capabilities. At present, IOT collection devices cannot automatically chain information, and the collection devices are unstable and vulnerable to attacks. In order to realize the direct chain of information, it is necessary to design a blockchain-specific module/chip, so that the blockchain can be deeply integrated with the IoT to realize automated and credible data collection, and in the future, it will be deeply combined with IoT devices to realize fast, low-latency and low-cost data credible chain of terminal devices.

Acknowledgements. This work is supported by the No. 62262030, 62067003, National Natural Science Foundation of China (NSFC) under Grant No. 61962026, the National Natural Science Key Foundation of China grant No. 61832014 and No. 62032016, the National Natural Science Foundation of China under Grant No. 62002143, the Natural Science Foundation of Jiangxi Province under Grant No. 20192ACBL21031 and the Foundation of Jiangxi Educational Committee under Grant No. GJJ210338.

References

1. Mi, Y.: Research on the optimization mechanism of cross-border e-commerce development model in china—based on the perspective of supply chain. Bus. Econ. Res. 136–140 (2022)
2. Chen, W., Zheng, Z.: Blockchain data analysis: status quo, trends and challenges. Comput. Res. Dev. **55**, 1853–1870 (2018)
3. Lee, H.L.: Material management in decentralized supply chains. Oper. Res. **41**, 835–847 (1993)
4. Ma, S.: Income distribution mechanism among supply chain partners based on Shapley's value method. Industr. Eng. Manage. **2006**, 1007–5420 (2006)
5. Chu, C.: Supply chain management: problems, determinants and implementation strategies. In: Proceedings of the First China- Japan Joint Conference on Industrial Engineering and Management, pp. 135–142 (1998)
6. Harland, C.: Supply chain operational performance roles. Integr. Manuf. Syst. **8**, 70–78 (1997)
7. Naif, A.: Block-supply chain: a new anti-counterfeiting supply chain using NFC and blockchain, pp. 30–35. Association for Computing Machinery (2018)

8. Bocek, T., Rodrigues, B.B., Strasser, T., Stiller, B.: Blockchains everywhere - a use-case of blockchains in the pharma supply-chain. In: 2017 IFIP/IEEE Symposium on Integrated Network and Service Management (IM), pp. 772–777 (2017)
9. Abeyratne, S.A.: Blockchain ready manufacturing supply chain using distributed ledger. Int. J. Res. Eng. Technol. **5**, 1–10 (2016)
10. Jangirala, S., Das, A.K., Vasilakos, A.V.: Designing secure lightweight blockchain-enabled RFID-based authentication protocol for supply chains in 5g mobile edge computing environment. IEEE Trans. Industr. Inform. **16**(11), 7081–7093 (2020)
11. Gupta, S.: Supply chain management in complex manufacturing. IIE Solut. **5**, 18–23 (1997)
12. Yang, H.: Construction of mutual trust and win-win supply chain information platform based on blockchain technology. Sci. Technol. Progr. Countermeas. **35**, 21–31 (2018)
13. Jelasity, M., Voulgaris, S., Guerraoui, R., Kermarrec, A.-M., van Steen, M.: Gossip-based peer sampling. ACM Trans. Comput. Syst. **25**(3), 8-es (2007)
14. Castro, M., Liskov, B.: Practical byzantine fault tolerance. In: Proceedings of the Third Symposium on Operating Systems Design and Implementation, OSDI 1999, USA, pp. 173–186. USENIX Association (1999)
15. Zhao, W.: On the quorum requirement and value selection rule for fast paxos. In: 2014 IEEE 5th International Conference on Software Engineering and Service Science, pp. 406–409 (2014)
16. He, P.: A review of blockchain technology and application prospects. Comput. Sci. **44**, 1–7+15 (2017)
17. Zhou, Y.: Design and implementation of invoicing inventory management system based on spring cloud microservice architecture. Industr. Control Comput. **31**, 129–130+133 (2018)
18. Shao, H.: Research on supply chain traceability model based on blockchain. J. Jiamusi Univ. (Nat. Sci. Edn.) **40**, 62–65 (2022)
19. Zhang, C.: Design of supply chain traceability system based on side chain technology. Comput. Eng. **45**, 1–8 (2019)
20. Yu, H.: Research on traceability information protection model of mybibliographyrice supply chain based on blockchain. Trans. Chin. Soc. Agric. Mach. **51**, 328–335 (2020)

A Multi-objective Optimization Method for Latency-Sensitive Applications in MEC-Enabled Smart Campus Using SMS-EMOA

Hanmeng Wang[1,2], Kai Peng[1,2(✉)], and Bohai Zhao[1,2]

[1] Huaqiao University, Quanzhou, China
[2] State Key Laboratory for Novel Software Technology, Nanjing University, Nanjing, People's Republic of China
kai.peng@hqu.edu.cn

Abstract. The Internet of Things (IoT) enables all devices to sense, communicate, which has given rise to the evolution of traditional educational planning. Benefiting from this revolution, a new paradigm, named smart campus came into being. More specifically, teaching way has changed significantly with the help of quite a few emerging real-time applications. However, the computing capabilities of smart devices (SDs) are constrained. Fortunately, mobile edge computing (MEC) has emerged as a scalable computing model to augment capacity of SDs by placing computing resources closer to users. However, the resources of the ESs in MEC are not inexhaustible. In view of this, we investigate computation offloading for latency-sensitive application which is modeled as workflow application in MEC-enabled smart campuses. Specifically, time consumption, energy consumption, and resource utilization are regarded as our optimized goals. To this end, a corresponding method is proposed. Extensive experimental results show that our method can achieve effective optimization effect in terms of given objectives.

Keywords: Smart Campus · Mobile Edge Computing · Workflow Applications · Multi-Objective Optimization

This work is supported by the National Science Foundation of China under Grant No. 61902133, the Fundamental Research Funds for the Central Universities under Grant No. ZQN-817, Quanzhou Science and Technology Project under Grant No. 2020C050R, Huaqiao University 2021 Teacher Teaching Development Reform Project under Grant No. HQJG202120.

Y. Cao and X. Shao (Eds.): MONAMI 2022, LNICST 474, pp. 63–77, 2023.
https://doi.org/10.1007/978-3-031-32443-7_5

1   Introduction

Combining the collected data with sensor devices enables people to experience intelligent services, realize information exchange through different media, and thus connect everything, this is Internet of Things(IoT) [1,2]. IoT has spawned many new applications, among them, smart campus is one of the most popular representatives [3–5].

Generally, smart campus is regarded as an information-based instance, which can provide networked teaching, research, management, and life services for students and teachers by collecting, integrating, and utilizing digital information. Different from the traditional model, smart campus facilitates smart devices (SDs), sensors, and campus servers to provide more accurate and timely information services, thereby improving school operations' efficiency [6–8]. In addition, with the development of IoT technologies, such as virtualization, wireless communication and RFID, it is credible that smart campus has ushered in its historical moment [9,10].

Generally, most campus networks mainly use large-scale cloud-like centralized service, this kind of service is simple and effective for the traditional campus and has been widely used for many years [11–13]. However, with the popularization of education and the expansion of electronic devices, the disadvantages of centralized service are gradually reflected. On the one hand, more and more SDs are flooding into the campus network, which means that the threshold of the central server load must be constantly breached, and thus requires continuous and cumbersome maintenance [14,15]. On the other hand, the bandwidth allocated to each device will drop rapidly as the number of SDs increases. To sum up, it is challenging to address above shortcomings [16,17].

Fortunately, the advent of mobile edge computing (MEC) offers hope for solving this problem [18]. In MEC scenario, edge servers (ESs) are usually arranged at the edge of the network closer to SDs to provide low response latency and high-quality services. Applications generated by mobile users (MUs) are allowed to be offloaded to the nearest ES for processing. Nevertheless, ESs are characterized as heterogeneous and resource-constrained. In addition, the coverage of ES services is also limited. Therefore, how to select the most suitable ES is a critical challenge.

In view of aforementioned description and challenge, we study the computation offloading for latency-sensitive applications in MEC-enabled smart campus scenario. The main contributions of this paper are summarized as follows.

- Firstly, the latency-sensitive applications are represented as sequential constrained workflow applications. In addition, computation offloading for workflow application is formulated as a multi-objective optimization issue where time consumption, energy consumption, and resource utilization are considered as the optimization objectives.
- Secondly, a corresponding system model and mathematical model are established. In what follows, a method based on overcapacity non-dominated sorting, called MOWASC, is proposed to get the optimal offloading strategy.

– Finally, we evaluate the advantages of our method through experimental tests under different scenarios. Extensive experiments have verified that our method can effectively reduce time and energy consumption, as well as improve the resource utilization of ESs.

The forthcoming portions of this paper is described as follows. First, we discuss the related work. Next, the definition of the computational model and optimization problems are illustrated. And then, the method and the related experimental evaluation are described. Finally, the conclusion and our future work are summarized.

2   Related Work

In this section, the existing work of computation offloading for general applications as well as workflow applications are reviewed, respectively.

Computation Offloading for General Applications. Computation offloading is a potent technology that can boost computing capacity while lessening the demand for MUs. Chang et al. [19] dynamically migrated the task to the edge fog node for execution to decrease service delay and energy usage. On the basis of hierarchical MEC networks, Li et al. [20] expanded the auxiliary cloudlets collaborative computing and relieved the user's operating costs. The complexity of the network architecture may lead to resource contention and unequal allocation. [21] focused on the resource allocation in MEC network, and the resource utilization and load balancing are framed as optimization goals in a heuristic algorithm. An online dynamic task assignment scheme was employed in [22], which can allocate resources dynamically, resulting in high-efficiency and low-latency communication. Similar contemporary techniques were used with MEC to increase computing effectiveness. Huang et al. [23] utilized the benefits of deep reinforcement learning to serve multiple wireless devices, which improves the quality of service for the MEC network.

Computation Offloading for Workflow Applications. Computation offloading strategies for general tasks cannot be directly applied to latency-sensitive and task-dependent items. Huang et al. [24] put data compilation into service, and customized differentiated offloading schemes for data-dependent and latency-sensitive programs. For the scheduling problem of workflow, Sun et al. [25] formulated the problem as an integer question and combined two algorithms to shorten the manufacturing time of workflow. Xu et al. [26] studied the computation offloading of workflow applications in cloud environments, which migrates tasks to the cloud and cloudlets to save energy consumption of SDs. Due to the particularity of the items in workflow, the completion time is attentively considered in the research. Ma et al. [27] proposed a deadline-constrained workflow service scheme that minimizes the application execution cost according to a cost-aware scheduling algorithm.

Different from the existing studies, in this paper, we focus on the computation offloading for latency-sensitive applications in MEC-enabled smart campus. Additionally, this study considers the dependence between sub-task while the time consumption, energy consumption, and resource utilization are jointly optimized.

3   System Model and Problem Formulation

In this section, the MEC-enabled smart campus system model is introduced firstly, followed by the description of workflow application, and then mathematical models for each optimization objective are introduced.

3.1   System Model

Figure 1 depicts the structure of the MEC-enabled smart campus, which guarantees the integration of management, teaching, and scientific research. Some MUs and infrastructures are included in the smart campus for teaching activities and campus management. The general MUs are students and teachers, who usually use mobile phones and laptops for socializing and learning online. Same for administrators, who frequently employ intelligent network equipment to monitor campus governance and network security issues. Among them, not only can MUs use the local area network (LAN) for data transfer with surrounding ESs, but they can interact with the Cloud Center (CC) over the wide area network (WAN).

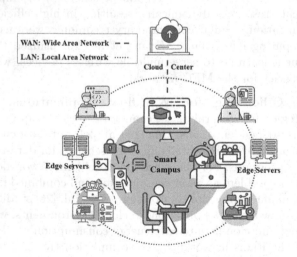

Fig. 1. An MEC-Enabled Smart Campus Architecture.

3.2 Workflow Application

One special feature, the multiple data dependencies that form a complicated application which can be reflected as a directed acyclic graph (DAG). Figure 2 shows a workflow consisting of eight items (I_1-I_8), they have different demands on resources. The weight of each edge represents the amount of data transferred between two tasks, while the order of task execution can be defined as a set $Ord = \{\, I_1,\ (I_2,\ I_3,\ I_4),\ I_5,\ (I_6,\ I_7),\ I_8\,\}$.

It can be seen from Fig. 2, except for the last item I_8, after each task is completed, some information will be transmitted to guarantee the next calculation, which is a special feature of workflow applications. After item I_1 is executed, 25, 15, and 20 pieces of data will be transferred to I_2, I_3, and I_4, respectively. After the calculation of I_2, I_3, and I_4 is finished, 30, 20, and 45 pieces of data will be transmitted to I_5, respectively. Similarly, after I_6, and I_7 are executed, the corresponding data will be transmitted to item I_8.

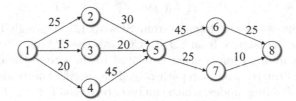

Fig. 2. An example of Workflow Application.

For those nodes that need to receive the data, they will work when all messages from their predecessor items are collected. When I_5 only gets one or two data among I_2, I_3, and I_4, it means that the preparation work for I_5 has not been completed. Likewise, I_8 only can start when I_8 receive complete data from I_6 and I_7.

P_i^w denotes a task to be processed, in which the value of w is the index of workflow, and i represents the index of the items in the workflow. The offloading strategies of tasks can be defined as S_i^w as follows.

$$S_i^w = \begin{cases} 0, & \text{if } P_i^w \text{ is executed on SDs,} \\ 1, ..., C, & \text{if } P_i^w \text{ is offloaded to ESs,} \\ C+1, & \text{if } P_i^w \text{ is offloaded to CC.} \end{cases} \tag{1}$$

$S_i^w = 0$ means that the computation task is executed on the SDs while $\{\, 1, \ldots,\ C\,\}$ represents that task is offloaded to the ESs and $C + 1$ indicates that task is migrated to the CC for execution.

3.3 Time Consumption Model

The system time consumption T_{sum} is introduced in this subsection, which is made up of task transmission time T_{tra}, queue waiting time T_{que} and task execution time T_{exe}.

Transmission Time. The time for tasks to migrate to the executing side and send processed data to the successor node constitutes task transmission time, which can be calculated as

$$T_{tra} = T_{tra}(P_a^w) + \frac{D_{a,b}}{B_{a,b}}. \tag{2}$$

The offloading time $T_{tra}(P_a^w)$ is the delay in data transmission when the task arrives at the associated server, which varies depending on where the work is carried out.

$$T_{tra}(P_a^w) = \begin{cases} 0, & S_i^w = 0, \\ L_{LAN}, & S_i^w \subseteq \{1, ...C\}, \\ L_{WAN}, & S_i^w = C + 1, \end{cases} \tag{3}$$

where L_{LAN} represents the latency from SDs to ESs through the LAN and L_{WAN} indicates the latency from SDs to CC over the WAN.

The time for information transfer is related to the size of the data $D_{a,b}$ and the bandwidth of the transmission path $B_{a,b}$. The specific bandwidth will change with different offloading modes, which can be categorized into the following three groups.

$$B_{a,b} = \begin{cases} \infty, & S_a^w = S_b^w, \\ B_{ee}, & S_a^w \subseteq \{1, ...C\}, & S_b^w \subseteq \{1, ...C\}, \\ B_{ce}, & S_a^w \subseteq \{1, ...C\}, & S_b^w = C + 1. \end{cases} \tag{4}$$

Among them, Bee is the bandwidth between ESs. When the task in ESs transfer data to CC, the packets will be transmitted through the WAN, and the bandwidth is Bce at this time.

Queue Waiting Time. ESs have an advantage in physical distance compared to the CC, which can reduce round-trip latency when tasks are offloaded. When many tasks are migrated to ESs, there is a need to queue for available resources if all the current resources are occupied, as resources are limited. The time consumed by queuing is called the queue waiting time.

Tasks typically arrive in queues at random. According to the queuing theory [28], the average queue time T_{que} is used to complete the model.

M parallel-running virtual machines (VMs), each with a service time that obeys negative exponential distribution with λ_s, are set up. Correspondingly, the time slots that tasks arrive successively obey the negative exponential distribution with λ_n. The average queue length L_a is composed of the average length of the line-up plus the average number of customers currently serving. The specific calculation of L_a is

$$L_a = \sum_{N=M+1}^{\infty} (N - M)P_N + \frac{\lambda_n}{\lambda_s}, \tag{5}$$

where P_N is the probability distribution state of the queue length N after the system reaches the equilibrium state. The average number of customers being served can be obtained by $\frac{\lambda_n}{\lambda_s}$. In summary, the average waiting time T_{que} can be calculated as

$$T_{que} = \frac{L_a}{\lambda_n} - \frac{1}{\lambda_s}. \tag{6}$$

Task Execution Time. The execution time T_{exe} is related to the amount of data and the computing rate of the device, which is calculated as

$$T_{exe} = \begin{cases} \frac{D_i^w}{H_e}, & S_i^w \subseteq \{1, ...C\}, \\ \frac{D_i^w}{H_c}, & S_i^w = C+1, \end{cases} \tag{7}$$

where D_i^w indicates the size of data while H_c and H_e represent the data processing capabilities of CC and ESs.

Total Time Consumption. After the above analysis and calculation of time consumption, the total time consumption T_{sum} can be expressed as

$$T_{sum} = \begin{cases} T_{tra} + T_{que} + T_{exe}, & S_i^w \subseteq \{1, ...C\}, \\ T_{tra} + T_{exe}, & \text{otherwise.} \end{cases} \tag{8}$$

3.4   Energy Consumption Model

As energy consumption usually has a positive correlation with time consumption, and thus the total energy consumption of the system E_{sum} can be expressed as

$$E_{sum} = \begin{cases} E_{tra} + E_{que} + E_{exe}, & S_i^w \subseteq \{1, ...C\}, \\ E_{tra} + E_{exe}, & \text{otherwise.} \end{cases} \tag{9}$$

Among them, E_{tra}, E_{que} and E_{exe} represent the energy consumption of task transmission, queuing, and execution, respectively.

3.5   Resource Utilization Model

Resource utilization, obtained by the number of VMs currently being occupied in the VM pool, reflects the usage of ES resources. The k-th VM VM_k in the VM pool has completed T tasks, and its resource utilization R_k is

$$R_k = \frac{1}{T} \cdot \sum_{w=1}^{W} \sum_{i=1}^{I} V_{w,i} \cdot F_{w,i}^k, \tag{10}$$

where $V_{w,i}$ is the VM workload occupied by P_i^w, and $F_{w,i}^k$ is a flag to determine whether the workload has been offloaded to the k-th ES.

$$F_{w,i}^k = \begin{cases} 1, & \text{if } V_{w,i} \text{ offloaded to the k} - \text{th ES,} \\ 0, & \text{otherwise.} \end{cases} \qquad (11)$$

By calculating the resource utilization of each ES, the average resource utilization A_R of the ESs can be expressed as

$$A_R = \frac{1}{E_E} \cdot \sum_{k=1}^{K} R_k, \qquad (12)$$

where E_E, the number of ESs occupied, can be defined as follows.

$$E_E = \sum_{k=1}^{K} FE, \qquad (13)$$

where FE is a flag to determine the status of ES.

$$FE = \begin{cases} 1, & \text{if the k} - \text{th ES is employed,} \\ 0, & \text{otherwise.} \end{cases} \qquad (14)$$

4   Algorithm Design

In this section, the basic framework and core steps of the multi-objective optimization method for latency-sensitive applications in MEC-Enabled Smart Campus (MOWASC)are introduced. First, task migration strategies are generated using SMS-EMOA. Then, the normalized fitness value is used to determine the optimal placement strategy.

4.1   Initialization

Some fundamental parameters need to be set for the algorithm, such as the population settings, the maximum number of evaluations, the probability and distribution indices for mutation and crossover, the comparator dominance comparator, and the number of matches.   In this paper, genes symbolize the task performed site and chromosomes represent the computational offloading scheme. Number 0 means the task is executed locally, 9 for CC, and number 1 to number 8 represents the task is executed in any of ESs.

4.2   Crossover and Mutation

Swapping the intersection genes in two coding strings, hoping to produce progeny of superior caliber, is the random crossover, which can be illustrated in Fig. 3. In the operation of Fig. 3, the number 3 is bartered with the number 5, which

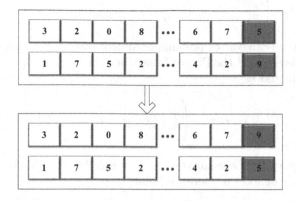

Fig. 3. Crossover operation.

means that the ES selected has shifted. The interchange of the numbers 5 and 9 indicates that the execution location is changed from ESs to CC.

The mutation is achieved by modifying chromosomes to ensure the diversity of the population and avoid early convergence of the solution set. An illustration of generating new individuals by mutation is shown in Fig. 4. After the mutation operation, the second task is executed locally, and the third task is executed by CC.

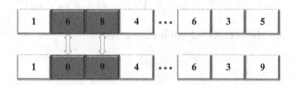

Fig. 4. Mutation operation.

4.3 Non-dominated Sorting

In multi-objective optimization, A dominates B signifying that the benefits of all objectives of solution A are superior to that of B, which can be defined as $A \prec B$. Non-dominance sorting is the process of sorting the solutions to distinct ranks $R_1, ...R_v$ by the dominance relationships.

4.4 Elimination Mechanism

$d(S, P)$ indicates the dominant points of the point S in the set P_t. $d(S, P)$ can highlight the sparse regions of the solution set and retain the diversity of the population, which can be measured as

$$d(S, P) = |\{y \in P \mid y \prec S\}|. \tag{15}$$

Hypervolume (HV) can convey the unique contribution of the current strategy. A benefit is HV also can get the Pareto front when the reference point is unknown. HV can be evaluated as

$$V(A, Y_{ref}) = \wedge \left(\bigcup_{y \in A} \{Y \mid y \prec Y \prec Y_{ref}\} \right), \tag{16}$$

where $\wedge$ symbolizes the Lebesgue measure, A signifies the Pareto optimal solution set, and Y_{ref} denotes a reference point.

$d(S, P)$ is employed as the selection criterion when the solution dominates. Otherwise, the size of HV is chosen as the requirement if all individuals of P_t are non-dominated [29, 30].

4.5 Optimal Selection

As computation offloading is a discrete problem, adaptation values for time consumption $V(T_{sum})$, energy consumption $V(E_{sum})$, and resource utilization $V(A_R)$ is required. The normalized fitness value fit is used for the determination of the optimal solution, which can be expressed as

$$fit = \alpha \cdot V(T_{sum}) + \beta \cdot V(E_{sum}) + \delta \cdot V(A_R), \tag{17}$$

where α, β and δ is the weight of each objective

4.6 Method Overview

Algorithm 1 illustrates the overall process of MOWASC. Firstly, some basic parameters are initialized (Lines 1–2). Then, a new generation is generated by crossover and mutation (Line 4). Then, Eqs. (8), (9), and (13) are used to calculate the time and energy consumption and resource utilization (Lines 5–7). Then, the solution is classified as different ranks by non-dominated sorting (Line 8). Then, $d(S, P)$ is used to complete the initial screening in the elimination mechanism, then the further disuse through HV to perform, and P_{t+1} is updated finally by calculating the fitness value (Lines 9–17). The algorithm will end when the maximum number of iterations is met (Lines 3–19).

5 Comparison and Analysis of Experimental Results

In this section, we demonstrate the effectiveness of MOWASC through extensive experiments. Firstly, the experimental setup is introduced. Then, the comparative algorithms and experimental evaluation are given.

Algorithm 1. MOWASC

Input: The max iterations
Output: The offspring population P_{t+1}
1: $P_0 \leftarrow$ Initial population
2: $t \leftarrow 0$
3: **while** max iterations fulfilled **do**
4:      Update P_t by crossover and mutation
5:      Calculate T_{sum} by Equation (8)
6:      Calculate E_{sum} by Equation (9)
7:      Calculate A_R by Equation (13)
8:      $\{ R_1, ... R_v \} \leftarrow$ non-dominated sort(P)
9:      **if** v>1 **then**
10:         Calculate $d(S, P)$ by Equation (15)
11:         r $\leftarrow R_v$ with highest $d(S, P)$
12:     **else**
13:         Calculate HV by Equation (16)
14:         r $\leftarrow R_1$ with lowest HV
15:     **end if**
16:     $P_{t+1} \leftarrow \{ P_t \setminus r \}$
17:     $t++$
18: **end while**
19:
20: Optimal selection through fit **return** P_{t+1}

5.1   Experimental Setting

All the simulation experiments are processed on a Win10 64-bit Operating System based on JAVA and the processor of physical machine is AMD Ryzen 7 PRO 4750U with Radeon Graphics 1.70 GHz.

In order to evaluate the applicability of these experiments in smart campus, two different groups of experiment are carried out. Firstly, to test the experimental utility when changing with the number of MUs, we study a test with 8 ESs serving, whose frequencies are distributed between 2000 and 2500.

Then, the second experiment is set up to test whether the effect would make adjustments for some challenging heterogeneous workflows. Two MUs by default in this experiment, each MU has an inconsistent workflow. The detailed parameter settings in experiments are listed in Table 1.

Next, the comparative methods, namely, Benchmark and FCFS are introduced in detail.

- **Benchmark** Tasks are distributed in a 2:3:15 ratio. Numbers 2, 3, and 15 indicate the probability that the task is executed locally, offloaded to CC, and migrated to ESs, respectively.
- **First Come First Service (FCFS)** Tasks are executed sequentially. Counting from 0, the 0-th arriving task is executed locally, and the tasks { 1, ..., C } are offloaded to the ESs for execution. Task $C + 1$ is offloaded to CC for execution.

Table 1. Parameters Setting

Parameter	Value
The computing frequency of SD	500 Mhz
The computing frequency of CC	3000 MHz
The computing frequency of ES	2000 MHz
The active power of SD	2 W
The idle power of SD	0.1 W
The transmission power of SD	0.8 W
The propagation time of LAN	0.5 ms
The propagation time of WAN	2 ms
The bandwidth of LAN	200 kps
The bandwidth of WAN	150 kps

5.2   Experimental Evaluation and Discussion

In this subsection, the optimized results of total time consumption, energy consumption, and resource utilization are comprehensively analyzed.

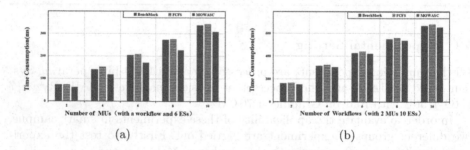

(a)   (b)

Fig. 5. Comparison of time consumption.

Comparison of Time Consumption. The total time consumption is obtained by Eq. (8) and the comparative outcomes of FCFS, Benchmark, and MOWASC in two distinct circumstances are depicted in Fig. 5. It can be seen that the time overhead of the methods FCFS and Benchmark is similar, while MOWASC consumes the least time. Focusing on Fig. 5(a), MOWASC requires 16% and 14% less time than FCFS and Benchmark, respectively. In Fig. 5(b), as the quantity of workflows changes, the optimization effect and trend are similar to the situation in Fig. 5(a). In conclusion, with the increase of MUs or workflows, MOWASC is the best method in reducing time consumption.

Comparison of Energy Consumption. The total energy consumption is calculated by Eq. (9) and Fig. 6(a) and Fig. 6(b) depict the experimental comparison of FCFS, Benchmark, and MOWASC. It can be seen that FCFS consumes the most energy, followed by Benchmark, while the energy depletion of MOWASC is always less than them under different situations. More specifically, compared with the other two methods, the overall energy optimization revenue of MOWASC reached 50%. In conclusion, MOWASC can obtain the best effect in reducing energy consumption.

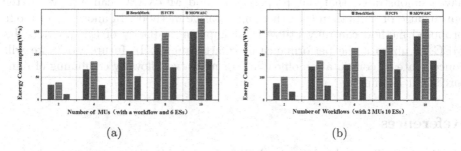

Fig. 6. Comparison of energy consumption.

Comparison of Resource Utilization. The resource utilization of ESs can be obtained by Eq. (13) and the related experiment effects of methods FCFS, Benchmark, and MOWASC can be found in Fig. 7(a) and Fig. 7(b). From Fig. 7(a) and Fig. 7(b), we can see that the resource utilization of method MOWASC is the highest under various conditions, with FCFS and Benchmark far behind. This means that, compared with other methods, method MOWASC adequately schedules the computing resources of ESs. When the number of workflows is 10, the magnitude of the rise in MOWASC slowed down. To sum up, MOWASC can obatin the best effect in optimizing resource utilization.

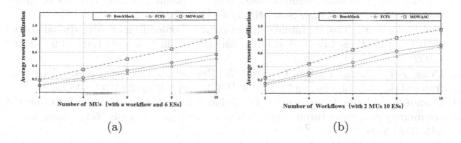

Fig. 7. Comparison of resource utilization.

6   Conclusion

The integration of smart campus and MEC is an awesome way to improve the service quality of the campus. Latency-sensitive applications are representative applications, and the execution of such applications affects the overall performance of the smart campus. In this paper, this kind of application is modeled as workflows. Furthermore, energy consumption, time consumption, and resource utilization are seen as the optimization goals. To this end, we proposed an intelligent computation offloading method using SMS-EMOA. Extensive experiments have demonstrated that our proposed method MOWASC can achieve better optimization results than the other comparative methods. In another word, our proposed method can fully utilize the computing capacity of ESs provided by MEC to improve the performance of smart campus. In future work, we will concentrate on computation offloading for multi-workflow by combining of reinforcement learning.

References

1. Gubbi, J., Buyya, R., Marusic, S., Palaniswami, M.: Internet of things (IoT): a vision, architectural elements, and future directions. Future Gener. Comput. Syst. **29**(7), 1645–1660 (2013)
2. Wu, H., Wolter, K., Jiao, P., Deng, Y., Zhao, Y., Xu, M.: EEDTO: an energy-efficient dynamic task offloading algorithm for blockchain-enabled IoT-edge-cloud orchestrated computing. IEEE Internet Things J. **8**(4), 2163–2176 (2020)
3. Xu, X., et al.: Edge content caching with deep spatiotemporal residual network for IoV in smart city. ACM Trans. Sens. Netw. (TOSN) **17**(3), 1–33 (2021)
4. Bastari, A., Bandono, A., Suharyo, O.S.: The development strategy of smart campus for improving excellent navy human resources. Global J. Eng. Technol. Adv. **6**(2), 033–043 (2021)
5. Chen, T.C.: Smart campus and innovative education based on wireless sensor. Microprocess. Microsyst. **81**, 103678 (2021)
6. Peng, G., Wu, H., Wu, H., Wolter, K.: Constrained multiobjective optimization for IoT-enabled computation offloading in collaborative edge and cloud computing. IEEE Internet Things J. **8**(17), 13723–13736 (2021)
7. Li, W.: Design of smart campus management system based on internet of things technology. J. Intell. Fuzzy Syst. **40**, 3159–3168 (2021)
8. Liu, P., Peng, K., Tao, P.: Intelligent computation offloading for educational virtual reality applications in smart campus using MoCell. Comput. Intell. **39**, 82–103 (2022)
9. Dong, Z.Y., Zhang, Y., Yip, C., Swift, S., Beswick, K.: Smart campus: definition, framework, technologies, and services. IET Smart Cities **2**(1), 43–54 (2020)
10. Prandi, C., Monti, L., Ceccarini, C., Salomoni, P.: Smart campus: fostering the community awareness through an intelligent environment. Mob. Netw. Appl. **25**(3), 945–952 (2020)
11. Bello, S.A., et al.: Cloud computing in construction industry: use cases, benefits and challenges. Autom. Constr. **122**, 103441 (2021)
12. Schleier-Smith, J., et al.: What serverless computing is and should become: the next phase of cloud computing. Commun. ACM **64**(5), 76–84 (2021)

13. Wu, H., Sun, Y., Wolter, K.: Energy-efficient decision making for mobile cloud offloading. IEEE Trans. Cloud Comput. **8**, 570–584 (2020)
14. Abdulqadir, H.R., et al.: A study of moving from cloud computing to fog computing. Qubahan Acad. J. **1**(2), 60–70 (2021)
15. Kourgiozou, V., Commin, A.N., Dowson, M., Rovas, D.V., Mumovic, D.: Scalable pathways to net zero carbon in the UK higher education sector: a systematic review of smart energy systems in university campuses. Renew. Sustain. Energy Rev. **147**, 111234 (2021)
16. Peng, K., Zhao, B., Bilal, M., Xu, X.: Reliability-aware computation offloading for delay-sensitive applications in mec-enabled aerial computing. IEEE Trans. Green Commun. Netw. **6**(3), 1511–1519 (2022)
17. Qu, G., Wu, H.: DMRO: a deep meta reinforcement learning-based task offloading framework for edge-cloud computing. IEEE Trans. Netw. Serv. Manag. **18**, 3448–3459 (2021)
18. Xu, X., Tian, H., Zhang, X., Qi, L., He, Q., Dou, W.: DisCOV: distributed COVID-19 detection on X-ray images with edge-cloud collaboration. IEEE Trans. Serv. Comput. **15**(3), 1206–1219 (2022)
19. Chang, Z., Liu, L., Guo, X., Sheng, Q.: Dynamic resource allocation and computation offloading for IoT fog computing system. IEEE Trans. Ind. Inf. **17**, 3348–3357 (2021)
20. Li, N., Yang, S., Wang, Z., Hao, W., Zhu, Y.: Multi-tier MEC offloading strategy based on dynamic channel characteristics. IET Commun. **14**, 4029–4037 (2020)
21. Sun, J., Yin, L., Zou, M., Zhang, Y., Zhang, T., Zhou, J.: Task offloading, load balancing, and resource allocation in MEC networks. IET Commun. **14**, 1451–1458 (2020)
22. Zhang, G., Zhang, W., Cao, Y., Li, D., Wang, L.: Energy-delay tradeoff for dynamic offloading in mobile-edge computing system with energy harvesting devices. IEEE Trans. Ind. Inf. **14**(10), 4642–4655 (2018)
23. Huang, L., Feng, X., Zhang, L., Qian, L., Wu, Y.: Multi-server multi-user multi-task computation offloading for mobile edge computing networks. Sensors **19**(6), 1446 (2019)
24. Huang, M., Liu, W., Wang, T., Liu, A., Zhang, S.: A cloud-MEC collaborative task offloading scheme with service orchestration. IEEE Internet Things J. **7**, 5792–5805 (2020)
25. Sun, J., Yin, L., Zou, M., Zhang, Y., Zhang, T., Zhou, J.: Makespan-minimization workflow scheduling for complex networks with social groups in edge computing. J. Syst. Archit. **108**, 101799 (2020)
26. Xu, X., et al.: Multiobjective computation offloading for workflow management in cloudlet-based mobile cloud using NSGA-II. Comput. Intell. **35**(3), 476–495 (2019)
27. Ma, X., Gao, H., Xu, H., Bian, M.: An IoT-based task scheduling optimization scheme considering the deadline and cost-aware scientific workflow for cloud computing. EURASIP J. Wirel. Commun. Netw. **2019**(1), 1–19 (2019)
28. Borodin, A., Kleinberg, J., Raghavan, P., Sudan, M., Williamson, D.P.: Adversarial queuing theory. J. ACM (JACM) **48**(1), 13–38 (2001)
29. Beume, N., Naujoks, B., Emmerich, M.: SMS-EMOA: multiobjective selection based on dominated hypervolume. Eur. J. Oper. Res. **181**(3), 1653–1669 (2007)
30. Koch, P., Kramer, O., Rudolph, G., Beume, N.: On the hybridization of SMS-EMOA and local search for continuous multiobjective optimization. In: Proceedings of the 11th Annual Conference on Genetic and Evolutionary Computation, pp. 603–610 (2009)

Research on the Development Model of Shenyang Rural Smart Tourism Based on Tourism Preferences in the Context of 5G Applications

Deli Xu[✉] and Yaning Ji

Shenyang Urban Construction University, Shenyang, Liaoning, China
xdlnhm@163.com

Abstract. We use the innovation of "5G + tourism" as an entry point and integrate it into the "smart+" model of the countryside in order to use smart tourism as an opportunity and a link to address the needs of the strategy for rejuvenating the countryside. The project will analyze the future development trend of the new "5G + Tourism" industry in rural Shenyang, suggest a route for the development of the new industry and an innovative development model, and suggest a planning reference point for enhancing the top-level design of the countryside, innovating the marketing model, and creating a public service platform. It gives local villagers, new tourism organizations, and tourism firms theoretical direction and practical reference for engaging in novel activities of "rural smart tourism," and it provides rural smart tourism fresh life.

Keywords: Application of 5G · Rural Smart Tourism · Preference for Travel · Mode of Development

1 Introduction

The "Document No. 1" of the Central Government has continued to emphasize the rural revitalization strategy in recent years. A number of pertinent policy recommendations were also put forth at the 2019 National Conference on 5G Applications. 5G applications are expanding into numerous fields in towns and villages thanks to favorable rules and chances for market expansion. Smart tourism is driving the change and modernization of the travel and tourism sector due to the close integration and development of IoT technology. For the towns and villages of Shenyang to expand in the future, the integration of 5G technology and the rural rejuvenation strategy is a necessity.

The General Office of the State Council proposed to construct 10,000 smart scenic places and smart tourism communities around the nation by 2020 in "Several Opinions

Source of the project: Project of the Liaoning Education Department's Scientific Research Fund for 2020《Researching strategies for improving rural landscape and architecture in Shenyang, Liaoning Province, in the context of rural revitalization》, Project No: LJKX202001.

Y. Cao and X. Shao (Eds.): MONAMI 2022, LNICST 474, pp. 78–101, 2023.
https://doi.org/10.1007/978-3-031-32443-7_6

on Further Promoting Tourism Investment and Consumption" published in August 2015. The "Notice on Accelerating the Construction of Smart Scenic Spots" was released by the National Tourism Administration in April 2016 [1]. The Action Plan for Promoting the Quality and Upgrading of Rural Tourism Development (2018–2020) was jointly released by the Ministry of Culture and Tourism, the National Development and Reform Commission, and 13 other departments. It includes proposals to encourage the integrated development of "tourism + agriculture + internet," promote collaboration between 1,000 important rural tourism villages and tourism e-commerce, modern logistics, and other related enterprises, and c. the special construction initiatives "back-up project" and "one village, one product." Encourage and direct the development of intelligent rural tourism by fusing rural tourism with the Internet and other contemporary information technology [2]. The Ministry of Culture and Tourism proposed to speed up the promotion of digital, networked, intelligent as the characteristics of intelligent tourism, speed up the construction of intelligent scenic spots in January 2021 in order to "start a good bureau to promote the work of culture and tourism to open up a new situation work report." Shenyang will utilize electronic information technologies, including the Internet of Things and cloud computing, to enhance rural tourism in the future. Information technology will permeate all facets of rural tourism activities through the smart collecting and analysis of tourism data [3]. Shenyang is urgently developing "5G + Tourism" to foster innovative rural tourism forms, boost rural tourism marketing and promotion, and create development momentum to raise the quality of rural tourism.

2 Situation of Shenyang's Rural Smart Tourism Presently

The province issued "Guiding Opinions of the People's Government of Liaoning Province on Promoting the Construction of Characteristic Townships" in 2016 and announced 100 provincial cultivation lists, 20 provincial characteristic townships, and 13 national characteristic small towns in response to the recent development boom in "rural revitalization," "characteristic township," "small town planning," and "livable country-side construction." The development of window top leisure tourism type township construction is one of the main tasks of the construction, according to the Implementation Plan for the Construction of Characteristic Townships in Shenyang City (2017–2020), which was published in 2017 by the General Office of the People's Government of Shenyang City.

2.1 National Rural Tourist Development

With over 100 billion yuan in yearly tourism income and 400 million annual visitors, rural tourism in China now accounts for roughly a third of all travel there. A wide range of agricultural enterprises are represented by the more than 500 agricultural tourism demonstration sites that are currently located around the nation in 31 provinces, autonomous regions, and municipalities on the mainland. About 70% of urban inhabitants choose rural travel for their vacations during the three Golden Weeks each year, and rural tourism has emerged as a new area of expansion for the tourist sector.

Rural tourism exhibits significant relevance to tourist destinations, agricultural production harvesting activities, and traditional festivals in the domestic tourism sector.

Folklore tourism, which focuses on "staying in a farmhouse, eating farm meals, doing farm work, and enjoying farming," and picking tourism, which focuses on harvesting various agricultural products and allows visitors to pick and taste fresh peaches, pears, apricots, and other fruits on their own, are the most frequently visited and returned to attractions.

2.2 Market Trends

In the past ten years, travel has become essential and there have been substantial changes in national tourism, particularly in terms of travel consumption and travel habits. Ten years ago, 19% of people did not even have time to travel, and 77% of people traveled for little more than 7 days annually. Today, 54% of people can plan trips lasting 7 to 10 days, while 15% can go on vacations lasting longer than a month.

2.3 The Tourism Industry's Trends

The country's tourism industry is expanding quickly, and beautiful areas have also demonstrated a new trend of diversification, progressively evolving into large-scale, varied, intelligent, and trendy (Table 1).

Table 1. Development Trends in the Tourism Industry Table.

The nation's tourist sector is expanding quickly	A tourism law was passed	New developments in landscape
1. Developmental characteristics Government priorities are very high The macro environment kept getting better Increasingly diverse products are offered in the tourism sector Deepening industrial convergence.	1. Challenges The bar for opening tourism attractions is too high. Obligations for landscape safety that are precisely stated.	Large scale Multifunctionality Intelligent Fashionable
2. Making four strides forward First, new product developments Second, advances in culture Thirdly, industrial breakthroughs Fourth, market innovation.	2.Opportunity For scenic locations to survive, their quality must be improved Strengthen administration and supervisory duties to ensure the tourism industry grows healthily.	

2.4 Market Research on Tourism

1. **The market's demand is still booming.** With more than RMB 6 trillion in tourist earnings and 155 million outbound journeys, China's domestic tourism air broke

4 billion trips in 2019. In terms of domestic travel, international travel, and combined spending on domestic and international travel, China ranked #1 in the world. According to data collected by the National Tourism Data Centre, 10.2% of all people working in China's workforce are employed in the tourism industry.

2. **New trends in the travel industry.** Tourism items that promote a return to nature, health, and oneself have emerged as the future development trend on a global scale. Ecology, health, and leisure will overtake conventional tourist attractions and forms of entertainment as the primary drivers of tourism development (Fig. 1).

Cultural tourism in the ascendant	Eco-tourism continue to heat up	Rural tourism sudden emergence	Wisdom tourism become fashionable
●The feasibility of expanding the source market is becoming more and more obvious, and cultural tourism will continue to increase. ●Cultural tourism will play a prominent role in the tourism system. ●Cultural tourism products tend to be personalized and diversified.	●The tourism experience is original and unique. ●Emphasis on the small scale of tourism, limited to affordability. ●Reinforcing the public participation of the tourist. ●It is a responsible tourism: a responsibility for the conservation of tourism resources and for the sustainable development of tourism.	Eight Rural Tourism Industries ●Country Hotel ●International Post ●Hedgerow picking ●Ecological fishing villages ●Leisure Farm ●Mountain Home ●Wellness Lodge ●Ethnographic Court	●A new form of tourism that focuses on the visitor experience. ●Innovation in means: using technologies such as cloud computing and the Internet of Things. ●Areas of application: tourism experience, industrial development, administration, etc. ●Service groups: public, business, government, etc.

Fig. 1. Chart for New Trends.

3 Analysis of a Travel Preference Survey

3.1 Simple Visitor Survey

In order to more effectively direct the construction of the project site, a total of 3,000 research questionnaires were distributed via the internet, friends, and paper questionnaires. 2,668 valid questionnaires were returned, yielding an efficiency rate of 88.9%, and they focused on consumer preferences for tourism products and travel methods.

64% of respondents were tourists from Northeast and North China, which corresponds to the target markets for the project areas; 43% of respondents said they were most interested in visiting rural vacation complexes. Rural communities and well-known mountains piqued the curiosity of the second-largest group of tourists. The trip's 2–5 day duration and focus on strengthening family ties show the growing appeal of short-haul family leisure and vacation travel (Figs. 2, 3, 4 and 5).

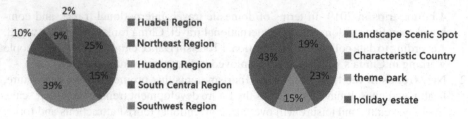

Fig. 2. Location Survey Figure.   **Fig. 3.** Optional Outings.

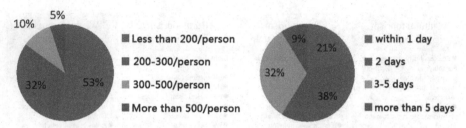

Fig. 4. Expenditures per person.   **Fig. 5.** Length of stay.

3.2 Travel Preferences and Tourism Consumption Survey

The era of the casual traveler has arrived as a result of the oversaturated tourism consumer market, with 43% of tour favorites choosing self-drive and 30%. Visitors preferred local specialties over cultural and artistic souvenirs by a margin of 43%, thus attention might be directed into developing tourism goods in the future. Customers expressed a high preference for flowery sceneries, waterfront views, old-world villages, and lush forests (Figs. 6, 7, 8 and 9).

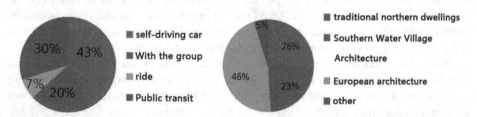

Fig. 6. Travel options.   **Fig. 7.** Architectural style selection.

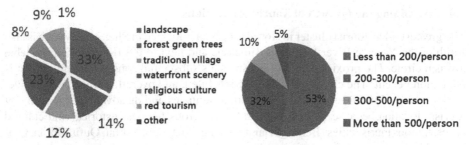

Fig. 8. Travel Preferences.   Fig. 9. Product selection for tourism.

3.3 Specific Market Analysis

Suitable to Families Market. A large consumer class that supports the family-friendly market and encourages parent-child entertainment, where parent-child entertainment tends to be more about fun and education than tourism per se, is the post-80s and post-90s generation, which is gradually entering the family stage and becoming a hot spot in the market for parent-child tours (Figs. 10, 11, 12 and 13).

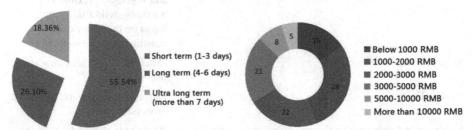

Fig. 10. Travel schedules for parents and children.

Fig. 11. An average breakdown of parent-child travel expenses.

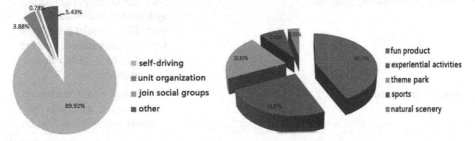

Fig. 12. Mode of travel.   Fig. 13. Preference for travel.

Self-drive Excursions. The self-drive tourism industry has a bright future and tremendous possibilities. There will be 395 million vehicles in the nation by the end of 2021, including 302 million cars. There were 481 million drivers, more than 444 million.

3.4 Examining the Growth of Tourist Attractions

The greatest urban tourist cluster in Northeast China is located in Shenyang, which is also south of the Yangtze River Delta tourism circle and next to the Beijing-Tianjin-Hebei tourism circle. The proximity to Northeast Asia's substantial source tourism market is a location benefit. The city is quite densely inhabited, and overall tourism competitiveness is at a medium level. The city has both advantages and disadvantages in terms of tourism location because it is surrounded by numerous famous historical and cultural cities, famous tourist cities (Beijing, Tianjin, Dalian, Qingdao, Yantai, Qufu, Tai'an, Qinhuangdao, etc.), and a variety of typical regional cultural landscapes (Guandong culture, grassland culture, farming culture, Qilu culture, Yanzhao culture, maritime culture). The key cities of the tourism region drive Shenyang to become a new tourism growth hub, and the city (Table 2).

Table 2. Analyses of Shenyang's various tourism project kinds.

Tourism Projects	Type of project
Eco Park	A tourism farm including agricultural sightseeing, fruit and vegetable picking, flower watching, wild fishing, etc., based on the historic city, the coastline, and the wetland park.
Seaside View	"Shelling" and "Seaside fishing"
Leisure Farm	Farming, tourism, and fine processing
Experiential farmhouses in the new socialist countryside	Working in the fields, assisting farmers, and sharing meals with them
Natural golden fishing grounds	Seawater farming, high-tech agricultural demonstration sites, 10,000 mu of greenhouse veggies, and leisure resorts are all visited by tourists who can buy things there.
Beachfront Resorts	Landscapes with a beachfront, a rocky beach, windmills that generate electricity, and others

(*continued*)

Table 2. (*continued*)

Tourism Projects		Type of project
Modern Ecological Agricultural Park		To build the greatest fruit trading and logistics hub and deep processing center for fruit in the northeast, a rural leisure resort and a new city of orchards are planned
Eco-Picker Leisure Resort		Fruit tree farms as the foundation
Small tourist towns		Innovative use of unique tourism offerings, backed by local folklore and religious history and culture
Specialty Tourist Goods		Building cold rich apples and mixed grains in Liaozhong District's Niu Xin Tuo in accordance with the principles of the environment
Other Fine Tourism Routes	Cultural Tour of Aisin Gioro Wine in BanLaShanZi Village, Faku County	Taste the Royal Wine Culture, Taste the Flavorful Food, and Old Northern Taste Wine Culture Tourism Area at Aisin Gioro Royal Museum
	Zhangyi Station Village ShengJing Stage Tour through History in the Tie Xi District	Picking apples and mushrooms at Sheng jing Station; shopping for specialty foods at the Old Town Station Visitor Center.
	A visit to the Sibe's house at Shen Bei New District's LaTa Lake Community	Welcome ceremony at the community's cultural center at Lata Lake (Xibe speciality village) fruit picking, the first national May 7 Cadre School, a farmhouse banquet (or a fish dinner at Lata Lake), and a visit to Seven Stars Wetland Park.
	Tong Jiayu and Wang Shi Lan Communities in Hunan District Take a Romantic Aegean Cruise	Aegean Resort Estate (Chapel, Lawn Wedding), Hiking, Kingoland Community Food Tasting, and Purchasing Organic Produce

Shenyang Tourism Bureau adheres to the working principle of "Benefiting the People, Promoting the Industry, and Good Governance" in order to carry out the spirit of "Opinions of the General Office of the State Council on Further Promoting Tourism Investment and Consumption" and actively support the development of "Smart Shenyang" and the integration of regional tourism. The "One Card, One Network, One Center" smart tourism construction model has been put out by the Shenyang Tourism Bureau.

The implementation of unified management, united planning, unified construction, and unified standards. By creating the Shenyang Economic Zone Wisdom Tourism Project Construction Guidance Funds, concentrating on the establishment of the Shenyang Economic Zone Wisdom Tourism Service Management Center Project, increasing wisdom tourism technology research, building the information technology infrastructure, hiring personnel, and other work investments, for the formation of the Shenyang Economic Zone Wisdom Tourism Service Management Center, to promote the scientific or otherwise.

The Shenyang Palace Museum is now working on building information technology in a variety of areas, including collection administration, a mobile website, a public We Chat platform, a QR code guide, a digital exhibition hall, and team digital tour guides.

3.5 A Study of the Variables Influencing the Dynamics of Rural Tourist Growth

We suggest the key elements that influence the growth of rural tourism through information technology and consumer demand, building on the excellent and well-known county wisdom tourism development model. The new tourism operation is focused on the needs of visitors and realizes intelligent tourism services, marketing, and management through the highly systematic integration and deep level activation of tourism information. It is supported by a new generation of information technology, such as the Internet of Things, cloud computing, and 5G+.

3.6 Issues with Rural Wisdom Tourism in Shenyang

Inadequate Management Strategies and a Lack of Logical, Scientific Planning. The majority of rural tourism in Shenyang is based on the city's picturesque mountain scenery, but it also has issues with poor rural infrastructure assistance, annoying traffic in specific areas, and poor environmental hygiene. Additionally, the use of technology and sophisticated marketing strategies is absent at rural tourist destinations, which makes it challenging to draw visitors over the long run and weakens the tourism attraction.

Serious Homogenous Competition, Comparable Development Initiatives, and Low Repurchase Rates. The development of rural intelligent tourism projects is urgently needed because Shenyang's rural tourism products are singular, homogeneous competition is severe, picking more than dozens of projects makes rural tourism development projects less distinctive and of lower quality, and the absence of intelligent technology means that tourists won't visit the same type of tourist destinations for repeated consumption.

Poor Marketing and Advertising, Little Knowledge About Tourism. The majority of tourism businesses don't have a marketing strategy for rural travel, lacking scientific packaging and planning, while government organizations invest little in rural travel marketing and promotion, lacking sensible and efficient demonstration and promotion.

There are numerous market and development potential in the future for rural intelligent tourism, which may be summed up as follows. At the present, it has become one of the hotspots and mainstream forms of rural tourist (Table 3).

Table 3. A SWOT analysis of Shenyang's rural smart tourism industry

Influencing factors	Swot analysis and strategy		Strategies
Internal elements	Advantage S		① Resource advantages ② Regional advantages ③ Advantages of urban infrastructure ④ Advantages of information technology infrastructure ⑤ Brand advantages
	Disadvantage W		① Clearly a low season for tourism and inadequate resources ② The hardware and information resources of the current information service platform are underutilized ③Tourism businesses only apply information to a limited extent
External environment	Opportunity O		① The Liaoning Coastal Economic Belt Strategy offers Shenyang's tourism industry limitless business potential ② Self-driving tours and high-speed rail increase the effectiveness of tourist travel ③ The vast tourism environment is boiling with limitless prospects ④ The internet travel services business is growing quickly
	Challenge T		① Cities compete fiercely with one another ② The growth of regional tourism e-commerce is being stifled by large platforms
Strategic response	Strategies	SO Strategy	① Thoroughly encourage the speed of intelligent tourism construction in order to standardize management as the foundation and raise the caliber of tourism services ② Resources coordinated by the government and used in tandem to create clever tourist projects

(continued)

Table 3. (*continued*)

Influencing factors	Swot analysis and strategy		Strategies
		WO Strategy	① Update hardware and software products, support business training, and enhance the use of smart tourism ② Create unique tourism initiatives, deeply integrate smart tourism, and raise the city's brand recognition
		ST Strategy	① Make use of beneficial resources and progressively encourage the development of intelligent tourism ② Make it a point to set the example and develop your skills to power clever applications across the tourism sector
		WT Strategy	① Development of the tourism business that is traditionally driven by smart tourism ② The growth of specialized intelligent rural tourism, which will aid the rural rehabilitation plan by establishing the lovely "one village, one product" pattern

4 Study on the Concepts and Strategies for Developing Rural Smart Tourism

4.1 Models for Smart Tourism Development to Study

In addition to these crucial components of smart tourism development, it is suggested that information technology, market demand, tourism resources, corporate and governmental behavior, regional environment, human resources, and geographic conditions serve as the main drivers of county smart tourism development (Table 4).

4.2 Summaries and Recommendations for Creating a "Rural Smart Tourism" Model

Big Field Agriculture-Focused 5G+ Field Agriculture Tour. Develop various thematic leisure activities with various characteristics, such as agricultural tours, forestry and fruit tours, flower tours, fishery tours, and pastoral tours to meet the psychological needs of tourists to experience agriculture and get back to nature. Integrate 5G+ into the idyllic rural landscape, agricultural production activities, and special agricultural products activities (Fig. 14).

Through clever techniques, tourists are better able to comprehend and experience agriculture through viewing agricultural production operations, tasting and purchasing organic food, learning about agricultural technologies, and participating in other

Table 4. Models for county-level smart tourism development.

Typical model	a summary of development concepts	Important motivators	
Wuyuan Model	① Active market activity; ② Adept at seizing chances; ③ Diverse tourism resources; strong economic foundation; chemical development; village-based tourism promotion; ④ Accentuate the development of connections between business operations and regional environments	① Resources for Travel; ② Business operations	The economy Regional environment
Taining Model	① Initiative in spite of the unfavorable surroundings; ② Government agencies first becoming active; ③ Developing a brand through tourism image promotion; ④ Restructuring of the industrial sector	① Resources for Travel; ② Government action	Conditions of location The economy Human Resources
Luanchuan Model	① A strong tourism county is always the development strategy and objective, led by a party and the government; ② Proactive industrial development that is focused on the market	① Resources for Travel; ② Government action	The economy Conditions of location
The Chun'an Model	① Government-led, unified leadership in development, management, and administration; integrated resources; mechanisms incentives; ② Model of a future development area with Qiandao Lake as the growth pole	① Resources for Travel; ② Government action ③ The economy ④ Conditions of location	Business operations
Shenyang Model	① Government-led, united leadership in development, management, and administration; integrated resources; mechanisms to promote; ② Model for the arrangement of future developments using Shenfu and Hunan as new growth poles	① Resources for Travel; ② Conditions of location	Business operations

Fig. 14. Charming agritourism

tourism-related activities. The agricultural science and technology tour also concentrates on contemporary agricultural science and technology parks and is designed to allow visitors to observe the parks' high-tech agricultural varieties, facility agriculture, and ecological agriculture in greenhouses in order to better understand contemporary agriculture. Visitors are exposed to actual agricultural production, farming culture, and a unique vernacular through taking part in agricultural production activities, eating, sleeping, and working with farmers.

5G+ Folk Customs Tourism Mode. Through rural customs and folk culture as the focus of tourism attraction, fully highlight the characteristics of farming culture, vernacular culture and folk culture, develop farming demonstrations, folk skills, seasonal folklore, festivals, folk songs and dances and other tourism activities to increase the cultural connotation of rural tourism. Through the application of 5G technology the farming culture tour, folk culture tour, vernacular culture tour ethnic culture tour are taken as the key development direction.

5G+ Folk Tourist Mode with Customs. Develop farming demonstrations, folk skills, seasonal folklore, festivals, folk songs and dances, as well as other tourism events to completely showcase the peculiarities of farming culture, vernacular culture, and folk culture. This will improve the cultural connotation of rural tourism. The agrarian culture tour, folk culture tour, vernacular culture tour, and ethnic culture tour are taken as the main development path through the application of 5G technology.

Use local folklore to develop farmhouses with a folklore theme, local agricultural production and farming life to develop agricultural tourism farmhouses, local old villages and houses to develop residential-style farmhouses, etc. to draw tourists to the area to visit, unwind, and engage in farming activities (Fig. 15).

Tourism Village Township Model with 5G. By creating tours of old homes and mansions, creating tours of ethnically distinct villages, creating tours of old townhouse structures, homes, streets, shops, and gardens, and creating tours of modern rural architecture, residential courtyards, street patterns, village greenery, and commercial and industrial operations.

5G+ Model for Leisure and Vacation Travel. Numerous leisure and recreational facilities have been built to offer visitors rest, entertainment, catering, and fitness services. These facilities rely on the natural beauty of the countryside, the comfortable

Fig. 15. Agritourism

and refreshing climate, the unique geothermal hot springs, the environmentally friendly and ecological green space, combined with the surrounding idyllic landscape and folk culture.

Leisure tourism is made available to guests by creating leisure resorts, leisure farms, and country hotels to complement the nearby natural and humanistic settings.

Model for 5G+ Science Tourism Education. Provide visitors with tourism activities to help them understand agricultural history, learn agricultural techniques, and broaden their knowledge of agriculture by using agricultural tourism parks, agricultural science and technology ecological parks, agricultural product exhibition halls, agricultural expositions, or museums. Through the development of agricultural science and technology education facilities, agricultural sightseeing and leisure parks, educational agricultural bases for kids, and agricultural expositions, as well as through agricultural sightseeing, participation and experience activities, and DIY educational activities using cutting-edge agricultural facilities, efficient agricultural production methods, and high-quality agricultural products. Allowing elementary and secondary school students to engage in extracurricular agricultural pursuits and obtain instruction in agricultural technology (Fig. 16).

Fig. 16. Experience with science tour

To enhance the tourist experience, it is also feasible to use local agricultural methods, agricultural goods, and agricultural culture for displays.

Back to Nature Tourism Model with 5G. Tourism activities like mountain watching, scenery appreciation, mountain climbing, forest bathing, skiing, and water skiing have been developed using the stunning natural landscape of the countryside, exotic mountains, green forests, and serene lakes to allow visitors to appreciate nature, get close to nature, and return to nature.

5   Advice for Making Decisions

5.1   Targeting

Build Shenyang into a key rural Liaoning Province core city, a golden rural wisdom tourism corridor in Northeast China, integrate it into the Bohai Sea tourism complex, develop the most rural wisdom tourism in Liaoning Province, establish a highly powerful rural wisdom tourism brand in Northeast Asia, and develop a rural wisdom tourism model demonstration area in Liaoning Province.

5.2   Ideas for Development

Establish a "5G+Tourism" system, pool resources, take the lead in the market, and establish a community with a unique wisdom tourism area (Fig. 17).

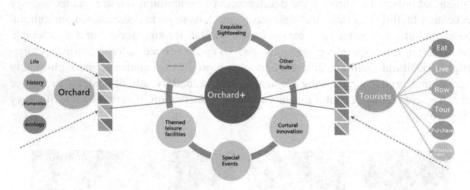

Fig. 17. Development ideas

5.3   Development Tools

5G+ Polarized Items for Sightseeing. Existing rural agricultural demonstration areas' landscapes to create high-end agricultural sightseeing destinations, fruit picking parks, etc.

Varied Holiday Goods for 5G+. To build varied 5G+ holiday products, rely on high-quality ecological tourist resources, enhance the variety of tourism products, add more holiday features, and implement special activities.

Incorporating 5G+ Tourist Components. The tourism sector should be improved, a holiday mood should be created for rural tourism, the resort's unique features should be highlighted, and a main attraction should be developed.

Innovative 5G+ Cultural Expression. The rural project site's basic resources will be imaginatively developed to build a leisure and wisdom resort of ecology+ and cultural creation+, incorporating elements of IP and cultural creation+.

5.4 Planning Ideas

See Fig. 18.

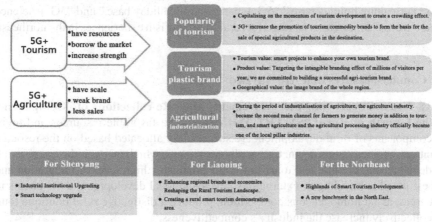

Fig. 18. Planning Ideas

5.5 Overarching Planning and Orientation Goals

It will completely integrate tourism resources, special planting resources, etc., close the 5G+ rural wisdom tourism market gap in Shenyang and even the entire Liaoning Province, and open up rural wisdom tourism quality, refinement, and branding operations with fashionable fields, exquisite landscape, sharing economy, and cultural creativity development concept, creating the first rural wisdom tourism model city in the Liaoning Province (Fig. 19).

Position in the Market. Core market: Tianjin, Beijing, and Hebei regions primarily offer 5G + agricultural leisure, 5G + rural tourist, and 5G + urban suburban parent-child vacation products. Shenyang serves as the center of the 300 km radiation area of urban inhabitants.

Opportunity Market: Products in the 5G+ parent-child vacation category and 5G+ cultural tourism category are primarily sold in Tianjin, Beijing, and Hebei.

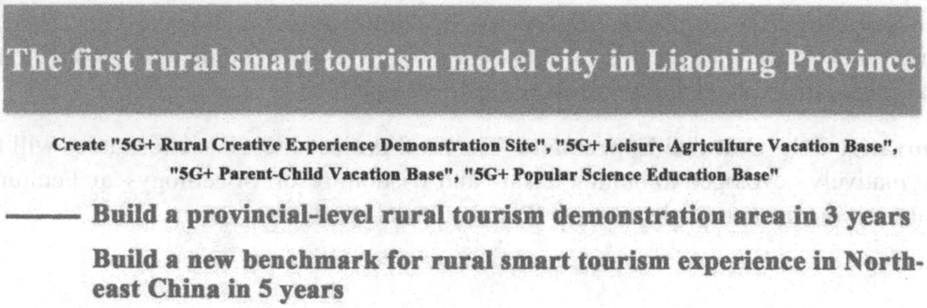

The first rural smart tourism model city in Liaoning Province

Create "5G+ Rural Creative Experience Demonstration Site", "5G+ Leisure Agriculture Vacation Base",
"5G+ Parent-Child Vacation Base", "5G+ Popular Science Education Base"

——— Build a provincial-level rural tourism demonstration area in 3 years

Build a new benchmark for rural smart tourism experience in North-east China in 5 years

Fig. 19. General guidelines

Objectives of the Planning. Create the first "rural smart tourism" pilot city in Liaoning Province as well as a "5G + countryside creative experience demonstration site," "5G + leisure agriculture holiday base," "5G + parent-child holiday base," and "5G + science education base" to set a new standard for rural smart tourism experiences in the northeast.

5.6 Countermeasures that Are Advised

Focus Your Efforts on the Movement and Re-collection of Components for the Growth of Rural "SMART TOUrism." The favorable resources and high-end components of rural development are successfully allocated based on the resource advantages of Shenyang's distinctive small (city) towns, which merge industry, research and development, culture, and tourism [8]. To establish a high level of integration and the best possible blending of external resources and local development components in rural areas, avoid homogeneous competition, produce a distinctive rural boutique tour, and collectively increase the industry's competitiveness.

Fostering the Modernization and Growth of Rural Smart Tourism as Well as the Digital ECONOMY's Development, and Accomplishing the Natural Fusion of One, Two, and Three Businesses. It successfully encourages the growth of the rural tourist business chain through the strategic allocation of components including rural nature, folk culture, and historical assets. The organic integration of one, two, and three industries can be accomplished in rural areas by utilizing the new industry of "5G+," which will enhance farmer income, promote rural development and industrial structure modernization, and address the three rural challenges.

Preservation of Historical Heritage and Creation of Original Rural Features. The development of the original natural qualities of the countryside while maintaining the historical lineage of the characteristic township, balancing the two, integrating the spatial environment, and defining the characteristic space. The town's current development needs are satisfied while also maintaining its small-town charm and giving the locals something to remember.

Expanding Channels, Creating Intelligent Experience Shops for Agritourism Commodities, and Turning Agricultural Products into Tourism Products. A single agricultural product is given a new connotation through the preferential selection and recommendation of various e-commerce platforms, realizing the conversion of tourism destination goods, becoming a significant carrier for the combination of agriculture and tourism, and expanding the channels for local farmers to increase their income [7]. In Jiande, Zhejiang, the "Fruit and Vegetable Paradise" served as inspiration for the establishment of the smart experience shop and marketing online shop for agricultural tourist goods.

5.7 "5G" Background to Support Innovation in "Smart Tourism"

Enhancing the Technical Base and Implementing the Technical Benefits of "SMART TOUrism." The platform integrates data center, data management, product management, customer relationship management, distribution management, consumption verification management and product booking, navigation guide, and other practical functional systems through the mobile internet and service cloud platform. The platform then develops intelligent mobile terminal APP applications for tourism management departments, rural tourism enterprises, and various tourists. To enable "smart tourism" technology and support the growth of the entire rural regeneration process, the "5G+" system will be promoted.

Experience Upgrade: Using 5G and VR to Create a New Tourism Model. An example of the new immersive tourism concept of 5G + VR, taken from the picturesque area of Xiongan New Area-Baiyangdian. Future immersive experiences in Shenyang will be made possible by the integration of 5G and VR technology. Remote VR cameras will be placed in remote, scenic areas, collecting 360-degree images of the surroundings before being sent to a cloud server for processing over the 5G network and being pushed to client-side devices [7]. Visitors can experience immersive scenery viewing using VR glasses powered by the 5G network or watch 360-degree views on a TV, making for a more relaxing, secure, and intelligent travel experience.

Building a Rural Smart Service Demonstration Area for Service Upgrade. Smart services will play a significant role in the future rural landscape of Shenyang. The creation of a rural intelligent Service demonstration area, the use of "one card", self-service navigation through mobile phone APP, two-dimensional code tour guides, multimedia information queries, real-time security monitoring, and dynamic traffic analysis; the realization of intelligent ordering, intelligent service, intelligent leisure, and intelligent management; and the one-stop customization of the best itinerary.

Creating an Interactive and Shared Platform for Tourism Information Through Sharing and Upgrading. The largest benefit of smart tourism is that cloud platforms are better able to address issues with information integration, sharing, interaction, and exchange. The "one-click release" of product information and marketing information from rural tourism enterprises to the OTA platform is made possible by integrating GDS (Global Distribution System) in the rural intelligent tourism service cloud platform. As a result, tourists can learn about the products and promotion information of the enterprises through the APP for the first time. Through the app, users may learn about the businesses' offerings and promotions.

Building a "5G + Smart Scenic Area" is the ultimate goal. Smart services, a number of new technologies to improve the quality of life Smart services, a number of new technologies to improve the quality of life.

China Mobile is currently in charge of completing 5G coverage in the Baiyangdian beautiful area and has established 30 base stations in the 5G scale networking and application demonstration project in Xiong'an [6]. To further capitalize on the benefits of 5G in smart tourism with the high speed, wide bandwidth, and low latency features of the 5G network, Shenyang's special townships and villages will be developed using 5G scale networking and demonstration project base stations.

Developing a Tourism Brand in Shenyang and Organizing a Rural Smart Tourism Fair. The ecological management of Wolong Lake, the Pu River, and the Hun River will be improved, together with the enhancement of the tourism and leisure environment and the upgrading of the tourism infrastructure in order to promote the image of the northern city.

Innovative Funding and Investment Strategies as well as Market-Based Promotion of the Operation of Small (City) Towns with Unique Characteristics.
Multiple funding channels. Deepen the reform of the investment and financing system of the typical town, mobilize all parties to raise construction funds through various channels and forms, realize the virtuous cycle of the town's construction inputs and outputs, implement market-oriented and industrialized operation techniques for the town's water supply, sewage treatment, and trash treatment, and design distinct financing models and debt servicing mechanisms for various project types. In order to encourage social capital to invest in and run urban public facilities, the government should also rationalize the pricing structure for municipal goods and services, relax access restrictions, enhance oversight, and create opportunities for businesses to enter the concessions market through PPPs and other means.

Releasing the money-channeling multiplier effect. The government, state-owned enterprises, and some private businesses are in charge of front-end capital investment, which is primarily used for town planning and design, infrastructure upkeep and improvement, habitat transformation, industrial projects that are still in the planning stage, and other areas. Increase the pace of the infrastructure construction that is typically driven by industrial expansion in small (city) towns.

Promotion of New Media Marketing in the Travel and Tourism Industry. Make full use of e-commerce trade, travel resources, and new media in the travel and tourism industry. Industry in Shenyang is actively planning for the future to improve tourism knowledge new media, strengthen marketing, and promote new media.

5.8 Strategies for "Rural Smart Tourism" in Shenyang

Building a "INTELLIgent Tourist Shenyang Model" Through Scientific Study and Planning. "Working to create and form a public service platform for intelligent tourism in Shenyang Economic Zone with perfect functions, convenience and practicality, and standardized operation" work idea, "investing in the construction of industry management, enterprise operation, and three information systems; piloting the construction of intelligent travel agencies, intelligent scenic spots, intelligent catering, intelligent hotels, and intelligent shopping malls; A long-term development plan has been created, and the project has been chosen as the focal point of the Shenyang smart tourist construction project.

Increase the Quality of Top-Level Design and Create Standards for Smart Tourism Building. A full-factor tourism wisdom construction standard system has been developed to control the construction of tourism wisdom in Shenyang in terms of construction standards, data interfaces, system construction, and other factors through the ten major aspects of tourism scenic spots, tourism accommodations, tourism transportation, tourism shopping, tourism catering, tourism countryside, tourism leisure and entertainment, etc. In order to achieve the objectives of "interconnection of government and enterprises, integration of enterprises, saving resources, and balanced development," the government has increased the construction of tourism wisdom infrastructure. This is done in order to support the balanced and orderly development of the city's tourism wisdom work.

Smart Tourism Cards are Being Issued by Innovative Application Carriers for the Shenyang Economic Zone. The Shenyang Tourism Bureau, along with the appropriate units, jointly founded and issued the Juyou-Smart Service Card, which has the service functions of data collection, fixed subsidy, and flash pass, in order to fulfill the work requirements of the General Office of the State Council's "Several Opinions on Further Promoting Tourism Investment and Consumption" to issue real-name national tourism cards and to realize the innovation of tourism wisdom application carriers.

Create a Smart Mobile Client for Tourism Based on Real-World Requirements. The tourism route marketing system, tourism ticket marketing system, tourism visa submission system, room booking system, catering booking system, and tour guide booking system are created to penetrate the tourism industry chain, realize one-stop and convenient online consumption, and promote the effective docking of tourism products from the perspective of meeting the needs of tourists, travel-related businesses, and industry supervision work. We will comprehensively promote the pilot construction of smart scenic spots, smart hotels, smart restaurants, and smart shopping malls, promote industrial integration, and strengthen the connectivity of information platforms of tourism through the development of enterprise resource management (ERP) systems, customer resource management (CRM) systems, interactive information distribution systems (CMS systems), and navigation guide tour guide systems, among others. We will achieve the automation of tourist information collecting, classification, processing, and release by creating tourism information management systems, tourism business approval systems, tourism consumer complaint systems, remote training systems for tour guides, etc.

Innovative Marketing Strategy to Enhance Wisdom Tourism's WeChat Public Platform We innovate to develop a new tourism wisdom marketing system that combines the features of scenic location promotion, quality improvement, and ticket distribution by creating the public WeChat platforms of JiuYuan and the Shenyang Tourism Bureau. Formation of tourism-related businesses, evaluation of tourism knowledge services, creative marketing by Moss, and enhancement of the WeChat public platform.

5.9   The Rural Smart Tourism Strategy in Shenyang's Liaozhong District

The offshore oasis and Pearl Lake were designated as the "primary tourism development direction" in the higher planning guidelines for water resources in Liaozhong District.

Development Proposals.

Proposal 1: Waterway Development.Proposal. It is conceivable to expand waterway tourism in the Liao River basin adequately and reconstruct the old ManDuHu ferry crossing to produce amphibious tourist, according to a previous estimate of the Liao River's yearly runoff.

Proposal II: Development suggestions for land transportation. To make it a popular tourist route and draw tourists, cooperative development of land and water transport will be fostered along with the development of water transportation.

Recommendation 3: A plan to increase traffic from virtual tourism. Some people may be able to take a journey around the globe without ever leaving their homes thanks to modern virtual display technologies. To pique viewers' interest, virtual tourism development can provide picturesque appreciation pathways along the Liao River (Figs. 20 and 21).

Development of Tourism.

Resources for travelers. The Liao and Jin ruins, Pearl Lake, the offshore oasis, and the ancient tomb complex were chosen as the "primary tourism growth direction" by the district's top planning of its tourism resources.

Water tourism is growing, especially in the Pearl Lake picturesque area, in Liaozhong District. Numerous ancient burial sites are scattered throughout the town of Tsiyutuo, and they, along with the excellent planning, are mostly used to create museums and other old cultural tourist initiatives. According to some planning research, the old city of Manduhu will primarily become a destination for folklore tourism. The Liaozhong District's rural experience tourist hub is situated in Liuzhang Township, reflecting the district's interpretation of its superior (Fig. 22).

Archival Materials. There are still some Liao and Jin sites in Liaozhong District that are useful for development. According to historical documents, the clan dates back to the early Qing Dynasty and was descended from Tabai, the sixth son of Nurhaci, the Qing Dynasty's great progenitor. For a moment, Manchu culture predominated. Due to the abundance of historical and cultural resources and the current presence of numerous

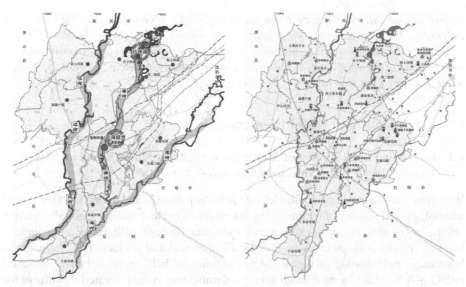

Fig. 20. Liaozhong District's Tourism Development

Fig. 21. Resources for Tourism are Distributed in Liaozhong

Fig. 22. Diagram of the development

ethnic groups, including the Han, Manchu, Mongolian, Hui, and Xibe, many different ethnic cultures can be produced and preserved.

Greater historical excavation opportunities could result from the expansion of the Liao and Jin sites and the construction of support structures surrounding them to create a circle for historical and cultural teaching.

Conclusion.

Utilizing the natural waterway, we will create a network of water ecological tourism, creating special wetland tourism in the spring and fall, special water tourism that incorporates 5G and folklore in the summer, and special ice tourism in the winter. A large-scale live interactive performance will be choreographed by renowned screenwriters on an outdoor stage that will be set up in the Liaohe wetland circle in accordance with the current natural scenery. With the help of high-tech virtual reality, a number of interactive historical and cultural VR experience projects have been created, allowing visitors to experience the natural beauty while getting a glimpse into the past of Manduhu Town.

Many interactive historical and cultural VR experience projects have been developed with the use of high-tech virtual reality, allowing tourists to take in the natural beauty while learning about the history of Manduhu Town.

6   Conclusions and Novel Elements

6.1   Innovation in Development Model: New Business Model Based on "5G + Tourism" and "VR + Internet of Things + Big Data"

We have created a development model for offline experiences and online sales using IoT technology and big data thinking, using innovative tourism products from Shenyang's unique towns and villages, including non-traditional heritage, calligraphy and painting, handicrafts, flower shops, cafes, and personalized agricultural products. [7]. The business has created the technological benefits of "smart tourism," built a new tourism model based on 5G + VR, created a rural smart services demonstration area, created a platform for the exchange of tourism-related information, and created a "5G + smart scenic site." Discover a new route for the quick expansion of rural smart tourism in Shenyang and develop into a new growth hub and pole for the city.

6.2   Innovation in Research Value: Multi-value Enhancement

Utilizing historical heritage, folk culture, architectural forms, and natural environments for their humanistic, aesthetic, environmental, and economic merits. The usage function and utilization value of the countryside are improved through functional compounding. Infusing new life into the growth of intelligent tourism in the countryside, the continuation of the cultural fabric and the creation of the original ecological style of the countryside will be accomplished.

6.3   Innovation in the Field of Study

Farmers can use the Internet, the Internet of Things, and other technologies to fully exploit the benefits of "5G" in rural tourism before, during, and after the tour by using the topic of "5G + Tourism," which has the depth of application of Internet of Things technology and is a smart greenway information system for rural intelligent tourism. In order to achieve a high level of integration between online and offline, to create a closed loop of service experience, to form a tourism data ecological chain, and ultimately to support the development of a beautiful economy, the system is designed to fully play to the advantages of "5G" in rural tourism before, during, and after the tour.

Providing wise management, wise service, wise marketing, wise operation, and wise experience for rural tourism in all aspects, "5G + Tourist" will lead the new trend of rural tourism development in Shenyang in the future, opening up a new road of "5G + Tourism" development in Shenyang. Additionally, it will support the modernization and development of rural intelligent tourism.

References

1. The nation released a number of laws to encourage the creation and use of intelligent tourism, Network for China's Security Industry
2. "Action Program to Promote the Development and Quality Upgrading of Rural Tourism (2018–2020)" Comprehensive Development and Reform [2018] No. 1465 (2018)
3. Li, M.: The development of connotations and interaction between intelligent tourism and tourism informationization. Northwestern Univ. Sch. Econ. Manag. (2012)
4. Chinese Academy of Social Sciences, number four. Report on China's Rural Tourism Development Index. Embrace the tour (2018)
5. Countdown to Internet conference: AI rooms, 5G networks debut in Wuzhen. People's Daily (2018)
6. The State Council's Commission for the Administration and Supervision of State-owned Assets. China Mobile and Huawei collaborate to present a new 5G + VR tourist model in Baiyangdian. Corporation of China Mobile Communications (2019)
7. Intelligent tourism for rural revitalization: building a rainbow bridge to connect rural and urban communities. China.com.cn (2018)

Computer Network and Machine Learning

A Dual-Stream Input Faster-CNN Model for Image Forgery Detection

Lizhou Deng[1], Ji Peng[2], Wei Deng[3], Kang Liu[1], Zhonghua Cao[1], and Wenle Wang[1(✉)]

[1] School of Software, Jiangxi Normal University, Nanchang 330027, Jiangxi, China
wenlewang@jxnu.edu.cn
[2] College of Information and Computer Engineering, Pingxiang University, Pingxiang 337055, Jiangxi, China
[3] School of Intercultural Studies, Jiangxi Normal University, Nanchang 330022, Jiangxi, China

Abstract. With the development of multimedia technology, the difficulty of image tampering has been reduced in recent years. Propagation of tampered images brings many adverse effects so that the technology of image tamper detection needs to be urgently developed. A faster-rcnn based image tamper localization recognition method with dual-flow Discrete Cosine Transform (DCT) high-frequency and low-frequency input is presented. For capturing subtle transform edges not visible in RGB domain, we extract high-frequency features from the image as an additional data stream embedding model. Our network model uses low-frequency images as the subject data to detect object consistency in different regions, further complements high-rate streams to strengthen image region consistency detection, and complements duplicate stream object tampering detection. Extensive experiments are performed on the CASIA V2.0 image dataset. These results demonstrate that faster-rcnn-w outperforms existing mainstream image tampering detection methods in different evaluation indicators.

Keywords: Image Forgery Detection · Faster-CNN · Dual-Stream Input

1 Introduction

Images have been widely used as carriers of information for rapid dissemination in the network, but with that comes the test of integrity and authenticity of images. With development of GAN [1–3] and the popularity of various PS tools, the threshold for tampering and forging fake pictures with no visual traces has been greatly reduced, and retouching has become relatively simple, but at the same time, many tampered pictures have been used to spread rumors, fabricate false news, and illegally seek benefits and other problems. Thus it can be seen that image tampering detection technology is particularly important, and there is a growing need for this new technology in society and the general public. The current research in digital image tampering is not mature enough, however, especially the research on multiple tampering detection. As a result, research on digital image tampering detection technology is of great significance. There are three ways to divide the type of image alteration.

Y. Cao and X. Shao (Eds.): MONAMI 2022, LNICST 474, pp. 105–115, 2023.
https://doi.org/10.1007/978-3-031-32443-7_7

1. Copy-move [4, 5]: By copying a region on the image, move the copied region to a location other than the copied one.This method applies to a single image.
2. Splicing [6–8]: Image splicing copies regions from a genuine image and pastes them to other images.This method applies to multiple images.
3. Removal eliminates [9]: regions from an authentic image followed by inpainting. This method applies to a single image.

In Fig. 1, tampered image areas are mostly item objects in order to enhance the tampering reliability, i.e., objects are added or removed in the tampering.

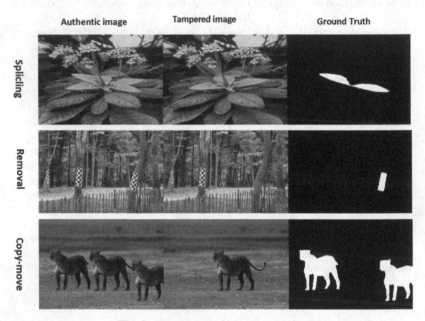

Fig. 1. Three ways of image tampering.

According to the literature [11], the images are transformed from the rgb domain to the frequency domain by Discrete Cosine Transform(DCT) then the high(or low) frequency component in the frequency domain are obtained as the input stream by high(or low) pass filter. The high-frequency component streams are further connected with the low-frequency component streams to complement each other. Motivated by this, in [12] we applied a dual-stream input model, where low-frequency images and high-frequency images are inputted separately at the input and fed to the network for training. Two channels are simultaneously trained to exchange training features and learn features in different frequency domains to accomplish consistency across objects, and cross-focus on both channels to back-propagate the enhanced algorithm. By iterating the object features, a global feature representation is achieved for later use in detection operations. Last, the detection region size is synchronously mapped to the original image using the consistency of the image position. After extensive experiments on publicly available datasets, we show that our faster-rcnn-w method outperforms most other methods in terms of evaluation metrics.

Our project currently contributes to the following:

(1) We innovatively ignore the rgb stream capture, but identify tamper artifacts by combining high-frequency transform with low-frequency features. This improves the prediction accuracy and reduces the speed of the coupled acceleration network.

(2) We make model improvements by performing a dual transformation on the input side and using a fusion pooling layer to reinforce the connection between the two channels. For the effect visualization, the results are mapped to the original image using image coherence with the tampered low frequency image position as a reference.

(3) We performed extensive experiments in multiple benchmark tests to demonstrate the advanced detection and localization properties of our method.

2 Related Works

In most image tampering detection, a single normal rgb stream image [13] is used as training object when image processing. Invisible image features and the intense intensity transform part often imply more tamper information [14]. This information is not visible in the rgb domain, so we propose a, multi-frequency domain joint modal approach and based on the faster-rcnn network model to find the image intense transformation information to achieve higher tampering recognition accuracy. At present, a lot of groundbreaking achievements have been made in image forgery detection. In the deep learning domain, in 2016 Bayar et al. Krishna et al. [15] innovated a novel convolutional layer structure to capture the correlation changes of adjacent pixels in the image when the image is tampered, and at the same time adaptively learn tampered features, and compress image content as much as possible. The detection effect. In 2017, a passive image forensics algorithm based on deep learning was proposed in the literature [10]. The image feature extraction part used CNN to learn features [16], and introduced the rich spatial model to initialize network parameters. Once the feature fusion is done, select The optimal features are used for classification and localization of tampered images and achieve high accuracy on public datasets. RGB-N [12] introduced a two-stream network for operation localization in 2018, where one stream extracted RGB features to capture visual artifacts, while the other exploited noise features to model the difference between tampered and unmodified regions. Inconsistencies between the two. It is the first method to use the dual-stream input model to complete the image detection problem, which further improves the tamper detection accuracy.

Image forgery is particularly critical in the medical field, In [17], We learned that in the Chest X-ray is a kind of medical image, [17] proposes a model for the detection of Chest-X-ray by Multi Attainment and Incorporating Background Information Model, Model focuses on how to improve the performance of decoders, for example, combining retrieval and generation for the template characteristics of the report. For image decoders, more mature convolutional neural networks (CNN) such as ResNet and DenseNet are used to extract features. We can learn from this that deep neural networks have a unique advantage in processing the abnormal part of the image. This aligns with the idea of identifying areas with image tampering.

3 Method

We aim to improve the dual-stream input network, input the network with dual Discrete Cosine Transform (DCT) [11] high-frequency and low-frequency images, improve prediction accuracy, and map the low-rate detection frame to the original image via the original input image when the result is returned. Figure 2 shows the steps of our approach. This chapter explains the three parts of preprocessing, Input and Model refinement.

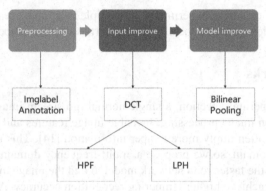

Fig. 2. Improvement steps of model.

Regarding the improvement of the model, namely as faster-rcnn-w, we will introduce three aspects: high-frequency image feature extraction, low frequency feature extraction and bilinear pooling. The structure of faster-rcnn-w model is shown as Fig. 3.

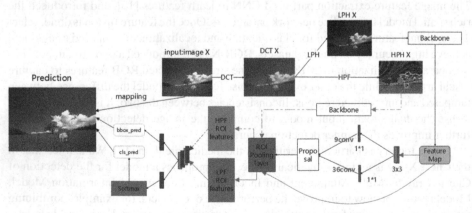

Fig. 3. Structure of faster-rcnn-w model.

3.1 High and Low Frequency Feature Extraction

Because manipulated images are often post-processed to hide tamper artifacts, capturing subtle tamper traces in RGB space is challenging. Thus, we extract features from the frequency domain to provide complementary cues for action sensing.

If an image X is taken as input, it is first converted from RGB to frequency domain using discrete cosine transform (DCT). The image processing process is shown in Fig. 4.

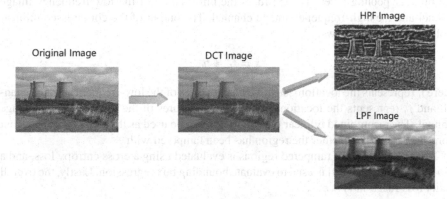

Fig. 4. Image Processing Flow

As there are no tamper marks hidden in normal images, capturing noise and image details in normal rgb space is challenging. With the goal of extracting more image features, we input the original image X of Fig. 3, first perform Discrete Cosine Transform (DCT) to convert It is transformed from the rgb domain to the Frequency Domain:

$$X = DCT(X) \tag{1}$$

where $X \in R^{H \times W \times 3}$.

The high frequency components are then obtained by a high pass filter to preserve the displacement invariance and local consistency of natural images:

$$DCT\,X = D^{-1}(H(X, a)) \tag{2}$$

where H is a high-pass filter, and a is a manually designed threshold that controls the low-frequency.

Similarly, we need to use the low frequency filter to let the DCT image enter and get the low frequency component:

$$DCT\,X = D^{-1}(L(X, b)) \tag{3}$$

where L is a low-pass filter, and b is a manually designed threshold that controls the high-frequency.

As shown in Fig. 4, we can see that the original image is converted into a DCT image, and the entire process of converting the DCT image into high frequency and low frequency.

Then, in Fig. 3, the two input streams enter the backbone pure convolutional layer at the same time to extract features and then divert the streams. The low frequency needs to go through the RPN network and then enter the ROI Pooling layer, while the high frequency image directly enters the ROI Pooling layer and joins the low frequency.

3.2 Bilinear Pooling

The bilinear pooling layer [16, 18] fuses the information of the low-frequency image channel and the high-frequency image channel. The output of the compressed bilinear pooling layer is as follows:

$$x = f_l^T * f_h \tag{4}$$

where f_l represents the location-sensitive map features of the low-frequency image channel, and f_h represents the location-sensitive map features of the high-frequency image channel. The recombined bilinear feature vector will be used as the basis for subsequent scores to determine whether the region has been tampered with.

The classification of tampered regions is evaluated using a cross entropy loss, and a smooth loss function [19] is used to evaluate bounding box regression. Lastly, the overall model loss function is:

$$L_a = L_r + L_c(f_l, f_h) + L_b(f_l) \tag{5}$$

Among them, L_a represents the total loss of the model, L_r represents the RPN network loss function, L_c represents the final cross-entropy classification loss, which is jointly determined by the dual-channel features f_l and f_h through the bilinear pooling layer, and L_b represents the final Bounding box regression loss, which is determined only by features fl from low-frequency image channels.

4 Experimental

This section evaluates the performance of faster-rcnn-w, conducts experiments on multiple tampered image datasets, uses a variety of evaluation criteria to obtain experimental data and compares with previous popular models, draws experimental conclusions.

4.1 Data Set Selection

The dataset contains the original image, the tampered image, and the corresponding master image. Existing image tampering detection datasets: CASIA dataset, RTD dataset, Columbia Uncompressed Image Splicing Detection dataset, Coverage dataset.

(1) CASIA 2.0, including two types of tampering, copy-move and splice
(2) Columbia Uncompressed Image Splicing Detection, this dataset only contains splice tampering, the dataset is small, only 183 tampered pictures, and the image resolution is high.

(3) The Coverage dataset only contains copy-move tampering, including 100 pairs of tampered images and the original image, and the image resolution is generally.

(4) RTD dataset, including three types of copy-move, splice, and remove, and the resolution is high.

For these four datasets, we have divided the training and test sets. After taking 90% of each dataset as training set and 10% as test set, we set the RPN network preselection rules, and anchors are finally determined as 16, 32, 64, 128. As the surface generation network filters anchors, IoU threshold of positive samples (samples containing tampered areas) is set to 0.7, and IoU of negative samples (those samples that do not contain tampered regions) is fixed to 0,3. According to the NMS (Non-Maximum Suppression) algorithm, the Samples with an IoU value greater than 0.7 are classified as foreground samples (tampered features), samples with an IoU value less than 0.3 are classified as negative samples (non-tampered features), and samples that are not within the above two ranges are selected. During training, the batch training method of small batch is selected, the batch size is set to 2, the number of iterations is 21600, the basic learning rate (learning_rate = 0.001), and the learning rate decays to one-tenth of the previous time for each iteration of 3240 times. Training of the algorithm consists of initializing the model first, and then starting the training of the detection model after parameter configuration.

In this paper, CASIA and RTD datasets are mainly used. The datasets' division for training and test is shown as Table 1.

Table 1. Division of training set and test set.

Dataset	CASIA 2.0	Columbia	Coverage	RTD
Training set	458	164	90	198
test set	50	18	10	22

4.2 Display of Experimental Results

We conducted experiments on the fusion dataset, obtained the experimental results of three tampering methods (Cp, Rm, Sp) respectively, and compared with the single-stream rgb domain faster-rcnn model and the RGB-N method. As we can see from the visual effects at first, our method is the closest to the tampered position of the ground truth among the three detections and has very high confidence, the comparison is shown as Fig. 5.

4.3 Evaluation Criteria and Description

The evaluation criteria used list as follow:

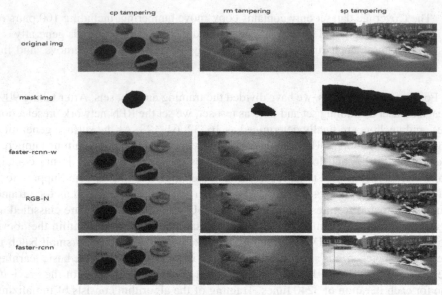

Fig. 5. Comparison with other models.

(1) F1 score precision and recall are generally used at the same time, and F1-score neutralizes the evaluation of both:

$$F1 = \frac{2 \times Precision \times Recall}{Precision + Recall} \tag{6}$$

(2) AP indicator PR curve concept: P in the PR curve represents precision, and R represents recall, which represents the relationship between precision and recall. The recall is set to the abscissa, and the precision is set to the ordinate. The AP index is the area enclosed by the PR curve and the x-axis.

(3) The AUC index roc curve refers to the false alarm probability P(y/N) obtained by the subjects under different judgment criteria under specific stimulation conditions as the abscissa, and the hit probability P(y/SN) as the ordinate, connecting the drawn points. AUC (Area Under Curve) is defined as the area under the ROC curve enclosed by the coordinate axis.

First, we compared our own model in three tampering methods, as shown in Table 2.

Table 2. Experimental evaluation diagram.

Tarmperway/Evaluation criteria	F1-score	AUC
Cp	35.4	45.4
Rm	53.4	74.4
Sp	63.4	87.4

Based on the data in the table, it can be seen that this method can realize three tamper detection schemes. This method is more effective among them for splicing detection, and the AUC value reaches 87.4, followed by the AU value of removal 74.4. The detection result of this method for copy-paste averages is not ideal, however, and the AUC value is only 45.4. According to the AUC and F1-score results, we can see that the method has better classification performance in detecting the effects of splicing and deletion. A F1-socre score for splicing and tainting is 63.4, and an F1 score for tainter removal is 60.4. Copy-paste detection results are not perfect.

Subsequently, we compared the performance of the model in this paper with the rgb single-stream faster-rcnn model and RGB-N on the same dataset, and evaluated with the above three evaluation indicators, as shown in Table 3.

Table 3. Comparison of evaluation indicators of different models.

Method	Tampering form	F1-score	AUC
Faster-rcnn-w	Cp	35.4	45.4
	Rm	60.4	74.4
	Sp	63.4	87.4
RGB-N	Cp	41.2	84.3
	Rm	58.6	78.4
	Sp	49.6	81.2
Faster-rcnn (rgb)	Cp	40.3	45.4
	Rm	35.4	50.3
	Sp	37.4	49.6

Table 3 shows that our dual-stream input model outperforms the faster-rcnn single-stream model by a large margin in each evaluation index. We conduct experiments on the fusion dataset, and benchmark the single-stream rgb input faster-rcnn model. As standard single-stream model, we not only add an input source to the input, but also perform image processing on the double-end, which is beneficial for the dct operation, and add high-frequency and low-frequency image filters to obtain high-rate and low frequency images of the dual-stream input end. The standard rgb stream represents the overall content of the image, while the high frequency side contains detail and noise. With the action of the high frequency input side, our network can analyze unseen details and noise in the rgb domain, which greatly improves the accuracy of model prediction.

When comparing with RGB-N, we observed that RGB-NN has lower F1-score metrics (49.6) and AUC metrics (81.2) on splicing (sp) than our model. RGB model – N only inputs a noise stream feature as an additional input, but the additional high frequency stream of our model input not only has noise features, but also changes edge details, which complements the insufficient noise stream and increases model accuracy. We replace the rgb stream with the low frequency data stream. This has the benefit of reducing coupling. We repeat the high frequency content repeated in the rgb stream with the high rate stream. The image is obtained in the low frequency domain with the high frequency content removed as the main body of the template. We show that the input model of the rgb domain can reduce coupling and improve model precision. However, in terms of copy and paste and tamper removal, RGB-N has a better effect than ours. This may be because when our model discards the rgb stream, it discards some content, causing some tampered regions belonging to high frequency content to be lost. Often when the tampered area is missing, the copy and paste content will be inconsistent with the copied area of the original image due to missing content, so faster-rcnn-w performs poorly in tampering cp. Similarly, under rm removal and tampering, our model and RGB-N have little difference in F1 and AUC indicators. It is because edge tearing is evident in tampered area, and the gray-scale contrast is strong whether it is high frequency input or SRM filtering. As the noise point of the image is enlarged, and the tearing edge is filled with such noise, under rm the performance of both is the same.

5 Conclusion

In today's society, image tamper detection is urgently needed to be developed, and our proposed faster-rcnn-w model is not inferior to the current mainstream image tampered detection templates. Above, complete dctization and extract high and low frequency features as input of dual-stream input, and inside the model, use dual-channel input and dual-pooling layer structure to complete the whole model improvement, no longer a simple overlay of convolution and rpn network, After the whole pattern is upgraded in three dimensions, the final result is presented on the low frequency image. We add rgb images at the output end to map the tamper area of low frequency images to complete the final result. Without changing the network hierarchy, this method improves the load speed, coupling and accuracy. At the same time, we have flaws. Out of the three tamper conditions we target, the tamper effect of cp copy-paste is not perfect. This is mainly because the tampered edges of the low frequency cp images are not consistent with the original image. Further research is warranted in future work. Enhance the tamper accuracy cp.

Acknowledgment. This work has been supported in part by the Natural Science Foundation of China under grant No. 62202211, the project supported by National Social Science Foundation under Grant No. 19CTJ014, the Science and Technology Research Project of Jiangxi Provincial Department of Education (No. GJJ170234).

Data Availability. The data in the experiments, used to support the findings of this study are available from the corresponding author upon request.

Conflicts of Interest. The authors declare that they have no conflicts of interest.

References

1. Goodfellow, I., et al.: Generative adversarial nets. In: NIPS (2014)

2. Zhu, J.-Y., Park, T., Isola, P., Efros, A.A.: Unpaired image-to-image translation using cycle-consistent adversarial networks. In: ICCV (2017)
3. Mirza, M., Osindero, S.: Conditional generative adversarial nets. arXiv preprint arXiv:1411. 1784 (2014)
4. Cozzolino, D., Poggi, G., Verdoliva, L.: Efficient dense-field copy–move forgery detection. IEEE Trans. Inform. Forensic. Secur. **10**(11), 2284–2297 (2015). https://doi.org/10.1109/TIFS.2015.2455334
5. Rao, Y., Ni, J.: A deep learning approach to detection of splicing and copy-move forgeries in images. In: WIFS (2016)
6. Huh, M., Liu, A., Owens, A., Efros, A.A.: Fighting fake news: image splice detection via learned self-consistency. In: Ferrari, V., Hebert, M., Sminchisescu, C., Weiss, Y. (eds.) ECCV 2018. LNCS, vol. 11215, pp. 106–124. Springer, Cham (2018). https://doi.org/10.1007/978-3-030-01252-6_7
7. Cozzolino, D., Poggi, G., Verdoliva, L.: Splicebuster: a new blind image splicing detector. In: WIFS (2015)
8. Kniaz, V.V., Knyaz, V., Remondino, F.: The point where reality meets fantasy: Mixed adversarial generators for image splice detection (2019)
9. Zhu, X., Qian, Y., Zhao, X., Sun, B., Sun, Y.: A deep learning approach to patch-based image in-painting forensics. Signal Process. Image Commun. **67**, 90–99 (2018)
10. Rao, Y., Ni, J.: A deep learning approach to detection of splicing and copy-move forgeries in images. In: IEEE International Workshop on Information Forensics and Security (WIFS), pp. 1–6. IEEE Computer Society, Abu Dhabi (2017)
11. Fridrich, J., Kodovsky, J.: Rich models for steganalysis of digital imagcs. IEEE Trans. Lnform. Forens. Secur. **7**, 868–882 (2012). https://doi.org/10.1109/TIFS.2012.2190402
12. Zhou, L.-N., Wang, D.-M.: Digital Image Forensics. Beijing University ol Posts and Telecommunications Press, Beijing (2008). (in Chinese)
13. Chen, S., Yao, T., Chen, Y., Ding, S., Li, J., Ji, R.: Local relation learning for face forgery detection. In: AAAI (2021)
14. Qian, Y., Yin, G., Sheng, L., Chen, Z., Shao, J.: Thinking in frequency: Face forgcry detection by mining frequency-aware clues. In: ECCV (2020)
15. Wang, J., Wu, Z., Chen, J., Jiang, Y.-G.: M2tr: Multi-modal multi-scale transformers for deep-fake detection. arXiv preprint arXiv:2104.09770 (2021)
16. Bianchi, T., Rosa, A.D., Piva, A.: Improved DCT coefficient analysis of forgery localization in JPEG images. In: Proceedings of the IEEE International Conference on Acoustics? Speech and Signal Processing (ICASSP), pp. 2444–2447. Prague, Czech Republic (2011)
17. Huang, X., Yan, F., Xu, W., Li, M.: Multi-attention and incorporating background information model for chest x-ray image report generation. IEEE Access **7**, 154808–154817 (2019)
18. Lin, T.-Y., RoyChowdhury, A., Maji, S.: Bilinear cnn models for fine-grained visual recognition. In: ICCV (2015)
19. Gao, Y., Beijbom, O., Zhang, N., Darrell, T.: Compact bilinear pooling. In: CVPR (2016)

Pneumonia Image Recognition Based on Transfer Learning

Tao Zhong[1], HuiTing Wen[1], Zhonghua Cao[2], Xinhui Zou[1], Quanhua Tang[1], and Wenle Wang[1(✉)]

[1] School of Software, Jiangxi Normal University, Nanchang 330027, Jiangxi, China
wenlewang@jxnu.edu.cn
[2] School of Software and Internet of Things Engineering, Jiangxi University of Finance and Economics, Nanchang 330013, Jiangxi, China

Abstract. With the rapid development of artificial intelligence (AI), the anomalies detection in biomedical has became important in patients' health monitoring. The pneumonia, including COVID-19, is a global threat. Detecting the infected patients in time is very critical to combating this epidemics. Thus, a rapid and accurate method for detecting pneumonia is urgently needed. In this paper, a deep-learning detection model, is designed to detect pneumonia efficient. Since training a neural network needs consuming a lot of time resources and computing resources, transfer learning is used for pre-training. At the same time, in order to improve the detection efficiency, we combine various deep learning models, and then perform prediction and classification. The simulation results show that comparing with the 91.5% accuracy of the traditional CNN model, the transfer learning model consisting of vgg16VGG16, vgg19VGG19, RresNnet50 and Xxecption reached 93.27%, 93.43%, 92.31% and 90.22% respectively. Most of the models are superior to the traditional models and have excellent stability with less time consuming.

Keywords: Transfer Learning · pneumonia detection

1 Introduction

As we all know, caused by an acute respiratory infection, the pneumonia has become one of the biggest threats to human society [1]. The key to combating this disease is identify the infected people in time. Because it can be caused by lots of factors, including viruses, bacteria, or fungus. Especially from the end of 2019, the COVID-19 has brought significant damage to the world. Many people have delayed treatment due to untimely diagnosis [2]. Because the pneumonia diagnosis is involves highly skilled analysis of a chest X-ray (CXR) using focused beam of radiation and professionally confirm the diagnosis with clinical history and laboratory tests, where the whole process is time-consuming [3].

The chest X-ray examining lungs, bones, and heart, are helpful to doctors to work out the placement and extent of the pneumonia [4]. The images brought by X-ray are

Y. Cao and X. Shao (Eds.): MONAMI 2022, LNICST 474, pp. 116–126, 2023.
https://doi.org/10.1007/978-3-031-32443-7_8

of the inside of body, where the thickness of body's tissues varies because the ratio of each part of body is different. The radiology technicians need to analyse a large number of CXRs every. And because different conditions may appear as opacity, it is difficult to identify the respiratory illness in CXR.

As artificial intelligence (AI) has recently become a topic of study in different applications, including healthcare, in which timely detection of anomalies can play a vital role in patient health monitoring [5]. With the potential of AI, it can minimize the repetitive task of clinicians, and automate the initial detection of potential respiratory illness to expedite the relevant review [6]. In the medical domain, the convolutional neural networks (CNN) methods are mostly used for classification. The [7] performed a study on the large pneumonia dataset containing the train, validation & test, which encountered that the smaller the image size, the better validation score. In [8], the DenseNet and MobileNetV2 CNN were used to train models on each dataset to classify, which achieved comparable performance to DenseNet, demonstrating the efficacy of CNNs for chest X-ray abnormality detection.

For these current deep learning models, it need to consume huge time resources and computing resources training a neural network. Therefore, reusing a pretrained deep learning model as a new model for another task, namely transfer learning, is a common approach in computer vision tasks [9]. Because most of the data and tasks are related, the parameters of the pre-training model can be transferred to the new model through transfer learning, thereby speeding up and optimize the learning efficiency of the model. Among them, the VGG CNN, including VGG16 and VGG19, are the most popular CNN model due to its simplicity and practicality. It shows good results in both image classification and object detection tasks [10].

In this paper, four models VGG16, VGG19, ResNet50 and Xeption are selected as the base learners of transfer learning, because these four models are classic convolutional neural networks, which are widely used, and have high recognition accuracy and generalization ability in the field of image recognition. Some outstanding achievements have also been made in transfer learning, which is an excellent base learner.

Therefore, a deep-learning pneumonia detection model, integrated with transfer learning model containing VGG16, VGG19, RresNet50 and Xecption, is proposed to detect pneumonia efficient. The contribution of this paper is as follows:

(1) A transfer learning model is constructed with VGG16, VGG19, ResNet50 and xecption, which obtains similar accuracy and less time consuming than single CNN method.
(2) Based on the designed transfer leaning model, we propose a ensemble learning model to retrive a better classfication accuracy to the traditional models.

2 Introduction to Data and Pre-processing

2.1 Dataset Description

The data set of this project comes from the public data of "chest X-ray images (pneumonia)" of kaggle. The data set contains more than 6000 pneumonia X-ray images, including two categories: pneumonia and normal. The images are divided into training set and test set of independent patients, marked as (disease) - (random patient ID) - (image number of the patient) and divided into four directories: CNV, DME, Drasen and normal. Table 1 shows the data composition of the training set, in which the ratio of positive and negative examples is 1:3.

Table 1. Data composition of training set.

Type	Count
Normal	About 1300
Pneumonia	About 3800

It can be seen that the data proportion difference is large, so the weight of the sample needs to be adjusted. At the same time, the number of data is small, so the data needs to be enhanced.

2.2 Dataset Description

Dataset processing is as follows:

(1) Use the image data generator provided by keras for enhanced preprocessing of datasets. First, tensor image data batches are generated by real-time data enhancement, and can be iterated circularly. The principle is to flip, pan, zoom and add noise to the original image. The degree range of random rotation is 20, the random width offset, the angle of random stagger transformation and the range of random scaling are all 0.1, and random horizontal flipping is allowed. Then, use flow_From_The directory method reads the data to realize the automatic enhancement of the data. The principle is to take the folder path as the parameter, generate the data after data promotion or normalization, and generate batch data infinitely in an infinite loop.
(2) Adjust the weight of the sample. Use the class in the fit function_weight method to map the value of the class index to the weight, which is used to weight the loss function (only during the training period). The calculation method is that the weight of normal samples = the number of pneumonia samples/total, and the weight of pneumonia samples = the number of normal samples/total.

3 Model

First of all, this chapter uses several commonly used and pre trained deep learning models for transfer learning, including VGG16, VGG19, ResNet50, Xecption. By freezing some weights of these models and consuming less time for model training, the transfer learning of these models is completed and four classifiers are obtained. Then, these four weak classifiers are fused by linear regression to form a strong classifier, which realizes the integration of the model. The fusion model of integrated learning is conducive to improving the recognition accuracy and generalization ability of the model. At the same time, we also trained the traditional CNN network model to compare with the fusion model, and we can find that the performance of the fusion model is better than the traditional model in all aspects.

3.1 Transfer Learning

The pre-training models used in this paper are VGG16, VGG19, ResNet50 and Xecption. Considering that the full connection layer structure added by VGG16 and VGG19 is similar, while the full connection layer structure added by ResNet50 and xeption is similar, we take VGG16and ResNet50 as examples.

(1) VGG16 model construction. First, keep VGG16 convolution layer parameters, remove the original full connection layer of the model, and rebuild it. The model network structure before the full connection layer is called the bottleneck layer, which is used to extract the features of the image and obtain a (4, 4, 4512) feature vector; The feature vector is extracted and transformed into the classification results we need through the full connection layer. The final model structure is shown in Fig. 1.

Layer (type)	Output Shape	Param #
vgg16 (Model)	(None, 4, 4, 512)	14714688
flatten_1 (Flatten)	(None, 8192)	0
dense_1 (Dense)	(None, 256)	2097408
dropout_1 (Dropout)	(None, 256)	0
dense_2 (Dense)	(None, 1)	257

Fig. 1. VGG16 network structure built

As Table1 shown, we have added a flatten layer, two Dense layers and a Dropout layer for VGG16. The first Dense layer uses Relu as the activation function to accelerate training and prevent information loss. The second Dense layer uses Sigmoid as the activation function to output the training results of the model. Dropout layer can effectively alleviate the occurrence of over fitting by randomly stopping a neuron with a certain probability p, and achieve the effect of regularization to a certain extent.

Next is the model's superparameters. Through multiple feedbacks of model training results to modify the superparameters, we get the final superparameters as follows. The optimizer of the model is Adam, and the loss function is binary_crossentropy, which is a loss function commonly used in binary classification problems. Because the number of the two types of pictures is uneven, this paper also uses class_weight is used to modify the weight of loss function of different categories of data to alleviate the problem of uneven sample number. At the same time, the first several layers of the bottleneck layer are frozen to reduce the training time of the model.

The output of the final model is a number between 0 and 1. The closer it is to 1, the greater the probability that the picture is pneumonia, otherwise the opposite is true.

(2) ResNet50 model building. ResNet50 and VGG16 are generally the same in the process of transfer learning, but there are still some differences. Here are the differences. The final model structure is shown in Fig. 2.

```
Layer (type)                     Output Shape              Param #
=================================================================
resnet50 (Model)                 (None, 5, 5, 2048)        23587712

global_average_pooling2d_1 (     (None, 2048)              0

dense_1 (Dense)                  (None, 512)               1049088

batch_normalization_1 (Batch     (None, 512)               2048

dropout_1 (Dropout)              (None, 512)               0

dense_2 (Dense)                  (None, 1)                 513
=================================================================
```

Fig. 2. Resnet50 network structure built

Firstly, the network structure of ResNet50 is more complex than VGG16, and there are many model parameters. Therefore, this paper uses the global pooling layer to replace the full connection layer. The advantage is that it can retain the spatial information extracted from the previous convolution layer and pooling layer, and can also effectively reduce the model parameters and reduce the training time of the model.

Because ResNet50 network structure is too deep, the network becomes difficult to train convergence and adjust parameters. This paper adds a batch processing layer, which whitens each batch, that is, the process of removing mean and variance. It can normalize the data, alleviate the gradient disappearance problem to a certain extent, accelerate the network convergence, and prevent the over fitting problem at the same time.

3.2 Integrated Learning

Because the output result of the model is between 0–1, the closer it is to 1, the greater the probability that the model considers pneumonia, and the closer it is to 0, the lower the probability that it considers pneumonia. We use linear regression to predict and build a linear regression model $y = a_1 x_1 + a_2 x_2 + a_3 x_3 + a_4 x_4 + b$, where x_1 reach x_4. They are the output results of VGG16, VGG19, ResNet50 and Xecption models for a picture respectively, and y is the prediction result. a_1, a_2, a_3, a_4 and b are the parameters that need training.

Through linear regression training, we can get that the prediction result of the fusion model is a value y. We believe that when the value y is greater than 0.5, the model predicts that the picture has pneumonia. Less than 0.5 is predicted to be a normal picture.

4   Experimental Results and Analysis

The experimental data set comes from the public data of "Chest X-Ray Images (Pneumonia)" of Kaggle. The data set contains more than 6000 pneumonia X-ray images, which are classified by many experts, and the data is highly reliable. Experimental machine Intel (R) Core (TM) i5-9300 H CPU @2.40 GHz (8 CPUs), ~2.4 GHz, CPU GTX650, memory 16G Windows10 operating system. All models use PyCharm as the integrated development environment, and are implemented using the deep learning framework keras. The Loss curve and accuracy curve of the experimental results are drawn by pyplot of matplotlib to analyze the convergence of the model.

4.1   Performance Index

Error rate and accuracy are the two most commonly used performance measures in classification tasks. Error rate refers to the proportion of the number of samples with classification errors in the total number of samples, which is defined as Eq. (1):

$$error = \frac{1}{m} \sum_{i=1}^{m} \| (f(x_i) \neq y_i) \tag{1}$$

Precision is the proportion of the number of samples with correct classification to the total number of samples, which is defined as:

$$acc = \frac{1}{m} \sum_{i=1}^{m} \| (f(x_i) = y_i) \tag{2}$$

Precision and recall are the detection values with high adaptability to evaluate the performance of applications. For the binary classification problem, the combination of real category and algorithm prediction category can be divided into four cases: true positive (T P), false positive (F P), true negative (T N) and false negative (F N). The precision P is defined as:

$$P = \frac{TP}{TP + FP} \tag{3}$$

The recall R's formula is as follow:

$$R = \frac{TP}{TP + FN} \tag{4}$$

F1 takes into account both precision P and recall R, is measured as below:

$$F1 = \frac{2 \times P \times R}{P + R} \tag{5}$$

where ALL is the total number of samples.

In this paper, F1 value is used as the main evaluation standard, and accuracy and recall are used as auxiliary evaluation standards.

4.2 Experimental Results of Each Transfer Learning Model

The superparameters of each model are shown as table 2.

Table 2. Superparameters of each model

model	Learning rate	epoch	Frozen network layers	Lower boundary of learning rate	Learning rate decline factor
VGG16	0.00001	24	16	0.000000001	0.8
VGG19	0.00001	16	12	0.000000001	0.8
Resnet50	0.00003	24	32	0.00000000001	0.8
Xception	0.00001	24	32	0.00000000001	0.8

The following Figs. 4 and 5 show the changes of accuracy and loss of each transfer learning model with the number of epoch. Obviously, it can be found that the accuracy and loss on the training set change slightly, while the change on the verification set is larger. This is due to the small number of validation sets. At the same time, it can be found that the accuracy of each model is more than 80% at the beginning, because the pre trained weights are used, which can also significantly reduce the time cost of the training model. The number of epochs of VGG 19 is 16, and the number of epochs of the other three models is 24. This is because it is found that VGG 19 is easier to over fit during training, so the number of epochs of the model is reduced. At the same time, it is found that ResNet50 performs best in this training set, followed by VGG16. This is because the residual structure of ResNet50 can effectively prevent the gradient disappearance caused by the deepening of the network structure, so it has better performance. At the same time, VGG16 outperforms other models in the validation set, which shows that VGG16 has high generalization ability and robustness. It can be seen that VGG19 model has a significant change in accuracy and loss in the 11th epoch, which is due to the oscillation phenomenon caused by the excessive learning rate.

The changes of accuracy and loss in training dataset is shown as Fig. 3.

The changes of accuracy and loss in validation dataset is shown as Fig. 4.

The performance of each transfer learning model in the test dataset is as Table 3.

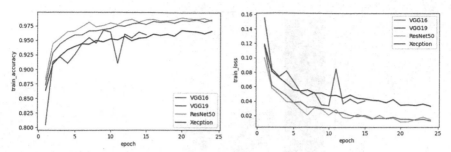

Fig. 3. The changes of accuracy and loss in training dataset.

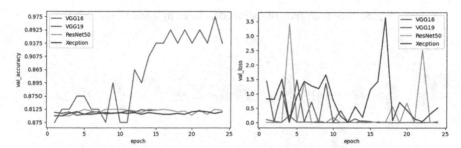

Fig. 4. The changes of accuracy and loss in validation dataset.

Table 3. Evaluation indicators of each model1

model	accuracy	recall	F1-score
VGG16	93.65%	91.97%	92.69%
VGG19	93.16%	92.78%	92.96%
Resnet50	92.80%	90.77%	91.61%
Xception	90.96%	88.16%	89.24%

4.3 Fusion Model

The Fig. 5 shows the weight diagram of four models fused by linear regression. It can be seen that VGG16 has the highest weight proportion, reaching 0.55, while Xecption has the lowest weight, reaching a point of almost negligible. It can be found that the higher the accuracy of the model, the greater the relative weight, which is in line with our expectations.

In order to compare the fusion model with the traditional model, this paper constructs a traditional CNN network, and the model structure is as follows Fig. 6.

The super parameter is set as: the number of iterations is 24, the learning rate is 0.00001, the learning rate reduction factor is 0.6, and the lower boundary of the learning rate is 0.000000001. It takes about seven hours to train in the local environment. The transfer learning model only needs more than three hours of training, which is twice as

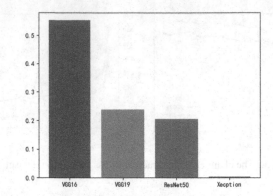

Fig. 5. Weight diagram of four models fused by linear regression

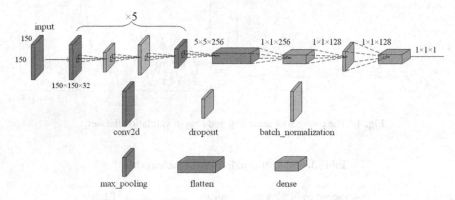

Fig. 6. The CNN network model structure constructed

fast as the ordinary CNN model. The Evaluation indicators of each model are listed in Table 4.

Table 4. Evaluation indicators of each model

model	accuracy	recall	F1-score
CNN	90.17%	94.10%	92.10%
Fusion model	94.40%	96.30%	95.34%

It can be found that the integration of multiple machine learning models can significantly improve the overall prediction ability. This is because different sub models have different expressive abilities in data. We can combine the parts they are good at to get an "accurate" model in all aspects. Through linear regression learning the weight of each model, we can get a relatively better weight of each model, which can well mine the strengths of each sub model and improve the effect of the final model.

5 Conclusion

X-ray detection of pneumonia is an important detection method in medicine. The traditional human eye detection is completely based on the judgment of doctors, which takes a long time to obtain the results and may be misjudged; CNN has a good foundation for pneumonia image detection, but the training time is long and the recognition accuracy is not high. This paper uses an integrated learning framework integrating multi transfer learning model, which greatly improves the accuracy of recognition and reduces the training time. In the model, we choose VGG16, VGG19, ResNet50, Xecption classifiers, and integrate multiple models into a strong classifier through linear regression. Compared with traditional CNN, it greatly reduces the training time of the model and improves the recognition ability of the model.

However, the model still has some limitations, including the inability to show the specific location of the lesion. This will be further studied in future work.

6 Conflicts of Interest

The authors declare that they have no conflicts of interest.

Acknowledgment. This work has been supported in part by the Natural Science Foundation of China under grant No. 62262030, the Science and Technology Research Project of Jiangxi Provincial Department of Education (No. GJJ170234).

Data Availability. The data in the experiments, used to support the findings of this study are available from the corresponding author upon request.

References

1. Gemelli Against COVID, Post-Acute Care Study Group, et al.: Post-COVID-19 global health strategies: the need for an interdisciplinary approach. Aging Clin. Exp. Res. **32**, 1613–1620 (2020)
2. Abbas, A., Abdelsamea, M.M., Gaber, M.M.: Classification of covid-19 in chest x-ray images using detrac deep convolutional neural network. Appl. Intell. **51**(2), 854–864 (2021)
3. Lin, T.-C., Lee, H.-C.: Covid-19 chest radiography images analysis based on integration of image pre-process, guided grad-cam, machine learning and risk management. In: Proceedings of the 4th International Conference on Medical and Health Informatics, pp. 281–288 (2020)
4. Wardlaw, T., Salama, P., Johansson, E.W., Mason, E.: Pneumonia: the leading killer of children. Lancet **368**(9541), 1048–1050 (2006)
5. Lakhani, P., Sundaram, B.: Deep learning at chest radiography: automated classification of pulmonary tu-berculosis by using convolutional neural networks. Radiology **284**(2), 574–582 (2017)
6. Vu, T.H., Murakami, R., Okuyama, Y., Ben Abdallah, A.: Efficient optimization and hardware acceleration of CNNS towards the design of a scalable neuro inspired architecture in hardware. In: 2018 IEEE International Conference on Big Data and Smart Computing (Big-Comp), pp. 326–332 (2018)

7. Stephen, O., Sain, M., Maduh, U.J., Jeong, D.-U.: An efficient deep learning approach to pneumonia classification in healthcare. J. Healthc. Eng. **2019**, 4180949 (2019)
8. Pan, I., Agarwal, S., Merck, D.: Generalizable inter-institutional classification of abnormal chest radiographs using efficient convolutional neural networks. J. Digit. Imaging **32**(5), 888–896 (2019)
9. Cai, C., Wang, S., Xu, Y., et al.: Transfer learning for drug discovery. J. Med. Chem. **63**(16), 8683–8694 (2020)
10. Wang, J., Nakamura, M., Ben Abdallah, A.: Efficient AI-enabled pneumonia detection in chest x-ray images. In: 2022 IEEE 4th Global Conference on Life Sciences and Technologies (LifeTech), pp. 470–474 (2022)

Surface Defect Detection Algorithm of Aluminum Sheet Based on Improved Yolov3

Liu Yang[1], Guoxiong Hu[1(✉)], and Li Huang[2]

[1] School of Software, Jiangxi Normal University, Nanchang 330027, China
huguoxiong@126.com
[2] School of Education, Jiangxi Normal University, Nanchang 330027, China

Abstract. The surface defect detection of aluminum sheet is of great significance to ensure the appearance and quality of aluminum sheet. The surface defects of aluminum sheets have the characteristics of different shapes, obvious size differences, and difficult to obtain defect samples, which make defect detection challenging. In order to solve this problem, we make the following improvements to YOLOv3: Adding attention mechanism modules after the three feature layers output by the model backbone and after neck upsampling; Freezing the model backbone and using pretrained for transfer learning. The proposed YOLOv3 + ECA model is compared with the target detection models such as YOLOv3 and Faster-RCNN. It is found that the mAP of our model reaches 96.22%, which is higher than the current conventional algorithm. The AP values for different types of defects have good detection results.

Keywords: Defect detection · Attention Mechanism · Few Shot · Small Target Detection

1 Introduction

Aluminum alloys are widely used in transportation, electronics, machinery and other fields [1]. In the process of production and processing, it is easy to have pinhole, scratch, dirty, fold and other surface defects. These surface defects will not only affect the appearance and fatigue strength of products, but also increase the production cost of enterprises. More seriously, it will threaten people's lives. Therefore, it is of great significance to detect defects on the surface of aluminum alloys in time.

In the defect detection of metal industrial products, the commonly used detection methods include manual inspection, magnetic flux leakage testing, radiography testing, traditional machine vision detection and deep learning detection [3–6]. Among them, manual inspection generally has the disadvantages of low precision, strong subjectivity and high labor intensity [2]; Magnetic flux leakage testing is not suitable for detecting cracks with complex shapes and narrow cracks, especially closed cracks; Radiography testing can easily determine the nature of defects, but it is expensive and harmful to human body; Compared with the previous detection methods, machine vision detection

© ICST Institute for Computer Sciences, Social Informatics and Telecommunications Engineering 2023
Published by Springer Nature Switzerland AG 2023. All Rights Reserved
Y. Cao and X. Shao (Eds.): MONAMI 2022, LNICST 474, pp. 127–137, 2023.
https://doi.org/10.1007/978-3-031-32443-7_9

has the outstanding advantages of high detection accuracy, fast detection speed and low cost. However, the traditional machine vision relies on artificial design features, and the robustness of the algorithm is poor. With the advent of the big data era and the improvement of computer computing power, deep learning has developed rapidly. Compared with traditional machine vision technology, deep learning achieves higher accuracy in image classification, image segmentation, target detection and other fields [5].

Owing to the superiority of deep learning algorithm in defect detection, the detection method based on deep learning has been widely concerned and studied. However, there are not many applications in actual industrial scenarios. The main reason is determined by the characteristics of defect data. The details are as follows: (1) The defect shapes are different. (2) Small target defect samples are few. (3) The size of different types of defects is obviously different. (4) It is difficult to obtain defect samples. This makes the practical application of surface defect method based on deep learning very challenging.

The attention mechanism has the properties of plug-and-play nature, which improves the detection accuracy of the model without significantly increasing the amount of computation. And it can also enable the network model to pay attention to more valuable information for the task, thereby improving the efficiency of task processing and the ability of feature extraction.

Therefore, this paper focuses on the attention mechanism and improves the YOLOv3 algorithm. The contribution of this paper are as follows:

1. Building defect dataset. The industrial defect images on the surface of aluminum sheet were collected by industrial camera and classified into four types of defects. Namely Pinhole, Scratch, Dirty and Fold.
2. Improving YOLOv3 model structure. We add attention mechanism modules to the neck of the network model to improve the feature extraction ability. It effectively solves the problem that small target defects are difficult to detect.
3. Model training with transfer learning. In view of the problem that it is difficult to obtain defect dataset, this paper uses pretrained weights to perform transfer learning by freezing the backbone of the model. This method not only speeds up the training speed of the model, but also enables the model to achieve better detection results on small datasets.

This paper is structured as follows: In the first section, we expound the background and significance of defect detection on the surface of aluminum sheets, enumerate the current main defect detection methods, and analyze their deficiencies. Section 2 introduces the related research on object detection algorithms and attention mechanisms. Section 3 proposes solutions to the problem that the surface defects of aluminum sheets are difficult to detect. Section 4 conducts a comparative experiment on the improved YOLOv3 algorithm and analyzes the performance of the algorithm. Section 5 briefly summarizes the content of the previous sections and draws conclusions.

2 Related Work

Object detection can obtain accurate positioning and category information of targets. At present, it is mainly divided into two-stages algorithms and one-stage algorithms. The former first generate candidate boxes that may contain targets, and then adjust the boxes and classify the targets. The latter does not generate candidate boxes, and the final detection result can be obtained after a single detection.

The main algorithm of the two-stage detection method is Faster-RCNN [7]. For example, Ding et al. [8] proposed a network dedicated to tiny defect detection (TDD-net). This method strengthens the fusion of information from the underlying structure and improves the detection accuracy of small defects. He et al. [9] proposed a method based on Faster R-CNN, using FPN, Soft Non-Maximum Suppression (NMS) and Region of Interest (ROI) alignment to improve the accuracy of the model. But the detection speed is slow. The main representatives of one-stage detection methods are YOLO and SSD. For example, Guo et al. [10] proposed MFST-YOLO model. Based on YOLOv5, this method combines Trans module designed by transformer and multi-scale feature fusion structure. It can quickly detect defects on steel surface, but the average detection accuracy still has great room for improvement.

Attention mechanism is widely used in the field of object detection due to its plug-and-play characteristics and the ability to capture valuable information. For example, Yao et al. [11] proposed an enhancing region and boundary Awareness Network (ERBANet). The author combines ERBANet with attentional feature enhancement (AFE) module. The method achieves faster detection speed and higher detection accuracy. Li et al. [12] proposed a hybrid attention mechanism, which is mainly composed of channel attention, spatial attention and aligned attention modules. Then the hybrid attention mechanism is combined with the single-stage target detection algorithm HAR to achieve target detection. The detection accuracy of the algorithm has been significantly improved.

Similarly, for the object detection task, the acquired image quality is also related to the accuracy of defect detection. Currently, the popular image quality assessment (IQA) methods are the no-reference(NR) techniques. For example, Hu et al. [14] proposed parametric models that describe general characteristics of chromatic data in natural images, which are unified in a common NR IQA metric. The proposed metric provides solutions to various color image processing problems. In addition to color images, night-time images are also used as objects for object detection. A night-time blind image quality assessment (BIQA) method based on support vector regression (SVR) [15] can effectively predict night-time image quality.

All of the above studies provide more possibilities for the detection of surface defects of aluminum sheets. At the same time, it can be seen from the above research that defect detection has produced a relatively large contradiction in accuracy and speed. This contradiction can be effectively alleviated by combining attention mechanism.

3 Methods

3.1 Improved YOLOv3 Model

YOLOv3 is a classic one-stage target detection algorithm. Compared with the two-stage detection algorithm, it can directly generate the object category probability and position coordinate value without going through the candidate region generation stage. So it has faster detection speed, but there is still room for improvement in detection accuracy. Therefore, while maintaining the detection speed, this paper introduces attention mechanism ECA module to improve the detection accuracy. The YOLOv3 network model combined with ECA module as show in Fig. 1.

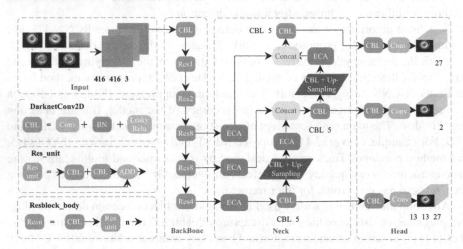

Fig.1. Improved YOLOv3 model

BackBone. The model can be divided into four parts: input, backbone, neck and head. Among them, the backbone feature extraction network is Darknet-53. This part has a total of 6 separate convolution layers and 23 residual blocks. As can be seen from Fig. 1, the input features of the residual block first go through a convolutional layer CBL with a kernel size of 1×1 and a stride of 1. Its number of channels is reduced to $\frac{1}{2}$ of the original, which is $\frac{Inchannels}{2}$. Then enter a 3×3 convolutional layer for feature extraction, and the number of channels is restored to *Inchannels*.

The output of the 3×3 convolution is directly added to the skip connection to obtain the output. After residual operation, the shape of the input feature map remains unchanged. The skip connections in it alleviate the gradient vanishing problem caused by increasing depth in deep neural networks. Secondly, the convolution part of Darknet-53 uses the unique darknetconv2d structure. The structure first performs a convolution and L2 regularization. After completing the convolution, Batch Normalization and LeakyReLU activation function are performed. The definition of LeakyReLU is shown in formula (1).

$$\text{LeakyReLU}(x) = \begin{cases} x & x > 0 \\ \alpha x & x \leqslant 0 \end{cases} \tag{1}$$

Neck. After Darknet-53 feature extraction, three effective feature layers are obtained. Their sizes are (52, 52, 256), (26, 26, 512), (13,13, 1024). Attention mechanism is a plug-and-play module. In order to successfully use the pretrained weight for transfer learning in the future, we do not add the attention module to the backbone network, but add the attention module after the three feature layers extracted from the backbone network and after two upsampling of the neck of the model. The introduction of the attention mechanism can make the model pay attention to the more valuable information for the task among the numerous information, so as to improve the efficiency and accuracy of task processing. Attention mechanism can be roughly divided into channel attention mechanism, spatial attention mechanism, and channel and spatial mixed attention mechanism.

ECA module is an implementation of channel attention mechanism. Adding this module to the model not only does not increase the complexity of the model, but also effectively improves the detection effect of the model. The structure of the ECA module is shown in Fig. 2. We first perform global average pooling(GAP) operation on the input feature $\chi \in R^{H*W*C}$ and compress it into $Z \in R^{1*1*C}$. The calculation formula is shown in formula (2). Then, we input Z into 1D convolution with a kernel size of k for feature learning to get the channel weights. The calculation formula of k is shown in formula (3). Finally, the results can be obtained by multiplying the weight to the feature directly.

$$z_c = \frac{1}{H * W} \sum_{i=1}^{H} \sum_{j=1}^{W} \chi_c(i, j) \tag{2}$$

$$k = \psi(C) = \left| \frac{\log_2(C)}{\gamma} + \frac{b}{\gamma} \right|_{odd} \tag{3}$$

where C indicates the number of channels; $|t|_{odd}$ represents the nearest odd number of t; $\psi(\cdot)$ indicates nonlinear mapping.

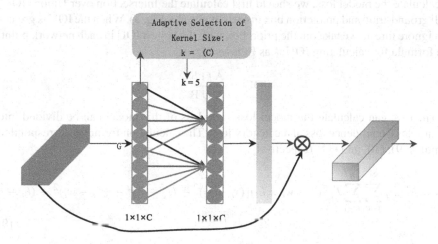

Fig. 2. ECA module.

Head. After the input features are passed through the neck network, three enhanced features can be obtained. Then these three enhanced features are passed into Head through the convolutional layer to obtain the prediction result. The shapes of the prediction results are (13, 13, 27), (26, 26, 27), (52, 52, 27). However, these prediction results do not correspond to the position of the final prediction box on the picture, so they still need to be decoded. The decoding process is to calculate the coordinates of the last displayed bounding box: b_x, b_y, and the width and height:b_w, b_h. In this way, we actually get the position of the predicted box. Each prediction box includes the position of prediction box, category information and confidence information. The calculation process is as follows:

$$b_x = \sigma(t_x) + c_x \tag{4}$$

$$b_y = \sigma(t_y) + c_y \tag{5}$$

$$b_w = p_w e^{t_w} \tag{6}$$

$$b_h = p_h e^{t_h} \tag{7}$$

where c_x and c_y are the coordinate of the upper left corner of the cell; p_w and p_h denote the edge length of priori box; $\sigma(t_x)$ and $\sigma(t_y)$ are the offset based on the grid point coordinates of the upper left corner of the center point of the rectangular box; t_w and t_h denote the width and height of the prediction box.

3.2 Loss Function

To calculate the model loss, we should first calculate the Intersection over Union (IOU) of all ground-truth and prediction box in each image (see Fig. 3). When the IOU is greater than ignore thresh, we take out the priori box with the largest IOU in each network point. The formula for calculating IOU is as follows:

$$IOU = \frac{A \cap B}{A \cup B} \tag{8}$$

Then we can calculate the model loss. The loss of this model can be divided into location loss, confidence loss and category loss. The calculation formulas correspond to formulas (9), (10) and (11) respectively.

$$lbox = \lambda_{coord} \sum_{i=0}^{S^2} \sum_{j=0}^{B} I_{ij}^{obj} (2 - w_i \times h_i)[(x_i - \hat{x}_i^j)^2 + (y_i - \hat{y}_i^j)^2 + (w_i - \hat{w}_i)^2 + (h_i - \hat{h}_i)^2] \tag{9}$$

$$lobj = \lambda_{noobj} \sum_{i=0}^{S^2} \sum_{j=0}^{B} I_{ij}^{noobj} (c_i - \hat{c}_i)^2 + \lambda_{obj} \sum_{i=0}^{S^2} \sum_{j=0}^{B} I_{ij}^{obj} (c_i - \hat{c}_i)^2 \tag{10}$$

$$lcls = \lambda_{class} \sum_{i=0}^{S^2} \sum_{j=0}^{B} I_{ij}^{obj} \sum_{c \in classes} p_i(c) \log(\hat{p}_i(c)) \tag{11}$$

where S is the grid size; B denotes the number of candidate boxes; I_{ij}^{obj} denotes whether there is a target object in the jth prior box of the ith grid. If there is, $I_{ij}^{obj} = 1$. Otherwise, $I_{ij}^{obj} = 0$.

The loss of the whole model is the sum of the above three. The calculation formula is as follows:

$$Loss = lbox + lobj + lcls \tag{12}$$

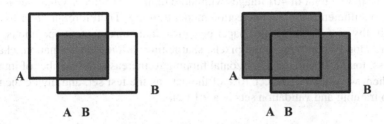

Fig. 3. IOU principle diagram.

4   Experimental Results and Analysis

4.1   Transfer Learning of Pretrained Mode

Transfer learning [13] is a technical means to apply the machine learning model trained in one field to another. It increases the utilization of the model to some extent, shows the superior performance when the amount of training data is small, and saves the training time and storage cost. For the neural network, it only needs to cut a trained neural network from the middle, and then splice it to other networks to realize the transfer learning. In the training phase, the topological structure and all super parameters of the migration module can remain unchanged, and the weight can decide whether to retrain according to needs. Transfer learning is divided into pretrained mode and fixed value mode according to whether to update the weight of the old module. Faced with the scarcity of training data for aluminum sheet surface defects, we have more advantages in using the pretrained transfer method.

We divide the training into two stages: freezing stage and unfreezing stage. In the freezing phase, the backbone of the model is frozen, and the feature extraction network is not changed, only the network is fine tuned. We set the initial learning rate to 0.01. During the training, we can adjust the batch size appropriately according to the use of the video memory. After unfreezing, all parameters of the network will be changed.

4.2   Experiment Description

All experiments were carried out on windows10 operating system with pytorch based on Python 3.8. The pretrained model is used in the training process. The batch size of the freeze phase is 16. The batch size in the unfreeze phase is 8. The initial learning rate is 0.001, and its decline mode is cos. Momentum is set to 0.937, IOU threshold is set to 0.5, and Adam optimizer is used.

4.3 Datasets

In the actual industrial production, the product yield is relatively high. So it is difficult for us to obtain a large number of defect image samples. The dataset in this paper is collected by industrial camera, including 4 types of aluminum sheet surface defects (see Fig. 4). We have a total of 401 images with more than 1000 defects. Quantitatively, this is far from sufficient for object detection model training. Therefore, in order to reduce the possibility of over fitting, this paper performs data enhancement operations, which include randomly removing some pixels, sharpening, affine transformation, changing brightness, tone following and horizontal flipping to increases the number of images to 2459. Then, we randomly select 10% of the data as the test set, and divide the rest of data into training and validation sets in a 9:1 ratio.

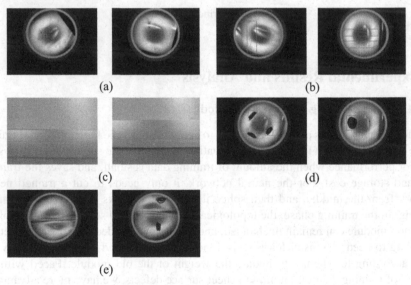

Fig. 4. Four types of aluminum sheet surface defects and corresponding label frames. (a) Pinhole: a circular small hole with an aperture less than or equal to 2 mm; (b) and (c) Scratch: linear scar with different length and depth; (d) Dirty: irregular black brown block; (e) Fold: part of the surface metal of the aluminum sheet is folded into the aluminum sheet, causing the metal to form overlapping layer defects.

4.4 Experimental Results

In order to verify the effectiveness of the attention adding mechanism proposed in this paper. We compare YOLOv3 + ECA with target detection models such as YOLOv3 and

Faster-RCNN. The evaluation indicators include Precision, Recall, Average Precisio (AP), mean Average Precision (mAP) and FPS. The definitions of Precision and Recall are shown in formulas (13) and (14) respectively:

$$\text{Precision} = \frac{TP}{TP + FP} \tag{13}$$

$$\text{Recall} = \frac{TP}{TP + FN} \tag{14}$$

where *TP* is the number of samples that are predicted to be positive and are actually positive; *TN* denotes the number of samples that are predicted to be negative and actually negative; *FP* denotes the number of samples with positive prediction and negative actual prediction; *FN* denotes the number of samples with negative prediction and positive actual prediction.

AP is the area enclosed by the precision-recall curve (P-R) and the coordinate axis. mAP denotes the mean value of AP, which reflects the comprehensive performance of the object detection algorithm. The definitions of AP and map are shown in formulas (15) and (16) respectively:

$$AP = \int_0^1 p(r)dr \tag{15}$$

$$mAP = \frac{1}{n} \sum AP \tag{16}$$

where $p(r)$ denotes the P-R curve,; n denotes the number of types of defects.

As can be seen from Table 1 and Fig. 5, the mAP of SSD is 92.56%, but the AP for the unclear defect such as scratch is only 78%. The mAP of Faster-RCNN reaches 94%, but the AP for small target defects such as pinhole is only 79%. The mAP of YOLOv3 is 66.42%, and the AP for different types of defects are all lower than the other three models. The mAP of YOLOv3 + ECA reached 96.22%. Detection speed is 20 FPS. Compared with the original YOLOv3, its detection rate has been greatly improved. At the same time, compared with SSD, YOLOv3 + ECA is slightly inferior in detection speed, but it can still meet the needs of industrial real-time detection. Although the AP and mAP of Faster-RCNN can also reach high values, their detection speed is only 6 FPS, which cannot meet the needs of industrial real-time detection. It can be seen that the effectiveness and superiority of the YOLOv3 + ECA.

Table 1. Performance comparison of different defect detection models.

Model	AP (%)				mAP (%)	FPS
	Pinhole	Scratch	Dirty	Fold		
SSD	94	78	100	98	92.56	**33**
Faster-RCNN	79	**98**	100	**100**	94.32	6
YOLOv3	89	10	100	95	73.54	8
YOLOv3 + Transfer Learning	60.70	7.60	99.96	97.41	66.42	21
YOLOv3 + Transfer Learning + ECA	**95**	91	**100**	99	**96.22**	20

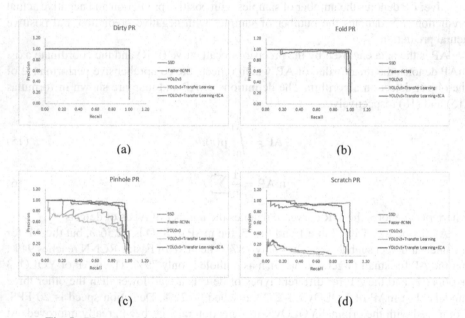

(a)   (b)

(c)   (d)

Fig. 5. PR curves of different target detection algorithms and different defects.

5   Conclusions

In this paper, we have improved YOLOv3 to detect surface defects of aluminum sheets. On the one hand, in order to solve the problem of small dataset size, this paper trains through transfer learning. On the other hand, in order to improve the detection accuracy of the algorithm for small target defects and unclear defects, this paper adds attention modules based on the original YOLOv3. The experimental results show that the mAP of the improved YOLOv3 algorithm is improved. Especially for scratch detection, the AP of the original YOLOv3 is only 10%, while the improved model improves to 91%. Moreover, the detection time of this model is 20 FPS, which can meet the needs of industrial real-time detection. Since there are not only four types of defects in aluminum sheets in reality, we will continue to study the automatic detection of different types of defects in the future.

Funding Statement. This work was supported by the Science and Technology Project of Jiangxi Provincial Department of Education under Grant no. GJJ200305 and GJJ191689, the Natural Science Foundation of Jiangxi Province under Grants no. 20202BABL202016.

References

1. Zhang, J., Song, B., Wei, Q., et al.: A review of selective laser melting of aluminum alloys: processing, microstructure, property and developing trends. J. Mater. Sci. Technol. **35**(2), 270–284 (2019)
2. Tao, X., Zhang, D., Ma, W., et al.: Automatic metallic surface defect detection and recognition with convolutional neural networks. Appl. Sci. **1575**, 1–15 (2018)
3. Dehui, W., Lingxin, S., Wang, X., et al.: A novel non-destructive testing method by measuring the change rate of magnetic flux leakage. J. Nondestr. Eval. **36**(2), 1–11 (2017)
4. Malarvel, M., Singh, H.: An autonomous technique for weld defects detection and classification using multi-class support vector machine in X-radiography image. Optik **231**, 166342 (2021)
5. O'Mahony, N., et al.: Deep learning vs. traditional computer vision. In: Arai, K., Kapoor, S. (eds.) CVC 2019. AISC, vol. 943, pp. 128–144. Springer, Cham (2020). https://doi.org/10. 1007/978-3-030-17795-9_10
6. Yang, J., Li, S., Wang, Z., Dong, H., Wang, J., Tang, S.: Using deep learning to detect defects in manufacturing: a comprehensive survey and current challenges. Materials **13**(24), 5755 (2020)
7. Ren, S., He, K., Girshick, R., et al.: Faster R-CNN: towards real-time object detection with region proposal networks. IEEE Trans. Pattern Anal. Mach. Intell. **39**(6), 1137–1149 (2017)
8. Ding, R., Dai, L., Li, G., et al.: TDD-net: a tiny defect detection network for printed circuit boards. CAAI Trans. Intell. Technol. **4**(2), 110–116 (2019)
9. He, D., Wen, J., Lai, Z., et al.: Textile fabric defect detection based on improved faster R-CNN. AATCC J. Res/ **8**(1_suppl), 82–90 (2021)
10. Guo, Z., Wang, C., Yang, G., et al.: MSFT-YOLO: improved YOLOv5 based on transformer for detecting defects of steel surface. Sensors **22**(9), 3467 (2022)
11. Yao, Z., Wang, L.: ERBANet: enhancing region and boundary awareness for salient object detection. Neurocomputing **448**, 152–167 (2021)
12. Li, Y.-L., Wang, S.: HAR-Net: Joint learning of hybrid attention for single-stage object detection. IEEE Transactions on Image Processing **29**, 3092–3103 (2020)
13. Pan, S.J., Yang, Q.: A survey on transfer learning. IEEE Trans. Knowl. Data Eng. **22**(10), 1345–1359 (2010)
14. Hu, R., Liu, Y., Gu, K., Min, X., Zhai, G.: Toward a no-reference quality metric for camera-captured images. IEEE Trans. Cybern. (2021)
15. Hu, R., Liu, Y., Wang, Z., et al.: Blind quality assessment of night-time image. Displays **69**, 102045 (2021)

Entity Relation Extraction of Traditional Chinese Medicine Influenza Based on Bi-GRU+GBDT

Yanhua Zhao[1], Jianxun Zhang[1(✉)], and Yue Li[2]

[1] Tianjin University of Technology and Education, Tianjin, China
zhangjx@tute.edu.cn
[2] Tianjin University of Traditional Chinese Medicine, Tianjin, China

Abstract. In this paper, an algorithm based on Bi-directional Gated Recurrent Unit (Bi-GRU) and Gradient Boosting Decision Tree (GBDT) is proposed to extract the entity relationship of Traditional Chinese Medicine influenza. Firstly, the word vector is used as the input data set and the word vector is constructed by the word embedding model Word2Vec tool. Then the sentence feature is extracted by Bi-GRU and the attention mechanism is integrated to improve the accuracy of feature extraction. Finally, the feature vector is input into the GBDT algorithm for classification training and prediction to complete the Traditional Chinese Medicine influenza entity relationship extraction. In this paper, a variety of different entity relation extraction algorithms are compared with this algorithm to verify the effectiveness of the algorithm. This algorithm improves the stability of the model and effectively solves the problem of insufficient generalization ability of the model. Therefore, when studying the relationship extraction of Traditional Chinese Medicine texts, we can give priority to using Bi-GRU+GBDT model. Also through the experiment to adjust the model parameters and comparison to get the optimal parameters of Traditional Chinese Medicine influenza relationship extraction experiment.

Keywords: relationship extraction · deep learning · gated cyclic neural network · gradient lifting tree · knowledge graph

1 Introduction

Traditional Chinese Medicine is the wisdom crystallization of several generations. After continuous inheritance and improvement, it has a complete theoretical system, has a good guiding significance for clinical practice, and provides a unique method for the diagnosis and treatment of diseases. As a substitute of modern medicine, Traditional Chinese Medicine is getting more and more attention all over the world, and a large number of Traditional Chinese Medicine

© ICST Institute for Computer Sciences, Social Informatics and Telecommunications Engineering 2023
Published by Springer Nature Switzerland AG 2023. All Rights Reserved
Y. Cao and X. Shao (Eds.): MONAMI 2022, LNICST 474, pp. 138–153, 2023.
https://doi.org/10.1007/978-3-031-32443-7_10

research papers are published every year [1]. At the same time, large-scale analysis of a large number of Traditional Chinese Medicine literature has become an interesting research field in recent years, because such an analysis can excavate the collective knowledge of Traditional Chinese Medicine researchers and supplement the main body of medical knowledge. In addition, Traditional Chinese Medicine is a very complex medical system, involving a variety of entities, and there can be many types of complex relationships among these entities [2]. Therefore, there are many ideas, methods and clinical experiences that have not been discovered. Therefore, it is necessary to further collate and analyze medical records and literature to dig out more knowledge content to supplement and improve the existing theoretical system of Traditional Chinese Medicine. Information technology is undoubtedly the most favorable assistant to this work, so how to use modern emerging information technology to explore the knowledge of Traditional Chinese Medicine is an important direction worthy of scholars' attention. In the vertical field, the medical field is one of the most widely used knowledge graphs [3]. Dan Zhu et al. [4] constructed the knowledge graph related to fatty liver disease. In the process, they used the methods of common and individual experience analysis, analyzed and studied the clinical trials of many famous Traditional Chinese Medicine on fatty liver disease, and found out the relationship between syndrome and treatment. Tong Ruan [5] and others construct the medical knowledge graph by using the medical concepts obtained from the medical website and the relationship between them. In the study of cervical radiculopathy, Kang Li [6] and others obtained the common syndrome type and commonly used drugs for treatment of cervical radiculopathy through association rule analysis. Their research data came from China knowledge Network. Hong Wu [7] constructed the knowledge graph of "symptom-disease-prescription-Traditional Chinese Medicine" by using the entities, attributes and relationships extracted from "Compendium of Materia Medica", "Collection of typical cases in China" and Traditional Chinese Medicine diagnosis and treatment data. Taking the obstetrics and gynecology textbooks as the data source. Xuejiao Zhao [8] and others proposed to use related technologies such as knowledge extraction to construct the gynecology and obstetrics knowledge graph in order to share the common knowledge of gynecology and obstetrics medicine related to science popularization. Entity relation extraction is a key step in the process of information extraction in the construction of knowledge graph. Relationship extraction (RE) refers to the extraction of the relationship between entities, so that scattered entities can be linked through relationship extraction [9], and then knowledge storage is carried out to form a related semantic network [10]. Relationship extraction (RE) refers to the extraction of the relationship between entities from unstructured text [11], which determines the category of the relationship according to the characteristics of the entity. Because the data in the field of Traditional Chinese Medicine is of great potential value and significance to human beings, the practical value of building a knowledge graph for the field of Traditional Chinese Medicine is highlighted.

2   Related Work

According to the form of the extracted corpus, the relation extraction model includes relation extraction for sentences and relation extraction for paragraphs. The difference between the two lies in whether two related entities appear in a sentence or in a paragraph. According to Chinese grammatical habits, generally speaking, two related entities and the relationship between them can be expressed clearly in a sentence. Therefore, this paper uses the relation extraction of sentences. According to whether the relationship type is predefined or not, the relationship extraction model can be divided into schema-based relation extraction and open relation extraction. The former means that the relationship of the entity pair can only be selected from the predefined category, while the latter means that the entity has no limit to the relationship. In the construction of domain knowledge graph, schema is fixed, so the relationship type of entity pair is predefined. This paper aims at relation extraction based on schema. Knowledge graph is used to describe concepts and their related relationships in the real world. In the medical field, that is, the composition of two medical entities with semantic relations and their semantic relations, it is a good intuitive knowledge representation. Entities are the nodes in the knowledge graph network, and the relationship is the type of semantic relationship between the two entities, that is, the edge of the network connection node [12]. Relationship category is the relationship between entities, and entities are connected through relationships, thus forming a complete semantic knowledge network. In this paper, according to the text data of influenza in Traditional Chinese Medicine, five kinds of relations are defined, which are symptomatic, dialectical, treatment, use and contain. Among them, there is a symptomatic relationship between "patient" and "symptom". The type of relationship is defined as "symptomatic" relationship, and the patient's syndrome is distinguished according to the patient's symptom. Therefore, there will be a dialectical relationship between "patient" and "syndrome", and the relationship type is defined as "dialectical" relationship, and the relative treatment method is adopted according to the syndrome differentiation. There will be a therapeutic relationship between "syndrome" and "treatment". The relationship type is defined as "treatment" relationship, and what prescription will be used to the patient after confirming the treatment method. Therefore, there will be a use relationship between "patient" and "prescription". The relationship type is defined as "use" relationship, according to what kind of Traditional Chinese Medicine is needed according to the prescription used, therefore, there will be an inclusive relationship between "prescription" and "Traditional Chinese Medicine". The relationship type is defined as a "contain" relationship. First of all, the entity pairs in the sentence are identified, and then the category of the relationship between the entity pairs is marked manually. A total of 1210 sample data are selected for entity relationship tagging, and the labeled data are divided into training set and test set according to the 80% and 20% standards. The distribution ratio accords with the common proportion of the data.

3 Design of Entity Relation Extraction Algorithm of Traditional Chinese Medicine Influenza Based on Bi-GRU+GBDT

There are two main methods used in entity relationship extraction, each of which has its own advantages and disadvantages. The first method is to use remote supervision to obtain training data, so that the labeling work can be reduced, but if the previous entity recognition errors will be passed on to the relationship extraction work. The second method is to combine the two tasks of entity recognition and relationship extraction between entities, so that the two can be more fully integrated, and the entity information can be fully utilized. However, the accuracy of this model is only 64%. When the accuracy of entity recognition is more than 80%, the first method is better than the second method. In the previous work, the entity recognition accuracy is much higher than 80%. The first method can be determined.

Entity relation extraction models can be divided into three categories [13]: pattern-based methods [14,15], statistical machine learning [16] and neural networks. The method based on pattern, that is, the traditional rule-based method, the rules need to be designed in advance, and the quality of the rule design determines the quality of the subsequent relationship extraction task. If the rule design is not good, it will not achieve the desired effect, and the waste of time has no effect. Statistical machine learning methods need to spend a lot of time and energy to extract relational features, which is also a very arduous task. Therefore, in comparison, in-depth learning in the field of neural network research can well complete the task of relationship extraction.

3.1 Framework of Bi-GRU+GBDT Entity Relationship Extraction Algorithm

Recurrent Neural Network (RNN) is a kind of artificial neural network and one of the representative algorithms of deep learning. It is a kind of neural network model with memory ability [17]. The advantage of cyclic neural network in relation extraction is that it can be used to extract long-distance dependent information in sentences, but it also has some disadvantages, such as easy to fall into gradient explosion [18]. The emergence of Gated Recurrent Neural Network solves this problem, and its principle is to control the flow of information through the door that can be learned [18]. The threshold Gated Recurrent Unit (GRU) used in this paper is one of the categories of gated cyclic neural networks, which is essentially similar to LSTM. Both belong to RNN.GRU, which is a variant of LSTM, and can be regarded as a LSTM without input gates, that is, from three gate functions of LSTM to two gate functions, including update gate and reset gate. Because there is no input gate, it writes all the contents of the memory unit to the overall network [18] at each time step, as shown in Fig. 1. Where r_t represents a reset door that determines the extent to which previous information is forgotten, and z_t represents an update door, which determines what information needs to be added and forgotten.

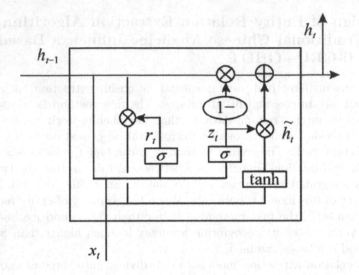

Fig. 1. GRU model structure.

$$\begin{cases} z_t = \sigma(W_z * [h_{t-1}, x_t]) \\ r_t = \sigma(W_r * [h_{t-1}, x_t]) \\ \widetilde{h}_t = tanh(W_{h_t} * [r_t * h_{t-1}, x_t]) \\ h_t = (1 - z_t) * h_{t-1} + z_t * \widetilde{h}_t \end{cases} \tag{1}$$

The problem of entity relationship extraction is usually regarded as multi-classification, and softmax is often used as the classifier in the deep learning model of relationship extraction, but the generalization ability of this classifier is insufficient, so the effect of relationship extraction is not very good. The Gradient Boosting Decision Tree (GBDT) is an integrated classifier, and the GBDT model can automatically find features and combine them effectively [19]. Gradient lifting decision tree is a lifting tree model based on CART regression tree model. Its core idea is to use negative gradient approximation to simulate residuals. In the process of generating each tree, the residual of the previous tree is calculated, and the next tree is fitted on the basis of the residual, so that the residual obtained on the next tree is reduced [20]. GBDT can combine and discretize features automatically. After the establishment of the decision tree, the path from the root node to each leaf node is a combination of different features, and each leaf node represents a unique feature combination. The lifting tree model can be expressed as an additive model of the decision tree:

$$f_M(x) = \sum_{m=1}^{M} T_m(x) \tag{2}$$

where: the decision T_m (x) represents the $m - th$ decision tree, and M represents the number of trees. The loss function is determined by negative gradient approximation, and the GBDT loss function is defined as L(y, f)

$$L(y, f) = \sum_{i=1}^{m} L(y_i, f(x_i)) \tag{3}$$

where: the loss function $L(y_i, f(x_i))$ represents the gradient to the tree $f(x_i)$. The process of gradient lifting tree algorithm (GBDT) is as follows: step1: During initialization, c is taken as the mean value of all the training samples, and the initial learner is obtained.

$$f_0(x) = c \tag{4}$$

step2: Iterative training m = 1, 2 ... N. Take the residual r_{mi} of the previous step as the new value of the sample, take the data as the training data of the next tree, get a new regression tree, its corresponding leaf node region is R_{mj}, and calculate the best fitting value is c_{mj}. j = 1, 2 ... J. The regression tree represented by J is the number of leaf nodes, and then update the learner:

$$r_{mi} = -[\frac{\partial L(y_i, f(x_i))}{\partial f(x_i)}]_{f(x)=f_{m-1}(x)} \tag{5}$$

$$c_{mj} = arg \min_{C} \sum_{x \in R_{mj}} L(y_i, f_{m-1}(x_i) + c) \tag{6}$$

step3: Get the final learner GBDT:

$$\hat{f}(x) = f_M(x) = f_M(x) + \sum_{m=1}^{M} \sum_{j=1}^{J} c_{mj} I(x \in R_{mj}) \tag{7}$$

where: I is the indicator function. If $x \in R_{m}j$, then I is 1, otherwise I is 0.

The Bi-GRU+GBDT entity relationship extraction model is mainly divided into the following parts, including input embedding layer, Bi-GRU layer, attention mechanism layer and output layer.

(1) Input embedding layer
    The input embedding layer serves as the input layer of the subsequent Bi-GRU layer. It represents the word vector of each sentence in the corpus, and then trains it by embedding words into the Word2vec to form the required input matrix of the subsequent model for use by the subsequent model.
(2) The Bi-GRU layer
    The GRU model selected in this paper has relatively few hyper-parameters, and the structure is simpler, so it is easier to train than other cyclic neural network models. In order to enable the neural network to learn both forward sequence information and reverse sequence information, the bi-directional GRU model is selected for training (Fig. 2).

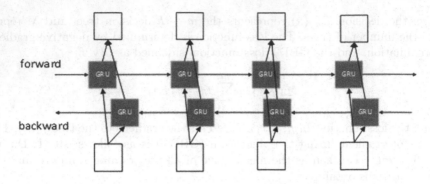

Fig. 2. Bi-directional GRU model.

(3) The attention mechanism layer The traditional RNN neural network model is not very effective in the overall sentence extraction, and the ability to learn context information is very poor, so in order to better learn the semantic information of the context, this paper adds the attention mechanism layer after the sentence feature extraction. It will focus on the characteristics of relational categories, and will consider the importance of key words or words to relational features. By assigning weights to different features, the forward and reverse sentence feature vectors transferred from the Bi-GRU layer can be calculated by stitching and weighting. The attention mechanism layer structure diagram is shown in Fig. 3.

a_{di}: The attention probability of the ith word to the dth word.

$$h_{di} = U_a * \tan(U_b * h_d + U_c * h_i + b) \tag{8}$$

$$a_{di} = \frac{exp(h_{di})}{\sum_{j=1}^{T} exp(h_{dj})} \tag{9}$$

Among them: U_a, U_b, U_c represent the weight matrix, h_d represents the forward output of the Bi-GRU layer, h_i represents the backward output, b represents the bias vector, and T represents the length of the sentence. After passing through the attention mechanism layer, the new output feature vector is H_t. As shown in formula (10).

$$H_t = \sum_{i=1}^{m} a_{di} * h_m \tag{10}$$

(4) The output layer inputs The feature vectors of sentences passing through the attention mechanism layer into the GBDT algorithm. This paper uses gradient lifting to train and predict classification, iterates to build a decision tree, and finally obtains the relationship categories between entities and entities contained in each sentence. The model architecture is shown in Fig. 4.

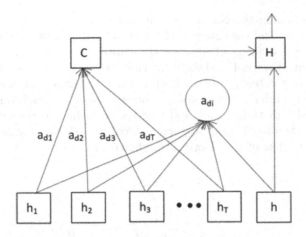

Fig. 3. Attention mechanism model.

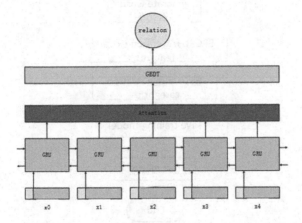

Fig. 4. Bi-GRU+GBDT model structure diagram.

3.2   Bi-GRU+GBDT Entity Relationship Extraction Algorithm Flow

Traditional Chinese Medicine influenza entity relationship extraction algorithm is mainly divided into six steps: acquisition of corpus data, pre-processing of corpus data, generation of word vector training model, training and learning relationship extraction model, test model, relationship category extraction. Using Word2vec to embed words into the training set samples to form a vector matrix as the input of the model, after the Bi-GRU model has forward output and backward output, the forward and reverse sentence feature vectors transferred from the Bi-GRU layer are spliced and weighted through the attention mechanism layer, and the sentence feature vectors are calculated. Finally, the final relation category is obtained by using the GBDT algorithm in the output layer. Among them, after obtaining the corpus data, a pair of related entities are extracted from the sentence, and the category of the relationship between the two entities in the sentence is tagged. There are 1210 sample data, and five relation categories are set in advance. For the specific category description, see the definition of the relationship category in the above work. The tagging format of each sample is (entity 1, entity 2, relationship, the sentence). In addition, the labeled data is divided into training set and test set according to the criteria of 80% and 20%, and the distribution proportion accords with the common proportion of the data. The flow of the algorithm is shown in Fig. 5.

Fig. 5. Algorithm flow chart.

4   Experiment and Result Analysis

In order to verify the effectiveness of this model, we use a variety of relational extraction models as comparative experiments, that is, the results of other models are compared with the experimental results of entity recognition of this model. Among them, the model comparison experiments include Bi-GRU model, GBDT model, Bi-GRU+GBDT model, and the m value of gradient lifting tree GBDT, that is, the optimization of the number of trees and the corresponding performance of the model.

4.1   The Source of Experimental Data

The data comes from Traditional Chinese Medicine ancient books such as "A hundred Clinical Books of Traditional Chinese Medicine in the past 100 years in China". Because these ancient books only contain PDF files and are scanned into picture format, these documents need to be processed regularly, and the text data about Traditional Chinese Medicine influenza can be extracted by OCR technology. According to the definition of the relationship between entities in the Traditional Chinese Medicine Language System (TCMLS), this paper defines the relationship among symptoms, dialectics and treatment of cases in ancient books of Traditional Chinese Medicine, and forms the SPO triple form of "entity 1, relationship, entity 2" [21]. At present, the triple in the sentences in the open domain data set is an one-to-one relationship. According to the writing format of medical records in the field of Traditional Chinese Medicine in real life, a sentence generally includes multiple entities, as well as multiple relationships, that is an one-to-many triple relationship. From this point of view, the corpus of the relationship extraction experiment in this paper is not limited to the one-to-one relationship of a sentence, but contains multiple relationships between multiple entities in a sentence [21]. In this experiment, a total of 1210 sentences are prepared, and then the entity pairs are identified and marked, and the labeled data are divided into training set and test set, accounting for 80% and 20% respectively.

4.2   The Experimental Instructions and Parameter Settings Preprocess the Data

After obtaining the corpus, then use the word embedding model Word2vec to construct the word vector and train it, using the word vector as the input of the bidirectional GRU [22], then extract the features through the bidirectional GRU and merge the coding sequences of the two directions, and then get the complete features of the sentence, and then pay attention to the features of the relation category through the attention mechanism layer. Assign weights to different features, calculate the output features and relationship category labels, and finally build a gradient lifting tree according to the output of the attention mechanism layer, and judge the final relationship category through model training and iteration.

The experiment is carried out in the Windows10 operating system based on Pytorch framework, and the experimental environment is shown in Table 1. The experimental steps and the hyper-parameter related settings of the model are as follows: first, the first word embedding layer trains the word vector through the Word2vec tool, and reads out the corpus that needs to be analyzed from the file. The dimension of the word vector is set to 128D. The value of this dimension is generally related to the size of the corpus. If it is a larger corpus, you can increase the dimension as needed. The default value of window is usually 5. In practical use, the size of the window can be adjusted dynamically according to the actual demand. The parameter min_count refers to the minimum word

Table 1. Configuration table of experimental environment.

Environment	configuration
memory	64G
CPU	Intel(R)Core(TM) i7-6700
operating system	Windows 10 64-bit
programming language	python 3.7
Deep Learning Framework	Torch 1.10.0
Compiler	PyCharm Community Edition

frequency of the word vector that needs to be calculated. This value can remove some obscure low-frequency words [23]. Because it contains more professional words, it can be set to 1, and the value can be adjusted according to the size of the corpus. Then, the word vector is read out from the pre-trained word vector model, which is used as the input data of the subsequent network model, and the data is divided into two parts: the training set and the verification set. Each word of the sentence in the sample of the training set has a labeled relational category tag, the words are converted into word vectors, and the sentences are input into the model in batches for training. The size of the batch_size can be adjusted according to the size of the corpus. Here, batch_size is set to 64, which means that 64 sentences are entered into the network model at a time, and the hidden layer in the network model maps the sentence features of the data to the high-dimensional space, and the next parameter neuron is used to further divide the features in the high-dimensional space, using linear division, so the more neurons are needed to achieve a high-precision model. With the structure of the network model will be more complex, and easily lead to over-fitting, to sum up, set the number of neurons to 128, before the model starts training, set a number of iterations, that is, the number of traversing samples. After each iteration, re-traverse the sample and continue to iterate until the specified number of iterations is reached. After the training, the model is tested, the test set is input into the model, and the accuracy of the model is tested [9]. The specific hyper-parameter settings are shown in Table 2.

4.3 Experimental Evaluation Criteria

In this paper, three models of Bi-GRU, GBDT and Bi-GRU+GBDT are added as the control group, and the three models are constructed by Word2vec [24]. In order to show the experimental results comprehensively and truly, when evaluating the model, this chapter mainly uses the following three factors as the evaluation index of the model: accuracy, recall and F value [25]. The accuracy is expressed by P, which refers to Precision, and the recall rate is expressed by R, which refers to the Recall. Accuracy refers to all the predicted results, the number of real samples in the predicted positive samples, that is, the proportion of the total number of results consistent with the actual results [26]. In popular

Table 2. Parameter related settings in the model.

Parameter name	Parameter setting
batch_size	64
learn_rate	0.003
epoches	60
min_count	1
window	5
emb_size	128
hidden_size	128
optimizer	Adam

terms, it is find the right. Recall rate refers to the number of predicted correct samples in the positive sample, that is, the proportion of the number of entities identified to all entities [27]. In reality, the accuracy and recall rate may contradict each other, at this time, the F value is needed to balance the two indicators. The F value is a combination of accuracy and recall rate to evaluate the model as a whole [24]. The relevant formulas for accuracy, recall and F value are shown in formula (3). The TP in the formula indicates that the identified entity is also the desired entity, that is, the number of identified entities, that is, the number of identified entities that are not relevant, that is, the number of useless entities, that is, the number of wrong entities identified, and TP+FP represents the total number of entities identified, whether useful or not. FN represents the number of unrecognized entities but in fact they are the number of entities needed, that is, the number of unrecognized but related entities [28], and TP+FN represents the total number of entities needed for manual labeling.

$$
\begin{cases}
P = \frac{TP}{TP+FP} * 100\% \\
R = \frac{TP}{TP+FN} * 100\% \\
F = \frac{P*R*2}{P+R} * 100\%
\end{cases}
\tag{11}
$$

4.4 Experimental Results and Analysis

Two model methods are designed and compared with this method, and the model training is carried out according to the parameters set in Sect. 3.2, and then in order to verify the effectiveness of the method used in Traditional Chinese Medicine influenza entity relationship extraction, the model is tested with the test set, and the parameter values of these groups are consistent. Table 3 and Fig. 6 are the final comprehensive comparison results of different entity recognition model experiments.

Table 3 and Fig. 6 show the final experimental results of the three relationship extraction models Bi-GRU, GBDT and Bi-GRU in Traditional Chinese Medicine influenza relationship extraction, and the evaluation indicators are the three elements mentioned above. First of all, comparing the recognition results of GBDT

Table 3. Comparison of final results of different models.

Model	Precision	Recall	F value
GBDT	80.47%	80.95%	80.71%
Bi-GRU	84.26%	84.03%	84.14%
Bi-GRU+GBDT	88.98%	88.59%	88.77%

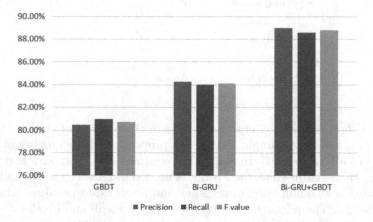

Fig. 6. Comparison of final results of different models.

and Bi-GRU, the result of Bi-GRU is better than that of GBDT model, because the ability of Bi-GRU model to automatically extract the deep relational features of sentences is stronger, so we can get better experimental results. Compared with Bi-GRU and GBDT, the effect of this model Bi-GRU+GBDT is improved, and GBDT is added as the classifier of the model on the basis of Bi-GRU. Because GBDT can improve the generalization ability of entity relationship recognition, thus improving the accuracy of relationship extraction. The experimental results of precision recognition of the model used in this paper in relation extraction are shown in Table 4.

Table 4. Bi-GRU+GBDT relation extraction experiment result table.

Model	Precision	Recall	F value
Symptomatic	89.36%	85.96%	87.63%
Dialectical	82.24%	85.48%	83.83%
Treatment	88.56%	89.33%	88.94%
Use	92.57%	90.61%	91.58%
Contain	92.16%	91.59%	91.87%
Synthesis	88.98%	88.59%	88.77%

From the test results, it can be seen that the better recognition effects of relation categories in relation extraction are "contain" and "use", while those with poor recognition results are "dialectics" and "therapy". The reason for this phenomenon is that there are fewer sentences related to these two kinds of relations in the data set for model training and learning, so the model recognition effect of this kind of relationship is worse than that of other categories. There is another part of the reason, when labeling data, there may be incomplete labeling, and some errors will lead to poor results.

In order to explore the effect of the number of decision trees m on the model, this paper sets the initial value to 10 when adjusting the number of gradient lifting trees m, and increases continuously with 10 as a unit, which is divided into 8 tests to test the effect of the model. The test results are shown in Table 5 and Fig. 7.

As can be seen from Table 5 and Fig. 7, m increases continuously from the initial value 10, and with the continuous increase of m, the corresponding F

Table 5. Comparison of experimental results of value adjustment.

m	Precision	Recall	F value
10	62.39%	62.73%	62.56%
20	73.66%	73.69%	73.67%
30	79.34%	78.92%	79.13%
40	83.79%	83.52%	83.65%
50	85.45%	85.39%	85.42%
60	88.98%	88.59%	88.77%
70	87.36%	87.51%	87.43%
80	87.34%	86.81%	87.07%

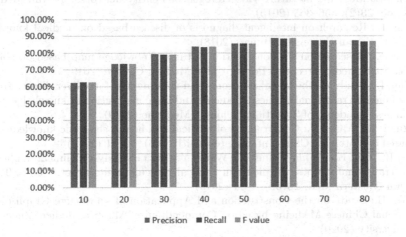

Fig. 7. Comparison of final results of different models.

value of the model increases gradually. When the m value reaches 60, the F value reaches the maximum, and the model effect is the best. When the m value continues to increase, the F value shows a small downward trend, but tends to be stable, so the model effect is the best when the number of gradient lifting trees m is 60.

5   Concluding Remarks

This paper mainly introduces the entity relation extraction of Traditional Chinese Medicine influenza based on Bi-GRU+GBDT algorithm, in which the Bi-GRU model has strong ability to automatically extract the deep relational features of sentences, and the traditional deep learning model is prone to lack of generalization ability in relation extraction, and GBDT just makes up for this deficiency, so adding GBDT on the basis of Bi-GRU model can improve the accuracy of the model. The three models of Bi-GRU, GBDT and Bi-GRU+GBDT are used for training, and then the effect of the model is evaluated by three evaluation indexes. Finally, the relationship recognition effects of the three models are compared, which verifies the effectiveness of this model in relation extraction compared with other models. Therefore, in the study of relationship extraction of Traditional Chinese Medicine texts, Bi-GRU+GBDT model can be given priority. In addition, through a large number of experiments to find the best performance of the model, the m value of the gradient lifting tree GBDT, that is, the number of trees, to provide experience for the future text relationship extraction of Traditional Chinese Medicine.

References

1. Wan, H.Y., Moens, M.F., Luyten, W., et al.: Extracting relations from Traditional Chinese Medicine literature via heterogeneous entity networks. J. Am. Med. Inf. Assoc. **23**(2), 356–365 (2015)
2. Liu, L.: Research on intelligent diagnosis of disease based on medical knowledge graph. Hunan University, Hunan (2018)
3. Xiu, X.: Research on the construction of tumor knowledge map based on Chinese electronic medical records. Peking Union Medical College (2019)
4. Zhu, D.: Study on the law of syndrome and treatment of fatty liver disease treated by famous Traditional Chinese Medicine and the construction of knowledge graph. Chinese Academy of Traditional Chinese Medicine (2019)
5. Ruan, T., Wang, H.: Construction of medical and health semantic knowledge base based on ontology. China Inf. Soc. (e-Health) (06), 50–51 (2014)
6. Li, K., Cui, K., Ao, F., Tang, X., Wang, Y., Li, Y.: Study on clinical application of Traditional Chinese Medicine in cervical radiculopathy. Pract. Comb. Tradit. Chin. Western Med. **19**(09), 7–11 (2019)
7. Wu, H.: Study on the Construction and Application of knowledge Graph of Traditional Chinese Medicine based on Compendium of Materia Medica. Zhengzhou University (2020)
8. Zhao, X.: Research and implementation of knowledge graph construction in obstetrics and gynecology. Chin. Digit. Med. **14**(01), 3–5 (2019)

9. Zhang, S.: Design and implementation of Intelligent question answering system for Coal Mine Industry. Hebei Engineering and Technology (2020)
10. Yuji, Y., Bin, X., Hu, J., Tong, M., Zhang, P., Zheng, L.: An accurate and efficient method for constructing domain knowledge graph. J. Softw. **29**(10), 2931–2947 (2018)
11. Di, Y.: Literature information extraction based on deep learning and its application in brain connection research. Huazhong University of Science and Technology (2020)
12. Qu, Q.: Research on Treatise on febrile Diseases based on Natural language processing. Anhui University of Traditional Chinese Medicine (2021)
13. Xu, H., et al.: More data, more relations, more context and more openness: a review and outlook for relation extraction. arXiv (2020)
14. Meng, J., et al.: MetaPAD: meta pattern discovery from massive text corpora. In: Proceedings of the 23rd ACM SIGKDD International Conference on Knowledge Discovery and Data Mining, pp. 877–886 (2017)
15. Zheng, S., Yu, P., Chen, L., Huang, L., Xu, W.: DIAG-NRE: a deep pattern diagnosis framework for distant supervision neural relation extraction, pp. 1419–1429 (2018)
16. Pawar, S., Palshikar, G.K., Bhattacharyya, P.: Relation extraction: a survey. arXiv (2017)
17. Du, S., Yu, H., Zhang, H.: Research progress of text classification based on deep learning. J. Netw. Inf. Secur. **6**(04), 1–13 (2020)
18. Song, Z., Yan, R.: Chinese text emotion classification model based on CNN-BIGRU. Comput. Technol. Dev. **30**(02), 166–170 (2020)
19. Gong, J.: Research and application of click rate prediction algorithm based on federated learning. Beijing Jiaotong University (2021)
20. Zhong, J.: Research on credit card fraud recognition based on feature combination of GBDT. Lanzhou University (2020)
21. Xie, X.: Study on the construction technology of disease knowledge graph for orthopedic consultation of Traditional Chinese Medicine. Kunming University of Science and Technology (2019)
22. Li, P.: Research on emotion Classification and Application of Stock investors based on Multi-core convolution Neural Network. Hangzhou University of Electronic Science and Technology (2020)
23. Lv, R.: Research and implementation of multi-tag text classification based on deep learning. Southeast University (2018)
24. Qu, Q., Kan, H.: Named entity recognition of Traditional Chinese Medicine text based on BERT-Bi-LSTM+CRF. Electron. Des. Process **29**(19), 40–43, 48 (2021)
25. Tang, L.: Information extraction method based on domain knowledge graph and its application in medical text. Southwest Jiaotong University (2020)
26. Meng, C., Dong, Y.: Text emotion analysis based on decomposed convolution neural network. Comput. Digit. Eng. **47**(8), 1970–1973, 2101 (2019)
27. Li, L.: Automatic bug allocation based on active learning. Dalian University of Technology (2013)
28. He, Y., Liu, S., Qian, L., Zhou, G.: Disease name recognition based on syntactic and semantic features. Chin. Sci. Inf. Sci. **48**(11), 1546–1557 (2018)

A Framework for Healthcare Data Integration Based on Model-as-a-Service

Yujie Fang[1], Chao Gao[1], Xinyue Zhou[1], Jianmao Xiao[2], and Zhiyong Feng[1](✉)

[1] Tianjin University, Tianjin, China
{fyj0328,gc_2019,zhouxinyue,zyfeng}@tju.edu.cn
[2] Jiangxi Normal University, Nanchang, Jiangxi, China
jm_xiao@jxnu.edu.cn

Abstract. More and more IoT detection devices are entering into healthcare domain. They collect remote data through the MQTT protocol. Along with the chaos of server subscription, data format, message structure, and content parsing, how to realize the end-to-end "model-as-a-service" in the healthcare scenario is an issue worthy of further study. This paper designs and implements a healthcare data integration framework that integrates the whole process from detected data subscription to model training deployment and data analysis automatically based on workflow, and provides users with a low-code workflow configuration method. First, this paper defined a custom description language for the workflow of the integration problem. Next, fully considering the situation of message parsing and storage of different devices, we build an end-to-end healthcare integration framework that realizes the dynamic management of access data and subscription clients. In addition, it provides customization and AutoML-based automation options to select machine learning models and parameters. Finally, the experiment shows that the framework completes the dynamic subscription, parsing, storage, model training and deployment, and data analysis of various device messages. This framework can further integrate techniques such as streaming data analysis and deep learning automation to perform complex tasks in different scenarios like real-time data analysis of elderly care and medical diagnosis.

Keywords: IoT · Healthcare · Model-as-a-Service · Workflow · Machine Learning · Data Analysis

1 Introduction

China has the largest number of elderly people in the world today, and the healthcare of the elderly is attracting more and more attention. Currently, elderly care in China has basically formed a combination of home, community, and institutional, where remote analysis of the elderly's physical data is critical.

The rapid development of IoT has brought new solutions to healthcare problems. A large number of IoT devices have entered into the healthcare domain, which is profoundly reshaping healthcare services. Nowadays, it is very convenient to collect physical data

Y. Cao and X. Shao (Eds.): MONAMI 2022, LNICST 474, pp. 154–168, 2023.
https://doi.org/10.1007/978-3-031-32443-7_11

such as blood pressure, heart rate, blood sugar as well as eye movement from various detection devices and sensors [1]. These devices use the MQTT protocol to distribute data with greatly low power consumption [2]. Users can subscribe to the data, making it possible to remotely monitor and analyze the health status of the elderly [3].

In addition, there is a wide range of applications that combine IoT with various technologies and tools like data storage and machine learning to improve the efficiency of diagnosis and treatment, and assist doctors in their work [4]. Guided by "model-as-a-service", training collected data, deploying machine learning models can further improve the added value of the business [5].

In the healthcare scenario, the ultimate realization of "model-as-a-service" needs to consider a series of issues. For IoT communication protocols, device data reception, data parsing, data storage, and integration are chaos. Different IoT devices generally have their own independent vertical IoT architecture. Device data will be published to their respective MQTT servers. Therefore, data consumers need to dynamically deploy and manage a large number of subscription clients to complete data subscription and collection tasks for multiple devices according to the changing situation of the collected devices. For data analysis, the subsequent complete data parsing, storage, and machine learning analysis process need to be done in collaboration with multiple technologies and systems. Machine learning-based models need to be deployed and trained separately on demand. Thus, the lack of seamless integration and management among IoT middleware, data systems, and machine learning systems is one of the main challenges in implementing "model-as-a-service" for remote health detection and data analysis services. Since data collection, data storage, and integration as well as data analysis of IoT devices are relatively fixed, the use of workflow to integrate the IoT data processing process and automate various end-to-end "model-as-a-service" integration tasks can effectively reduce user's operational difficulty and learning costs. In summary, the contributions of this paper are as follows.

- We proposed a set of unified custom description language from the perspective of workflow to abstract and model the "model-as-a-service" problem in the healthcare scenario, and use the custom language to unify the description of different types of task flows, tasks, and related dynamic configuration resources in the integrated workflow.
- We specified the workflow analysis and processing process corresponding to the custom description language, which provided the basis for the realization of the workflow integration framework of "model-as-a-service".
- The functions provided by the design and implementation of the "model-as-a-service" workflow integration framework in the healthcare scenario: data subscription, data analysis, data storage, machine learning model training and deployment, data analysis, etc.
- Verification of the usability and ease of use of the integration framework: In the case of a healthcare scenario. The user defines a personalized workflow, uses this framework to dynamically subscribe, parse and store data for a variety of health testing devices, and utilizes The data set is used for model training and deployment, and the entire process of model loading and data analysis is completed by fetching data from different devices.

The subsequent part of this paper is structured as follows. Section 2 introduces the related work. Section 3 outlines the methodology of the framework implementation. Section 4 reports the experimental results. Section 5 concludes this paper and points out the future work.

2 Related Work

In the past few years, IoT sensors and devices have been gradually applied in areas such as health and disease detection, and the reliance on IoT technologies for health and disease detection is increasing [6]. For example, the Mi Smart Band can detect the heart rate of the human body and diagnose conditions such as arrhythmia in time [7]. Yang et al. [8] proposed an ECG monitoring system, which collects and transmits ECG signals using Wi-Fi in the IoT infrastructure, and uses HTTP and MQTT to transmit and collect data in the IoT cloud server. In the work of Laport et al. [9], the signals from the EEG sensors are used to classify the eye status, where the ESP8266 Wi-Fi module is used to send the raw EEG signals and the MQTT protocol handles the communication between the different IoT agents. Moreover, fall detection is an important application in healthy aging. Yacchirema et al. [10] proposed a 3D-axis accelerometer embedded in a 6LoWPAN device and used the MQTT protocol to send emergency alert notifications to caregivers. Kadarina et al. [11] applied blood oxygen sensors to collect heart rate and blood oxygen from mothers and infants and then uploaded the data to their own IoT platform via the MQTT platform. The proliferation of detection sensors and devices such as these is the backdrop for this work, and they provide a variety of data sources needed for health and disease detection and analysis using techniques such as machine learning [12]. However, since the detection of health or disease often involves a large number of analytic metrics, the functionality of a single sensor or device cannot cover all the analytic metrics alone, and therefore remote data collection from multiple devices is often required for further analysis.

Table 1. Workflow Reference Model

Application	Workflow Development Language	Process Definition Forms	Workflow Framework
Business Process Management	Java	XML	jBPM Activiti
Data Task Management	Python	Python Python YAML	Ariflow Perfect DVC

The healthy aging integration framework proposed in this paper is based on workflows [13], whose main purpose is to effectively organize different tasks to collaboratively accomplish the set goals, and is applicable to scenarios and domains where a large number of complex tasks exist. Based on different directions, a series of different workflow frameworks and process definition methods are derived [14], as shown in Table 1.

The framework uses perfect core as a workflow engine kernel to call data access, data integration, and data analysis sub-modules to achieve a complete end-to-end "model-as-a-service" process.

3 Methodology

Guided by the idea of "model-as-a-service", the IoT data integration solution for the healthcare domain opens up the entire end-to-end process from data subscription, analysis, storage to model training, deployment, analysis, and service.

The solution mainly faces the following technical challenges. This framework organically bonds and expands different technical links, and provides a necessary support for the implementation of automated applications of remote health data collection and analysis.

- The integration of health data involves multiple types of business such as IoT subscription, database storage, data analysis, etc. How to formalize the workflow issues to represent the basis for subsequent custom language design and framework design.
- The business process workflow is generally defined in XML form and the data analysis workflow is generally defined in python. How to design a custom description language for integration solutions to take into account the legibility of business process workflow and the good support of python workflow framework for machine learning tasks, and provide it for healthcare industry personnel.
- Designing the corresponding parsing process to execute the workflow tasks using the workflow engine.

3.1 Formalization of Integration Program Issues

The workflow is described by a directed acyclic graph $G = (T, E)$, where $T = \{t_1, t_2,....t_N\}$ is the set of N workflow tasks, and E denotes the dependency between workflow tasks. The subscription client of the MQTT data should remain continuously open after the task is opened, and the data analysis task depends on the data subscription [15]. The execution of the task should not depend on the end of the data subscription task. Therefore, it is appropriate to split the health aging IoT data integration workflow into a data subscription task flow and multiple data analysis task flows.

Definition 1 (Healthcare IoT data integration workflow): The senior care data integration workflow can be written as a two-tuple $Flow=<flowName, taskFlowSet>$, where *flowName* denotes the unique representation of the workflow and *taskFlowSet* denotes the set of task flows contained in the workflow.

Definition 2 (Task Flow): Task flow can be divided into data subscription task flow and data analysis task flow in terms of task flow type. Task flow can be divided into timed workflow and one-time workflow in terms of execution conditions. A task flow can be represented as a six-tuple *taskFlow=<taskFlowName, taskFlowType, Resource,*

scheduleType, scheduleValue, taskSet>, where *taskFlowName* indicates the unique name of the task flow, and *taskFlowType* denotes the type of the task flow, *Resource* denotes the dynamic task resource on which the task flow depends, *scheduleType* denotes the type of task flow execution, *scheduleValue* denotes the timed execution interval, and *taskSet* denotes the set of tasks contained in the task flow.

Definition 3 (Task): A task flow consists of one or more tasks and can be defined as a four-tuple *Task<taskName, taskType, taskParmSet, taskState>*. Where *taskName* represents the unique representation of the task, *taskType* represents the specific type of the task, *taskParmSet* represents the set of parameters needed to execute the task, and *taskState* represents the completion status of the task.

Definition 4 (Task Parameter): A task parameter can be represented as a two-tuple, which can be written as *Parm=<ParmName, ParmValue>*, where *ParmName* represents the name of the parameter and *ParmValue* represents the value of the parameter.

3.2 Custom Description Language for Integration-Oriented Solutions

The Basque paradigm (BNF) is a specification for the definition of a set of computer language symbols expressed in a recursive way of thinking [16]. The BNF paradigm is used to give a strict syntactic definition of the custom description language of the scheme, which serves as a standard interface for the outside world to interact with this framework. The basic meta-symbols for BNF [17] and their descriptions are shown in Table 2.

Table 2. BNF main meta symbol description

Symbol	Explanation
X::=Y	X is defined as Y
<X>	X is required
[X]	X is optional
{X}	X is a repeatable option
X|Y	X or Y

The specific important tags and attributes in the custom description language are explained below.

IoTWF::=<[TaskFlow,…]\|[TaskResource]>: The IoTWF tag is a root tag that can contain multiple TaskFlow tags or a TaskResource tag. The IoTWF tag is used to describe the workflow when it contains multiple TaskFlow tags, and to describe the dynamically configured resources for data subscription tasks when it contains a TaskResource tag.

A general form of a workflow defined by an IoT integration domain-driven language is given, as shown in Fig. 1.

Lines 1–8 define a data subscription task flow, and line 5 defines the address of the dynamic configuration resource on which the task flow depends. Lines 10–20 define a data analysis task flow. Lines 12–15 define a data query task, and lines 16–18 define a model prediction task.

```
1    <!--Data Subscription Task Flow Example-->
2    <IotWF>
3        <TaskFlow taskFlowName = "FN_0001" taskFlowType = "SubscribeFlow" scheduleType = "Rolling" scheduleValue = "60">
4            <task taskName = "t0" taskType = "DataCollection">
5                <parm parmName = "resource">...</parm>
6            </task>
7        </TaskFlow>
8    </IotWF>
9    <!--Data Analysis Task Flow Example-->
10   <IotWF>
11       <TaskFlow taskFlowName = "FN_0002" taskFlowType = "AnalysisFlow" scheduleType = "Once" scheduleValue = "0">
12           <task taskName = "t1" taskType = "SQL">
13               <parm parmName ="SQL">...</parm>
14               <parm parmName = "outgoing">...</parm>
15           </task>
16           <task taskName = "t2" taskType = "M1Predict">
17               <parm parmName = "joblib">...</parm>
18           </task>
19       </taskFlow>
20   </IotWF>
```

Fig. 1. General form of a Workflow

3.3 Workflow Analysis Execution Process

The parameters and task sets of different task flows are heterogeneous, and the execution process of the task flow engine is divided into three main steps: task flow parameter construction, task instantiation construction, and task flow instantiation execution, as shown in Fig. 2.

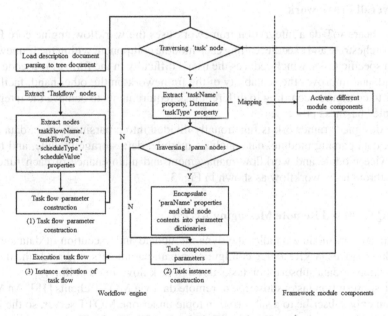

Fig. 2. Workflow Analysis Execution Flowchart

Task Flow Parameter Construction. The workflow engine first loads the description document and parses it, and then saves the parsed structure as a tree structure. After that, the TaskFlow node in the tree structure is extracted and the taskFlowName, task-FlowType, scheduleType, and scheduleValue properties under this node are obtained to represent the name, type, timing type, and timing interval parameters of the task flow respectively for constructing the parameters of the task flow.

Task Instantiation Constructs. The next step is to construct the task collection under the task flow, first by traversing the task nodes under TaskFlow, extracting the taskName property as the task name parameter, extracting the taskType property, and calling different framework modules and components according to their property types. Then, by traversing the parm nodes under task, we obtain the parmName property and the content of the child nodes to encapsulate the parameters, which can be represented as a dictionary: TASK_PARM:{<key, value>,...} where key is the parameter name parmName attribute and value is the child node content parmValue. After completing the parameter encapsulation, different components are called and passed as parameters to complete the instantiation of a single task. Then the instantiation of the entire task set is completed by analogy.

Task Flow Instantiation Execution. When the task flow parameters and all tasks under the task flow are constructed, the instantiation of the current task flow is finally completed and executed.

3.4 Overall Framework

The healthcare IoT data integration framework uses the workflow engine core Prefect Core to orchestrate and execute, calling each module component within the framework to perform specific tasks, which reduces the user's difficulty in the form of low code on the one hand, and improves the scalability of the framework on the other hand, facilitating the user to configure according to different task requirements to achieve the integration of complex business processes.

The designed framework is functionally divided into a parsing engine, data access module, data parsing module, data analysis module, data storage module, and model-as-a-service module and workflow management and maintenance of each functional module through the workflow as shown in Fig. 3.

3.5 MQTT-Based Remote Messaging Access

The Data Access module handles the dynamic update and execution of data subscription tasks, receives taskResource configuration path parameters, and reads the dynamic configuration of data subscription tasks through task flow timed polling.

Data subscription tasks subscribe to remote data via MQTT clients [18]. An MQTT client can only subscribe to a subscription topic under one MQTT server, so the framework regularly reads the dynamic configuration in taskResource and assembles MQTT clients according to the corresponding parameters to correspond to different servers or subscription topics with different parsing storage mechanisms under the same server [19]. At the same time through the configuration of the state identifier for subscribing clients to mention the destruction mechanism to achieve dynamic message subscription.

Example of Device Data Subscription Topic Client Description Snippet is shown in Fig. 4.

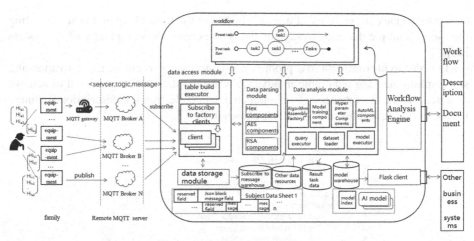

Fig. 3. IoT Data Integration Framework

The two attributes db and flag in the subject node are used to identify the table build status (0-not built, 1-built) and subscription status (0-not subscribed, 1-subscribed, 2-need to cancel, 3-canceled) of the subscribed topics, respectively.

```
1    <equipmentsub>
2        <server>******</server>
3        <port>****</port>
4        <subject db = "1" flag = "1">oldTopic/device01</subject>
5        <subject db = "1" flag = "1">oldTopic/device02</subject>
6        <username>*****</username>
7        <password>*****</password>
8    </equipmentsub>
9    <equipmentsub>
10       <server>*****</server>
11       <port>*****</port>
12       <subject db = "0" flag = "0">newTopic/#</subject>
13       <username></username>
14       <password></password>
15   </equipmentsub>
```

Fig. 4. Example of automatic creation of description fragment for a data table of a device data subscription topic IoT Data Integration Framework

The data access module obtains the corresponding server IP address, port number, and the list of subscribed topics of all subject nodes under the node by traversing all equipmentsub nodes. Based on the db identification status, the table builder is started, and the flag identification status starts the subscription client assembly factory or closes the client instance. Finally, we update the corresponding db and flag identifiers and taskResource configuration to achieve the dynamic update of data subscription tasks.

Build Table Actuator. The subscribed message data comes from different devices, and the parsed message bodies vary widely. Message body fields and data meaning of the corresponding structure using sql, including complex JSON type of messages using nosql for storage. The framework uses postgresal, using the characteristics of postgresql to maximize the compatibility of message bodies in the form of sql and nosql, avoiding the use of multiple database storage methods to increase the complexity of the system [20].

In order to prevent data loss problems, it is necessary to create the corresponding subscription message data table in advance when the data is first accessed to achieve data persistence. An example of an automated data table creation description fragment for the device data subscription topic is shown in Fig. 5.

```
1    <equipmentdb>
2        <sub>oldTopic/device01</sub>
3        <type>jsonField</type>
4        <table>device01</table>
5    </equipmentdb>
6    <equipmentdb>
7        <sub>oldTopic/device02</sub>
8        <Type>customField</Type>
9        <table>device02</table>
10       <field type = "VARCHAR(255)">humidity</field>
11       <field type = "VARCHAR(255)">content_co</field>
12   </equipmentdb>
```

Fig. 5. Example of automated data table creation description fragment for device data subscription topic

When executing data subscription stream tasks, the framework regularly reads the dynamic configuration in taskResource. The table executor performs two types of operations through the type tag value: when the type is customField, the above description fragment is first parsed as a table CREATE statement and takes the table tag value as the table name, the default necessary fields include id field incremental primary key and createtime field to indicate the current record insertion time; when the type of attribute "type" is When the type is JSON field, the ALTER statement is executed after the completion of the table build operation by adding a JSON type data field for storing complex message bodies.

Subscription Client Factory. The subscription client factory receives parameters such as the IP address of the subscription topic server and completes the instantiation of the client based on the python version of the MQTT client paho library. The factory first writes the subscription topic and the current process u number to the database, which is used by subsequent modules to perform dynamic additions and deletions to the client instance, and then instantiates the data parsing module and the data saving module. In the callback function on_connect, it subscribes to the corresponding topic, and in on_message, it calls the parsing and saving instances. Finally, the factory instantiates the client, assigns the callback function to the client instance and starts the MQTT client connection.

3.6 Data Parsing and Preservation Based on Pass-Through and Encryption Components

This framework receives data from users via MQTT messages, and IOT detection devices connected to the server may be located in an insecure network environment where messages may be listened to and tampered with. Some IoT detection device providers safeguard the confidentiality, integrity, and authenticity of the data by encrypting the MQTT messages. Therefore, a parsing module is needed to decrypt specific device data. The framework builds several parsing components to adapt to various third-party encryption parsing according to the actual business situation, and the data decoding can be performed for the accessed data by adding the corresponding description in the workflow. The network layer where different devices are located is complex, so the control of data security is mainly carried out in the application and transport layers of the MQTT protocol, where data security can be protected by adding MQTT user names and passwords to the workflow.

Hexadecimal Pass-Through Parsing Component. Most of the communication methods of up and down computers, such as serial and CAN ports, and many Bluetooth modules, are based directly on hexadecimal hardware commands transmitted in the form of pass-through. Therefore, for devices that transmit data in hexadecimal format, we need to provide a set of hexadecimal parsing components to convert the hexadecimal strings in transmissive form into the commonly understood JSON format. This component is specified to take two parameters, the first being a hexadecimal string converted to utf¬8, and the second specifying the name of the field to be parsed and the number of bytes in the original message for a JSON format body.

Table 3. Body temperature sticker hexadecimal message format

Name	Number of Bytes	Meaning
Id	4	Request sequence number
Temperature	2	Temperature property value
Voltage	2	Voltage property value

The hexadecimal transmission format of a temperature sticker is shown in Table 3. For example, the data of a temperature sticker is 0x0022334400260003, according to the format description, the first four bytes 0x00223344 represent the id number 2241348, the next two bytes 0x0026 represent the temperature of 38 degrees, and the last two bytes 0x0003 represent the current voltage of 3 V. In the workflow configuration In the workflow configuration, the workflow engine automatically calls this parsing component after parsing the subscription into the parsing format of { "id":4, "temperature":2, "voltage":2}. After parsing, this parsing component will be called automatically, and the message to be parsed and the parsing rules will be passed into the component, and finally the component will parse the message body { "id":2241348, "temperature":38, "voltage":3} is returned to the subsequent workflow, so the parsing of hexadecimal format messages can be completed.

3.7 Machine Learning Automated Data Analytics

The main function of the data analysis module is to provide support for the health aging data analysis task and to satisfy the user to train and utilize the model using the workflow. The machine learning algorithm library module in this framework defaults to the user already having data suitable for model training, so the module starts from the consideration of the process after feature engineering and designs a series of components to meet the needs of tasks such as data loading, model and parameter selection, model training, and model saving.

Data Loader. The module abstracts the data loader DataExtract component, the function of the data loader is mainly to load the data and return the data needed by the algorithm to learn the classification, and try to be compatible with more file formats and data description methods. The instance method of the DataLoader component class receives the dataset file path parameters and target column parameters passed by the workflow. The component determines the file type by parsing the suffix string of the dataset file path, and then calls the appropriate method to read the file.

Algorithm Assembly Factory. The data analysis module provides ModelueSet algorithm assembly factory, through the reflection mechanism based on python to achieve dynamic loading of user-specified algorithm modules and classes, while the dynamic assembly of algorithm modules and classes also provides a strong ability to extend the framework to use algorithm libraries other than scikit-learn library. First, the instance method of ModelueSet class component receives two string real parameters for the module name and class name passed by the workflow, and uses the importlib() function in the python standard library to dynamically import the required algorithm module by string, then calls hasattr() and getattr() functions to get the specific class name under the module, thus The algorithm classes selected by the user are loaded and assembled.

Model Training Component. After the training data and the specified algorithm module are dynamically loaded, the model needs to be trained. The training module receives the training data, assemblies, and the algorithms, hyperparameters, and model save names passed through the workflow.

Hyperparametric Components. For hyperparametric search problems, grid search and stochastic search can generally be used to solve them. The stochastic search method trades a small reduction in the efficiency of the low-dimensional space for a large increase in the efficiency of the high-dimensional search space, thus avoiding violent optimization search for a large number of parameters. Using the stochastic search method, the Ml_RSCV hyperparametric component provides its concrete implementation.

AutoML Component. If the user of the framework is very little knowledge of machine learning, it is still difficult to operate, so the framework combined with the recent rise of AutoML technology, the introduction of an automatic machine learning library ATM, and its packaging as AutomlTrain components. ATM all the algorithms are based on scikit-learn while supporting the popular classification algorithms, so can be well integrated with this framework. By combining with the workflow engine, the framework can be used to make calls to ATM through user-defined workflows.

```
1  ∨ <task taskType = "AutoMLTrain" taskName = "step2">
2        <parm parmName = "url">D:\heart_disease\heart.csv</parm>
3        <parm parmName = "joblib">heart_aTM1.pkl</parm>
4     </task>
```

Fig. 6. Example of workflow

When the user gives the following workflow as shown in Fig. 6.

The instance method of the AutoML component class receives the file path and target column name parameters and the model save path, then calls ATM and passes in the relevant parameters, completes the model and hyperparameter search, outputs the best model and parameters, and saves the model to the specified path.

4 Experiments and Results

4.1 Experiment Preparation

This section utilizes the proposed framework for validation based on the above requirements proposed in the healthy aging scenario. The experimental environment consists of a pilot community service center and a separate unit room, with the service center and the unit room each connected to the network through fiber optics. A server is deployed in the community service center with a hardware configuration of CPU Intel Xeon 5220 memory 32G and operating system of 64-bit windows server system.

4.2 Cases Based on Behavioral Anomaly Detection Scenarios

The proposed framework is validated to give a case study based on an abnormal behavior detection scenario. Activity detection sensors are installed in the home environment of the elderly, activity data such as activity points and durations of the elderly are recorded, and the labeled data are classified by labeling the normal and abnormal activity data of the elderly over a period of time, the labeled data are learned, and after the training is completed, the saved model is invoked to detect the abnormal data of the elderly user for the latest period of time according to the requirements of the elderly user.

The body detection sensor connects to its own gateway via the Zigbee protocol and forwards MQTT messages outwards. The MQTT message body of the device itself is: {"battery": "100", "mac": "30:ae: 7b:e2:e5:53", "value": "0",...}.

To add the function of recording the start time and duration of the person's activity, the nodered project based on js was used to logically determine and forward the messages of the device, adding the number of hours the person's activity started and the number of minutes the activity lasted. The new MQTT message body is {"start_time": "12", "duration": "15", "mac": "30:ae:7b:e2:e5:53", "create_date": "2022-05-01"}.

Data Subscription Task Flow. The user first defines a workflow that is executed at regular intervals and contains a data subscription task flow. The data subscription task dynamically subscribes to the device data by reading the corresponding resources from the taskResource dynamic resource configuration. Since the device data does not require special parsing, there is no need to define the parsing part and then start the data subscription task flow to complete the data access. The original message structure of the device is shown below. The dynamic resource configuration of the human activity detector is shown in Fig. 7.

```
1   <IotWF>
2       <taskResourse resourceName = "RN_0002">
3           <equipmentsub>
4               <server>101.43.***.**</server>
5               <port>18**</port>
6               <subject db = "0" flag = "0">t</subject>
7               <username></username>
8               <password></password>
9           </equipmentsub>
10          <equipmentdb>
11              <sub>t</sub>
12              <type>customField</type>
13              <table>pir</table>
14              <field type = "VARCHAR(255)">start_time</filed>
15              <field type = "VARCHAR(255)">duration</filed>
16              <field type = "VARCHAR(255)">create_date</filed>
17          </equipmentdb>
18      </taskResourse>
19  </IotWF>
```

Fig. 7. Dynamic resource allocation of human activity detection sensors

```
1   <IotWF>
2       <TaskFlow taskFlowName = "FN_003" TaskFlowType = "AnalysisFlow" scheduleType = "Once" scheduleValue = "0">
3           <task taskName = "t1" taskType = "SQLExtract">
4               <parm parmName = "SQL">D:\ecgPytorch\heart_disease\pir.csv</parm>
5               <parm parmName = "targetCol">3</parm>
6           </task>
7           <task taskName = "t2" taskType = "ModuleSet">
8               <parm parmName = "module">sklearn.neighbors</parm>
9               <parm parmName = "class">KNeighborsClassifier</parm>
10          </task>
11          <task taskName = "t3" taskType = "M1_TRAIN">
12              <parm parmName = "alg">KNeighborsClassifier</parm>
13              <parm parmName = "p">{n_neighbors = 5, weights = 'distance'}</parm>
14              <parm parmName = "joblib">knn01.joblib</parm>
15          </task>
16          <task taskName = "t4" taskType = "SQL">
17              <parm parmName = "SQL">SELECT start_time, duration FROM pir where create_date > '2022-05-05'</parm>
18              <parm parmName = "outgoing">t5</parm>
19          </task>
20          <task taskName = "t5" taskType = "M1Predict">
21              <parm parmName = "joblib">knn01.joblib</parm>
22          </task>
23      </taskFlow>
24  </IotWF>
```

Fig. 8. Data Analysis Task Definition in Behavior Anomaly Detection Scenario

Data Analysis Task Flow. After visualizing the elderly behavior data, we can find that the normal activity time of the elderly is mainly concentrated around 13:00 to 16:00, and the activity length is mainly concentrated around 10 to 20 min, and there are four abnormal activities around 0:00 to 5:00, which may be related to the elderly's health condition and need to find medicine urgently. The data were therefore pre-labeled and formed into a dataset before training. As shown in Fig. 8, this data analysis task flow first performed the data loading task in lines 3–6 and loaded this dataset. Lines 7–10 define an algorithm assembly task calling the algorithm assembler to dynamically assemble the sklearn.neighbors module and classes. Lines 11–16 define a machine learning training task that uses manual determination of model parameters and saves the generated KNN machine learning model. Lines 17–20 define a data query task that selects data in the pir table after May 5. Finally, a model execution task is defined to call the specified model from the model repository to detect the above data and return the model results.

5 Conclusion and Future Work

This paper provides an integration framework that presents an overall solution for complex healthcare devices integration, data storage, and machine learning analysis. It improves the scalability of the framework through flexible configuration, improves ease of use, and realizes "model-as-a-service" in healthcare scenarios. Based on the current work, this framework can further integrate technologies such as streaming data analysis, deep learning automation, etc. In the future to perform more complex tasks in different scenarios such as real-time data analysis for healthy aging and medical diagnosis.

Acknowledgment. This work is supported by the National Natural Science Foundation of China (61832014,61972276,62032016), and the Foundation of Jiangxi Educational Committee (GJJ210338).

References

1. Mutlag, A.A., Abd Ghani, M.K., Arunkumar, N.A., Mohammed, M.A., Mohd, O.: Enabling technologies for fog computing in healthcare IoT systems. Futur. Gener. Comput. Syst. **90**, 62–78 (2019)
2. Thangavel, D., Ma, X., Valera, A., Tan, H.X., Tan, C.K.Y.: Performance evaluation of MQTT and CoAP via a common middleware. In: 2014 IEEE Ninth International Conference on Intelligent Sensors, Sensor Networks and Information Processing (ISSNIP), April, pp. 1–6. IEEE (2014)
3. Sworna, N.S., Islam, A.M., Shatabda, S., Islam, S.: Towards development of IoT-ML driven healthcare systems: a survey. J. Netw. Comput. Appl. **196**, 103244 (2021)
4. Kulkarni, A., Sathe, S.: Healthcare applications of the internet of things: a review. Int. J. Comput. Sci. Inf. Technol. **5**(5), 6229–6232 (2014)
5. Santos, J.: E-service quality: a model of virtual service quality dimensions. Managing Serv. Qual.: an Int. J (2003)
6. Laplante, P.A., Laplante, N.L.: A structured approach for describing healthcare applications for the internet of things. In: 2015 IEEE 2nd World Forum on Internet of Things (WF-IoT), pp. 621–625. IEEE (2015) December
7. Alfian, G., Syafrudin, M., Ijaz, M.F., Syaekhoni, M.A., Fitriyani, N.L., Rhee, J.: A personalized healthcare monitoring system for diabetic patients by utilizing BLE-based sensors and real-time data processing. Sensors **18**(7), 2183 (2018)
8. Yang, Z., Zhou, Q., Lei, L., Zheng, K., Xiang, W.: An IoT-cloud based wearable ECG monitoring system for smart healthcare. J. Med. Syst. **40**(12), 1–11 (2016)
9. Laport, F., Dapena, A., Castro, P.M., Vazquez-Araujo, F.J., Iglesia, D.: A prototype of EEG system for IoT. Int. J. Neural Syst. **30**(07), 2050018 (2020)
10. Yacchirema, D., de Puga, J.S., Palau, C., Esteve, M.: Fall detection system for elderly people using IoT and big data. Procedia Comput. Sci. **130**, 603–610 (2018)

11. Kadarina, T.M., Priambodo, R.: Monitoring heart rate and SpO2 using thingsboard IoT platform for mother and child preventive healthcare. In: IOP Conference Series: Materials Science And Engineering, vol. 453, No. 1, p. 012028. IOP Publishing (2018) November
12. Otto, C., Milenković, A., Sanders, C., Jovanov, E.: System architecture of a wireless body area sensor network for ubiquitous health monitoring. J. Mob. Multimedia 1, 307–326 (2006)
13. Xiao, F., Zhang, W.H., Wang, D.H.: Overview of workflow technology in scientific process. Appl. Res. Comput. 28(11), 4013–4019 (2011)
14. Hollingsworth, D., Hampshire, U.K.: Workflow management coalition: the workflow reference model. Document Number TC00-1003 19(16), 224 (1995)
15. Light, R.A.: Mosquitto: server and client implementation of the MQTT protocol. J. Open Source Softw. 2(13), 265 (2017)
16. Russel, S.J., Norvig, P.: Artificial Intelligence–A Modern Approach, pp. 736–741. Person Education Inc., New Jersey (2003)
17. McCracken, D.D., Reilly, E.D.: Backus-naur form (bnf). In: Encyclopedia of Computer Science, pp. 129–131 (2003)
18. Mishra, B., Kertesz, A.: The use of MQTT in M2M and IoT systems: a survey. IEEE Access 8, 201071–201086 (2020)
19. Babu, B.S., Ramanjaneyulu, T., Narayana, I.L., Srikanth, K., Sindhu, D.H.: Smart vehicle management through IoT. Int. J. Emerg. Trends Technol. Comput. Sci. (IJETTCS) 5(3), 26–31 (2016)
20. Young, M.: An automated framework to derive model variables from open transport data using R, PostgreSQL and OpenTripPlanner (2016)

A Deep Reinforcement Learning-Based Content Updating Algorithm for High Definition Map Edge Caching

Haoru Li[1], Gaofeng Hong[1(✉)], Bin Yang[2], and Wei Su[1]

[1] School of Electronic and Information Engineering, Beijing Jiaotong University,
Beijing, China
{21120074,honggf,wsu}@bjtu.edu.cn
[2] School of Computer and Information Engineering,
Chuzhou University, Chuzhou, China

Abstract. Edge caching is a promising technique to alleviate the communication cost during the content update and retrieving. Particularly, it is suitable for the High Definition Map (HDM) caching which needs frequent updates to avoid its contents becoming staleness. In this paper, we aim at minimizing the response latency while satisfying the content freshness of the vehicle's HDM request under the edge caching scenario. We first depict the change of the content freshness difference, in term of the Age of Information (AoI) difference value, of each request, which are determined by both the vehicular requirements and the content update decision of the Road Aide Unit (RSU). Then, we formulate the HDM content update optimization problem, which jointly considering the AoI difference and the extra responding latency of each request. On this basis, we transform the problem into a Markov Decision Process (MDP), and propose an optimization algorithm based on the deep reinforcement learning-based theory to obtain the optimal update decision by maximizing the long-term discounted reward. Finally, extensive simulations are presented to verify the effectiveness of the proposed algorithm by comparing it with various baseline policies.

Keywords: Vehicular Networks · High Definition Map · Edge Caching · Deep Reinforcement Learning · Content Update · Age of Information · Transmission Latency

1 Introduction

The High Definition Map (HDM) is an essential tool to help autonomous vehicles make path planning and relative driving decision [1]. Generally, the HDM can be roughly divided into two layer called the static layer and the dynamic layer [2]. The static layer contains the road topology information while the dynamic layer contains the real-time traffic condition of the specific road section which

Y. Cao and X. Shao (Eds.): MONAMI 2022, LNICST 474, pp. 169–181, 2023.
https://doi.org/10.1007/978-3-031-32443-7_12

needs to update frequently. To better support the time-critical and the location-dependent features of the autonomous driving, caching the dynamic layer contents of the HDM at the network edge corresponding to their geographical location is a promising solution [3–5]. However, how to ensure the freshness of the requested content is still a fundamental problem in mobile edge caching by considering the limited network resource [6, 7].

To better characterize the freshness characteristic of the dynamic contents, a novel metrics named Age of Information (AoI) has been proposed [8]. The AoI of a cached content is defined as the time elapsed since the content was generated from the source [9]. Based on the concept of AoI, researches on the dynamic content caching strategies have been carried out [10–15]. Relevant studies can be divided into two categories: minimizing the average/(peak) AoI [10–12] of a local cache system and realizing a tradeoff between AoI and request latency [13–15]. The former aims at exploring a content update policy to minimize the average/(peak) AoI of a local cache system by considering other factors such as content popularity as well while the latter jointly optimizes content freshness and request latency during the content update process (Existing research points out that delay-optimal may not be AoI-optimal [16]). Notice that, both categories of the above studies have their defects when applied to the edge HDM dynamic layer caching: 1) The former focuses on the AoI of cached items on the edge network, while the freshness of contents received by the user which acts as a more important performance indicator in a practical situation has been ignored. 2) Both of which make the analysis with the queuing theory frameworks where the request patterns of users are regarded as a prior knowledge. However, the dynamic layer contents of the HDM requested by different vehicles are almost infeasible to estimate since they depend on the vehicle's autonomous driving level and target path planning.

Recently, learning-based methods such as Markov Decision Process (MDP) and Reinforcement Learning (RL) [17–21] have been applied to make AoI optimization in a variety of caching problems. In particular, most of these methods are efficient in solving the cache update problems under no prior request condition. Their objectives are to minimize the AoI when the energy of the information collector is limited [17,18] or minimize the average AoI of all the contents under a transmission resource limited scenario [19–21]. However, for autonomous vehicles, they are more concerned with obtaining HDM's dynamic layer contents which can meet their AoI requirements within the possible lowest request latency [2]. Therefore, the existing learning-based methods still have their limitations when apply to the HDM dynamic layer contents caching.

In this paper, we investigate a dynamic HDM content update algorithm to satisfy the AoI requirements by autonomous driving vehicles and minimize the content request latency in an edge network, where the RSU doesn't know the vehicles' request patterns in advance. To balance the AoI requirement of vehicle and the content request latency with limited transmission resource, we consider the content update optimization as a discrete time slot decision problem to minimize the long-term discounted cost brought by the AoI difference (the difference of the AoI requirement value and its actual value in a specific time slot) and the request latency. To solve the problem, we model the edge-cached HDM content update problem as an MDP and apply an RL-based algorithm [22] to obtain the optimal update decision. The proposed algorithm can well address the curse of dimensionality problem brought by the large state or action space, and doesn't need the prior information of the vehicular request. Extensive simulation results verify the efficiency of the proposed algorithm.

The rest of the paper is organized as follows. Section 2 introduces our concerned network model and formulates the problem. In Sect. 3, we transform the problem into an MDP and solve it with a model-free RL-based algorithm. Extensive simulation results are provided in Sect. 4. Finally, Sect. 5 concludes this paper.

2   System Model and Problem Formulation

2.1   Network Model

We consider a typical vehicular network scenario with a single Road Side Unit (RSU), F traffic information acquisition sensors and several vehicles under its communication range. Assuming that the RSU combined with the storage capability of the edge cloud server, and each sensor is responsible for refreshing the specific HDM content with the same size l cached on the RSU. The vehicular request and HDM dynamic content sets are denoted by $\mathcal{N} = \{1, 2, ..., N\}$ and $\mathcal{F} = \{1, 2, ..., F\}$ respectively. We focus on a discrete time slots system, where a time step $T(t)$ is defined to represent each decision epoch. $T(t)$ can be defined as the integral multiple of a constant time slot τ. During each time step, the RSU may receive the vehicular HDM content request, it then will decide whether to pull the up-to-date states of HDM contents from the relevant sensors due to the content AoI demands of vehicles, if any, the content update will be executed. On the other hand, the RSU will respond to the vehicular HDM content requests with its local cached contents.

Each vehicular request n includes its query details, which containing the requested HDM contents and the relevant content AoI demands based on the vehicle's driving path planning and autonomous driving level. Here, we use a query procontent $d_n(t) = \left\{ d_n^1(t), d_n^2(t), ..., d_n^F(t) \right\}$ to represent the query details of the request n in time step t, where $d_n^f(t) \in \{d_{mid}, d_{high}, 0\}$ $(d_{mid} > d_{high})$, d_{mid} and d_{high} are two integers which depends on the autonomous driving level of each vehicle. We define that all the requested HDM contents in a same vehicular request n have the same AoI demand $(d_{mid}$ or $d_{high})$. $d_n^f(t) = 0$ indicates that content f hasn't been requested in n at time step t. Meanwhile, the request indicator $\tilde{d}_n(t)$ is set to represent whether request n exists in the time step t.

$$\tilde{d}_n(t) = \begin{cases} 0, & \sum_{f=1}^{F} d_n^f(t) = 0 \\ 1, & Otherwise \end{cases} \tag{1}$$

The RSU can obtain the query procontents $D(t) = \{d_1(t), d_2(t), ..., d_N(t)\}$ of all the requests in time step t, but it has no prior knowledge of the vehicular request arrival rates and the popularity of each cached HDM content.

After the RSU received the query procontents $D(t)$, it will make the HDM dynamic content update decision based on the requested HDM contents and the relevant AoI demands. We use $U(t) = \{u_1(t), u_2(t), ..., u_F(t)\}$ to represent the HDM content update decision in time step t, where $u_f(t) \in \{0,1\}$, $f \in \mathcal{F}$. $u_f(t) = 1$ represents that the RSU decides to refresh content f and pull the up-to-date states from the relevant sensor in time step t, otherwise $u_f(t) = 0$. The RSU will select content f to refresh in time step t based on the comparison of its real-time AoI on the RSU and the AoI demand in the query procontent $D(t)$. Notice that, when there is no query of content f in the query procontents $D(t)$, content f may also be updated to reduce the transmission delay caused by the temporary request update if there is available transport resources. Then, the RSU responds the vehicular requests with its cached HDM contents.

In our network model, we consider that the RSU is assigned with limited transmission resource blocks which are orthogonal to each other, the number of its whole available resource blocks is H_b. The maximum number of requests which can be served by the in a time step is N. Each resource block is allocated to a different communication point for the wireless data transmission. The actual number of requests in each time step $|\mathcal{N}(t)|$ is defined as:

$$|\mathcal{N}(t)| = \sum_{n=1}^{N} \widetilde{d}_n(t) \tag{2}$$

Typically, $(H_b - |\mathcal{N}(t)|)$ is the number of available resource blocks which can be divided for the HDM content updating. Therefore, at most $(H_b - |\mathcal{N}(t)|)$ sensors can execute the HDM content refreshing simultaneously in time step t. We use the content transmission occupancy rate $\beta(t)$ to denote the proportion of resource blocks occupied for transferring contents from RSU to the vehicles. As for the HDM content update decision $U(t)$ made by the RSU in the time step t, some contents whose $u_f(t) = 1$ may not be refreshed due to transmission resource constraints. We set an update success indicator $y_f(t) \in \{0,1\}$ $(y_f(t) \leq u_f(t))$ to represent whether a content f whose $u_f(t) = 1$ has been refreshed successfully or not, which satisfies: $\sum_{f=1}^{F} y_f(t) \leq H_b - |\mathcal{N}(t)|$.

Without loss of generality, we assume that the content update time consumption of each HDM content remains the same in different time steps due to the identical content update size and transmission time, which can be abstracted as $\mathbb{T}_r = \{\mathcal{T}_r^1, \mathcal{T}_r^2, ..., \mathcal{T}_r^F\}$ $(\mathcal{T}_r^f < T(t), f \in \{1, 2, ..., F\})$.

2.2 AoI Analysis

Based on the proposed network model, we analyse the real-time change in the value of cached HDM contents' AoI on the RSU and the influence of content response latency on AoI when the requested content received by the vehicle.

In order to prevent the impact on the vehicle caused by the staleness of the requested HDM contents, we define a metric α_{max} called the maximum allowable AoI, which represents the maximum AoI a content cached on the RSU can reach. Specifically, the value of α_{max} can be set to d_{mid}. For the RSU, the real-time AoI value of its cached HDM content f can be expressed as:

$$\alpha_0^f(t) = \begin{cases} T(t-1), & y_f(t) = 1 \\ min\left\{\alpha_0^f(t-1) + T(t-1), \alpha_{max}\right\}, & Otherwise \end{cases} \quad (3)$$

Figure 1 illustrates the AoI variation for the RSU cached HDM content due to the vehicular requests and the pre-defined maximum AoI threshold.

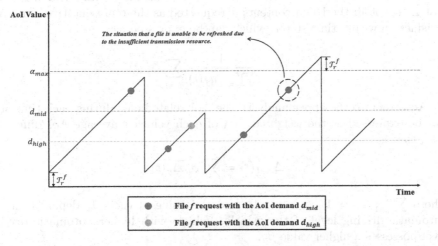

Fig. 1. The AoI variation for the cached HDM content on the RSU.

For the vehicle that makes the request n, the transmission latency brought by the content respond process also increases the staleness of the information. To ensure a requested content f which can be directly responded without updating still meets the vehicular AoI demand when it received by the vehicle, we redefine the actual AoI demand of each request as $d_{mid} - T_{lat}^{max}$ and $d_{high} - T_{lat}^{max}$, where T_{lat}^{max} represents the maximum data transmission latency of a request n that can be generated under the proposed network model in this paper.

$$L_n(t) = \begin{cases} 0, & \sum_{f=1}^{F} d_n^f(t)y_f(t) = 0 \\ max\left\{T_r^f \mid T_r^f \in \mathbb{T}_r, d_n^f(t)y_f(t) = 1\right\}, & Otherwise \end{cases} \quad (4)$$

2.3   Problem Formulation

In this paper, our objective is to meet the AoI requirements of vehicles with limited transmission resources and reduce the extra request latency by designing a dynamic content update mechanism. The extra request latency cost $L_n(t)$ of the vehicular request n in time step t is depended on whether the requested HDM contents need to be updated or transmit to the vehicle directly, which is expressed in the Eq. (4).

To better characterize the satisfaction with the AoI of the requested HDM content, we define a new metric called AoI difference cost $\Delta_n^f(t)$ to represent the overhead caused by the request HDM content f not meeting the corresponding AoI requirements when it received by the vehicle, which can be expressed as:

$$\Delta_n^f(t) = \begin{cases} 0, & \alpha_n^f(t) - d_n^f(t) \leq 0 \quad or \quad d_n^f(t) = 0 \\ \alpha_n^f(t) - d_n^f(t), & Otherwise \end{cases} \tag{5}$$

As for the vehicle who sent the request n, we use the average AoI difference cost $\overline{\Delta}_n(t)$ of all the HDM contents it requested as the representative of its AoI satisfaction within time step t, which can be expressed as:

$$\overline{\Delta}_n(t) = \frac{1}{\sum_{f=1}^{F} u_f(t)} \sum_{f=1}^{F} \Delta_n^f(t) \tag{6}$$

According to the above analysis, the AoI related cost during each time step can be expressed as the weighted sum of each vehicle's average AoI difference cost, that is:

$$\Delta_{AoI}(t) = \sum_{n=1}^{N} \beta_n \overline{\Delta}_n(t) \tag{7}$$

where $\sum_{n=1}^{N} \beta_n = 1$ $\beta_n \in [0,1]$, and the value of each β_n depends on the automatic driving level of the vehicle. Vehicle with higher automatic driving level possesses a higher value β_n.

The overall system cost in each time step t can be expressed as:

$$C_{tot}(t) = \omega_{AoI}\Delta_{AoI}(t) + \omega_L \frac{1}{N} \sum_{n=1}^{N} L_n(t) \tag{8}$$

where $\omega_{AoI} + \omega_L = 1$, ω_{AoI} and ω_L can realize a tradeoff update decision between the AoI difference cost of vehicles and the extra request latency cost in each time step. We adopt a larger ω_{AoI} than ω_L in this paper, for the AoI requirements of the requested HDM content is more important than the content request latency for an automatic driving vehicle.

Based on the cost function (8), the average future cost of the HDM content requests can be defined as:

$$C_{ave} = \lim_{T_{max} \to \infty} \frac{1}{T_{max}} \mathbb{E}(\sum_{t=0}^{T_{max}} C_{tot}(t)) \tag{9}$$

The RSU should make optimal HDM contents refreshing decisions by interacting with the environment to minimize C_{ave}.

3   Deep Reinforcement Learning-Based HDM Updating Algorithm

To achieve the expected performance, we formulate the HDM content update process on the RSU as an MDP, for which we build a DRL-based algorithm to obtain the optimal content update strategy.

3.1   MDP Model

Our MDP is modeled as a 4-tuple $\langle S, A, P, R \rangle$, relevant details are described as below:

- **Modeling of System State Space S:** $s(t) = (s_0(t), s_1(t), ..., s_N(t))$ is defined as the system state at time step t, which is composed of the real-time HDM content AoI value on the RSU $s_0(t) = (\alpha_0^1(t), \alpha_0^2(t), ..., \alpha_0^F(t))$ and the vehicular content AoI demands $s_n(t) = (d_n^1(t), d_n^2(t), ..., d_n^F(t))$ $n \in \mathcal{N}$. The whole state space S can be regarded as a combination of communication node states $(S = s_0 \times s_1 \times s_2 \times ... \times s_N)$ in the proposed network, which is finite due to the maximum AoI value restriction.
- **Modeling of System Action Space A:** $a(t) = (u_1(t), u_2(t), ..., u_F(t))$ is defined as the system action at time step t, which represents the HDM content update decision of the RSU. The action space A of the system can be expressed as:

$$A = \{U \mid u_n \geq y_n, u_n \in \{0,1\}, y_n \in \{0,1\}, \forall n \in \mathcal{N}\} \tag{10}$$

- **System State Transition Probability P:** $P = S \times A \times S \rightarrow [0,1]$ represents the distribution of the transition probability $P(s' \mid s, a)$ from the system state s to a new system state s' $(s, s' \in S)$ when an action $a \in A$ is chosen, which is largely effected by the real environment conditions, such as the HDM content request rate, the HDM content transmission occupancy rate $\beta(t)$ of the RSU resource blocks etc.
- **Modeling of Reward Function R:** $S \times A \rightarrow R$ maps a state-action pair to a value $R(s(t), A(t))$. Our objective in this paper is to minimize the average future cost $C_{ave}(t)$ given in Eq. (9), so that we define the reward function as $R(s(t), a(t)) = -C_{ave}(t)$.

We define the policy π as an action $a \in A$ that the RSU will execute by given a specific system state $s \in S$. Policy π is uncorrelated to the time step length. The difficulty here is to find an optimal policy π^* to maximize the long-term average reward, that is:

$$\arg\max_{\pi^*} \lim_{T_{max} \to \infty} \frac{1}{T_{max}} \mathbb{E}\left[\sum_{t=0}^{T_{max}} R(s(t), a(t)) \mid s(0)\right] \tag{11}$$

3.2   HDM Updating Algorithm Design

With the MDP model aforementioned, we need to design an adaptive and efficient HDM dynamic layer update strategy, which can proactively make content update decision in each state, so as to earn a higher reward by considering the long-term system performance.

Deep Reinforcement Learning (DRL) is a model-free method to solve MDP problems with large state or action space [22]. The goal of DRL is to maximize the long-term discounted reward by utilizing the deep neural network (DNN) as an approximation function to learn policy and state value. The agent can obtain enough experience by interacting with the environment, and train its policy network model. The well-trained model can quickly perform the optimal actions for executing content update. The state value function $V_\pi(s)$ and the state-action value function $Q_\pi(s, a)$ of the DDQN can be expressed as follows:

$$V'_\pi(s) = \mathbb{E}\left[\sum_{k=0}^{\infty} \gamma^k R(s(t+k), \pi(t+k)) \mid s(t) = s\right] \tag{12}$$

$$Q'_\pi(s, a) = \mathbb{E}\left[\sum_{k=0}^{\infty} \gamma^k R(s(t+k), a(t+k)) \mid s(t) = s, a(t) = a\right] \tag{13}$$

where γ is the discount factor.

The optimal policy π^* can be obtained by utilizing the Bellman Optimality Equation:

$$V_{\pi^*}(s) = max_{a \in A} Q_{\pi^*}(s, a) \tag{14}$$

The architecture of our DRL-based HDM dynamic layer update mechanism is presented in Fig. 2. θ and θ^- are the DNN parameters of the main network and the target network respectively. The agent interacts with the environment and observes the real-time system state. Based on the current state $s(t)$, the agent selects an action by utilizing the ϵ-greedy strategy (select the action $max_a R(s, a, \theta)$ with probability $(1 - \epsilon)$, and randomly select action $a \in A$ with probability ϵ, where $\epsilon \in [0, 1]$). After the agent performs an action $a(t)$, the corresponding reward $R(s(t), a(t))$ can be obtained from environment, and the system state $s(t)$ transfers to $s(t + 1)$. So that a new experience tuple $\mathcal{E}(t) = (s(t), a(t), R(s(t), a(t)), s(t + 1))$ is generated and will be cached in the experience replay buffer $\mathbb{M}$. Then, the former steps go into a loop to obtain enough experience in the replay buffer for the future training. The oldest experience tuple will be discarded when the experience buffer $\mathbb{M}$ is full.

As for the training procedure, a mini-batch of the cached experience tuples $\mathbb{W} = \{\mathcal{E}_1, \mathcal{E}_2, ..., \mathcal{E}_{W_m}\}$ will be sampled randomly from the experience replay buffer. The goal of the training procedure is to minimize the loss function $L(\theta)$, which can be expressed as:

$$L(\theta) = \mathbb{E}\left[\left(R(s_j, a_j) - \gamma \max_{a'_j} Q'(s'_j, a'_j; \theta^-) - Q(s_j, a_j; \theta)\right)^2\right] \tag{15}$$

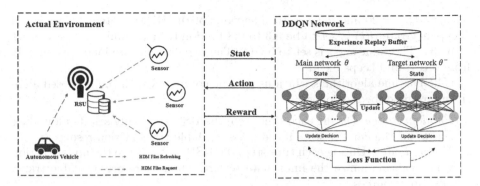

Fig. 2. The architecture of the proposed mechanism

The DNN parameter θ updates iteratively as Eq. (16):

$$\theta' = \theta + \xi \nabla_\theta L(\theta) \tag{16}$$

where ξ is the learning rate. The parameter θ of the main network is updated every step while the parameter θ^- of the target network will be updated every i steps, that is $\theta_t^- = \theta_{t-i}$.

4 Simulation Results and Discussions

In this section, we evaluate the performance of the proposed HDM updating algorithm. Firstly, we describe our simulation settings and the present the baseline algorithms used for the performance comparison. Then, we show the performance comparison of the proposed algorithm with the baseline policies in different environments and give the relevant analysis. The whole experiment is implemented by the Tensorflow frame and runs on a PC with an Intel Core i7-6700 CPU @2.6 GHz, Memory 16G.

4.1 Simulation Settings

We build a simulation scenario with one RSU (integrated with an MEC server), N connected vehicles and 10 traffic information acquisition sensors. The value of N ranges from 10 to 40. We set the available number of the orthogonal transmission resource blocks as $H_b = 50$. In each time step, we set each vehicular request for each edge-cached HDM content subjecting to a random distribution. For each sensor, the relevant content update latency is randomly selected from the value set $\{0.8\tau, 0.9\tau, 1.0\tau, 1.1\tau, 1.2\tau\}$, where $\tau = 1$ is the length of the unit time slot. Once the content update latency of each sensor has been determined, their values will remain unchanged during the whole simulation process. Based on this, we set the extra request latency of a specific content to be the same as its update latency. Without loss of generality, we set the value of maximum allowable AoI

$\alpha_{max} = d_{mid} = 20$ and $d_{high} = 10$. The value of the HDM content transmission occupancy rate $\beta(t)$ is set to be 0.3 to 0.8 randomly. The mini-batch size is set to be 64. The value ω_{AoI} is set to be 0.6. The exploration rate increases linearly from 0 to 1 and keeps fixed.

The baseline algorithms which used to be compared with the proposed algorithm are described as follows:

Random Policy: During each time step, the RSU randomly selects an update action for the current state if there are available transmission resources.

Greedy Policy: During each time step, the RSU will execute the update action which can maximize the immediate reward when there are available transmission resources.

4.2 Simulation Results

Convergence Performance. To ensure the reliability of our proposed method, we first verify its convergence performance.

Figure 3 shows the convergence comparison of the proposed algorithm and the baseline policies when $N = 30$. Here, we also evaluate the performance of the proposed algorithm under different discount factor γ. It can be seen from Fig. 3 that the long-term reward becomes higher with a bigger γ. However, the network model became hard to converge when the value of γ is too big (0.98). Meanwhile, compared with the greedy policy and the random policy, our proposed algorithm obtained a significant high reward.

Based on the above analysis, we find that when the value of the discount factor is 0.95, the proposed policy shows its best performance. So in the subsequent simulation, we set $\gamma = 0.95$ in the proposed policy.

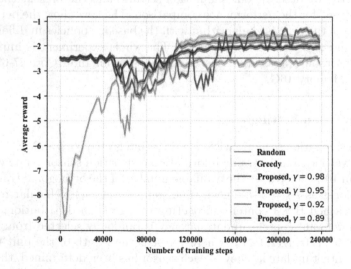

Fig. 3. The training rewards comparison under different policy.

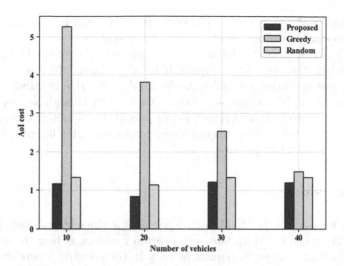

Fig. 4. Performance comparison in AoI cost.

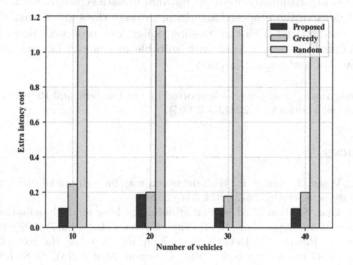

Fig. 5. Performance comparison in extra latency cost.

Efficiency Analysis. To verify the efficiency of our proposed method, we make performance comparison with the mentioned baseline policies.

Figure 4 shows the AoI cost which brought by the AoI difference when vehicle requests the cached HDM contents under different number of vehicles. It can be observed from Fig. 4 that while the RSU adopts the proposed policy, the AoI cost maintains a relatively low and stable value compared with the baseline policies. The proposed policy considers to maximize the long-term discounted reward, it can execute optimal update actions in response to the vehicular requests. So that proposed policy can ensure the stability of the AoI cost performance and realize a reasonable utilization of the network resources.

Figure 5 shows the extra latency cost which brought by the instant content updating when the content is requested by the vehicle. It can be seen from Fig. 5 that the proposed algorithm keeps a relatively stable latency cost with the number of vehicle increasing. Notice that, even though we have already emphasized the effect of the AoI cost in our previous parameter settings ($\omega_{AoI} = 0.6$), the performance of the proposed algorithm on the extra latency cost is much better than the baseline policies.

5 Conclusion

This paper focused on the HDM update problem in the edge caching system. We first formulated the HDM update optimization problem as how to minimize the AoI difference and the extra request latency in the scenario where transmission resources are limited. Then, we modeled the problem as an MDP and utilized a DRL-based algorithm to obtain the optimal update strategy. We have verified the performance of the proposed algorithm through the simulations, The results shown that, compared with the baseline policy, our proposed algorithm could achieve higher long-term reward with suitable discounted factor, and realized relative low AoI and request latency.

Acknowledgment. This paper is supported by the Fundamental Research Funds for the Central Universities (No. 2022JBGP005).

References

1. Liu, R., Wang, J., Zhang, B.: High definition map for automated driving: overview and analysis. J. Navig. **73**(2), 324–341 (2020)
2. Xu, X., Gao, S., Tao, M.: Distributed online caching for high-definition maps in autonomous driving systems. IEEE Wirel. Commun. Lett. **10**(7), 1390–1394 (2021)
3. Bastug, E., Bennis, M., Debbah, M.: Living on the edge: the role of proactive caching in 5G wireless networks. IEEE Commun. Mag. **52**(8), 82–89 (2014)
4. Vu, T.X., Chatzinotas, S., Ottersten, B.: Edge-caching wireless networks: performance analysis and optimization. IEEE Trans. Wirel. Commun. **17**(4), 2827–2839 (2018)
5. Yuan, Q., Zhou, H., Li, J., Liu, Z., Yang, F., Shen, X.S.: Toward efficient content delivery for automated driving services: an edge computing solution. IEEE Netw. **32**(1), 80–86 (2018)
6. Qiao, G., Leng, S., Maharjan, S., Zhang, Y., Ansari, N.: Deep reinforcement learning for cooperative content caching in vehicular edge computing and networks. IEEE Internet Things J. **7**(1), 247–257 (2020)
7. Yao, J., Han, T., Ansari, N.: On mobile edge caching. IEEE Commun. Surv. Tutor. **21**(3), 2525–2553 (2019)
8. Kaul, S., Yates, R., Gruteser, M.: Real-time status: how often should one update? In: 2012 Proceedings IEEE INFOCOM, pp. 2731–2735 (2012)

9. Kosta, A., Pappas, N., Angelakis, V.: Age of Information: A New Concept, Metric, and Tool (2017). https://ieeexplore.ieee.org/xpl/articleDetails.jsp?arnumber=8187436

10. Tang, H., Ciblat, P., Wang, J., Wigger, M., Yates, R.: Age of information aware cache updating with content- and age-dependent update durations. In: 2020 18th International Symposium on Modeling and Optimization in Mobile, Ad Hoc, and Wireless Networks (WiOPT), pp. 1–6 (2020)

11. Yang, L., Zhong, Y., Zheng, F.-C., Jin, S.: Edge caching with real-time guarantees (2019). arXiv:1912.11847

12. Kam, C., Kompella, S., Nguyen, G.D., Wieselthier, J.E., Ephremides, A.: Information freshness and popularity in mobile caching. In: 2017 IEEE International Symposium on Information Theory (ISIT), pp. 136–140 (2017)

13. Zhang, S., Wang, L., Luo, H., Ma, X., Zhou, S.: AoI-delay tradeoff in mobile edge caching with freshness-aware content refreshing. IEEE Trans. Wirel. Commun. **20**(8), 5329–5342 (2021)

14. Cao, J., Zhu, X., Jiang, Y., Wei, Z.: Can AoI and delay be minimized simultaneously with short-packet transmission? In: IEEE Conference on Computer Communications Workshops (INFOCOM WKSHPS), IEEE INFOCOM 2021, pp. 1–6 (2021)

15. Zhang, S., Li, J., Luo, H., Gao, J., Zhao, L., Shen, X.S.: Low-latency and fresh content provision in information-centric vehicular networks. IEEE Trans. Mob. Comput. (Early Access) (2020)

16. Najm, E., Nasser, R.: Age of information: the gamma awakening. In: 2016 IEEE International Symposium on Information Theory (ISIT), pp. 2574–2578 (2016)

17. Hatami, M., Leinonen, M., Codreanu, M.: AoI minimization in status update control with energy harvesting sensors. IEEE Trans. Commun. **69**(12), 8335–8351 (2021)

18. Wang, S., et al.: Distributed reinforcement learning for age of information minimization in real-time IoT systems. IEEE J. Sel. Top. Signal Process. (Early Access) (2022)

19. Ceran, E.T., Gündüz, D., György, A.: A reinforcement learning approach to age of information in multi-user networks with HARQ. IEEE J. Sel. Areas Commun. **39**(5), 1412–1426 (2021)

20. Kam, C., Kompella, S., Ephremides, A.: Learning to sample a signal through an unknown system for minimum AoI. In: IEEE Conference on Computer Communications Workshops (INFOCOM WKSHPS), IEEE INFOCOM 2019 (2019)

21. Sert, E., Sönmez, C., Baghaee, S., Uysal-Biyikoglu, E.: Optimizing age of information on real-life TCP/IP connections through reinforcement learning. In: 2018 26th Signal Processing and Communications Applications Conference (SIU), pp. 1–4 (2018)

22. van Hasselt, H., Guez, A., Silver, D.: Deep reinforcement learning with double Q-learning. In: AAAI, vol. 30, no. 1 (2016)

Edge Computing and Fog Computing

Docker-Based Full Life-Cycle Experimental Cloud Platform Design and Implementation

Huilin Song[1](✉) and Qilong Li[2]

[1] School of International Economics and Trade, Jiangxi University of Finance and Economics, Nanchang 330013, China
songhuilin@jxufe.edu.cn
[2] Department of Computer Science and Technology, Tongji University, ShangHai 201804, China

Abstract. The university laboratory that adopts the virtual machine method has problems such as the large maintenance workload of the experimental environment, complex configuration, fixed experimental time, and the inability to save the process. We propose a lightweight experimental environment based on Docker. Monitoring service, high availability session management, and resource protection mechanism of Docker runtime are designed. The full life cycle service runs after the Docker container is created and provides a management interface for the upper cloud platform. The prototype system of the cloud experimental platform is realized, which simplifies the construction and management of the cloud experimental platform in colleges and universities.

Keywords: Docker · Full life-cycle · Cloud Platform

1 Introduction

The traditional laboratory in colleges and universities has the defects of large infrastructure investment and high equipment loss rate. Due to the fixed location of the experiment, it is difficult for the instructor to grasp the experimental progress in the limited time, let alone to carry out the expansion of teaching. At present, most of the experimental platforms in colleges and universities are based on virtual machine technology, not only resource utilization but also can not carry out the full life-cycle management.

With the rapid development of computer networks [1–4], the emergence of cloud computing provides a new idea for the experimental platform of colleges and universities [5–7]. By reintegrating and encapsulating resources such as computer hardware, software, and computing capability, and providing them to students in the form of services, this new computing mode can be more flexible and make full use of computing resources. Based on lightweight virtualization technology, such as Docker [8]. Docker directly shares the kernel and hardware of the host, so the performance gap between the application running in the Docker container and the application running on the host is almost negligible. Unlike virtual machines, containers do not require hardware virtualization or run a complete operating system. This benefits higher resource utilization, a faster application running, and more efficient data storage.

Y. Cao and X. Shao (Eds.): MONAMI 2022, LNICST 474, pp. 185–195, 2023.
https://doi.org/10.1007/978-3-031-32443-7_13

In general, the cloud platform for experiments based on Docker should meet the following points: (1) Ability to deploy and distribute lab environments. (2) Can manage the full life cycle of containers. (3) Have a certain experimental preservation ability. However, the virtualization scheme provided by native Docker cannot meet the above requirements. Based on the above requirements and deficiencies, we first redesigned the Docker container from three aspects: monitoring service, high availability session management, and resource protection mechanism, providing a management interface for the upper cloud platform and realizing full life cycle management. Then the prototype system of the cloud experimental platform is designed and implemented, which simplifies the construction and management of the cloud platform.

2 Related Work

None of the three scheduling algorithms built into Docker's native resource scheduling management tool Swarm can give full play to the overall performance of Docker clusters, and many studies have improved Docker container scheduling strategies [9–11]. Kaewkasi et al. [12] proposed an algorithm based on ACO(Ant Colony Optimization, ACO), and experimental results show that ACO placed workload is about 15% better than greedy algorithm workload on the same host configuration. McDaniel et al. [13]. Proposed a two-layer approach to extend Docker and Docker Swarm so that both can monitor and control the I/O of Docker containers and improve resource utilization without being affected by competition. Zhang et al. [14]. Proposed an effective adaptive scheduler by modeling the scheduling problem as integer linear programming, which achieved significant cost savings. Wu et al. [15]. Developed an availability guarantee buffer layer priority scheduler, which could use the local buffer layer on nodes in Docker Swarm to reduce network traffic and speed up the start of service-related tasks. To ensure maximum utilization of system resources, idle containers are closed by recycling resources. To realize this process, it is necessary to monitor and manage the state of the container and to be able to save and restore the memory state of the container. Jimenez et al. implemented CoMA [16], a container monitoring agent for OS-level virtualization platforms.

However, the experimental platform has two special scenarios: (1) Different services are sensitive to different resource types. (2) A large number of concurrent requests may occur in a short time. Previous studies have not discussed this, so it is worth studying how to design corresponding algorithms for different scenarios and propose a multi-algorithm collaborative scheduling strategy to meet scheduling requirements in different scenarios by using different algorithms in turn to process requests.

3 Full Life-Cycle Management

3.1 Monitor Service

To obtain monitoring information on each node, it is necessary to require nodes to be able to transmit data to each other. Therefore, we adopt a centralized architecture, and the nodes in the cluster are divided into master nodes and slave nodes. The overall monitor service is divided into a monitor agent, a monitor center, and the monitoring data processing logic on the server-side. Since the system uses the monitoring data in the way of active requests, and the demand of the request is real-time data, there is no need to store the data. The data that the monitoring service needs to collect is mainly divided into two categories: container-oriented monitor and host-oriented monitoring.

3.1.1 Monitor Agent

The monitor agent is deployed on each node in the cluster. As a data collector, the monitor agent collects various performance data of the node host, keeps monitoring status, and responds to data requests from the server. The structures used to record performance data are shown in Table 1.

Table 1. Structure for recording host information

Variable	Type	JSON
CoreNum	int	json:"core_number"
CpuRatio	float64	json:"cpu_ratio"
MemCap	float64	json:"memory_capacity"
MemUsage	float64	json:"memory_usage"
MemRatio	float64	json:"memory_ratio"
NetIO	float64	json:"net_io"
BlockIO	float64	json:"block_io"

The structure records basic host performance parameters: number of CPU cores, CPU usage, total memory, memory usage, network, and disk I/O throughput. In addition to basic configuration data, such as the number of CPU cores and memory capacity, other performance data must be collected and calculated in real-time. The CPU usage is calculated as follows:

$$CPU(N_i) = \left(\frac{us + sy}{us + sy + id}\right) \times 100\% \tag{1}$$

where, us, sy, and id respectively indicate the kernel state, user state, and idle id in Linux. The memory usage is read by the values of MemTotal and MemAvailable in /proc/meminfo. Then the following formula is calculated:

$$Mem(N_i) = \frac{MemTotal - MemAvailable}{MemTotal} \times 100\% \tag{2}$$

The network load of the system in a certain period can be expressed as formula 3:

$$Net(N_i) = \frac{(ReceByte2 - ReceByte1) + (TransByte2 - TransByte1)}{(T2 - T1) \times Throughput} \tag{3}$$

3.1.2 Monitor Center

The main responsibility of the monitoring center is to collect the global image information of the cluster, the basic information of docker containers and the operation performance data of containers. The structure design for recording performance data is shown in Tables 2 and 3. The image structure records the basic parameters of the Docker image: image repository, tag, and ID.

Table 2. Image structure

Variable	Type	JSON
Repository	string	json:"image_repository"
ID	float64	json:"image_id"
Tag	float64	json:"tag"

In the container structure, the ID, Name, CPU, and memory capacity are all basic information after a container is generated. BlkIO indicates the average I/O speed of disk data, and NetIO indicates the average I/O speed of network data flows.

Table 3. Container structure

Variable	Type	JSON
ID	string	json:"container_id"
Name	string	json:"container_name"
CpuCap	float64	json:"cpu_capacity"
MemCap	float64	json:"memory_capacity"
Host	string	json:"host_name"
Cpu	float64	json:"cpu_usage"
Mem	float64	json:"memory_usage"
BlkIO	float64	json:"block_io"
NetIO	float64	json:"net_io"

3.2 Session Services

We use port mapping to expose the host computer to external users for access. However, Docker itself does not provide the function of managing ports. If the port number is not specified when creating containers, Docker will randomly allocate host ports, which is not conducive to management in a multi-host cluster environment. To this end, we designed a highly available session management service based on an *etcd* cluster.

3.2.1 *Etcd* Storage Directory

Etcd's cluster awareness can quickly respond to the addition and removal of nodes. Can provide high availability for the cluster, so that the cluster can cope with node failure and expansion problems. The directory structure of the storage system node is shown in Fig. 1. The cluster contains multiple node information and builds a Swarm, so the node information format is a string composed of IP and the port monitored by the Swarm, and the key and value are the same, and these key-value pairs store the Swarm cluster information required by the Swarm manager.

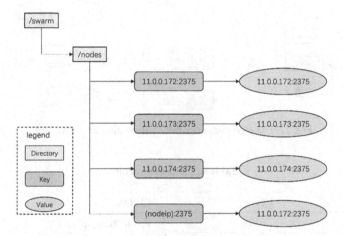

Fig. 1. Information directory structure of etcd cluster nodes

The container information used by users, including port information, container state, container access links, and so on, is maintained by the *etcd* instead of database storage, which improves the portability of the system. As shown in Fig. 2, container information for the entire cluster is stored in the *user* directory of the *etcd*. The *user* directory is a subdirectory named in the format of the username. To effectively utilize system resources, each user can use only one container at a time. Therefore, there is a one-to-one relationship between users and containers. Each subdirectory contains five key-value pairs that record details of containers created by that user. IP indicates the IP address of the host running the container. Port records the cluster port corresponding to the container. ConID records the container id. Status records the status of the container, including None, created, and saved. Url records the URL that accesses the container. The above data is subject to change frequently and can be kept up to date using *etcd's* key-value store.

3.2.2 Port List

The session structure for recording the port session is shown in Table 4. The variables in the session structure correspond to the port storage of *etcd*.

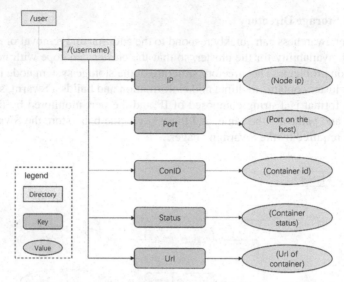

Fig. 2. The *etcd* container information directory structure

Table 4. Session structure

Variable	Type	JSON
IP	string	json:"host_ip"
Port	string	json:"container_port"
ConID	string	json:"container_id"
Status	string	json:"container_status"
Url	string	json:"container_url"

3.3 Resource Conservation

Although the resource utilization of the Docker container is much more efficient than that of the virtual machine, it is difficult to determine the demand for system resources of the application that needs to run for a long time when it is started in the Docker container, and some applications are transient. If the quota is allocated according to the maximum possible demand, when the application demand is in a slow period, Most of the resources allocated cannot be used efficiently. We designed a resource protection mechanism to obtain the container operating status information with the assistance of the monitoring system. The main functions are as follows: (1) If the container resource is tight, the resource quota is dynamically increased. (2) If the container is not in use for a long time, save the container on-site and recycle the container resources.

3.3.1 Dynamic Increases

The monitoring center designed in Sect. 3.1 can collect the basic information and performance data of Docker containers in the global scope of the cluster. The resource usage of a container can be determined based on the CPU and memory usage. If the resource usage of a container is high, it indicates that the container needs more resources to ensure normal running. In this case, the monitoring center triggers the resource protection mechanism to increase the resource quota for the container. In the case of wasted resources, the system does not do much because the container does not have a good prediction of whether it will need its allocated resources in the future.

When a container resource is scarce and the usage of a certain resource (memory or CPU) reaches 90%, the system increases the allocated resource quota by 20% to ensure the normal running of the container. For example, if the memory limit of container A is 200M and the monitoring center detects that the memory usage of container A is 92%, the resource protection mechanism is triggered and the docker update command is executed to reset the memory limit of container A to $(200 + 200 \times 20\%)$ M.

3.3.2 Storage of Containers

The monitoring center collects global container information every 15 min. When BlkIO and NetIO are both 0, it means that the user has not used the container for at least 15 min. Trigger the resource protection mechanism to save the container. When saving a container, you need to take into account what is being edited in the saving container. The storage algorithm of the container is shown in Table 5.

Table 5. EclipseSave.sh

```
1.  #!/bin/bash
2.  WID=`xdotool search --
    name "Eclipse Platform" | head -1`
3.  if [ -n "$WID" ]
4.  then
5.  xdotool windowactivate $WID
6.  xdotool windowfocus $WID
7.  xdotool key ctrl+S
8.  xdotool key --window $WID Return
9.  xdotool windowkill $WID
10. else
11. echo "eclipse is not running"
12. fi
```

4   Cloud Platform Implementation

4.1   System Structure

Based on the full life-cycle management mechanism, we designed the overall architecture of the system, as shown in Fig. 3. When a user initiates a request through the front-end page, the management center will route to different execution modules according to the corresponding API of the request, and these execution modules will complete the user's request. System users have two roles: teacher and student. As an administrator, teachers can view the basic information of Docker images and Docker containers and have certain management rights, such as setting experimental images. The operation of students is mainly the creation, saving, recovery, and destruction of the experimental environment (Docker container).

Specifically, the request to create the container is distributed to the scheduling module, which is responsible for scheduling the container in the cluster. When the container is created, the session management module allocates ports and records connection information for remote sessions. The monitoring module will constantly detect the health status of the container, and provide the host load information and container status information for the scheduling module and the runtime module. The runtime module is responsible for saving and restoring the container runtime. The data module is responsible for allocating storage directories to containers.

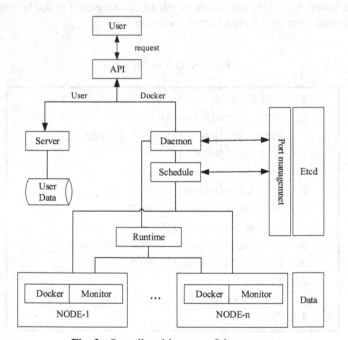

Fig. 3. Overall architecture of the system

4.2 Module Page

The experimental platform is B/S mode. Students create, save, restore, and destroy the web page. Teachers can view containers and set up experimental mirrors, including the status information of hosts in the cluster and the list of remotely connected ports (Fig. 4).

Fig. 4. Interface corresponding to experimental environment operation

5 Conclusion

In this paper, the full life-cycle management system of the cloud experimental platform is designed and implemented. First, the monitoring service is designed and implemented, the docker monitoring tool is analyzed and the monitoring agent and monitoring center are introduced in detail. Secondly, by analyzing the forwarding mechanism of the Docker network, the port management storage structure of *etcd* is designed, and a port list is maintained for each node in the cluster. Thirdly, the corresponding dynamic increment and container saving operations are described in two cases of resource shortage and container idle respectively. Fourthly, the prototype system of the cloud experimental platform is designed. In the future, we will study the customized Settings of different experimental environments combined with Docker images.

Funding. This study was supported by the Science and Technology Research Project of Jiangxi Provincial Department of Education (No. GJJ200318 and GJJ210520).

References

1. Sadeeq, M.M., Abdulkareem, N.M., Zeebaree, S.R.M., et al.: IoT and Cloud computing issues, challenges and opportunities: a review. Qubahan Acad. J. **1**(2), 1–7 (2021)
2. Huang, X., Yi, W., Wang, J., Xu, Z.: Hadoop-based medical image storage and access method for examination series. Math. Probl. Eng. **2021**, 1–10 (2021)
3. Cao, Y., Ji, R., Ji, L., Lei, G., Wang, H., Shao, X.: l2-MPTCP: a learning-driven latency-aware multipath transport scheme for industrial internet applications. IEEE Trans. Ind. Inform. **18**, 8456–8466 (2022)
4. Cao, Y., Ji, R., Huang, X., Lei, G., Shao, X., You, I.: Empirical mode decomposition-empowered network traffic anomaly detection for secure multipath TCP communications. Mobile Netw. Appl. **27**, 2254–2263 (2022)
5. Ali, M.B., Wood-Harper, T., Mohamad, M.: Benefits and challenges of cloud computing adoption and usage in higher education: a systematic literature review. Int. J. Enterp. Inform. Syst. **14**(4), 64–77 (2018)
6. Baldassarre, M.T., Caivano, D., Dimauro, G., et al.: Cloud computing for education: a systematic mapping study. IEEE Trans. Educ. **61**(3), 234–244 (2018)
7. Zhang, Z., Min, H.: Analysis on the construction of personalized physical education teaching system based on a cloud computing platform. Wireless Commun. Mobile Comput. **2020**, 1–8 (2020)
8. Merkel, D.: Docker: lightweight linux containers for consistent development and deployment. Linux J. **2014**(239), 2 (2014)
9. Marathe, N., Gandhi, A., Shah, J.M.: Docker swarm and kubernetes in cloud computing environment. In: 2019 3rd International Conference on Trends in Electronics and Informatics (ICOEI). IEEE, pp. 179–184 (2019)
10. Huang, C.H., Lee, C.R.: Enhancing the availability of Docker Swarm using checkpoint-and-restore. In: 2017 14th International Symposium on Pervasive Systems, Algorithms and Networks & 2017 11th International Conference on Frontier of Computer Science and Technology & 2017 Third International Symposium of Creative Computing (ISPAN-FCST-ISCC), pp. 357–362. IEEE (2017)
11. Magableh, B., Almiani, M.: A self healing microservices architecture: a case study in docker swarm cluster. In: Barolli, L., Takizawa, M., Xhafa, F., Enokido, T. (eds.) Advanced Information Networking and Applications: Proceedings of the 33rd International Conference on Advanced Information Networking and Applications (AINA-2019), pp. 846–858. Springer International Publishing, Cham (2020). https://doi.org/10.1007/978-3-030-15032-7_71
12. Kaewkasi, C., Chuenmuneewong, K.: Improvement of container scheduling for docker using ant colony optimization. In: 2017 9th international conference on knowledge and smart technology (KST), pp. 254–259. IEEE (2017)
13. McDaniel, S., Herbein, S., Taufer, M.: A two-tiered approach to I/O quality of service in docker containers. In: 2015 IEEE International Conference on Cluster Computing, pp. 490–491. IEEE (2015)
14. Zhang, D., Yan, B.H., Feng, Z., et al.: Container oriented job scheduling using linear programming model. In: 2017 3rd International Conference on Information Management (ICIM), pp. 174–180. IEEE (2017)
15. Wu, Y., Chen, H.: Abp scheduler: Speeding up service spread in docker swarm. In: 2017 IEEE International Symposium on Parallel and Distributed Processing with Applications

and 2017 IEEE International Conference on Ubiquitous Computing and Communications (ISPA/IUCC), pp. 691–698. IEEE (2017)

16. Jimenez, L.L., Simon, M.G., Schelén, O., et al.: CoMA: Resource monitoring of docker containers. In: International Conference on Cloud Computing and Services Science: 20/05/2015–22/05/2015, vol. 1, pp. 145–154. SCITEPRESS Digital Library (2015)

17. Cérin, C., Menouer, T., Saad, W., et al.: A new docker swarm scheduling strategy. In: 2017 IEEE 7th international symposium on cloud and service computing (SC2), pp. 112–117. IEEE (2017)

Edge Computing-Based Multitasking Strategies in Smart Grids

Han Zhao[1]([⊠])(iD), Mengxuan Dai[2](iD), Kaiwen Ji[3](iD), Wenshan Wei[4](iD), Xinghong Jiang[2](iD), Yong Ma[2](iD), Yunni Xia[5](iD), and Bingbing He[6](iD)

[1] School of Digital Industry, Jiangxi Normal University, Shangrao, China
zhaohan@jxnu.edu.cn

[2] School of Computer and Information Engineering, Jiangxi Normal University, Nanchang, China
{dmx,jxh,may}@jxnu.edu.cn

[3] Jiangxi Institute of Economic Development, Jiangxi Normal University, Nanchang, China
54745348@qq.com

[4] School of Foreign Languages, Beihang University, Beijing, China
gram594@buaa.edu.cn

[5] School of Computer Science, Chongqing University, Chongqing 400030, China

[6] Hefei Youer Electronic Technology Co., Hefei, China
hebingbing@youotech.com

Abstract. In order to promote the digital development of the smart grid, power data needs to be analyzed and processed in real time, but because the number of power grid terminal devices is vast, the massive amount of data generated will incur additional network latency and communication costs if processed directly by cloud servers, and there is also a risk of data leakage. Therefore, power data is considered to be placed on edge servers for processing to overcome many problems in the current cloud computing paradigm for power systems, such as the inability to fully realize the requirements of high bandwidth and low latency. This paper thus proposes a multitask assignment strategy (MPA) for smart grid terminals based on edge computing. The method first classifies grid end tasks into different classes based on the size of data, security level, and computational workload; it then selects a suitable edge server for the smart grid terminal tasks using the particle swarm algorithm. The simulation results show the effectiveness of the method in this paper.

Keywords: edge computing · Smart grid · task assignment · particle swarm algorithm · multi-objective constraints

Y. Cao and X. Shao (Eds.): MONAMI 2022, LNICST 474, pp. 196–211, 2023.
https://doi.org/10.1007/978-3-031-32443-7_14

1   Introduction

The Internet of Things (IoT) [1] and artificial intelligence [2] are two cutting-edge information technologies that combine to create the smart grid, a modern grid system that plays an essential role in the energy infrastructure. To collect and upload various power data in real-time, massive terminal devices need to be deployed for the smart grid. The development of technologies such as cloud computing [3] and artificial intelligence has created favorable conditions for the intelligence of grid terminal devices. Efficient analysis and process of the tasks generated by these terminals are one of the challenges facing the smart grid. Cloud computing, a technology that provides on-demand computing resources, can be a solution. However, for end devices, cloud servers are usually in a relatively centralized location. Transferring tasks to cloud servers consumes a lot of bandwidth and other resources, resulting in high communication costs. In addition, in extreme cases, it will lead to serious delay and congestion, and even cause data loss and slow processing efficiency, which will not only bring losses to the power grid company, but also reduce system QoS [4]. In order to solve the above problems, the concept of edge computing [5] has been introduced in smart grids.

Edge computing is an open platform that integrates core functions such as networking, computing, storage, and applications at the network edge near the source or data source. It can also provide nearby edge intelligence services to meet critical needs of industry digitization such as agile connectivity, real-time business, data optimization, application intelligence, security, and privacy protection. Edge computing differs from cloud computing in that edge computing allows users to offload the deployment of computing tasks to servers at the edge of the network, localizing the service, significantly reducing the amount of remote data transmission, lowering network transmission latency, decreasing the cost of equipment consumed during the transmission of computing tasks, and abating placement costs. This paper selects appropriate edge servers for grid end tasks through an edge computing-based multi-task assignment strategy (MPA) in order to process tasks from grid end devices efficiently and with almost no delay, which not only saves the transmission time of massive data to and from the cloud but also improves data transportation efficiency and ensures real-time data processing while reducing the possibility of network congestion.

The remaining chapters of this paper are organized as follows. In Sect. 2, related work on smart grids, edge computing, and particle swarm algorithms are introduced. In Sect. 3, the system model is introduced. In Sect. 4, the effectiveness of the proposed strategy is verified by simulation experiments. In Sect. 5, the paper is summarized and the future research directions are discussed.

2   Related Work

The problem of task allocation is widely discussed in edge computing, which enables resource-constrained edge servers to provide satisfactory services to end devices by solving the problem of how computational tasks generated by end applications are distributed among edge servers [6]. It also reduces computational latency and bandwidth consumption, balances the load [7], and improves network QoS. In addition, how to introduce the edge computing paradigm into the smart power grid domain has also become a focus of research. A distributed computing architecture for smart grid IoT devices based on edge computing is proposed in the reference [8]. The architecture introduces an edge node coordinator to achieve collaborative work among smart grid edge nodes. Reference [9] proposes the security and confidentiality of communication information when users access cloud resources, combined with application security to ensure legitimate user permission to operate.

Edge computing is a technology developed in the context of high-bandwidth and time-sensitive IoT integration, where the energy consumption and latency of edge computing migration are essential metrics to measure migration decisions. Reference [10] considered the singularity of optimized resource strategies in mobile edge computing and proposed a multiple resource computing migration energy consumption model based on particle swarm task scheduling algorithm to ensure sufficient reduction of edge device energy consumption under delay constraints. Reference [11] proposed an efficient asynchronous federated learning mechanism for edge network computing, which compresses the redundant communication between nodes and parameter servers during the training process according to an adaptive threshold. Reference [12] for a multi-user serial task offloading problem with latency and energy consumption as the optimization objectives, following the first-come, first-served principle, to make a near-optimal offloading decision for users. Reference [13] constructs an objective function for joint optimization of the average offload delay and resource allocation balance in the context of 3GPP long-term evolution technology application to effectively reduce the average offload delay of multiple users while balancing the workload of each mobile edge computing server. Reference [14] proposed a strategy integrating abundant computing resources of Mobile Cloud Computing (MCC) and the low transmission delay of MEC to formulate computing offloading decisions, and it provided an Iterative Heuristic MEC Resource Allocation (IHRA) scheme. The scheme extends the single-user offloading problem to multi-user offloading while integrating resource constraints and interference among multiple users to achieve collaborative execution of tasks at the edge and in the cloud and reduce task execution latency. Reference [15] presents a one-to-many task assignment problem and designs a task assignment optimization algorithm based on the Lagrange multiplier method. Reference [16] propose a novel stochas-tic approach that jointly optimizes the usage of transmission resources (e.g., bandwidth), and transcoding resources (e.g., CPU) in CLS systems that leverage the cooperation of Cloud, Edge, and Crowd technologies.

The swarm intelligence algorithm, which simulates the collaborative group search in nature, is widely used with its robust global search and optimization capability, less computational cost, and faster convergence speed. The particle swarm optimization algorithm is the first choice for solving some practical engineering problems because of its fast convergence and low setting parameters. The formula for calculating the inertia coefficient of the particle swarm algorithm was improved in reference [17] and reference [18] by dynamically changing the inertia coefficient according to the fitness value of the particles. The second category combines particle swarm algorithms with other evolutionary algorithms. Reference [19] combined particle swarm algorithm with genetic algorithm to solve the decision problem of offloading the middle layer of deep networks. The third one uses particle swarm algorithms to solve subproblems in the task unloading problem. As in reference [20], to solve the computational offloading problem in ultra-dense heterogeneous networks, a coarse-grained search using a genetic algorithm is followed by a fine-grained search using particle a swarm algorithm to derive the optimal computational offloading decision. Reference [21] proposed a combined particle swarm and genetic algorithm for the migration decision problem of large deep neural networks and proposed a layer merging upload algorithm to solve the upload problem. Reference [22], on the other hand, decomposes the probabilistic task unloading problem into multiple unconstrained subproblems and uses a particle swarm algorithm to solve each subproblem to obtain an optimal solution to the probabilistic task unloading problem.

This paper focuses on overcoming the current problems of large data volume and complicated task processing in power systems and selecting suitable edge servers for different levels of smart grid terminal tasks for processing. A new edge computing-based multitasking strategy for smart grid terminals is proposed in this paper, which optimizes the distance of data transmission to the edge server, the cost, matching constraints, and load rate.

3   System Model

The system model scenario in this paper is an application scenario with multiple terminal devices and multiple edge servers, as shown in Fig. 1, where the terminal device is a smart meter belonging to the edge device level node [23], which can meet the real-time terminal requirements.

Suppose there are N end devices with M edge servers, and each edge server is connected through a wireless communication link. In this paper, we assume that each end-device can offload its computation of the execution task, and the task can only be offloaded to one MEC server for computation when offloading, and each end-device is within the range of the wireless connection. However, every MEC server has limited computing power and cannot accept offload requests from every endpoint at the same time, assuming that the maximum number of load tasks per edge server is h. The set of end devices is $U = \{u_1, u_2, u_3 \ldots u_n\}$, The set of edge servers is $S = \{s_1, s_2, s_3 \ldots s_m\}$.

3.1   Task Model

Smart grid terminal devices generate different types of tasks randomly. In order to solve the problem of task assignment in smart grid [24], this paper classifies

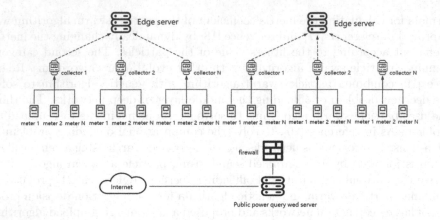

Fig. 1. System model

smart grid terminal task types into four different types according to computational workload, security level and data size, which are general tasks, predictive tasks, statisticaltasks, and top-secret tasks, and selects suitable edge servers according to different levels of smart grid terminal tasks.

Consider a set of tasks $T = \{t_1, t_2, \ldots, t_n\}$, where n is the total number of input tasks in the edge computing system. Each task is denoted by $t_i = \{D_i, W_i, \delta_i, S_i\}$, where D_i denotes the computational workload of task t_i, W_i denotes the security level of the data generated by task t_i, δ_i denotes the data size of task t_i, and S_i denotes the task level.

Table 1. provides a detailed breakdown of the types of tasks randomly generated by the smart grid terminals

Task Type	Calculating workload	Security Level	Data Size	Task Level
General tasks	1	1	1	1
Predictive tasks	3	2	2	2
Statistical tasks	2	2	3	3
Top-Secret Tasks	4	3	2	4

General tasks refer to the collection of power data, which is less computationally intensive and generally does not have security issues; however, the direct delivery of power data to the cloud center will lead to congestion in the communication channel, and standard edge servers can be selected for distribution to reduce costs. Predictive tasks are slightly more computationally intensive and have a higher security level than regular tasks. Generally, predictive tasks are based onhistorical electricity consumption data to predict future electricity consumption at a specific time. A statistical task is usually to count a large amount of electricity data and find the electricity consumption pattern, which can be used for abnormal data detection, such as electricity theft analysis. The statistical task is not heightened in computational power but very large in data volume, so selecting an edge server that can receive a large amount of data is necessary. Top-secret tasks generally involve power data critical military institutions and state-owned enterprises.

After determining the level of tasks generated by the smart grid terminals, the security level of the edge servers also needs to be considered. If the task level is smaller than the edge server's encryption level, the data security is at risk, and if the task level is higher than the encryption level of the edge server, it will cause additional resource waste because that a higher encryption level means more computational power, storage capacity, and bandwidth capacity is required to encrypt and decrypt the original data. Based on this, a more suitable edge server needs to be matched to suit the level of the task. The security level corresponding to task t of edge server number m is selected and noted as $safe_{mt}$, the target constraint for the overall security level is expressed as follows.

$$\text{Max}\,(O_{\text{safe}}) = \sum_{j=1}^{M} \sum_{n=1}^{h} \text{safe}_{jn} \tag{1}$$

$$\text{s.t. } 0 < \text{safe}_{jn} \tag{2}$$

3.2   Load Model

The edge server needs to consider four aspects in its operating state: processor utilization, disk read/write rate, memory utilization, and bandwidth occupancy. The server state is evaluated by combining these four factors, representing the busy level of the server CPU, the throughput of data operations, the system operating state, and the amount of received data, respectively. The set of edge servers is known to be $S = \{s_1, s_2, s_3 \ldots s_m\}$, and the overall performance of its servers is denoted as $C^{S_m} = \left(C_{\text{cpu}}^{S_m}, C_{\text{i/o}}^{S_m}, C_{\text{mem}}^{S_m}, C_{\text{band}}^{S_m} \right)$, where $C_{\text{cpu}}^{S_m}$, $C_{\text{i/o}}^{S_m}$, $C_{\text{mem}}^{S_m}$, $C_{\text{band}}^{S_m}$ denote the maximum processor utilization, disk read/write rate, memory utilization, and bandwidth occupancy that edge server m can carry, respectively. The load state of the edge server m is $\text{Load} = \left(\text{Load}_{\text{cpu}}^{S_m}, \text{Load}_{\text{i/o}}^{S_m}, \text{Load}_{\text{mem}}^{S_m}, \text{Load}_{\text{band}}^{S_m} \right)$, where $\text{Load}_{\text{cpu}}^{S_m}, \text{Load}_{\text{i/o}}^{S_m}, \text{Load}_{\text{mem}}^{S_m}, \text{Load}_{\text{band}}^{S_m}$ denote the current processor utilization, disk read/write rate, memory utilization, and bandwidth usage of server m, respectively. $F_{\text{cpu}}^{S_m}$, $F_{\text{i/o}}^{S_m}$, $F_{\text{mem}}^{S_m}$, $F_{\text{band}}^{S_m}$ denote the percentages of the four metrics of processor utilization, disk read/write rate, memory utilization, and bandwidth occupancy of server m, respectively. Then:

$$\text{Load}_{\text{cpu}}^{S_m} = F_{\text{cpu}}^{S_m} C_{\text{cpu}}^{S_m} \tag{3}$$

$$\text{Load}_{\text{i/o}}^{S_m} = F_{\text{i/o}}^{S_m} C_{\text{i/o}}^{S_m} \tag{4}$$

$$\text{Load}_{\text{mem}}^{S_m} = F_{\text{mem}}^{S_m} C_{\text{mem}}^{S_m} \tag{5}$$

$$\text{Load}_{\text{band}}^{S_m} = F_{\text{band}}^{S_m} C_{\text{band}}^{S_m} \tag{6}$$

The total load can be expressed as:

$$\text{Load}_{\text{all}} = \alpha_{\text{cpu}} \text{Load}_{\text{cpu}}^{S_m} + \alpha_{\text{i/o}} \text{Load}_{\text{i/o}}^{S_m} + \alpha_{\text{mem}} \text{Load}_{\text{mem}}^{S_m} + \alpha_{\text{band}} \text{Load}_{\text{band}}^{S_m} \tag{7}$$

$$\alpha_{\text{cpu}} + \alpha_{\text{i/o}} + \alpha_{\text{mem}} + \alpha_{\text{band}} = 1 \tag{8}$$

Among them, α_{cpu}, $\alpha_{\text{i/o}}$, α_{mem} and α_{band} denote the weights occupied by each index of processor utilization, disk read/write rate, memory utilization, and bandwidth occupancy, respectively, and higher values indicate that the proportion of corresponding resources is more significant and more dependent.

The edge server can maintain stable service support when the total load is low enough during the overall task migration. When the load on a single edge server exceeds 1, tasks may not be completed as scheduled, negatively impacting user perception. By denoting Load_{jn_l} the load generated when the smart grid terminal distributes task n to the jth edge server for processing, then the target constraint for the total load can be expressed as:

$$\text{Min}\left(O_{\text{Load}}\right) = \sum_{i=1}^{M}\sum_{n=1}^{h} \text{Load}_{jn\_l} \tag{9}$$

$$\text{s.t. } 0 < \sum_{n=1}^{h} \text{Load}_{jn\_l} \leq \text{Load}_{all} \tag{10}$$

3.3 Communication Distance Model

Smart grid end devices allocate their computing tasks to edge servers with more abundant computing resources to reduce task execution latency and save cost and energy. Smart grid end devices are connected to the edge server via a wireless channel, and the transmission rates are as follows:

$$R_{u,s} = W \log_2 \left(1 + \frac{G_{u,s} P_{u,s}}{\sigma^2}\right) \tag{11}$$

$$\text{s.t. } 0 < P_{u,s} \leq P_{u,s}^{\text{max}} \tag{12}$$

$G_{u,s}$ denotes the channel gain between a grid terminal device u and an edge server s [25] in dB; W denotes the bandwidth of the link; σ^2 denotes Gaussian white noise; $P_{u,s}$ is the transmission power between a grid terminal device u and an edge server s, and defines the maximum transmission power of device m as $P_{u,s}^{\text{max}}$. The communication transmission distance is as follows:

$$Dis_{u,s} = R_{u,s} t_{u,s} \tag{13}$$

$t_{u,s}$ is the transmission time between the grid terminal device u and a certain edge server s.

$$\text{Min}\,(O_{dis}) = \sum_{j=1}^{M}\sum_{n=1}^{h} Dis_{jn\_dis} \tag{14}$$

$$\text{s.t. } 0 < Dis_{jn\_dis} \le Dis_{max} \tag{15}$$

3.4   Cost Model

Grid terminal tasks incur costs when computed on the edge server side, and grid companies prefer to choose edge service nodes with lower costs per unit as offload targets to reduce costs. Assume that each edge server has a different price and that each edge server has a standby cost (As long as there is a successful migration of services and standard calculation will incur standby costs, this cost will only be calculated once). Set the standby cost as Cost_Standby, The collection of service prices is as follows:

$$\text{Cost}_s = \{cost_{s1}, cost_{s2}, cost_{s3} \ldots, cost_{sk}\} \tag{16}$$

Record the active status of the edge server as ac:

$$\begin{cases} ac_m = 1 \\ ac_m = 0 \end{cases} \tag{17}$$

Among them, $ac_m = 1$ means that edge server m is active;$ac_m = 0$ means that edge server m is inactive. The set of its state is Activate $= \{ac_1, ac_2, ac_3 \ldots, ac_k\}$, the task security level is Tsafe $_n$, which is denoted as the security level of the nth task of the jth base station, and the set of security levels for edge servers is as follows:

$$\text{Bsafe} = \{\, \text{Bsafe}_1,\ \text{Bsafe}_2,\ \text{Bsafe}_3 \ldots,\ \text{Bsafe}_m\} \tag{18}$$

γ_{jn} is the task cost multiplier, and the individual task cost is calculated as follows:

$$\gamma_{jn} = \begin{cases} 1, \text{Tsafe}_j \le \text{Bsafe} \\ \text{Bsafe}_j - \text{Tsafe}_n + 1, \text{Tsafe}_j > \text{Bsafe}_n \end{cases} \tag{19}$$

$$\text{TaskCost}(j, n) = cost_{sj} * \left(\text{Load}_{cpu}^{S_m} + \text{Load}_{i/o}^{S_m} + \text{Load}_{mem}^{S_m} + \text{Load}_{band}^{S_m}\right) * \gamma_{jn} \tag{20}$$

The formula for calculating the total service cost is as follows:

$$\text{Cost} = \sum_{j=1}^{M}\sum_{n=1}^{h} \text{TaskCost}(j, n) + \sum_{j=1}^{M} ac_j * \text{Cost\_Standby} \tag{21}$$

The target constraint for the total service cost is expressed as follows:

$$\text{Min}\left(O_{\text{Cost}}\right) = \sum_{j=1}^{M}\sum_{n=1}^{h} \text{cost}_{sj} * \sum_{j=1}^{M}\sum_{n=1}^{h} \text{Load}_{jn\_l} + \sum_{j=1}^{M} ac_j * \text{Cost\_Standby} \quad (22)$$

$$\text{s.t. } 0 \leq cost_{sj} \quad (23)$$

3.5   Multi-objective Constraint Conversion

In the computing situation mentioned in this paper, multiple task offload requests are issued by grid end devices simultaneously. Due to the limited resources of the edge server, there is no guarantee that the task will be assigned to the most appropriate edge server under any circumstance. In this case, it is necessary to consider the optimal overall benefit and enable the grid end devices to utilize the edge end resources equitably and maximally [26]. Based on this, the four influencing factors of consumption cost, communication distance, edge server load factor, and security level are combined and defined as the combined cost to evaluate whether the task allocation can maximize the use of the edge server resources. A joint optimization model is established, and the normalized transformation function of the cost is obtained using the min-max normalization process [27] as follows:

$$\overline{\text{cost}}_{i,j} = \frac{\text{cost}_{i,j} - \text{cost}_{\min}}{\text{cost}_{\max} - \text{cost}_{\min}} \quad (24)$$

$\text{cost}_{\max}$ and $\text{cost}_{\min}$ are the maximum and minimum values of the consumption cost, respectively, and $\overline{\text{cost}}_{i,j}$ is the normalized consumption cost. The communication distance is normalized to obtain the following:

$$\overline{\text{dis}}_{i,j} = \frac{\text{dis}_{i,j} - \text{dis}_{\min}}{\text{dis}_{\max} - \text{dis}_{\min}} \quad (25)$$

where $\text{dis}_{\max}$ and $\text{dis}_{\min}$ are the maximum and minimum values of the communication distance, respectively, and $\overline{\text{dis}}_{i,j}$ is the normalized communication distance value. In order to minimize the cost, transmission distance, and load factor, it is only needed to minimize the cost affiliation function value, transmission distance function value, and load factor function value, where the security level of the task corresponding to the base station should be as high as possible, and the specific transformation process is expressed as follows:

$$\text{Min}(O) = \mu_1 \text{MinO}_{\text{Cost}} + \mu_2 \text{MinO}_{dis} + \mu_3 \text{MinO}_{\text{load}} + \mu_4 \text{Max} O_{\text{safe}} \quad (26)$$

where: $\text{Min}(O)$ is the minimum expected objective, μ_1 is the cost weight, μ_2 is the distance weight, μ_3 is the load weight, μ_4 is the matching restriction weight, and the following equation is satisfied:

$$\sum_{i=1}^{4} \mu_i = 1 \quad (27)$$

For different needs, it can be satisfied by changing the values of μ_1, μ_2, μ_3 and μ_4.

4 Particle Swarm Algorithm

The particle swarm optimization (PSO) algorithm is a swarm intelligence algorithm proposed by Dr. Eberhart and Dr. Kennedy by studying the predatory behavior of birds [28]. Bird flock search for food is based on information sharing and collaborative cooperation among individual members of the flock. The PSO algorithm is relatively simple to implement and does not require many parameters to be tuned. It has been widely used for solving optimization problems and training neural networks [29].

The PSO algorithm designs a flock of massless particles to simulate the behavior of a flock of birds, and each particle has two essential properties, namely, position X and velocity V, where the position of the particle represents a feasible solution to the problem to be solved in the search space, and the velocity of the particle represents the rate and orientation of the particle to be flown. Each particle adjusts its position according to the individual extremum pbest and the global extremum gbest, thus approaching the optimal position in the search space, where pbest is the best position found so far for the particle itself and gbest is the best position found so far for the particle population. In addition, each particle calculates the corresponding fitness value based on its current position and uses this value to evaluate the individual extremum pbest and the global extremum gbest. Iterative operation on particle swarm (the primary purpose is to calculate the velocity and position of the particle, update the two poles), finally, all particles will converge to the optimal position, thus finding the optimal solution of the problem to be solved.

The PSO algorithm is inspired by the flock of birds foraging in nature. When a bird is foraging for food, in addition to following its target flight, it has to refer to the flight path of other birds in the flock, especially the one close to the food.

In particle swarm algorithms, each particle is a candidate solution, and each particle has N dimensions, which depend on the particular research problem. In our research problem, N is the task to be assigned, and assigning N tasks to M data centers minimizes the processing time, transmission time, processing cost, and transmission cost. Each particle is iteratively updated until the desired result is obtained or the iterative set-point is reached. The process of implementing PSO is shown in Algorithm 1.

1. Initialize a population array of particles with random positions and velocities on D dimensions in the search space.
2. loop.
3. For each particle, evaluate the desired optimization fitness function in D variables.
4. Compare the particle's fitness evaluation with its pbesti.
5. Identify the particle in the neighborhood with the best success, and assign its index to the variable g.

6. Change the velocity and position of the particle according to the following
   equation:

$$
\begin{cases}
v_i^{(t+1)} = wv_i^t + c_1 r \left(\mathrm{pb}_i^{(t)} - x_i^{(t)} \right) + \\
\qquad c_2 R \left(\mathrm{gb}^{(t)} - x_i^{(t)} \right) \\
x_i^{(t+1)} = x_i^{(t)} + v_i^{(t+1)}
\end{cases}
\tag{28}
$$

7. If a criterion is met (usually a sufficiently good fitness or a maximum number
   of iterations), exit loop.
8. end loop

where v_i^t and $x_i^{(t)}$ denote the velocity and position of the particle, $\mathrm{pb}_i^{(t)}$ denotes
the individual historical optimum of the ith particle, $\mathrm{gb}^{(t)}$ denotes the global
optimum of the whole population, r and R are random values within [0,1], respectively, and w, c_1, and c_2 are the weight values.

5   Experiments

5.1   Parameter Setting

To verify the effectiveness of the MPA algorithm, the authors of this paper
compare five algorithms and simulate the randomly generated tasks of electricity
meters as data sets for simulation experiments. The four aspects, namely cost,
communication distance, edge server load factor, and matching constraint, are
analyzed respectively.

Most of the code is implemented in Python 3.8, and the experiments were
conducted on a server with a 3.8 GHZ AMD CPU and 32 G of RAM.

5.2   Comparison of Algorithms and Metrics

Table 2 shows the algorithms considering combined factors and multiple algorithms considering single factors.

The proposed algorithms are tested and compared using the following four
evaluation metrics.

1. Cost: represents consumption; the lower the indicator, the lower the cost.
2. Communication Distance: represents the communication distance metric, and
   the lower the metric, the closer the edge server selected for the task.
3. Load Rate: represents the edge server load factor; the lower the metric, the
   more stable the edge server is.
4. Matching Constraints: represents the matching constraints metric of tasks
   and edge servers; the lower the metric, the more edge servers the task can
   choose.

Table 2. Task classification

Algorithm	Specific description
MPA	The algorithm proposed in this paper considers a combination of factors cost, communication distance, load factor, and matching restriction parameters to select a suitable edge server to handle the grid terminal device tasks.
MLA	A greedy algorithm that prioritizes edge server load factor to select edge servers
MDA	A greedy algorithm that prioritizes communication distance to select edge servers.
MCA	A greedy algorithm that prioritizes consumption costs to select edge servers.
MRA	Randomly select edge servers for tasks.
MTA	Consider both communication distance and consumption cost (Reference [15]).

5.3   Analysis

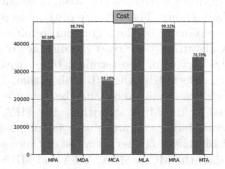

Fig. 2. Cost

Comparative Cost Analysis: A particular cost is consumed in assigning grid terminal tasks to the appropriate servers. Figure 2 indicates that algorithm MLA consumes the highest cost, while algorithm MCA consumes the lowest cost and accounts fTor only 58.28% of the cost generated by the MLA algorithm. Because that the MLA algorithm gives preference to edge servers with a lower load, which incur relatively higher costs, while the MCA algorithm focuses on selecting the edge servers with the lowest selection cost. Algorithm MTA considers both distance and cost, so the consumed cost is between the range of cost consumed by algorithm MCA and MDA. In contrast, MDA, MPA, and MRA, all three algorithms consume relatively high costs because they consider only one factor. The cost of the MPA algorithm proposed in this paper accounts for 90.39% of the cost of the MLA algorithm. This is because the MPA algorithm takes into account the cost and also integrates other factors, and finally selects an edge server with moderate cost.

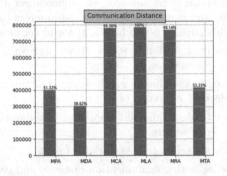

Fig. 3. Communication Distance

Comparative Analysis of Communication Distance: As shown in Fig. 3, the MLA algorithm prioritizes the edge server load, in assigning the grid terminal tasks to the appropriate servers. The distance of the selected edge server is not the first factor to be considered by the algorithm, resulting in a long distance. In contrast the MDA algorithm prioritizes the distance of the edge server and selects the closest edge server for the terminal tasks, with a distance of only 38.82% of the distance selected by the MLA algorithm. The MTA algorithm considers the cost as well as the distance, and the distance accounts for 53.23% of the distance selected by the MLA algorithm. The MPA algorithm proposed in this paper, after considering comprehensive factors, selects an edge server distance for the end task that is farther than the distance selected by the MDA algorithm but closer than the MCA, MLA, MTA and MRA algorithms which is a moderate distance.

Comparative Load Rate Analysis: The lower the edge server load ratio, the more stable the edge server runs, so when assigning edge servers to grid terminal tasks, the load ratio must be considered so that some nodes do not stop responding because of excessive load or remain idle and cause a waste of resources. Figure 4 reveals that the edge server selected by the MCA algorithm is overloaded, which is because the MCA algorithm only considers the cost, and the lower the cost, the higher the load rate; the MLA algorithm gives priority to the server with lower load, which only accounts for 33.36% of the load rate of the edge server selected by the MCA algorithm. After considering the comprehensive factors, the load rate of the edge server selected by the MPA algorithm proposed in this paper only accounts for 38.02% of the load rate of the edge servers selected by the MCA algorithm, which is in a moderate range.

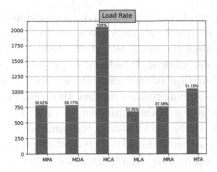

Fig. 4. Load Rate

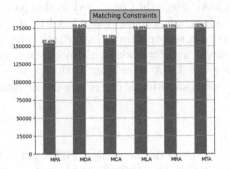

Fig. 5. Matching Constraints

Comparative Analysis of Matching Constraints: The tasks generated by the smart grid terminal have a certain security level. When assigning tasks to appropriate edge servers, the security level of tasks cannot be higher than the security level of edge servers, and tasks with a low-security level can be offloaded to high-security level servers. In contrast, tasks with high security levels cannot be offloaded to low-security level servers. Otherwise, the data will have security risks. The lower the matching constraint parameter, the more edge servers the task can be assigned to. As shown in Fig. 5, the matching constraints of the proposed MPA algorithm in this paper is the lowest among all experimental algorithms, indicating that the grid end tasks can choose to offload more edge servers.

6   Conclusion and Outlook

With the development of the IoT industry, the data from grid terminals has increased dramatically. When transferring data to cloud servers for computing, there are problems such as increased transmission costs, network delays, and data loss or distortion, and edge computing technology can effectively solve these problems. Selecting the appropriate edge server for grid terminal tasks becomes a challenge. The authors propose an edge-computing-based smart grid terminal multitasking assignment strategy (MPA) to solve this problem. Compared with traditional task assignment methods, the MPA algorithm divides smart grid terminal tasks into different classes. It selects appropriate edge servers for tasks by considering a combination of factors such as cost, communication distance, server load, and matching constraints so that the total energy consumed by all terminal devices and edge servers is minimum. In order to verify the performance of the algorithm MPA, the authors conducted simulation experiments, and the experimental results show that the MPA algorithm proposed in this paper can effectively select the appropriate edge server for different levels of grid terminal tasks, reduce the network transmission delay, and reduce the various costs consumed in the process of task transmission.

Nevertheless, the MAP algorithm proposed in this paper still has some limitations. In the task allocation scenario considered in this paper, although the edge server acts as the main resource provider for task computing, the computing resources are still limited, and for tasks with more data volume and computation and lower latency, the MPA algorithm in this paper can be considered to be integrated with cloud computing architecture in the future.

References

1. Ashton, K.: That 'internet of things' thing. RFID J. **22**(7), 97–114 (2009)
2. Charniak, E.: Introduction to Artificial Intelligence. Pearson Education India (1985)
3. Sadiku, M.N.O., Musa, S.M., Momoh, O.D.: Cloud computing: opportunities and challenges. IEEE Potentials **33**(1), 34–36 (2014)
4. Kumar, K., Liu, J., Lu, Y.H., et al.: A survey of computation offloading for mobile systems. Mobile Netwo. Appl. **18**(1), 129–140 (2013)
5. Shi, W., Cao, J., Zhang, Q., et al.: Edge computing: vision and challenges. IEEE Internet Things J. **3**(5), 637–646 (2016)
6. Wang, S., Zafer, M., Leung, K.K.: Online placement of multi-component applications in edge computing environments. IEEE Access **5**, 2514–2533 (2017)
7. Dai, Y., Xu, D., Maharjan, S., et al.: Joint load balancing and offloading in vehicular edge computing and networks. IEEE Internet Things J. **6**(3), 4377–4387 (2018)
8. Wang, P., Liu, S., Ye, F., et al.: A fog-based architecture and programming model for IoT applications in the smart grid. arXiv preprint arXiv:1804.01239 (2018)
9. Bo, Y., Ma, Y., Ma Z., Shao, S., Yang, S., Wang, M.: Research on key technologies for secure access management of resource pools. J. Jiangxi Normal Univ. (Nat. Sci. Edn.), **44**(06), 639–643 (2020). https://doi.org/10.16357/j.cnki.issn1000-5862.2020.06.16
10. Tang, L., He, S.: Multi-user computation offloading in mobile edge computing: a behavioral perspective. IEEE Netw. **32**(1), 48–53 (2018)
11. Shahidinejad, A., Farahbakhsh, F., Ghobaei-Arani, M., et al.: Context-aware multi-user offloading in mobile edge computing: a federated learning-based approach. J. Grid Comput. **19**(2), 1–23 (2021)
12. Zhou, S., Jadoon, W.: The partial computation offloading strategy based on game theory for multi-user in mobile edge computing environment. Comput. Netw. **178**, 107334 (2020)

13. Yang, X., Yu, X., Huang, H., et al.: Energy efficiency based joint computation offloading and resource allocation in multi-access MEC systems. IEEE Access **7**, 117054–117062 (2019)
14. Huang, P.Q., Wang, Y., Wang, K., et al.: A bilevel optimization approach for joint offloading decision and resource allocation in cooperative mobile edge computing. IEEE Trans. Cybern. **50**(10), 4228–4241 (2019)
15. Jianbin, X., Yaning, A.: A novel task offloading and resource allocation strategy based on edge computing. Comput. Eng. Sci. **42**(06), 959–965 (2020)
16. Chen, X., Xu, C., Wang, M., Wu, Z., Zhong, L., Grieco, L.A.: Augmented queue-based transmission and transcoding optimization for livecast services based on cloud-edge-crowd integration. IEEE Trans. Circuits Syst. Video Technol. **31**(11), 4470–4484 (2021). https://doi.org/10.1109/TCSVT.2020.3047859
17. Deng, X., Sun, Z., Li, D., et al.: User-centric computation offloading for edge computing. IEEE Internet Things J. **8**(16), 12559–12568 (2021)
18. Wang, Y., Wu, L., Yuan, X., et al.: An energy-efficient and deadline-aware task offloading strategy based on channel constraint for mobile cloud workflows. IEEE Access **7**, 69858–69872 (2019)
19. Chen, X., Zhang, J., Lin, B., et al.: Energy-efficient offloading for DNN-based smart IoT systems in cloud-edge environments. IEEE Trans. Parallel Distrib. Syst. **33**(3), 683–697 (2021)
20. Zhou, T., Qin, D., Nie, X., et al.: Energy-efficient computation offloading and resource management in ultradense heterogeneous networks. IEEE Trans. Veh. Technol. **70**(12), 13101–13114 (2021)
21. Xue, M., Wu, H., Li, R., et al.: EosDNN: an efficient offloading scheme for DNN inference acceleration in local-edge-cloud collaborative environments. IEEE Trans. Green Commun. Netw. **6**(1), 248–264 (2021)
22. Liu, Z., Dai, P., Xing, H., et al.: A distributed algorithm for task offloading in vehicular networks with hybrid fog/cloud computing. IEEE Trans. Syst. Man, Cybern. Syst. (99), 1–14 (2021)
23. Dinh, T.Q., Tang, J., La, Q.D., et al.: Offloading in mobile edge computing: task allocation and computational frequency scaling. IEEE Trans. Commun. **65**(8), 3571–3584 (2017)
24. Wang, P., Yao, C., Zheng, Z., et al.: Joint task assignment, transmission, and computing resource allocation in multilayer mobile edge computing systems. IEEE Internet Things J. **6**(2), 2872–2884 (2018)
25. Diao, X., Zheng, J., Wu, Y., et al.: Joint computing resource, power, and channel allocations for D2D-assisted and NOMA-based mobile edge computing. IEEE Access **7**, 9243–9257 (2019)
26. Aki, H.: Better than net benefits: rethinking the FERC v. EPSA test to maximize value in grid-edge electricity markets. Ecology Law Q. **44**(2), 419–444 (2017)
27. Robinson, M.D., Oshlack, A.: A scaling normalization method for differential expression analysis of RNA-SEQ data. Genome Biol. **11**(3), 1–9 (2010)
28. Xinchao, Z.: A perturbed particle swarm algorithm for numerical optimization. Appl. Soft Comput. **10**(1), 119–124 (2010)
29. Singh, N., Singh, S.B., Houssein, E.H.: Hybridizing SALP swarm algorithm with particle swarm optimization algorithm for recent optimization functions. Evol. Intell. 1–34 (2020)
30. Tsai, H.C., Lin, Y.H.: Modification of the fish swarm algorithm with particle swarm optimization formulation and communication behavior. Appl. Soft Comput. **11**(8), 5367–5374 (2011)

A Cloud-Side Task Scheduling Algorithm with Multiple Evaluation Metrics

Yong Ma[1] , Xinghong Jiang[2] , Chenyang Lv[2] , Tao Tao[3] ,
Liang Zhou[4](✉) , Qilin Xie[5] , and Lingguo Zhen[6]

[1] School of Computer and Information Engineering, Jiangxi Normal University,
Nanchang, China
[2] School of Computer and Information Engineering, Jiangxi Normal University,
Nanchang, China
{jxh,cyang_lv}@jxnu.edu.cn
[3] School of Digital Industry, Jiangxi Normal University, Shangrao, China
[4] China Electric Power Research Institute, Beijing, China
zhouliang@epri.sgcc.com.cn
[5] School of Electronic and Information Engineering, Jinggangshan University,
Jian, China
1809102045@jgsu.edu.cn
[6] YUFENG Technology Corporation Limited, Shenzhen, China

Abstract. With the popularity of intelligent terminal devices, edge computing has been fully developed. Power patrol robot is widely used in power grid information collection, and edge computing can effectively shorten response time, improve processing efficiency and reduce network pressure, so as to meet the real-time requirements. However, the following problem is how to realize the scheduling strategy of edge cloud and central cloud and optimize multi performance indicators. To solve this problem, this paper proposes a task scheduling model combining genetic algorithm with Docker container technology and taking cloud computing center and edge cloud into comprehensive consideration. Firstly, the task is classified by condition analysis. Assign tasks to cloud computing centers or edge nodes according to the task type; Genetic algorithm is used to assign tasks to edge nodes. Finally, the performance of the model is verified in the simulation environment. The experimental results show that this task allocation method greatly improves the resource utilization of edge server equipment on the basis of considering the needs of tasks, the limited resources of edge server, and meeting the needs of task proposers.

Keywords: Genetic algorithm · Edge cloud · Amulti-objective restriction · task scheduling

1 Introduction

Substation is one of the core hubs of the power system. Inspection of the equipment in the station is a basic measure to ensure the safety of the system and the

Y. Cao and X. Shao (Eds.): MONAMI 2022, LNICST 474, pp. 212–229, 2023.
https://doi.org/10.1007/978-3-031-32443-7_15

effective operation of the equipment. Domestic power grid enterprises are put forward to realize the new target of "machine patrol+ person patrol" exploring the application of intelligent operation, aims to develop flexibly carrying variety, high-performance and high-precision sensors of intelligent robot, push to "intelligent equipment and intelligent wisdom" transformation and upgrading, alleviate the pressure of the structural vacancies, improve operation quality and equipment health level.

With the boom in IoT, AI and the proliferation of mobile end devices, the scale of users, resources, tasks and workflows is increasing, along with the scale of edge clouds. Task execution and scheduling in the edge cloud in conjunction with the cloud computing centre is of paramount importance. It affects the overall task running efficiency, user quality of service, resource load balancing, etc. In order to improve the efficiency of resource use in the cloud computing environment, optimise performance indicators and meet the requests of multi-user and multi-computing tasks, the problem of resource allocation and task scheduling optimisation has received widespread attention.

Cloud computing environment is a typical distributed computing environment. The services provided by cloud computing include the following three categories: software as a service (SaaS), platform as a service (PAAS) and infrastructure as a service (IAAs) [1]. Task scheduling refers to the process of assigning tasks to appropriate resources to execute according to the actual situation of tasks and resources in IAAs layer [2]. The task scheduling mechanism of cloud computing system mainly focuses on multi performance indicators such as load balancing of edge cloud devices and quality of service parameters (QoS). In recent years, the academic research on task scheduling algorithm is mostly meta-heuristic algorithm, which is the combination of random algorithm and local search algorithm. [3] meta-heuristic algorithm does not depend on specific issues, but as a general heuristic strategy, it can be widely used in function combination optimization and function calculation. The high-precision solution and short overall scheduling cycle are its remarkable features, it can provide a search process for large-scale optimization problems. Therefore, meta-heuristic algorithm is always used to find the approximate optimal solution of NP hard problems.

At present, the research focus of meta-heuristic algorithm is how to balance local search and global search and avoid local optimal solution effectively. These algorithms can be roughly divided into two categories: swarm intelligence optimization and random search optimization [3]. Swarm intelligence optimization algorithm refers to the behavior taken by insects, herds and other groups to complete a certain goal. There is a task selection mechanism and division of labor in the group. Individuals constantly change the search direction according to local rules and the interaction between adjacent individuals, so as to ensure that the global group behavior can achieve a certain goal in the way of approximate optimal solution. On the other hand, the random search optimization algorithm is based on the traditional local search and global search, and further improves the search mode and adds a specific random algorithm to avoid the local optimal, so as to find the global optimal.

This paper proposes a task scheduling model combining genetic algorithm with Docker container technology and taking cloud computing center and edge cloud into comprehensive consideration. Firstly, the task is classified by condition analysis. Assign tasks to cloud computing centers or edge nodes according to the task type; Genetic algorithm is used to assign tasks to edge nodes. Finally, the performance of the model is verified in the simulation environment.

2   Related Work

In recent years, a variety of methods of task scheduling based on random search optimization have been proposed in academia. Zhang MAO et al. [4] put forward an adaptive individual-assessment scheme based on evolutionary states, and adjust the evolutionary parameters accordingly to handle the constraints in multi-objective optimization problems, which can meet the quality of service needs of users and efficiently utilize cloud resources. [5] proposes a temporal task scheduling algorithm (TTSA) to effectively dispatch all arriving tasks to private CDC and public clouds. In each iteration of TTSA, the cost minimization problem is modeled as a mixed integer linear program and solved by a hybrid simulated-annealing particle-swarm-optimization. H. Krishnaveni et al. [6] proposes an efficient algorithm namely Execution Time Based Sufferage Algorithm (ETSA). By establishing the expected calculation schedule, the difference between the two minimum execution time and completion time is calculated to achieve the best performance in load balancing. [7] using DEA and adaptive optimization strategy, an algorithm is proposed to enhance the fitness by modifying the mutation crossover operation, so as to optimize the execution time and energy consumption. Although the above methods can meet the accuracy requirements of higher solutions, it is limited to numerical solutions, multiple iterations and slow convergence speed.

Many scholars have proposed the task scheduling method based on swarm intelligence optimization. B. Gomathi et al. [8] proposed the Epsilon-fuzzy dominance based composite discrete artificial bee colony (EDCABC) approach. The Epsilon-fuzzy dominance sort approach is used to choose the best solutions from the Pareto optimal solution set in the multi-objective domain. And EDCABC with composite mutation strategies and fast local search method are used to enrich the local searching behaviours which help to avoid the premature convergence. Mandeep Kaur et al. [9] proposed a multi-objective bacterial foraging optimization algorithm (MOBFOA). Based on the improvement of the bacterial foraging algorithm, the method selects the bacteria positions from both the dominant as well as non-dominant fronts to obtain diversity in the solutions obtained. By introducing adaptive step size in chemotactic step, the accuracy and speed of the convergence of the BFOA has been improved. Huang Weijian et al. [10] proposed a multi-objective task scheduling model based on chaotic cat swarm algorithm (CCSO), in which the scheduling algorithm is carried out through search and tracking modes, and Logistic chaos mapping is used to process experimental data, thus obtaining the optimal task scheduling solution set. Li Hongwei [11] proposed a cloud computing task scheduling strategy based on the improved moth optimization algorithm, introduced the dynamic inertia weight, and used the lateral mutation strategy for the optimal moth position in the algorithm iteration process, so as to avoid the particles falling into local optimization in the later stage of the iteration and improve the multi-objective efficiency. However, the above schemes are complex to implement, highly dependent on parameters and prone to fall into local optimization, which is difficult to meet the requirements of multi-latitude task scheduling optimization objectives. Xingyan Chen [12] proposes a new stochastic approach to optimise the use of resource transfer and resource transcoding in systems that utilise cloud, edge and crowd technologies in collaboration. A joint resource allocation problem is proposed using stochastic optimisation arguments and an accelerated gradient optimisation (AGO) algorithm is designed to solve this optimisation problem in a scalable way that reduces system cost while having higher QOE performance.

Therefore, it is still a difficult problem to achieve the high-precision and multi-dimensional optimization goal of task scheduling and explore the scheduling algorithm with better optimization performance.

3 Preliminaries

This part mainly introduces Docker technology, Linux task scripting technology and genetic algorithm used in the task scheduling model.

3.1 Docker

Traditionally, when we receive a task and want to assign it to an idle edge server, we usually need the server to set up the corresponding runtime environment, configuration files, class libraries, etc. However, different cloud server resources have different environment configurations. In this case, tasks may fail to run due to complex running environment configurations and memory overload. At the same time, when cloud computing resources are dealing with multi-tasks, it is obviously unrealistic to constantly change configurations because different tasks need different configuration environment requirements. To solve this problem, Docker container technology is used in this paper.

Docker container technology provides us with a very standardized solution in cloud computing. Docker technology can be used to easily achieve system migration, provide the virtualization environment required by the task and so on. Traditional applications generally refer to "code as application", in order to run the application, if the environment does not meet the requirements of the application, the application must temporarily configure the environment. However, Docker technology uses the concept of "image is application", which packages all applications into an image starting from the kernel of the system to be run. It can run quickly in the new computer environment through Docker

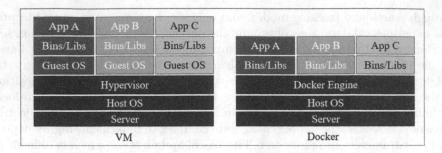

Fig. 1. Compare the traditional VM mode with the Docker container mode

engine. This not only solves the problem of task running environment configuration, but also enables the task scheduling and allocation calculation to get the most suitable cloud computing resources without considering the problem of running environment, thus improving the efficiency of task scheduling (Fig. 1).

3.2 Linux Task Scripting Technology

In actual scenarios, it is often necessary to schedule a large number of tasks, including the selection of edge services, configuration of the operating environment and data collection, etc. Obviously, it is unrealistic to configure each task manually (Fig. 2).

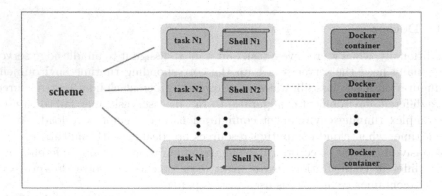

Fig. 2. Deployment principles of Shell task scripts

Therefore, in combination with the Docker technology introduced above, this paper installs the Docker environment for the edge server in advance. Based on the Docker container and Linux scripting technology, the system generates specific task scripts for specific tasks. After finding the optimal allocation scheme, script automation is implemented to build the running environment of tasks and the execution operation of programs.

3.3 Genetic Algorithms

Multiple edge devices may be available when scheduling a task. The system hopes to improve resource utilization and reduce energy consumption as much as possible. Therefore, in the selection process, the link bandwidth of edge devices, the storage size of tasks, and the deployment and operation time after receiving tasks should be considered comprehensively. When there are multiple tasks to be assigned, we hope to take all factors into consideration and finally arrive at an optimal task assignment scheme. In order to solve this problem, genetic algorithm is used in this model.

Genetic algorithm (GA) is a global optimization adaptive probabilistic retrieval algorithm developed according to the mechanism of natural selection and genetic evolution, hoping to select the optimal population of individuals through many high-quality iterations. In this model, for a set of task assignment scheme, the optimal assignment scheme for each task to be assigned to each edge server should be given according to the type of task and parameters of edge server (Fig. 3).

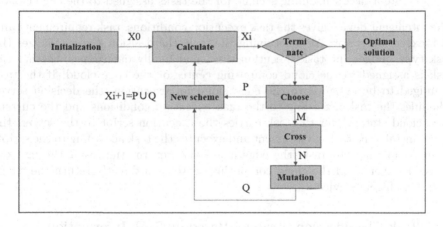

Fig. 3. Basic process diagram of genetic algorithm

4 A Cloud Side Task Scheduling Scheme Based on Task Deadline

This chapter first introduces the system model and application scenario, and then introduces the proposed comprehensive objective genetic algorithm scheme in detail.

4.1 System Model

The system model of this paper is shown in Fig. 4. The edge cloud in the figure refers to the computing and storage resources deployed around the decision server; The function of decision server is to collect the surrounding edge resource information, receive task information and generate task scheduling strategy. The decision server receives a certain range of task requests, and stores a certain number of tasks in the task queue within a period of time.

The tasks in the task queue may be executed in the cloud computing center or in the edge cloud. The task flow direction is mainly determined according to the specific requirements of the task.

The execution steps of the model task are as follows:

1. The decision server collects edge cloud device information.
2. The decision server receives the task information and generates a task queue.
3. Judge the task type according to the task information.
4. Generate a task scheduling scheme for the tasks assigned to the edge cloud.

The intelligent device gives the task execution conditions, task requirements and task execution script; After receiving the task, the decision server analyzes the task type, judges the task execution time, and finally determines whether the task is assigned to the cloud computing center or the edge cloud. If the task is judged to be assigned to the edge cloud for execution, the decision server schedules the task according to the task execution conditions and the current edge cloud state; After the task carries the execution script to the server, the server installs the task environment and executes the task according to the script. After completing the task, the edge cloud also returns the result through the decision server. And the cloud computing center can directly return the result to the intelligent device.

4.2 Task Classification Strategy Based on Task Information

After receiving the task information, the decision server simply classifies the task. See Table 1 for specific task types. In reality, due to the limited storage resources of mobile devices, large data contents are stored in cloud data centers. This paper defines such task as Scale Task. Considering the task execution deadline and measurement time, the task is divided into Immediate Task and Edge Timely Task. Immediate task is executed in the cloud computing center, while edge timely task is executed in the edge cloud. Measurement time refers

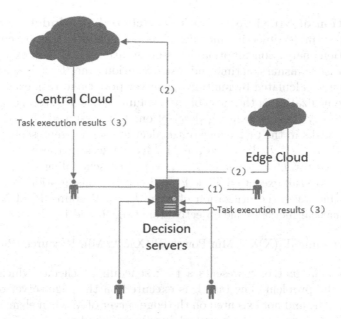

Fig. 4. Schematic diagram of system model

to the shortest time for the cloud computing center to perform tasks set by the model considering the network delay; The specific value is obtained by averaging the response speed of historical tasks under the LAN, and then making a fuzzy judgment incombination with the task size.

Table 1. Task classification

Task Name	Attribute
Scale task	The tasks consume a lot of storage and computing resources
Immediate task	The task deadline is greater than or equal to the measurement time
Edge timely task	The task deadline is less than measurement time

4.3   Edge Task Scheduling Scheme Based on Genetic Algorithm

The genetic algorithm considers the Task Size (TS), Task Deadline (TD), Task Number (TN) given by the edge timely task, and generates a set of task assignment scheme combined with the information of edge cloud devices at the current time. Edge cloud device information includes three parameters: CPU frequency, storage size and number of edge servers.

Construction of Multi-objective Task Scheduling Model

In this paper, multi-objective includes three parameters: task execution time, task execution energy consumption and storage utilization; Task execution time consists of task transmission time and task execution time; Task execution energy consumption is calculated by multiplying server power and task execution time, and storage utilization is the ratio of task volume to device storage space.

Edge Timely Task scheduling description: it is assumed that there are N edge timely tasks in the task queue of the decision server, represented by vector $P = \{P_1, P_2, P_3, \cdots, P_N\}$; There are M edge devices in the edge cloud, represented by vector $D = \{d_1, d_2, d_3, \cdots, d_M\}$. The scheduling scheme hopes to minimize the overall execution Time[P] and energy consumption Power[P] of N tasks, and maximize the utilization of edge device Resource[P] of N tasks. So the mathematical model of the objective function should be Eq. (1).

$$\text{Min Time } [P](X) \&\& \text{ Min Power } [P](X) \&\& \text{ Min Resource } [P](X) \quad (1)$$

X is the N × M matrix represents a task scheduling scheme, which is also a solution of the problem. The task L is executed on the edge server of M when element $x_m^l = 1$, and not executed on the edge server of M when element $x_m^l = 0$. In order to reduce the complexity, a task is only executed on one device by default in this paper, that is, only one element in a row of X matrix can have a value of 1 and the rest are 0.

$$X = \begin{bmatrix} x_1^1 & x_2^1 & \cdots & x_M^1 \\ x_1^2 & x_2^2 & \cdots & x_M^2 \\ \cdots & \cdots & \cdots & \cdots \\ x_1^N & x_2^N & \cdots & x_M^N \end{bmatrix} \quad (2)$$

The total execution time of a single task P_l on device d_m can be expressed as T_m^l. The total time consists of task transmission time and task execution time. The calculation formula is as follows:

$$T_m^l = tt_m^l + tc_m^l \quad (3)$$

$$m \in [0, M] \quad (4)$$

$$l \in [0, N] \quad (5)$$

tt_m^l represents the time when task is uploaded to edge server m. TS_l represents the size of task l, BT_m^l represents the bandwidth of the upload link when task l is transmitted to edge server m, and d represents the interference of data during transmission. The calculation formula is as follows:

$$tt_m^l = \frac{TS_l * d}{BT_m^l} \quad (6)$$

tc_m^l represents the running time of the task l on the edge server m, which is equal to the size of the task divided by the frequency of the edge server CPU, TS_l

represents the size of the task l, f_m represents the frequency of the edge server CPU, and the calculation formula is as follows:

$$tc_m^l = \frac{TS_l}{f_m} \tag{7}$$

The calculation formula of T_m^l obtained from (3) (6) (7) is as follows:

$$T_m^l = \frac{TS_l * d}{BT_m^l} + \frac{TS_l}{f_m} \tag{8}$$

After calculating the execution time of each task on each edge server, it is necessary to limit T_m^l not to exceed the deadline T_m^l of task l. If it exceeds the deadline, it means that server does not have the ability to execute task l. If the execution time of the task l on all edge servers exceeds the deadline, the execution time of the task is deemed to have failed. Therefore, all task assignments need to meet the following constraints:

$$T_m^l < TD_l \tag{9}$$

Finally, output the execution time of each task on each device. T matrix is used here. T is $N \times M$ matrix. The elements in the matrix comply with the constraints of Eq. (8), and the calculated time is filled in the specified position of the matrix. If not, the maximum value is filled in the corresponding position.

$$T = \begin{bmatrix} T_1^1 & T_2^1 & \cdots & T_M^1 \\ T_1^2 & T_2^2 & \cdots & T_M^2 \\ \cdots & \cdots & \cdots & \cdots \\ T_1^N & T_2^N & \cdots & T_M^N \end{bmatrix} \tag{10}$$

The resource utilization of a single task P_l on the device d_m can be expressed as M_m^l, and the calculation formula of the resource utilization is as follows, where D_m represents the overall storage space of the edge server m:

$$M_m^l = \frac{TM_l}{D_m} \tag{11}$$

$$M_m^l < 1 \tag{12}$$

After calculating the memory utilization of each edge server, the M matrix is used to store the utilization of each task on each edge server. M is $N \times M$ matrix. Each element in the M matrix needs to meet the condition that the value is less than 1 to ensure that the server can run this task.

$$M = \begin{bmatrix} M_1^1 & M_2^1 & \cdots & M_M^1 \\ M_1^2 & M_2^2 & \cdots & M_M^2 \\ \cdots & \cdots & \cdots & \cdots \\ M_1^N & M_2^N & \cdots & M_M^N \end{bmatrix} \tag{13}$$

The task execution energy consumption C_m^l is related to the calculation power P_m and calculation time T_m^l of the edge server. The calculation formula of C_m^l is as follows:

$$C_m^l = P_m * T_m^l \tag{14}$$

The calculated power P_m of the edge server is related to the CPU frequency and k_m is a parameter related to the CPU structure. The calculated power P_m can be obtained from the following formula:

$$P_m = k_m * (f_m)^2 \tag{15}$$

After simplifying the task execution energy consumption in combination with formula (8) (14) (15), it is as follows:

$$C_m^l = k_m * (f_m)^2 * \left(\frac{TS_{l*}d}{BT_m^l} + \frac{TS_l}{f_m} \right) \tag{16}$$

After calculating the execution energy consumption of each task by each edge server, the C matrix is used to store the corresponding execution energy consumption. C is N × M matrix.

$$C = \begin{bmatrix} C_1^1 & C_2^1 & \cdots & C_M^1 \\ C_1^2 & C_2^2 & \cdots & C_M^2 \\ \cdots & \cdots & \cdots & \cdots \\ C_1^N & C_2^N & \cdots & C_M^N \end{bmatrix} \tag{17}$$

Multi-objective Conditional to Single Objective Scheduling Scheme
A good task scheduling scheme X has relatively low time cost, low energy consumption and high resource utilization. According to the above analysis, it can be found that the lowest time often brings high power consumption. In order to achieve a relatively good index for both of them and resource utilization, the following single-objective evaluation function is designed in this paper:

$$f(X) = C(X) * t_1 + \frac{1}{M(X)} * t_2 + T(X) * t_3 \tag{18}$$

t_1, t_2, t_3 respectively represent the weights of three different parameters. Different values can be set considering different scene requirements. $C(X), M(X), T(X)$ represent the total value of the three parameters under scheme X. According to the requirements of Eq. (1), the objective function of the system can be obtained:

$$\text{Min} f(X) \tag{19}$$

The generation steps of single objective scheduling scheme are as follows:

1. The random algorithm is used to generate s sets of task scheduling schemes satisfying the constraints.
2. The evaluation values of all schemes are calculated according to the single objective evaluation function.
3. Sort the evaluation values from small to large. Combined with the objective function, we can know that the scheme with small evaluation value is more in line with the expectation of the model.
4. Select s schemes from the initial s schemes according to the evaluation value, and the same scheme can be selected repeatedly.

Algorithm 1. Crossover operator algorithm

Require: Father matrix,Mother matrix
Ensure: Child matrix
1: Calculate $f($ father $),f($ mother $)$
2: Father=Min($f($ father $),f($ mother $))$
3: Mother=Max($f($ father $),f($ mother $))$
4: i=0
5: **while** $i < task\_num/2 + 1$ **do**
6:     Child[i]=father[i]
7:     i=i+1
8: **end while**
9: **while** $i < task_num$ **do**
10:     Child[i]=mother[i]
11: **end while**
12: **return** Child;

Algorithm 2. Mutation operator algorithm

Require: Child matrix
Ensure: Child matrix
1: x =random(task)
2: y =random(device)
3: Child[x][y]= 1
4: i=0
5: **while** $i < device\_num$ **do**
6:     **if** $i == y$ **then**
7:         i=i+1
8:     **end if**
9:     Child[x][i]=0
10:     i=i+1
11: **end while**
12: **return** Child;

---

5. Cross judge the selected s set of schemes. If it fails, keep it unchanged and cross it successfully. Crossover operation, crossover operator is given in algorithm 1. After the population crossover is completed, s sets of schemes are also generated.
6. According to the mutation probability set and the mutation operator algorithm given in algorithm 2, the mutation operation is performed on the s schemes.
7. View evolutionary algebra
   (a) If the set evolutionary algebra is reached, the scheme with the minimum evaluation value is selected as the final scheme from s schemes.
   (b) If the set evolutionary algebra is not reached, go back to the first step and continue (Fig. 5).

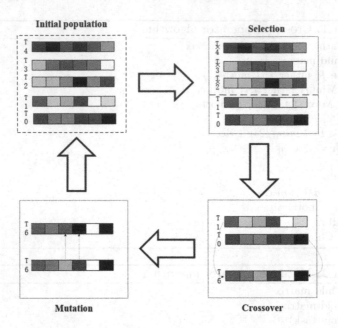

Fig. 5. Schematic diagram of population evolution

5   Simulation Experiment and Result Analysis

In this chapter, by comparing different evolutionary algebras, we find out the most suitable evolutionary algebra as the value of model evolution algebra. On the other hand, the performance differences between single target and comprehensive target in time, energy consumption and resource utilization are compared to prove the advantages of this model.

5.1   Experimental Setup

All experiments in this section are completed on laptops running windows10 system, and the specific configuration is as follows:

Intel (R) Core (TM) i7-8550UCPU@1.80 GHz processor, NVIDIA GeForce 940MX core graphics card with 8 GB of running memory. All the experimental code is written in Python language. Manual generation of 100 edge servers, a dataset containing 10 tasks and a dataset containing 20 tasks. The edge server parameters contain server cpu frequency, server storage space size. Task data contains task volume size, task deadline. By processing data to find out the edge and timely tasks, the task scheduling scheme is obtained by using genetic algorithms. Comparison algorithm:

1. Genetic algorithms of different evolutionary algebras: In this paper, evolutionary algebras were set as 10, 50, 100 and 150 respectively.

2. Genetic algorithms with different evaluation functions: Time first genetic algorithm, power consumption first genetic algorithm, storage resource utilization first genetic algorithm, comprehensive objective genetic algorithm.
3. Min-min algorithm: find the server with the smallest running time in the edge cloud to execute based on the order of the tasks in the task queue.

Comparison parameters:

1. Time: the average cost time of each task in the task scheduling scheme.
2. Energy consumption: the average energy consumption of each task in task scheduling scheme.
3. Storage usage: the average storage usage of each task in a task scheduling scheme (the amount of task computation compared to the storage size of the server).

5.2 Experimental Results and Analysis

As shown in Fig. 6, 7 and 8, For the same number of evolutionary generations, the task scheduling solution generated by the time-first genetic algorithm has the lowest time cost and the task scheduling solution generated by the power-first genetic algorithm has the lowest energy cost. The storage utilisation-first genetic algorithm generates the best utilisation solution. This is because time, energy consumption and storage utilisation are evaluated as separate measures of population evolution, so that the population always moves towards the optimal one for each of them.

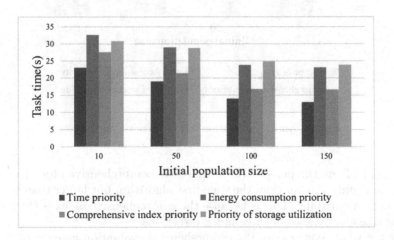

Fig. 6. The time cost of four genetic algorithms

It can be found from the information in the analysis figure that the performance of the comprehensive index cannot reach the optimal value in any evaluation direction, but it is always the sub-optimal value in all evaluation directions.

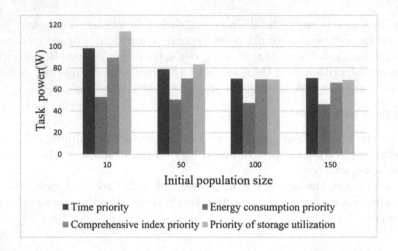

Fig. 7. Task power consumption of four genetic algorithms

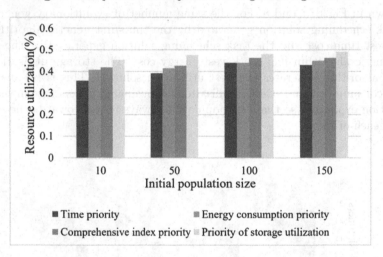

Fig. 8. Storage utilization of four genetic algorithms

For example, from the perspective of time, the comprehensive objective genetic algorithm is only smaller than the time-first algorithm but larger than the other two genetic algorithms. This is because the comprehensive index is the result of making a relative choice in three index directions.

For the whole edge cloud, the comprehensive evaluation index is often more helpful to the performance of the whole cloud.

Analysis of the information in Fig. 9 shows that as the number of evolutionary generations increases, the final solution performs better and better in time, while the decline in time decreases as the number of evolutionary generations increases. When the evolutionary generation is set to 100 and 150 respectively, the final solution no longer changes much in time. With the same task scenario and the same evaluation index, there must be a perfect final individual, and the increase in evolutionary generation can help the population to approach the final individual indefinitely. When the initial test population evolves to 100 generations, the population is already close to the final solution. Therefore, the population will not change much if it continues to evolve.

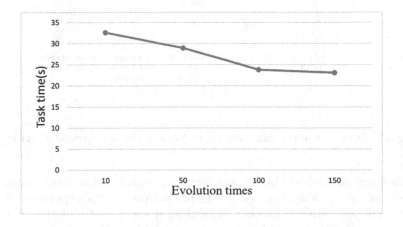

Fig. 9. Time cost of synthetic objective genetic algorithm

The analysis in Fig. 9 reveals that the genetic algorithm can deduce excellent task allocation schemes when the evolutionary generation is set to 100. Therefore, when comparing with the min-min algorithm, the evolutionary generation of the genetic algorithm is set to 100. In order to discover the advantages of the integrated genetic algorithm in dealing with complex situations. In this paper, two task sets, named task1 and task2, are set up, containing 10 and 20 tasks respectively.

Analysis of the information in Fig. 10 shows that the time-first genetic algorithm outperforms the min-min algorithm for either a task count of 10 or 20. For a task count of 10, the min-min algorithm outperforms the integrated goal genetic algorithm, and for a task count of 20, the results are reversed. The time-first genetic algorithm performs best as it finds the task allocation solution in the context of the whole population. When the number of tasks is 10, the min-min algorithm outperforms the integrated goal genetic algorithm because the number of tasks is much larger than the number of devices. As the number of tasks increases, the min-min algorithm's effectiveness drops and the integrated goal genetic algorithm outperforms the min-min algorithm.

In summary, the integrated goal genetic algorithm outperforms the power-first genetic algorithm and the storage resource utilisation-first genetic algorithm in terms of time; it outperforms the time-first and storage resource utilisation-first genetic algorithm in terms of energy consumption; and it outperforms the

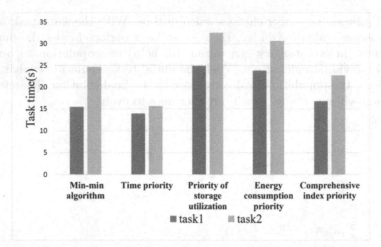

Fig. 10. Time cost of the mim-mim algorithm and the four genetic algorithms

time-first and power-first algorithm in terms of storage resource utilisation; and the value of a reasonable evolutionary algebra is found for the experimental data. In a comparison with the min-min algorithm, it was found that the integrated goal genetic algorithm could handle more complex situations.

6   Conclusion

In order to improve the efficiency of task scheduling and the overall resource utilization rate of edge cloud, a task scheduling model based on comprehensive objective genetic algorithm is proposed in this paper. Firstly, simple tasks are performed according to the task information, and then the edge cloud task scheduling scheme is generated by using comprehensive objective genetic algorithm for edge timely tasks. Other types of tasks are assigned to cloud computing centers. In order to improve the execution efficiency of the task, docker container technology and Linux script technology are combined to deploy and execute the task environment. Finally, the performance of the comprehensive objective genetic algorithm is verified in the simulation environment. The experimental results show that the comprehensive objective genetic algorithm can achieve good performance in the three dimensions of time, energy consumption and storage utilization.

References

1. He, J., Sun, G.: Multi-objective task scheduling based on cuckoo particle swarm optimization algorithm. Inf. Technol. **44**(5), 37–40 (2020)
2. Tian, Y., Huang, Z., Zhang, Y.: A survey of task scheduling methods in cloud computing environment. Comput. Eng. Appl. **57**(2), 1–11 (2021)

3. Wang, Q.: Application of meta-heuristic algorithm in discrete location selection. Nanjing University of Aeronautics and Astronautics (2010)
4. Zhang, M., Li, H., Liu, L., et al.: An adaptive multi-objective evolutionary algorithm for constrained workflow scheduling in clouds. Distrib. Parallel Databases **36**(2), 339–368 (2018)
5. Yuan, H., Bi, J., Tan, W., et al.: TTSA: an effective scheduling approach for delay bounded tasks in hybrid clouds. IEEE Trans. Cybern. **47**(11), 3658–3668 (2016)
6. Krishnaveni, H., Sinthu Janita Prakash, V.: Execution time based sufferage algorithm for static task scheduling in cloud. In: Peter, J.D., Alavi, A.H., Javadi, B. (eds.) Advances in Big Data and Cloud Computing. AISC, vol. 750, pp. 61–70. Springer, Singapore (2019). https://doi.org/10.1007/978-981-13-1882-5_5
7. Shishido, H.Y., Estrella, J.C., Toledo, C.F.M., et al.: Genetic-based algorithms applied to a workflow scheduling algorithm with security and deadline constraints in clouds. Comput. Electr. Eng. **69**, 378–394 (2018)
8. Gomathi, B., Krishnasamy, K., Balaji, B.S.: Epsilon-fuzzy dominance sort-based composite discrete artificial bee colony optimisation for multi-objective cloud task scheduling problem. Int. J. Bus. Intell. Data Min. **13**(1–3), 247–266 (2018)
9. Kaur, M., Kadam, S.: A novel multi-objective bacteria foraging optimization algorithm (MOBFOA) for multi-objective scheduling. Appl. Soft Comput. **66**, 183–195 (2018)
10. Huang, W., Xin, F., Huang, Y.: Multi-objective task scheduling in cloud computing based on chaotic cat swarm algorithm. Microelectron. Comput. **36**(6), 55–59 (2019)
11. Li, H.: Cloud computing task scheduling strategy based on improved moth optimization algorithm. J. Taiyuan Univ. (Nat. Sci. Ed.) **38**(1), 61–67 (2020)
12. Chen, X., et al.: Augmented queue-based transmission and transcoding optimization for livecast services based on cloud-edge-crowd integration. IEEE Trans. Circuits Syst. Video Technol. **31**(11), 4470–4484 (2020)
13. He, J.-Y., Sun, Q.-K.: Cuckoo particle swarm optimization algorithm for multi-objective task scheduling. Inf. Technol. **44**(5), 37–40 (2020)
14. Wang, L., Wu, C., Fan, W.: A review of resource allocation and task scheduling optimization for edge computing. J. Syst. Simul. **33**(3), 509 (2021)
15. Zhao, X., Zhao, Y., Li, B., et al.: A delay- and energy-aware approach to edge server placement. Comput. Eng. (2021)
16. Tian, J.J., Huang, Z., Zhang, Y.: A review of task scheduling methods for cloud computing environments. Comput. Eng. Appl. **57**(2), 1–11 (2021)
17. Nardini, G., Stea, G., Virdis, A.: A low-latency and reliable multihop D2D transmissions scheduling algorithm for guaranteed message dissemination. Ad Hoc Netw. **126**, 102755 (2022)
18. Priya, V., Kumar, C.S., Kannan, R.: Resource scheduling algorithm with load balancing for cloud service provisioning. Appl. Soft Comput. **76**, 416–424 (2019)
19. Lin, Y., Song, H., Ke, F., et al.: Optimal caching scheme in D2D networks with multiple robot helpers. Comput. Commun. **181**, 132–142 (2022)
20. Zhao, H., Bai, K., Cui, B., Han, L., Ma, Y.: Research on the key path of enterprise-level data warehouse construction based on DAMT. J. Jiangxi Normal Univ. (Nat. Sci. Ed.) **42**(06), 634–638 (2018). https://doi.org/10.16357/j.cnki.issn1000-5862.2018.06.15

Multi-objective Computation Offloading in MEC-Empowered Smart Warehousing

Liangfei Yang[1,2], Kai Peng[1,2,3(✉)], and Bohai Zhao[1,2]

[1] Huaqiao University, Quanzhou, China
[2] State Key Laboratory for Novel Software Technology, Nanjing University, Nanjing, People's Republic of China
[3] Sincetech (Fujian) Technology Co., Ltd., Quanzhou, China
kai.peng@hqu.edu.cn

Abstract. As a typical application of the Industrial Internet of Things (IIoT), smart warehousing has attracted widespread attention. In addition, smart warehousing is regarded as a key part of logistics and supply chain management. The main idea of smart wareshousing is to deploy a large number of smart devices (SDs) to collect large amounts of data for improving the efficiency of digital management. However, it is difficult for SDs to process large amounts of data due to their limited computing capacity, meanwhile, traditional cloud-based smart warehousing paradigm often suffers from high latency disadvantage. Fortunately, mobile edge computing (MEC) can make up for the above shortcoming. Nevertheless, it is challenge to effectively integrate edge computing and smart warehousing. In view of this, we investigate the computation offloading problem in MEC-empowered smart warehousing, and propose an intelligent computation offloading algorithm to optimize time consumption and energy consumption of SDs as well as the resource utilization of the edge server cluster in this paper. Finally, we conduct several group of experiments to prove the effectiveness of our proposed method, and the results indicate that our method outperforms the other comparison methods in the given optimization objectives.

Keywords: MEC · Computation Offloading · Smart Warehousing

This work is supported by the National Science Foundation of China under Grant No. 61902133, the Fundamental Research Funds for the Central Universities under Grant No. ZQN-817, Quanzhou Science and Technology Project under Grant No. 2020C050R, China Postdoctoral Science Foundation under Grant No. 2022M710700.

1   Introduction

The implementation of the Industrial Internet of Things (IIoT), which combines intelligence, data sharing, and more extensive computerization [1], has profoundly changed the way of living and working [2,3]. As a symbol of the IIoT, smart warehousing is proposed. Smart warehousing is an integrated hyperconnected platform which highly relies on the combination of intelligent devices and traditional industrial facilities.

Additionally, smart warehousing is a space to store goods for different fields, which aims to increase the overall intelligence, automation and integration of the warehouse. In addition, smart warehousing is a traceability and unmanned place when performing the operation of purchase, inbound, and outbound [4]. Smart devices (SDs) such as Automated Guided Vehicle (AGVs) and sensors are deployed in corresponding areas to control and manage the entire process of different segments in the warehouse. The maximum efficiency of the warehouse is guaranteed due to the participation of SDs [5]. Nevertheless, SDs have to process huge amount of digital data during the whole process [6,7]. However, due to the limited computing capacity of SDs, especially for the limited battery capacity, their efficiency will be greatly reduced when the amount of data becomes very large [8,9].

Fortunately, mobile edge computing (MEC) is regarded as one of the promising solutions to address the above shortcoming. MEC provides service by deploying ESs around SDs in smart warehousing. As an effective method to extend the computing capacity of SD, computation offloading has been extensively studied [10,11]. A large amount of data generated by SDs are offloaded to the ES, which can effectively provide fast and high-quality services for warehousing.

On the other hand, real-time information processing is very important for smart warehousing system. In another word, untimely cargo information adversely affects the entire warehouse management system [12]. And therefore, the optimization of time consumption in MEC-enabled smart warehousing is a critical issue. In addition, the computing resources of ES is usually characterized as limited, and how to use the limited resources to process more cargo information for high-efficiency warehouse is becoming critical. In view of this, we investigate the computation offloading in MEC-empowered smart warehousing. The main contributions of this paper can be concluded as the following points.

- We take into account the time consumption and energy consumption of SDs and the resource utilization of the ES cluster as the objectives in such a system. And we establish corresponding mode for the above objectives.
- A computation offloading algorithm called multi-objective optimization in smart warehousing (MOSW) is proposed based upon the traditional genetic algorithm, aiming at obtaining an appropriate offloading strategy.
- Finally, we conduct comprehensive experimental to verify the validity of our proposed method. The experimental results and analysis show that MOSW outperforms comparison methods under different situations.

The remainder of this paper is laid out as follows. Section 2 illustrates related work. Section 3 presents the model for multi-objective optimization in MEC-empowered smart warehousing scenario. Then, the proposed algorithm is illustrated in Sect. 4. Section 5 introduces experiments under different scenarios and the analysis of the results. Finally, we describe conclusion and our future work.

2 Related Work

In this part, we review the existing research from the perspectives of computation offloading in IIoT and computation offloading for MEC.

Computation offloading in IIoT. There has been extensive research on computation offloading in IIoT. Aiming at solving the problem of resource allocation and computation offloading, a task offloading method was proposed in [13]. This method introduced reinforcement learning to achieve an optimal binary computation offloading decision, which effectively reduced the computational cost and delay in IIoT scenarios. The multi-hop computation offloading problem was studied in [14], they proposed two distributed algorithms to provide stable performance gains for IIoT. Considering the high requirements of IIoT in terms of time and energy consumption, Chen et al. [15] focused on an energy-optimized non-static computation offloading program in fog computing scenarios with the goal of reducing energy cost. Similarly, Ren et al. [16] investigated a deep learning approach to minimize system energy consumption across multiple IIoT devices and multiple fog access points.

Computation Offloading for MEC. The concept of computation offloading is to migrate computing tasks generated by SDs to edge nodes. Computation offloading in MEC has been studied, either aims to optimize the delay [17,18], or energy consumption [19,20] or optimize the above two objectives jointly [21,22] . The time minimization problem was studied in a MEC system consisting of mobile users and heterogeneous ESs [17]. The optimal offloading node was selected by Markov decision process and the minimum offloading time was finally obtained. Wu et al. [18] studied an online method based on quality of service and real-time prediction of user trajectory aiming at minimizing response time of ES while considering user mobility. Wang et al. [19] researched the selective migration strategy problem by ARIMA-BP model with the aim of minimizing energy consumption of mobile devices, while meeting latency constraints. The ARIMA-BP model was used to estimate the computing power of the edge cloud. Zhang et al. [20] investigated the energy-saving computation offloading problem of MEC in 5G heterogeneous networks, aiming at minimizing the energy consumption of the MEC system. Tao et al. [21] studied a low-complexity sorting method to solve the multi-objective resource assignment issue. Finally, the joint optimization of task delay and device energy consumption is obtained. Wang et al. [22] studied the energy minimization optimization problem in MEC. They applied the Karush-Kuhn-Tucker to solve this problem and proposed a task offloading scheme to tradeoff time and energy consumption.

Different from previous studies, we study the computation offloading problem in MEC-empowered smart warehousing. And we consider both SDs and the server cluster with the aims of improving the overall service quality of smart warehousing. For one thing, time and energy consumption are taking into consideration to meet real-time applications requirements. For another, the resource utilization is considered to improve the system management efficiency. Meanwhile, an intelligent offloading method is leveraged.

3   System Model and Problem Formulation

In this part, the system model of MEC-empowered smart warehousing is illustrated, where the system model consists of time consumption, energy consumption model and resource utilization model, followed by the multi-objective optimization problem.

3.1   System Model

As illustrated in Fig. 1, our proposed system model of computation offloading in MEC-empowered smart warehousing is presented. In this system, AGVs and sensors are regarded as SDs to deliver and identify cargos. SDs in the warehouse are labeled as $ITD = \{i_1, i_2, i_3, \ldots, i_n\}$. The collection of ESs are deployed around SDs which is represented as $ES = \{es_1, es_2, es_3, \ldots, es_m\}$. The data center has more computing resources than ES but which is far from SDs.

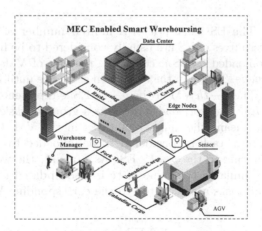

Fig. 1. An MEC-Enabled Smart Warehousing Architecture.

There are different offloading strategies for SDs. And choosing an appropriate offloading strategy is an important step to achieve multi-objective optimization. It is supposed that the offloading strategy of the $j - th$ task of the $i - th$ SD is denoted as S_i^j. The tasks of SDs are assigned to the local, ES and data center according to the offloading strategy. These different offloading strategies are denoted as L, S, R, respectively.

$$\begin{cases} S_i^j = L & \text{The task is executed locally,} \\ S_i^j = S & \text{if } S_i^j \text{ is offloaded to the ES,} \\ S_i^j = R & \text{if } S_i^j \text{ is offloaded to the data center.} \end{cases} \quad (1)$$

3.2   Time Consumption Model

The total time consumption of SDs consists of three parts, including execution time TD_e, waiting time TD_w and transmission time TD_t.

Executing Time. Tasks are executed on the virtual machines (VMs) and the execution time is generated. Execution time is related to task workload and frequency of different SDs which is expressed as

$$TD_e(S_i^j) = \begin{cases} \frac{tw_{i,j}}{f_m}, & S_i^j = L, \\ \frac{tw_{i,j}}{f_e}, & S_i^j = S, \\ \frac{tw_{i,j}}{f_c}, & S_i^j = R, \end{cases} \quad (2)$$

where $tw_{i,j}$ represents the task workload. The f_m represents the computing frequency of SDs, f_e represents the computing frequency of ES, and f_c represents the computing frequency of data center.

Waiting Time. The ES usually uses a limited number of VMs to provide resources, so the resources of ES are usually considered to be limited. When the number of tasks offloaded to ES exceeds the number of VMs, tasks $tw_{i,j}$ will join the waiting queue. Task join the execution sequence until ES has computed the previous task. The $a - th$ VM of the $b - th$ ES is represented by a two-tuple $v_{b,a} = (workload, tc)$. The workload represents a group of tasks workload of the $a - th$ VM and tc means the number of tasks in the VM. Corresponding to the migration strategy, task is considered to be offloaded to the VM with the smallest occupancy rate in the $p - th$ ES. As a result, the workload increases $tw_{i,j}$ on its basis. Similarly, the value of tc is also updated to tc+1. Loop the above steps until all tasks are allocated to the corresponding VM. And TD_w is expressed as

$$TD_w(S_i^j) = \sum_{i=1}^{N} \sum_{j=1}^{|tw_i|} TD_e(p(S_i^j)) \cdot \varepsilon_i^j, \quad (3)$$

where ε_i^j is to ensure whether $tw_{i,j}$ is assigned to the waiting queue, and the $TD_e(p(S_i^j))$ means the execution time of previous task.

Transmission Time. The transmission time between the SDs and ESs or data center is relevant to destination of task offload. If a task is assigned to execute locally, its transmission time is zero. And transmission time TD_t is expressed as

$$TD_t(S_i^j) = \begin{cases} 0, & S_i^j = L, \\ \frac{tw_{i,j}}{B_e}, & S_i^j = S, \\ \frac{tw_{i,j}}{B_c}, & S_i^j = R, \end{cases} \tag{4}$$

where B_e and B_c represent the bandwidth of the ESs and the data center, respectively.

Total Time Consumption. In summary, $TD^{(total)}(S)$ is used to represent the total time of the SDs, which can be expressed by

$$TD^{(total)}(S) = \sum_{i=1}^{N} \sum_{j=1}^{|tw_i|} (TD_e(S_i^j) + TD_w(S_i^j) + TD_t(S_i^j)). \tag{5}$$

3.3 Energy Consumption Model

Energy consumption is positively correlated with time consumption, corresponds to time consumption, energy consumption of SDs consist of execution energy consumption EC_e, waiting energy consumption EC_w and transmission energy consumption EC_t. The total energy consumption of SDs is shown below.

$$EC^{(total)}(S) = \sum_{i=1}^{N} \sum_{j=1}^{|tk_i|} (EC_e(S_i^j) + EC_w(S_i^j) + EC_t(S_i^j)). \tag{6}$$

3.4 Resource Utilization Model

In this paper, resource utilization is a key index for judging the performance of the ES cluster. When ESs process tasks from SDs, the resources of VMs in ESs are consumed. The value of resource utilization is obtained by the ratio of the used resources to the total resources. Utilized resources and total resources are represented by active VMs instances and VMs instances, respectively. The total number of VM instances of the $k-th$ ES is expressed as V_k. The resource utilization of ESs is as follows.

$$S_k = \frac{1}{V_k} \cdot \sum_{w=1}^{W} \sum_{m=1}^{M} p_{m,n} \cdot q_{m,n}^k, \tag{7}$$

where $p_{m,n}$ represents the number of VMs instances corresponding to s_i^j and $q_{m,n}^k$ is to judge whether the computing task is run on the kth ES. Therefore, the number of ESs performing tasks in this system be expressed as

$$PE = \sum_{s=1}^{m} O_k, \tag{8}$$

and the resource utilization of the ES cluster can be expressed as

$$AV(S) = \frac{1}{PE} \sum_{s=1}^{m} S_k. \tag{9}$$

3.5   Problem Formulation

We concentrate on minimizing the time consumption and energy consumption of SDs and the resource utilization of the ES cluster in this paper. subsequently, optimization goals are established. It is expressed as

$$\text{Min}\{\text{TD(S)}\}, \text{Min}\{\text{EC(S)}\}, \text{Max}\{\text{AV(S)}\} \tag{10}$$

$$TD^{(total)}(S) < deadline \tag{11}$$

Equation (11) indicates that the total time consumption of SD cannot exceed the set deadline.

4   Algorithm Design

In this part, we propose a multi-objective optimization genetic algorithm called multi-objective optimization in smart warehousing. MOSW has the advantages of traditional multi-objective genetic algorithms. On the one hand, MOSW divides individuals into several frontiers and MOSW does not rely on Pareto dominance but uses a scalarizing function. On the other hand, MOSW adopts the weight vector to maintain the diversity of the Pareto front (PF). Moreover, some traditional algorithms only consider ideal points as reference points in the fitness function, MOSW considers both the utopia point p^i and nadir point p^u at the same time, so that can be closer to PF.

The following introduces the main steps of MOSW. First of all, coding computation offloading strategies. Secondly, initialize the first generation population pop^f. Thirdly, the new generation population pop^n is obtained through crossover and mutation steps. Afterwards, populations are sorted by achievement scalarizing function (ASF) and use tournament selection to select next populations $pop^{(f+1)}$. Finally, SAW and MCDM are used for selecting optimal individual in the PF.

4.1   Encoding

In this part, the chromosomes of individuals in the population represent different computation offloading strategies for running applications in SDs. As shown in Fig. 2, the gene sequence in the chromosome is composed of $(0, 1, ..., S + 1)$. Different genes represent different ways of task offloading. And 0 means that the computing task is performed locally and S+1 represents that the task is migrated to the data center.

Fig. 2. Gene encoding.

4.2   Initialization

The first thing that a genetic algorithm does is perform initialization work. Initialization including set the size of the population, the probability of crossing genes p_c, the probability of gene mutation p_m, total number of iterations I_{tot} and the generations of the current iteration I_{now} in MOSW. Finally, it is assumed that initial population is established randomly.

4.3   Crossover and Mutation

During the crossover of chromosomes, two selected parent chromosomes exchange partial genes to form a better offspring chromosome. The purpose of the crossover operation is to pass on the chromosome segments of the excellent individuals to the offspring. As shown in Fig. 3, we assume that an individual has five genes and the crossover operation of the two genes takes place. It is obvious that crossover operation occurs between 1 and 5, 3 and 6 at the same time. The exchange of gene fragments is equivalent to the relevant offloading strategy is altered.

The mutation operator acts on the entire population, and the mutation probability p_m ensures the number of chromosomes to be mutated. An instance of a mutation operation be seen in Fig. 4. The gene in the chromosome 2 is turned into 5 means that the tasks originally offloaded to the 2-ed ES will be offloaded to the 5-th ES now. The mutation operation is to maintain population diversity by modifying some genes in chromosomes. New offspring are formed after completing these two operations.

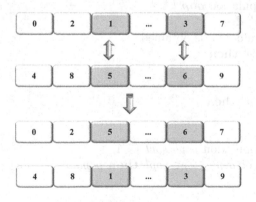

Fig. 3. Crossover operation.

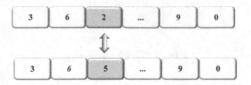

Fig. 4. Mutation operation.

4.4 ASF Sorting

In this subsection, we introduce the sorting process based on achievement scalarizing function. ASF is represented as the fitness function of this algorithm and is obtained by Chebyshev distance. The individuals in the population are divided into different frontiers by the value of ASF. This formula contains the objective function f and the reference point $q = \{q_1, q_2, ..., q_i\}$. The selection of reference points is generally considered to alternately select utopian points and nadir points. It is represented as

$$s = \max_{j \in 1,...,i} u_j(f - q_j) + p \sum_{j=1}^{i} (f - q_j) \tag{12}$$

where $u = \{u_1, u_2, ..., u_i\}$ represents vector of strictly positive weights. And p is regarded as augmentation coefficient. And augmentation term (the term $p \sum_{j=1}^{i} (f - q_j)$ in Eq. (12)) is set to ensure that minimizing the value of s can obtain a Pareto optimal solution. In Eq. (12), the reference points need to be updated when utopian points and nadir points are improved by an individual in offspring solutions.

Algorithm 1. ASF sorting

Input: initial population pop^f reference point p^i and p^u
Output: next population $pop^{(f+1)}$
 1: **while** $x \in pop^f$ **do**
 2:     The ASF value $x.n$ is obtained
 3:     **if** $x.n < x.p^i$ **then**
 4: $x.p^i \leftarrow x.n$
 5:     **end if**
 6:     **if** $x.n > x.p^u$ **then**
 7: $x.p^u \leftarrow x.n$
 8:     **end if**
 9:     rank the population pop^f $sort \leftarrow 1$
10:     **if** Number of($pop^{(f+1)}$)$< pop^f$ **then** $pop.sort \leftarrow sort$
11:     **end if**
12: $sort \leftarrow sort+1$
13: **end while**

4.5   Selection

Generally, each offspring have two parents. The parents are selected from the parent population through a tournament selection. In the parent population, all individuals are considered to have the same probability of being selected. Individuals with lower ASF values are regarded as the next parent population. Repeat the above operations until the next generation of population.

4.6   Optimal Selection by SAW and MCDM

When the number of iterations reaches the maximum iteration, the collection of Pareto frontiers is generated. It is necessary to choose the optimal individual among the population. And SAW [23] and MCDM [24] are regarded as an efficient method to select optimal solutions with higher speed and better convergence.

4.7   Method Overview

Algorithm 1 shows the detailed process of ASF sorting and Algorithm 2 demonstrates the steps of MOSW. The purpose of MOSW is to form an appropriate migration strategy to achieve the above-mentioned objective optimization. It is known that diverse chromosome represents different offloading strategies. Frist of all, the chromosomes of the population are initialized and called pop^f and total iterations called I_{tot}. Secondly, select two reference point, the nadir point and utopian points, respectively (Line 1). Then, perform ASF sorting to assign individuals to different fronts (Line 2). In Algorithm 1, we use ASF to divide the non-dominated solution set. The population is generated after the above steps are completed. Afterwards, select better individuals through the tournament selection, crossover and mutation operations to obtain the next generation (Lines 3-4). Calculate the three goals of the population separately by different formulas (Line 5-7). The population of 2N is selected as the population of N after the above operations (Line 8). Afterwards, evaluate population and update reference points including utopia points and nadir points, and perform the ASF sorting by Algorithm 1 (Lines 9-10). The population needs to be equal to the population size of P0. The population begins to iterate until it reaches the maximum number of iterations and obtain the collection of PF (Line 11).

5   Evaluation of Experimental Results

In this section, the superiority of MOSW is demonstrated by experiments under different conditions. Firstly, we introduce the experimental setting. Afterwards, experimental performance and analysis are shown.

Algorithm 2. MOSW

Input: The population pop^f and total number of iterations I_{tot}
Output: The best solution S
 1: Select the reference point p^i and p^u
 2: Perform ASF sorting algorithm by algorithm 1
 3: **while** $I_{now} < I_{tot}$ **do**
 4:     Execute tournament selection, crossover and mutation procedures to pop^f
        and structure a population pop^n with N
 5:     Time consumption is calculated by Equation (5)
 6:     Energy consumption is calculated by Equation (6)
 7:     Resource utilization is calculated by Equation (9)
 8:     $pop^t \leftarrow pop^n \bigcup pop^f$
 9:     Update reference points p^i, p^u
10:     Perform ASF sorting algorithm by algorithm 1
11:     Next population $pop^{(f+1)}$
12: **end while**
13: SAW and MCDM to select an optimal offloading strategy
14: **return** S

5.1 Experimental Setting

In our experiments, we set up several sets of experiments under different conditions to verify the superiority of MOSW. In multiple applications experiments, it assumes the number of applications is from 10 to 50 or 100 to 300, and the fixed number of SDs is 2. In multiple SDs experiments, the number of SDs is from 5 to 20 and each SD has 10 applications and the number of ESs is set to 5. More specific information about the experimental parameters is shown in Table 1.

Table 1. Parameters Setting

Parameter	Value
The active power of the smart device L_{v2d}	0.6 W
The idle power of the smart device L_{v2c}	0.01 W
The clock frequency of ESs	1800-2500 MHz
The clock frequency of data center	5000 MHz
The bandwidth between smart device and ES	300 kps
The bandwidth between ES and data center	200 kps
The maximum number of ESs	20
The population size	100
The maximum number of iterations	300

In order to highlight the superiority of MOSW in MEC-empowered smart warehousing. We introduce two comparison methods, namely, Benchmark and FCFS, which are shown as follows.

- **Benchmark** All applications are randomly migrated to ES cluster or data center. If VMs are not enough to handle applications, the new coming applications enter the waiting queue until the free VMs are released.
- **First Come First Service (FCFS)** All applications are offloaded in an orderly manner. More specifically, the first edge server handles the first application, the following applications are executed on the corresponding ES in order. Finally, the last one is executed by cloud.

The above experiments are all run based on JAVA language on a PC with 8 Intel Core i5-8250U 1.60 GHz processor and 8 GB RAM.

5.2 Experimental Evaluation and Discussion

We conduct rigorous and diverse comparative experiments to evaluate the performance of the three methods in terms of time and energy consumption of SDs and resource utilization of the ES cluster. Figure 5, 6 and 7 illustrate the experimental results.

5.3 Comparison of Time Consumption

The total time consumption is obtained by Eq. (5). Figure 5(a)–Fig. 5(c) shows the time consumption result of Benchmark, FCFS and MOSW under different conditions. Figure 5(a) reveals the comparison of time consumption with different numbers of SDs. In the case of different application numbers, the performance results of the three above-mentioned methods are indicated in Fig. 5(b) and Fig. 5(c). It can be observed that the time consumption increases with the number of SDs or applications from the experimental results. Therein, when the number of tasks becomes larger, the superiority of MOSW is more obvious under different conditions. Compared with the other algorithm, MOSW is superior in terms of time consumption because it has a more reasonable offloading strategy. Finally, we can conclude that MOSW is more suitable for time consumption optimization.

5.4 Comparison of Energy Consumption

The total energy consumption is obtained by Eq. (6). The positive correlation between energy consumption and time consumption has been shown in the model section. Their correlation also be reflected in the experimental results. Figure 6(a) reveals the comparison of energy consumption under different scales of SDs. And the performance results under different scales of applications of the three above-mentioned methods are shown in Fig. 6(b) and Fig. 6(c). It can be observed that the energy consumption increases with the number of SDs or applications.

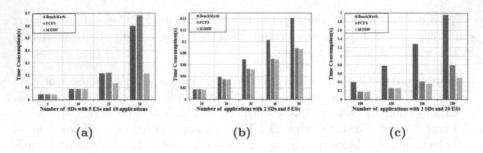

Fig. 5. Comparison of time consumption

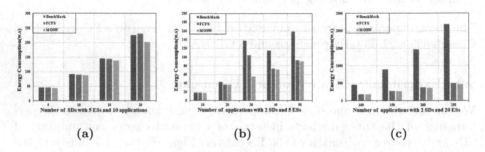

Fig. 6. Comparison of energy consumption

Therein, when the number of tasks becomes larger, the superiority of MOSW is more obvious. In summary, we can conclude that MOSW has advantages in energy optimization in various scenarios.

5.5 Comparison of Resource Utilization

The computing capacity of ESs is limited, and thus the resources should be fully utilized. The resource utilization is obtained by Eq. (9). Figure 7(a) reveals the comparison of resource utilization under different scales of SDs. In the case of different numbers of applications, the performance results of the three methods

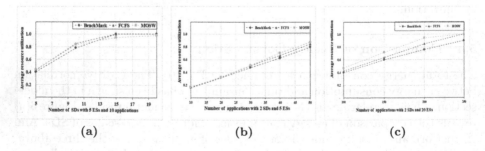

Fig. 7. Comparison of resource utilization

are indicated in Fig. 7(b) and Fig. 7(c). In the comparison results, MOSW has different degrees of optimization effect compared with the other two methods under different scenarios. Especially when the workload is heavy, the optimization effect is better. In conclusion, MOSW is more effective compared with other comparison methods.

6   Conclusion

The combination of MEC and warehouse provides a solution for realizing smart warehousing. In this paper, we have studied computation offloading for MEC-empowered smart warehousing, the purpose is to meet the demands of latency-sensitive applications with limited resources, we consider multiple optimization objectives, namely, time consumption and energy consumption of SD and resource utilization of ESs. Subsequently, a multi-objective optimization model is established and a computation offloading algorithm is proposed. Our proposed algorithm trades off three optimization objectives to get the optimization effect. Adequate results indicate that the proposed method has superior performance in terms of pre-optimization goals compared to the comparative methods. In future work, we will utilize deep learning to address the multi-objective optimization problem.

References

1. Wu, Y., Dai, H., Wang, H.: Convergence of blockchain and edge computing for secure and scalable IIoT critical infrastructures in industry 4.0. IEEE Internet Things J. **8**, 2300–2317 (2021)
2. Xu, X., Tian, H., Zhang, X., Qi, L., He, Q., Dou, W.: DisCOV: distributed COVID-19 detection on x-ray images with edge-cloud collaboration. IEEE Trans. Serv. Comput. **15**, 1206–1219 (2022)
3. Peng, K., Huang, H., Zhao, B., Jolfaei, A., Xu, X., Bilal, M.: Intelligent computation offloading and resource allocation in IIoT with end-edge-cloud computing using nsga-iii. IEEE Trans. Netw. Sci. Eng. 1–15 (2022). https://doi.org/10.1109/TNSE.2022.3155490
4. Liu, Y., Su, Z., Wang, Y.: Energy-efficient and physical layer secure computation offloading in blockchain-empowered internet of things. IEEE Internet Things J. (2022)
5. Peng, G., Wu, H., Wu, H., Wolter, K.: Constrained multiobjective optimization for IoT-enabled computation offloading in collaborative edge and cloud computing. IEEE Internet Things J. **8**, 13723–13736 (2021)
6. Qu, G., Wu, H., Li, R., Jiao, P.: Dmro: a deep meta reinforcement learning-based task offloading framework for edge-cloud computing. IEEE Trans. Netw. Serv. Manage. **18**(3), 3448–3459 (2021)
7. Kekana, P., Bakama, E.M., Mukwakungu, S.C., Sukdeo, N.: The impact of smart-warehousing on a local foodservice equipment-company's external customers. In: 2020 IEEE International Conference on Industrial Engineering and Engineering Management (IEEM), pp. 771–775 (2020)

8. Wang, K., Ding, Z., So, D.K.C., Karagiannidis, G.K.: Stackelberg game of energy consumption and latency in MEC systems with NOMA. IEEE Trans. Commun. **69**, 2191–2206 (2021)
9. Wu, H., Wolter, K., Jiao, P., Deng, Y., Zhao, Y., Xu, M.: Eedto: an energy-efficient dynamic task offloading algorithm for blockchain-enabled IoT-edge-cloud orchestrated computing. IEEE Internet Things J. **8**, 2163–2176 (2021)
10. Xu, X., et al.: Edge content caching with deep spatiotemporal residual network for IoV in smart city. ACM Trans. Sens. Networks **17**, 29:1–29:33 (2021)
11. Peng, K., Huang, H., Bilal, M., Xu, X.: Distributed incentives for intelligent offloading and resource allocation in digital twin driven smart industry. IEEE Trans. Ind. Inf. (2022)
12. Wu, H., Sun, Y., Wolter, K.: Energy-efficient decision making for mobile cloud offloading. IEEE Trans. Cloud Comput. **8**(2), 570–584 (2018)
13. Hossain, M.S., Nwakanma, C.I., Lee, J.M., Kim, D.S.: Edge computational task offloading scheme using reinforcement learning for IIoT scenario. ICT Express **6**, 291–299 (2020)
14. Hong, Z., Chen, W., Huang, H., Guo, S., Zheng, Z.: Multi-hop cooperative computation offloading for industrial IoT-edge-cloud computing environments. IEEE Trans. Parallel Distrib. Syst. **30**, 2759–2774 (2019)
15. Chen, S., Zheng, Y., feng Lu, W., Varadarajan, V., Wang, K.: Energy-optimal dynamic computation offloading for industrial IoT in fog computing. IEEE Trans. Green Commun. Netw. **4**, 566–576 (2020)
16. Ren, Y., Sun, Y., Peng, M.: Deep reinforcement learning based computation offloading in fog enabled industrial internet of things. IEEE Trans. Industr. Inf. **17**, 4978–4987 (2021)
17. Yang, G., Hou, L., He, X., He, D., Chan, S., Guizani, M.: Offloading time optimization via markov decision process in mobile-edge computing. IEEE Internet Things J. **8**, 2483–2493 (2021)
18. Wu, C., Peng, Q., Xia, Y., Lee, J.: Mobility-aware tasks offloading in mobile edge computing environment. In: 2019 7th International Symposium on Computing and Networking (CANDAR), pp. 204–210 (2019)
19. Zhao, M., Zhou, K.: Selective offloading by exploiting ARIMA-BP for energy optimization in mobile edge computing networks. Algorithms **12**, 48 (2019)
20. Zhang, K., et al.: Energy-efficient offloading for mobile edge computing in 5g heterogeneous networks. IEEE Access **4**, 5896–5907 (2016)
21. Tao, X., Ota, K., Dong, M., Qi, H., Li, K.: Performance guaranteed computation offloading for mobile-edge cloud computing. IEEE Wireless Commun. Lett. **6**, 774–777 (2017)
22. Xu, X., et al.: Game theory for distributed IoV task offloading with fuzzy neural network in edge computing. IEEE Trans. Fuzzy Syst. (2022)
23. Afshari, A., Mojahed, M., Yusuff, R.M.: Simple additive weighting approach to personnel selection problem (2010)
24. Aruldoss, M., Lakshmi, T.M., Venkatesan, V.P.: A survey on multi criteria decision making methods and its applications (2013)

A Community Discovery Algorithm Using Increment of Modularity to Optimize the Label Propagation Process

Xinqi Xu$^{(\boxtimes)}$ (iD) and Xiaoyan Zheng

Tianjin University of Technology and Education, Tianjing 300222, China
xxq_0414@163.com

Abstract. Due to the strong randomness of label selection, the label propagation algorithm makes the community results unstable. Especially in asynchronous updates, the final results are quite different due to the different order of selecting listeners. This paper proposes a community discovery algorithm using increment of modularity to optimize the label propagation process. In the process of label propagation, the increment of modularity is introduced to ensure that the increment of modularity is positive in each update. At the same time, the selection of popular nodes in traditional label propagation algorithms is retained. Combining these two methods, each node selection improve the division of the community and reduce the possibility of poor results due to asynchronous updates. The algorithm is verified in real network, and the results show that the algorithm is feasible and effective.

Keywords: Community detection · Label propagation · Modularity · Optimization

1 Introduction

A complex network is an abstraction of a complex system. In a complex network, nodes represent individuals in a complex system, and edges between nodes represent connections between individuals according to specific rules. There are also some statistical characteristics commonly found in complex networks, such as the "scale-free characteristic" [1], which reflects the characteristics of network nodes obeying a power-law distribution, the "small-world" [2], which reflects the characteristics of short path length and high clustering coefficient of the network. As well as the "community structure" that reflects the tight connections between nodes in the same community and the sparse connections between nodes in different communities. It is ubiquitous in complex networks [3].

With the rapid development of computer and information technology, especially the emergence of social networks, people are divided into countless small groups for various reasons. Meanwhile, the study of community structure has become increasingly valuable. It can help people to extract useful association

© ICST Institute for Computer Sciences, Social Informatics and Telecommunications Engineering 2023
Published by Springer Nature Switzerland AG 2023. All Rights Reserved
Y. Cao and X. Shao (Eds.): MONAMI 2022, LNICST 474, pp. 245–252, 2023.
https://doi.org/10.1007/978-3-031-32443-7_17

information from known social networks in complex networks. Therefore, community discovery has more and more applications in scientific research, commercial promotion, public safety and other fields. More and more researchers are devoted to related fields.

The rest of the paper is arranged as follows: Section 2 discusses the preparatory work related to the algorithm; Sect. 3 describes how the increment of modularity helps labels to spread better; Sect. 4 verifies the feasibility of the algorithm in real networks; Finally, the full text is summarized. and discuss the next stage of work.

2   Related Work

After years of exploration, researchers have proposed many classic community discovery algorithms.

The Label Propagation Algorithm (LPA) was proposed by Zhu et al. [4] in 2002, which uses the relationship between samples to build a relational complete graph model. In 2007, Raghavan et al. [5] first proposed the application of LPA to community discovery, which is referred to as the RAK algorithm for short. The algorithm will give each node a unique label, select the most popular label to record in the iterative process, and finally the nodes with the same label will be combined into the same community.

Since most of the communities in the real network are not independent of each other, the study of overlapping communities becomes very important. Gregory [6] extended the RAK algorithm. The algorithm allows each node to retain multiple labels, so that the node can select multiple different communities to discover overlapping community structures. However, as the number of iterations increases, the performance decreases significantly, which is not suitable for today's huge dataset environment. Xie et al. [7] proposed the SLPA algorithm, which retains the charac-teristics of low complexity and high efficiency of the LPA algorithm. Label all nodes with different labels, scan all labels of the nodes, the record with the most occurrences is the candidate label, the label with the most occurrence of the candidate label is the node community name, and the final community division is obtained after multiple traversals.

Modularity, as an important indicator for evaluating community structure, has been applied in label propagation by many scholars. In order to avoid all nodes in LPA selecting the same community, Barber et al. [8] proposed a modularity-specialized label propagation algorithm (LPAm), which is a constraint-based LPA monitoring network community. A variable is introduced to maximize the modularity value of the community. The community discovery problem is transformed into a solution problem of objective function optimization. On the basis of the number of connected vertices with the same label, an objective function H is defined, and the LPA algorithm is used to find the local optimal value of the H function. Qiao et al. [9] proposed an overlapping community detection algorithm in complex network big data, based on the idea of modularity clustering, graph computing and optimal modularity. A balanced binary tree is used to index the increment of modularity to alleviate the impact of multiple modularity computations on the performance of the algorithm. Leung et al. [10] also pointed out that the module maximization method is not a scale-free interval measure method, and it is not feasible to detect communities only by relying on it. Therefore, modularity is generally not used as the final objective function, but it can still help us improve the quality of the found community structure.

Through numerous algorithm studies, we found that the LPA algorithm has low complexity and can be well adapted to the monitoring of large-scale communities. It does not require optimization of a predefined objective function, nor does it require prior information about the number and size of communities, and there is no limit to the size of communities. However, due to the uncertainty of label selection, the final community division result is unstable. This paper chooses the community structure evaluation index - modularity, to help nodes select labels. It avoids the shortcomings of modularity as an objective function, and at the same time, it can help nodes choose labels that are beneficial to themselves as much as possible. The increment of modularity after each label propagation is kept positive, so that each node label selection can improve the overall community division and reduce the possibility of poor results due to updates.

3   Description of the Proposed Algorithm

This chapter introduces the specific calculation formula of the increment of modularity, describes the community discovery algorithm using increment of modularity to optimize the label propagation process (IMO-LPA) in detail, and finally verifies that the time complexity of algorithm is close to linear.

3.1   The Increment of Modularity

Modularity [11] is an important indicator for calculating community accuracy. The specific formula is as follows:

$$Q = \sum_{c=1}^{n_c}(\frac{l_c}{m} - (\frac{d_c}{2m})^2)$$

(1)

where, m is the total number of edges in the network, n_c is the number of communities, l_c is the total number of edges in community c, and d_c is the sum of the degrees of all nodes in community c.

If the node i in the community c_2 is allowed to enter the community c_1, that is, the increment of modularity generated by the node i selecting the label represented by the community c_1

$$Q_{before} = \frac{l_{c_1}}{m} - (\frac{d_{c_1}}{2m})^2 + \frac{l_{c_2}}{m} - (\frac{d_{c_2}}{2m})^2$$

(2)

$$Q_{after} = \frac{l_{c_1} + k_{i\_c_1}}{m} - (\frac{d_{c_1} + k_i}{2m})^2 + \frac{l_{c_2} + k_{i\_c_2}}{m} - (\frac{d_{c_2} - k_i}{2m})^2 \qquad (3)$$

Formula (3)–(2) can obtain formula (4):

$$\Delta Q = \frac{1}{m} [k_{i\_c_1} - k_{i\_c_2} - \frac{k_i(d_{c_1} - d_{c_2} + k_i)}{2m}] \qquad (4)$$

where, $k_{i\_c_1}$ represents the number of connecting edges between node i and nodes in community c_1. $k_{i\_c_2}$ represents the number of connecting edges with the nodes in the community c_2. If there is only node i itself in the community c_2, then $k_{i\_c_2} = 0$.

3.2 IMO-LPA Algorithm

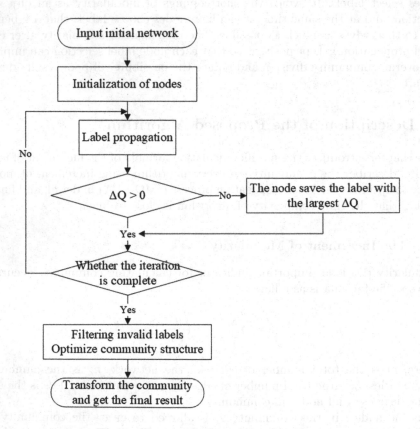

Fig. 1. The specific flow of the algorithm

Modularity, also known as modularity metric, characterizes the accuracy of the division of node communities in the network. The general basic idea of using modularity for community division is: If the connection strength between nodes in a subgraph of a network is much greater than the connection strength between nodes in the subgraph under random division of the network, then the subgraph can be considered as a community of the network. The increment of modularity is the increase of the calculated modularity. If two nodes are in the same community and have a positive effect on the entire community structure, then the increment of modularity is positive. Similarly, the closer the connection between the two nodes is, the greater the increment of modularity will be. Due to the high randomness of label propagation, generally speaking, the higher the influence of the label, the faster the propagation, but there are a large number of random selections in the selection process, especially in the initial stage. At this time, the increment of modularity can be added to help nodes select more suitable nodes for message interaction. The specific process is as Fig 1:

3.3 Complexity Analysis

We perform a time complexity analysis of the IMO-LPA algorithm. The time complexity of initializing nodes and communities is $O(N)$. Each node will act as a listener, and the number of iterations is t_0, and the sounding nodes are the nodes of the listener, that is, the node degree $k_{listener}$ of the listener. For the calculation of the increment of modularity, at least $O(1)$, the most popular labels meet the judgment conditions; at most $O(k_{listener})$, then each label has the same weight. The final label optimization, if the final number of communities obtained is $N_{community}$, the time complexity is $O(NN_{community})$. The time complexity is $O((2+t_0 k_{listener}^2 + N_{community})N)$. In general, t_0 and $N_{community}$ tend to a fixed value, and $k_{listener}$ is much smaller than the number of nodes N, so the time complexity of the algorithm tends to be linear.

4 Experiments

4.1 Experiment Preparation

This paper also compares the IMO-LPA algorithm in four different real networks and one artificial synthetic network. The information and parameters of the experimental network are shown in Table 1.

Table 1. General information of the real network.

Network	Description	Nodes	Edges
Dolphins [12]	Lusseau's dolphins	62	159
Polbooks [13]	Amazon's american political book	105	441
Football [3]	American College football union	115	616
Powergrid [1]	The topology of the powergrid of the United States	4941	6594

The experiment will use two evaluation indicators to verify the community division results. For communities with accurate community division results, the Normalized Mutual Information (NMI) [14] can quantify the similarity between the generated algorithm partition community and the standard community, and measure the accuracy of the algorithm results. For communities without accurate division results, the overlapping modularity (Qov) [15,16] is used to help evaluate the merits of the division results. At the same time, Qov can also help us judge whether the impact of overlapping modularity on the algorithm is positive.

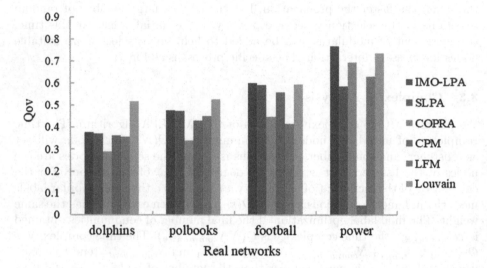

Fig. 2. Qov comparison experiment in real networks

4.2   Result Analysis

In this paper, a total of five classic algorithms and MIO-LPA algorithms are selected for comparison experiments, namely SLPA, COPRA, CPM [17], LFM [15] and Louvain [18]. As can be seen from Fig. 1, the IMO-LPA algorithm has the best modularity in the network football and power, and is slightly lower than the algorithm Louvain in the network dolphins and polbooks. Overall, the IMO-LOA algorithm outperforms most experimental algorithms in real networks Among the four real networks selected in the experiment, the network dolphins, polbooks and football all have accurate community division results. NMI is used for evaluation in these three networks. The evaluation results are shown in Fig. 2. It can be seen from the figure that the accuracy of the IMO-LPA algorithm is significantly higher than that of other algorithms. In general, the modularity of general real networks is close to 0.5, and the IMO-LPA algorithm is not the best in overlapping modularity, but has better accuracy. Therefore, it shows that the increment of modularity can indeed help the label to propagate better (Fig. 3).

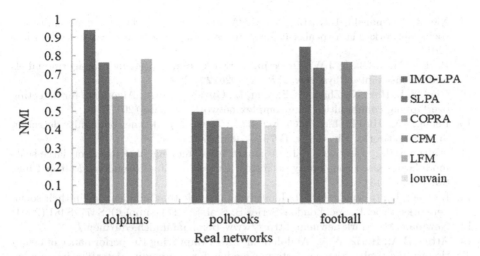

Fig. 3. NMI comparison experiment in real networks

5   Conclusion

Because the LPA algorithm has the characteristics of low complexity and high performance, it is more in line with the needs of today's huge data. However, because of the large amount of randomness in the process, the results of the algorithm are sometimes not as good as expected. In this paper, the increment of modularity is added to the label propagation process to help nodes select more reasonable labels and reduce the adverse effects of uncertainty. Experiments in real networks show that the algorithm increases the accuracy of the algorithm while retaining the advantages of the LPA algorithm.

Acknowledge. This work is supported by Tianjin Science and Technology Planning Project (Grant No. 64822KPXMRC00170), Science and Technology Think Tank Young Talent Program, China (Grant No. 64920220615ZZ07110153).

References

1. Watts, D.J., Strogatz, S.H.: Collective dynamics of 'small-world'networks. Nature **393**(6684), 440–442 (1998)
2. Barabási, A., Albert, R.: Emergence of scaling in random networks. Science **286**(5439), 509–512 (1999)
3. Girvan, M., Newman, M.E.J.: Community structure in social and biological networks. Proc. Natl. Acad. Sci. **99**(12), 7821–7826 (2002)
4. Zhu, X.: Learning from labeled and unlabeled data with label propagation. Technical report (2002)
5. Raghavan, U.N., Albert, R., Kumara, S.: Near linear time algorithm to detect community structures in large-scale networks. Phys. Rev. E **76**(3), 036106 (2007)
6. Gregory, S.: Finding overlapping communities in networks by label propagation. New J. Phys. **12**(10), 103018 (2010)

7. Xie, J., Szymanski, B.K., Liu, X.: SLPA: uncovering overlapping communities in social networks via a speaker-listener interaction dynamic process. arXiv e-prints (2011)
8. Barber, M.J., Clark, J.W.: Detecting network communities by propagating labels under constraints. Phys. Rev. E **80**(2), 026129 (2009)
9. Qiao, S.J., Han, N., Zhang, K.F., Zou, L., Gutierrez, L.A.: Algorithm for detecting overlapping communities from complex network big data (2017)
10. Leung, I.X., Hui, P., Lio, P., Crowcroft, J.: Towards real-time community detection in large networks. Phys. Rev. E **79**(6), 066107 (2009)
11. Waltman, L., Van Eck, N.J.: A smart local moving algorithm for large-scale modularity-based community detection. Eur. Phys. J. B. Condens. Matter Phys. **86**, 1–14 (2013)
12. Lusseau, D., Newman, M.E.J.: Identifying the role that animals play in their social networks. Proc. R. Soc. London. Series B: Biol. Sc. **271**(suppl_6), S477–S481 (2004)
13. Newman, M.: Mark newman. http://www-personal.umich.edu/mejn/
14. Attea, B.A., Hariz, W.A., Abdulhalim, M.F.: Improving the performance of evolutionary multi-objective co-clustering models for community detection in complex social networks. Swarm Evol. Comput. **26**, 137–156 (2016)
15. Lancichinetti, A., Fortunato, S., Kertész, J.: Detecting the overlapping and hierarchical community structure in complex networks. New J. Phys. **11**(3), 033015 (2009)
16. Nicosia, V., Mangioni, G., Carchiolo, V., Malgeri, M.: Extending the definition of modularity to directed graphs with overlapping communities. J. Stat. Mech: Theory Exp. **2009**(03), P03024 (2009)
17. Palla, G., Derényi, I., Farkas, I., Vicsek, T.: Uncovering the overlapping community structure of complex networks in nature and society. Nature **435**(7043), 814–818 (2005)
18. Blondel, V.D., Guillaume, J.L., Lambiotte, R., Lefebvre, E.: Fast unfolding of communities in large networks. J. Stat. Mech. Theory Exp. **2008**(10), P10008 (2008)

Mobile Networks and Management

Evaluating the Coverage of 5G Signals: Coupling Spatial Autocorrelation and 3D Sight Lines Based on GIS

Lei Wen[1], Hua Tan[1]([✉]), Weihong Li[2], Yang Liu[1], Guohua Dai[1], Xinzhang Yang[1], Yimeng Liu[1], Haitao Zhang[1], Tao Zhang[1], and Li Chen[1]

[1] Research Institute of China Telecom Corporation Limited, Guangzhou 510630, China
{wenlei,tanhua,liuyang8,yangxz11,liuym11,daiguoh,zhanghait,
zhangt33,chenl45}@chinatelecom.cn
[2] South China Normal University, Guangzhou 510631, China

Abstract. 5G communication network has been developed and applied in recent years, the researches on 5G communication network planning have become gradually sufficient. However, the previous researches on the coverage planning of 5G signals are mostly based on 2D spatial framework, for the constructed 5G communication network, there is still a research gap in the evaluation of the coverage of 5G signals in outdoor environment of modern cities from the perspective of 3D spatial framework. We selected several blocks from Shenzhen city as the study area. In this study, we conducted spatial autocorrelation analysis on the spatial distribution of 5G base stations in the study area, and found that the characteristic of the spatial distribution of 5G BSs illustrates a kind of random rather than aggregate or discrete. And, we established a 3D model of the buildings and 5G BSs distribution in the study area, combined with the height of the buildings and the construction height of the 5G BSs, the 3D sight lines of the 5G BSs to the road network represents the LOS service coverage of the 5G BSs to the road network. The value of the Global Moran's I approaches to 0, the coverage ratio of the roads in the study area is about 18.89%.

Keywords: 5G · GIS · Spatial autocorrelation · 3D sight lines

1 Introduction

To meet the demand of mobile communication network in the rapidly development of economy and science, fifth-generation mobile communication technology (5G) has been developed and applied in recent years. 5G, which with the characteristics of enhanced mobile broadband (eMBB), massive machine type of communication (mMTC), ultra-reliable and low latency communications (URLLC), can be widely applied in Internet of Things (IoT), artificial intelligence (AI), virtual reality (VR) and self-driving cars [1, 2]. 5G unmanned vehicles will be one of the most valuable application scenarios, which can provide safer and more efficient transportation services [3]. The coverage of 5G signals

© ICST Institute for Computer Sciences, Social Informatics and Telecommunications Engineering 2023
Published by Springer Nature Switzerland AG 2023. All Rights Reserved
Y. Cao and X. Shao (Eds.): MONAMI 2022, LNICST 474, pp. 255–264, 2023.
https://doi.org/10.1007/978-3-031-32443-7_18

to road networks in modern cities directly affects the realization of unmanned vehicles, meanwhile, it would characterize the coverage of 5G signals to urban outdoor area to a certain extent.

A high-frequency millimeter wave was adopted in 5G communication technology as a basic wireless network technology, which with the characteristic of huge amount of data carriage but over a short distance [4], so the effective coverage radius of most 5G base stations (BSs) are between 100 and 300 m [5, 6]. In modern cities, the high density of urban buildings limits the transmission of 5G signals, and building materials can almost isolate indoor and outdoor millimeter wave transmission signals [7], hence, in modern cities, densely buildings distribution is the main factor affecting the coverage of 5G signals, which will cause a penetration loss of 5G millimeter wave [8–10]. Attenuation of wireless communication signals during transmission is called the line-of-sight (LOS) effect [5, 11, 12]. To ensure the quality of service (QoS) of 5G network is sufficient, the LOS effect must be considered in the demand area of 5G communication network [13].

In recent years, with the commercial construction and usage of 5G communication network, the researches on 5G communication network planning have become gradually sufficient. For instance, Palizban et al. [7] used a computational geometry to plan an outdoor millimeter wave network in a dense city, Su et al. [14] used Voronoi tessellation to design the radio access level of 5G mobile networks for the placement of BSs, Ahamed et al. [15] proposed an updated cell architecture with six sectors and an advanced antenna system that provides better 5G coverage. As a valuable tool, geographic information system (GIS) was coupled in 5G communication network planning, Wang et al. [16] based on GIS to explicate the propagation of 5G signals in two-dimensional (2D) spatial framework.

Since the commercial construction and usage of 5G communication network in 2019, it has been planned and constructed for more than 3 years in China. However, the previous researches on the coverage planning of 5G signals are mostly based on 2D spatial framework, for the constructed 5G communication network, there is still a research gap in the evaluation of the coverage of 5G signals in outdoor environment of modern cities from the perspective of 3D spatial framework. Spatial autocorrelation analysis is an important approach to assess the extent of spatial aggregation for variables of interest characterized with global Moran's I index [17], which evaluates whether the pattern expressed is clustered, dispersed, or random. Based on GIS, we analyze the spatial distribution characteristic of 5G base stations with global Moran's I index, and simulate the coverage of 5G signals to the urban road network from the perspective of 3D spatial framework in view of the construction height of 5G BSs in the study area.

2 Study Area and Data

We selected several blocks from Shenzhen city as the study area (see Fig. 1). Shenzhen located in the south of Guangdong Province, China, adjacent to Hong Kong. Guangdong Province, located in the south of Chinese Mainland, is the province with the highest GDP in Chinese Mainland. As of the end of 2021, the GDP of Guangdong had exceeded 2 trillion US dollars, of which Shenzhen had exceeded 464.60 billion US dollars, which is the third city in Chinese Mainland after Shanghai (654.70 billion US dollars) and

Beijing (610.10 billion US dollars). The population of the city is 17 million. The study area of this paper was selected from downtown area of Shenzhen. The total area of the study area is approximately 2.78 km². Shenzhen is one of the cities with the largest scale of 5G communication network construction in Chinese Mainland.

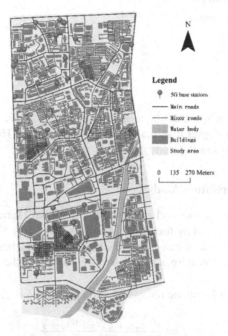

Fig. 1. Map of the study area.

According to the nature of land use, the study area is divided into building area, urban road area and water area. The total area of buildings in the study area is about 0.76 km², accounting for about 27% of the study area. The average height of buildings in the study area is about 33.30 m. In this study, we abstract the roads as vector lines. We classify the roads as main roads and minor roads according to the road width. The length of the main roads is about 18.16 km, and of the minor roads is about 68.22 km, the density of the road network in the study area is about 31.07 km/km². In addition, there is a section of river in the study area, covering an area of about 0.06 km².

We obtained the location and construction height of 5G BSs in the study area from Chinese telecom operators. There are 29 outdoor 5G BSs in the study area, of which 25 BSs were built at the top edge of the building and 4 BSs were erected on the ground, with the height of 4 m to 6 m. The average construction height of the 5G BSs in the study area is about 20.13 m. The data we used in this evaluation research listed in Table 1.

Table 1. Attributes of the data used for 5G signals evaluation in the case study.

Data	Source	Format	Geometry	Spatial reference
Existing 5G BSs	Chinese telecom operators	ESRI Shapefile	Point	GCS_WGS_1984
Buildings	Map world		Polygon	
Roads			Line	

3 Methods

The building density in the study area is approximately 27%, the average height of buildings (33.30 m) is higher than that of 5G BSs (20.13 m). Hence, most 5G signals are blocked by buildings in the study area.

3.1 Spatial Autocorrelation Analysis

Spatial autocorrelation analysis is characterized with global Moran's I index, the z-score and p-value will be returned by the Global Moran's I analysis. Hoping the z-score and the p-value will indicate that we can reject the null hypothesis, because it would indicate that rather than a random pattern at the probability of 10% if the value of the z-score $<$ -1.65 or $>+1.65$.

The global Moran's I statistic for spatial autocorrelation is given as:

$$I = \frac{n}{S_0} \frac{\sum_{i=1}^{n} \sum_{j=1}^{n} w_{i,j} z_i z_j}{\sum_{i=1}^{n} z_i^2} \tag{1}$$

where z_i is the deviation of an attribute for feature i from the mean $(x_i - \overline{X})$, $w_{i,j}$ is the spatial weight between feature i and j, n is equal to the total number of features, S_0 is the aggregate of all the spatial weights:

$$S_0 = \sum_{i=1}^{n} \sum_{j=1}^{n} w_{i,j} \tag{2}$$

The z_I-score for the statistic is computed as:

$$z_I = \frac{I - E[I]}{\sqrt{V[I]}} \tag{3}$$

where:

$$E[I] = -1/(n-1) \tag{4}$$

$$V[I] = E[I^2] - E[I]^2 \tag{5}$$

$$E[I^2] = \frac{A - B}{C} \tag{6}$$

$$A = n\left[\left(n^2 - 3n + 3\right)S_1 - nS_2 + 3S_0^2\right] \tag{7}$$

$$B = D\left[\left(n^2 - n\right)S_1 - 2nS_2 + 6S_0^2\right] \tag{8}$$

$$C = (n - 1)(n - 2)(n - 3)S_0^2 \tag{9}$$

$$D = \frac{\sum_{i=1}^{n} z_i^4}{\left(\sum_{i=1}^{n} z_i^2\right)^2} \tag{10}$$

$$S_1 = (1/2) \sum_{i=1}^{n} \sum_{j=1}^{n} \left(w_{i,j} + w_{j,i}\right)^2 \tag{11}$$

$$S_2 = \sum_{i=1}^{n} \left(\sum_{j=1}^{n} w_{i,j} + \sum_{j=1}^{n} w_{j,i}\right)^2 \tag{12}$$

The relationship between the null hypothesis rejection and the z-score and the p-value is demonstrated in Fig. 2.

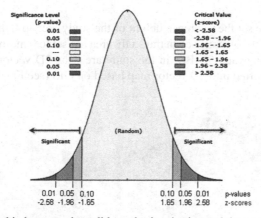

Fig. 2. The relationship between the null hypothesis rejection and the z-score and the p-value.

3.2 Analysis of the Coverage of 5G Signals to Road Network

Wang [16] conducted a coverage model for 5G signals based on the LOS characteristics of 5G signals: discretizing a continuous service space with sampling a series of regular grid points, buildings in study area were modeled as 2D vector polygons in GIS, simulating the 5G LOS service coverage for the maximum effective radius of 200 m of a 5G BS. In this study, the road network in the study area is discretized into points with an interval of 10 m. Combined with the height of the buildings and the construction height of the 5G BSs, the 3D sight lines (see Figs. 3 and 4) of the 5G BSs to the road network represents the LOS service coverage of the 5G BSs to the road network.

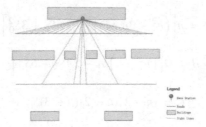

Fig. 3. Propagation of 5G signals in 2D spatial framework.

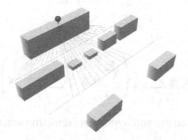

Fig. 4. Propagation of 5G signals in 3D spatial framework.

In this study, we set the reference height of the study area to 0 m, so the heights of the road network and water surface in the study area are set to 0 m. In combination with the height of buildings and 5G BSs in the study area, the 2D vector map of buildings and 5G BSs is converted into 3D vector map based on GIS (see Fig. 5).

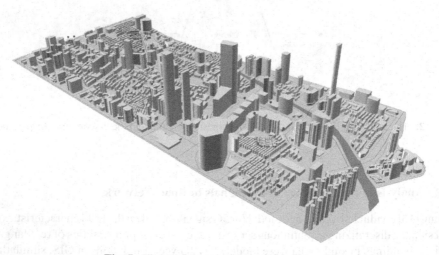

Fig. 5. The study area in 3D spatial framework.

GIS is used to construct the 3D sight lines of the 5G BSs to road network. The coverage radius is set to 200 m [7, 14, 16], count the length of roads covered by 5G signals and calculate the coverage proportion of road network respectively.

4 Results and Discussion

4.1 Spatial Autocorrelation Analysis

The total area of the study area is approximately 2.78 square kilometers. There are 29 5G BSs in the study area, and the density of BSs is about 10.43 BSs/km^2, which is less than the research result of Ge et al. [18] on the construction density of 5G BSs (40–50 BSs/km^2). The value of the Global Moran's I is 0.14, the value of the z-score is 1.06, and of the p-value is 0.28. The value of the Global Moran's I approaches to 0, which can be seen that the spatial distribution of 5G BSs in the study area does not show a significant spatial aggregate or discrete characteristic, but illustrates a kind of random.

Due to the high investment of 5G communication network construction [16], The energy consumption of a single 5G BS is about 4 times that of a 4G BS, meanwhile, the energy consumption of a 5G network is about 12 times that of a 4G network due to the high-density construction of 5G BSs [19]. Hence, 5G communication network construction is not a once-off action, but a step-by-step process [20]. Since the commercial construction and usage of 5G communication network in 2019, the construction of 5G communication network in China has transited from policy-led to technology-driven, and is experiencing a transition from business-led to market-driven [20].

To 5G communication service providers, the profits earned from enterprise users are higher than individual users. At current period, the construction of 5G communication network in China gives priority to serving enterprises to develop applications such as IoT and AI. 5G unmanned vehicles application in open roads is limited by native laws. The construction of 5G network which to cover urban outdoor area mainly serves individual 5G users, 5G communication service providers tend to choose relatively high population density area in urban outdoor environment as priority to the coverage of 5G signals.

4.2 Analysis of the Coverage of 5G Signals to Road Network

Combined with the height of the buildings and the construction height of the 5G BSs, the 3D sight lines (see Fig. 6 and Fig. 7) of the 5G BSs to the road network represents the LOS service coverage of the 5G BSs to the road network. The total length of the roads in the study area is about 86.38 km, and the length of the roads covered by 5G signal is 16.32 km after simulation, with a coverage ratio of about 18.89%. Among them, the coverage length of the main roads is 6.78 km, and the coverage proportion is 37.32%, which of the minor roads is 9.54 km, with a coverage ratio of 13.98%.

In researches of the coverage of 5G signals in urban outdoor area, Wang [16] discretized a continuous service space with sampling a series of regular grid points as the demand and coverage area of 5G signals. The road area is one of the areas with the largest demand for 5G communication network services in urban outdoor area. We take the urban road network as the research object of 5G signals coverage, which represents

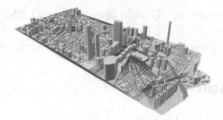

Fig. 6. The 3D sight lines of the BSs to the road network in the study area.

Fig. 7. The 3D sight lines of the BSs to the road network in the study area with 200 m coverage radius.

the coverage of 5G signals to urban outdoor environment to some extent. Palizban et al. [7] and Wang et al. [16] explicated the propagation of 5G signals in 2D spatial framework, Su et al. [14] designed the placement of base stations at low and high network load in the same perspective. Wang [16] simulated the propagation of 5G signals using Buffer and LOS analysis.

With high building density in modern cities, the construction height of 5G BSs must be considered. The LOS coverage research on 5G signals based on the construction height of 5G BSs from the perspective of 3D spatial framework would provide decision support for 5G communication networks construction and optimization in modern cities.

5 Conclusions

5G will play an essential role in the development of science and technology. A high-frequency millimeter wave was adopted in 5G communication technology as a basic wireless network technology, which with the characteristic of huge amount of data carriage but over a short distance, so the effective coverage radius of most 5G BSs is shorter than the previous communication networks, such as 3G and 4G. Since the commercial construction and usage of 5G communication network in 2019, it has been planned and constructed for more than 3 years in China. Approaches to evaluate the coverage of 5G signals in outdoor environmental in modern cities in China deserves to be explored. The road area is one of the areas with the largest demand for 5G communication network services in urban outdoor area. We take the urban road network as the research object of 5G signals coverage, which represents the coverage of 5G signals to urban outdoor environment to some extent.

Spatial autocorrelation analysis is an important approach to assess the extent of spatial aggregation for variables of interest [17]. In this study, we conducted spatial autocorrelation analysis on the spatial distribution of 5G base stations in the study area, and found that the characteristic of the spatial distribution of 5G BSs illustrates a kind of random rather than aggregate or discrete.

Due to the construction investment and energy consumption of 5G communication network are higher than the previous communication networks, such as 3G and 4G [16, 19], the construction of 5G communication network needs to be built on demand. The construction of 5G network which to cover urban outdoor area mainly serves individual 5G users, 5G communication service providers tend to choose relatively high population density area in urban outdoor environment as priority to the coverage of 5G signals.

In the previous 5G network planning studies, most of them are in the 2D spatial framework. In the 5G BSs construction issues, the height is the natural attribute of the base stations. For the evaluation of the coverage of 5G signals, the construction height of 5G BSs needs to be considered. The LOS coverage research on 5G signals based on the construction height of 5G BSs from the perspective of 3D spatial framework would provide decision support for 5G communication networks construction and optimization in modern cities.

In the paper, we established a 3D model of the buildings and 5G BSs distribution in the study area, combined with the height of the buildings and the construction height of the 5G BSs, the 3D sight lines of the 5G BSs to the road network represents the LOS service coverage of the 5G BSs to the road network. The result shows that the length of the main roads which covered by 5G signals in the study area is about 3 times that of the minor roads. As urban main roads were built to carry more traffic and people than minor roads, the research result also verifies the on-demand construction mode of the construction of 5G communication networks in Chinese modern cities to a certain extent.

Nevertheless, limitations still exit in this study. Further researches should focus on the space-time distribution of population density in the study area. According to the population density, the construction and optimization of 5G communication network in the study area needs to be carried out at the next step, and the energy consumption of 5G BSs in the study area could be precisely controlled according to the temporal and spatial distribution of the population.

References

1. Pi, Z., Khan, F.: An introduction to millimeter-wave mobile broadband systems. IEEE Commun. Mag. **49**(6), 101–107 (2011)
2. Khan, F., Pi, Z., Rajagopal, S.: Millimeter-wave mobile broadband with large scale spatial processing for 5G mobile communication. In: 2012 50th Annual Allerton Conference on Communication. Control, and Computing, pp. 1517–1523. Illinois, Allerton (2012)
3. Ma, X., Li, X., Tang, X., et al.: Deconvolution feature fusion for traffic signs detection in 5G driven unmanned vehicle. Phys. Commun. **47**, 1–11 (2021)
4. Bai, T., Heath, R.W.: Coverage and rate analysis for millimeter-wave cellular networks. IEEE Trans. Wireless Commun. **14**(2), 1100–1114 (2015)

5. MacCartney, G.R., Zhang, J., Nie, S., et al.: Path loss models for 5G millimeter wave propagation channels in urban microcells. In: GLOBECOM 2013 – Wireless Communication Symposium, pp. 2948–3953 (2013)
6. Sulyman, A.I., Nassar, A.T., Samimi, M.K., et al.: Radio propagation path loss models for 5G cellular networks in the 28 GHz and 38 GHz millimeter-wave bands. IEEE Commun. Mag. **52**(9), 78–86 (2014)
7. Palizban, N., Szyszkowicz, S., Yanikomeroglu, H.: Automation of millimeter wave network planning for outdoor coverage in dense urban areas using wall-mounted base stations. IEEE Wireless Commun. Lett. **6**(2), 206–209 (2017)
8. Al-Dabbagh, R.K., Al-Aboody, N.A., Al-Raweshidy, H.S.: A simplified path loss model for investigating diffraction and specular reflection impact on millimeter wave propagation. In: 2017 8th International Conference on the Network of the Future (NOF), pp. 153–155. IEEE, London (2017)
9. Lu, M., Hsu, S., Chen, P., Lee, W.: Improving the sustainability of integrated transportation system with bike-sharing: a spatial agent-based approach. Sustain. Cities Soc. **41**, 44–51 (2018)
10. Rappaport, T.S., MacCartney, G.R., Mellios, E.: Overview of millimeter wave communications for fifth-generation (5G) wireless networks—with a focus on propagation models. IEEE Trans. Antennas Propag. **65**(12), 6213–6230 (2017)
11. Al-Falahy, N., Alani, O.: Coverage and capacity improvement of millimeter wave 5G network using distributed base station architecture. IET Networks **8**(4), 246–255 (2019)
12. Qamar, F., Hindia, M.N., Dimyati, K., et al.: Investigation of future 5G-IoT millimeter-wave network performance at 38 GHz for urban microcell outdoor environment. Electronics **8**(5), 1–26 (2019)
13. Rappaport, T.S., Gutierrez, F., Ben-Dor, E., et al.: Broadband millimeter-wave propagation measurements and models using adaptive-beam antennas for outdoor urban cellular communications. IEEE Trans. Antennas Propag. **61**(4), 1850–1859 (2013)
14. Su, J., et al.: 5G multi-tier radio access network planning based on voronoi diagram. Measurement **192**, 110814 (2022)
15. Ahamed, M.M., Faruque, S.: 5G network coverage planning and analysis of the deployment challenges. Sensors **21**(19), 6608 (2021)
16. Wang, Q., Zhao, X., Lv, Z., Ma, X., Zhang, R., Lin, Y.: Optimizing the ultra-dense 5G base stations in urban outdoor areas: coupling GIS and heuristic optimization. Sustain. Cities Soc. **63**, 102445 (2020)
17. Li, L., Tang, H., Lei, J., Song, X.: Spatial autocorrelation in land use type and ecosystem service value in Hainan Tropical Rain Forest National Park. Ecol. Indic. **137**, 10872. (2022)
18. Ge, X., Tu, S., Mao, G., et al.: 5G ultra-dense cellular networks. IEEE Wirel. Commun. **23**(1), 72–79 (2016)
19. Chih-Lin, I., Han, S., Bian, S.: Energy-efficient 5G for a greener future. Nat, Electron. **3**(4), 182–184 (2020)
20. Cheng, X., Hu, Y., Varga, L.: 5G network deployment and the associated energy consumption in the UK: a complex systems' exploration. Technol. Forecast. Soc. Change **180**, 121672 (2022)

A Performance Evaluation Method for a Class of Cross-Chain Systems

Ou Wu[1,2](✉), Binbin Huang[3], Shanshan Li[1], Yanze Wang[1], and Haoming Li[1]

[1] State Key Laboratory of Novel Software Technology, Software Institute,
Nanjing University, Nanjing, China
`lss@nju.edu.cn, ouwu123@126.com`
[2] Department of Basic Courses, The PLA Army Engineering University,
Nanjing, China
[3] School of Computer, Hangzhou Dianzi University, Hangzhou, China
`huangbinbin@hdu.edu.cn`

Abstract. In recent years, the heterogeneity among the blockchains has become the driving force behind the development of cross-chain technologies. Due to the limited processing speed of cross-chain system, excessive cross-chain transactions in the short term may cause network congestion and negatively impact. For this reason, it is essential to evaluate and optimize the performance of the cross-blockchain transaction process. However, existing research ignores the limitations of cross-chain systems. Much research is carried out to model, simulate and analyze the performance of traditional blockchain systems rather than cross-blockchain processes. To bridge this gap, our study proposes a queuing theoretical model based on system finite space, using the case of Cosmos, a typical cross-blockchain implemented by the relay mode. The solution of the steady-state equations are established by two-dimensional continuous time Markov process, and the performance measures such as average queue length, transaction rejection probability, and transaction response time are given. Finally, we simulated the analytical solutions of the relevant performance measures through experiments to verify the model's effectiveness. We believe this analytical approach can be generalized to other cross-blockchain systems.

Keywords: Blockchain · Cross-blockchain · Relays · Performance modeling · Queueing theory · Simulation

1 Introduction

Most of the blockchains in the current mainstream blockchain platforms are independent, vertical closed systems [1]. In commercial application scenarios with increasingly complex business forms, the interconnection between chains has become particularly important. As an important technical means for blockchain to achieve interoperability and improve scalability, cross-chain technology has been valued by more and more scholars.

© ICST Institute for Computer Sciences, Social Informatics and Telecommunications Engineering 2023
Published by Springer Nature Switzerland AG 2023. All Rights Reserved
Y. Cao and X. Shao (Eds.): MONAMI 2022, LNICST 474, pp. 265–281, 2023.
https://doi.org/10.1007/978-3-031-32443-7_19

As a bridge connecting multiple blockchains, cross-blockchain technology can overcome the problem of blockchain interoperability and save the blockchain from the island of decentralization. Many solutions and tools have been proposed to further solve the problem of blockchain interoperability [2,3]. Among them, the side chain/relay mode, Cosmos, Polkadot and Irisnet, are widely used by many representative solutions for asset portability, atomic exchange or any other more complex use cases [4,5]. In terms of the specific technology using the side chain/relay pattern, Cosmos is a highly scalable, robust, and easily upgradeable blockchain cross-chain network architecture. Each of its blockchains is supported by the BFT algorithm and can be used as a blockchain, providing reliable underlying technical support for the formation of the Internet.

Nowadays, performance has become a major factor hindering the expansion of blockchain systems. This is particularly true for high-performance systems such as real-time payment system [6]. Therefore, it is necessary to compare, evaluate and optimize the new solutions to show their efficiency and effectiveness. In addition, performance evaluation of the blockchain can also identify the system's performance bottlenecks. This can be used to further optimize the blockchain system in a specific ways. For these reasons, many researches have proposed performance evaluation solutions for blockchain systems based on mathematical modeling methods [7–12].

To our knowledge, there is no research on the use of mathematical modeling methods to evaluate the performance of cross-blockchain system. Due to the difference of consensus algorithm and communication protocol, the process of cross-blockchain technologies may be different. And the mathematical modeling method involves the complexity of theoretical derivation and the application of conditions [6,13]. Therefore, it is promising to use this way to study, analyze, and set up the fundamental understanding about the performance capability and bottleneck of specific cross-blockchain processes.

This paper takes the typical solution Cosmos as a case, and applies queuing theory to model its cross-blockchain process.

This paper has the following contributions.

(1) For the complex cross-chain process of Cosmos, consider several key factors, such as transaction arrival rate, block size and block generate time, transaction pool capacity, etc., we propose a model for transaction batch service based on queuing theory.
(2) Considering that the transaction service process is block generation and k-round block consensus. Through the established two-dimensional continuous time Markov process, we solve the state probability vector of stationary equations with faster convergence of the sub-rate matrix. Finally, the expressions of system queue length, transaction rejection probability, transaction execution time and other performance measures are obtained.
(3) We built MATLAB R2016a software platform to simulate the established model. The system capacity, transaction arrival rate, block size and other parameters are adjusted to simulate the impact on the system performance measures. Experiments show that the stability of our proposed model is good and efficient.

2 Related Work

The use of mathematical modeling methods to evaluate blockchain performance has been studied by many scholars. Kasahara et al. [14] gave the earliest study on the analysis of Bitcoin transaction confirmation time performance using queuing theory, where they provided some abstract ideas and queuing theory model to inspire the follow-up research. Based on the work of Kasahara, Li et al. [15] divided the service process into block generation and blockchain construction, established a $G/M/1$ queuing model and provided system expressions. Jiang et al. [16] provided a series model of transaction processing on the Hyperledger Fabric platform. The performance indexes such as system throughput, transaction rejection probability and transaction response delay are derived by using the state transition graph of queuing theory. Memon et al. [17] using queuing theory models $M/M/1$ and $M/M/c$ to simulate and model the memory and mining pool of the blockchain system, and provide transaction performance indicators through the memory and mining pool. Ricci et al. [18] proposed an optimized framework that combines machine learning and queuing theory model to identify confirmed transactions and characterizes confirmation times.

However, there is no research on performance modeling and analysis of cross-blockchain system. So we use queuing theory to model the process of a typical case system to solve this problem. It can support a better understanding of the performance characteristics of the cross-blockchain system.

3 Cosmos Architecture

So far, the cross-chain projects in the side chain/relay mode account for the largest proportion of the entire cross-chain projects, and the proportion is still increasing [19]. At the same time, there have been many mature solutions for the side chain/relay model, which have a great impact on cross-chain technology, the most representative of which is Cosmos[1] in 2016.

3.1 Cosmos Architecture and Consensus

Cosmos is a scalable, easy-to-use, and interoperable decentralized network of multiple independent parallel blockchains. There are three important components: The Hub is the relay chain, maintained by the government and used as a trust center for cross-chain messages. Zones are parachains participating in the Cosmos network. To support cross-chain interoperability between parachains, Cosmos proposes the Inter-Chain Communication Protocol (IBC) to perform cross-chain operations with Hub [20]. The Hub is used for cross-chain management in the parachain area. It connects the blockchain developed based on the Cosmos-SDK module to the Hub, and uses the Tendermint consensus algorithm to achieve cross-chain. As the first central chain, Cosmos hub enables network changes and updates through a simple administrative mechanism.

---

[1] https://github.com/cosmos.

In a single hub system, cross-chain transactions are queued in the mempool of the proposer node through different zones, waiting for the tendermint core to perform consensus verification. Tendermint's consensus mechanism is based on the Byzantine fault-tolerant algorithm. According to the rules, validators must reach a consensus on each block in rounds. Each round consists of three steps:

- Proposal stage. The proposer in each round is selected deterministically from an ordered list in proportion to the voting weight. The voting ratio in the whole process is calculated based on the Stake ratio, and each validator node has a different voting weight according to the number of tokens pledged by each validator node.
- Prevoting stage. Each validator broadcasts their own prevote. When a block in the round receives more than 2/3 of the prevote, it enters the next stage.
- Precommit phase. Each validator broadcasts their precommitted vote. When the vote exceeds 2/3, it enter the next stage.

The process is shown in Fig. 1. The block can only enter the commit phase when the adivators of 2/3 is consistent in the prevoting and precommit phases. Otherwise, it means that the block submission failed. In this case, the Tendermint protocol will choose the next validator to propose a new block at the same height and start voting again. At this time, the consensus time of this block is much longer than that of other blocks, but there is no rollback phenomenon.

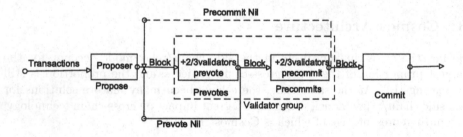

Fig. 1. Cosmos consensus process

4   Modeling Using Queuing Theory

Queuing theory is a mathematical method for solving different types of queuing system performance and service quality. In this paper, we model and test the core cross-blockchain processes of Cosmos, and use the batch service queuing theory to evaluate the performance of Cosmos hub system.

4.1   Cosmos Cross-Blockchain Queuing Representation

In the cross-chain activities of Cosmos, multiple Hub (relay)-centric blockchain alliances will form a huge network. Due to the complexity of the blockchain alliance, we first solve the cross-chain process problem of a single-relay system.

In the Cosmos hub, n validators are randomly selected to form a validator group to provide consensus verification for cross-chain transactions. The consensus process of the validator group is briefly as follows: Firstly, one of the validators be selected as the proposer node (generated by the validator in turn), then the proposer node starts to monitor and collect all transactions of the whole network, and store them in the memory pool to wait for consensus. Secondly, the proposer node will assemble a new block of cross-chain transactions, the proposal block, and broadcast it to other validators. Finally, when all validator nodes in the entire network receive the proposal block, they read all transactions in this block, vote after confirming that there is no problem, and broadcast the voting message to all validators again. However, when the prevote or precommit fails to pass the vote, the block is sent back for verification, and this process loops until the block is successfully verified. The process is shown in the Fig. 2.

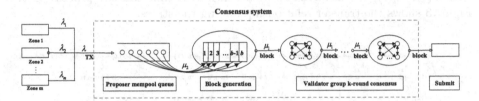

Fig. 2. Cross-chain process of Cosmos hub system.

We build a queuing system for Cosmos as follows.

Arrival Process: Assuming there are m zones in the system, the ith zone sends λ_i cross-chain transactions per second on average, which is equivalent to randomly receiving $\lambda = \sum_{i=1}^m \lambda_i$ cross-chain transactions per second in mempool. That is, in the entire Cosmos hub system, the number of cross-chain transactions that arrive is a Poisson process with parameter λ.

Service Rules: For cross-chain process of Cosmos, we set the service rule as first-come, first-served (FCFS).

Service Process: The first stage of the service is the process of generating blocks for a transaction. We assume that the block generation time of a transaction follows the exponential distribution with μ_2. Then the proposer broadcasts the packaged blocks to other validators, and verifies the transactions in the block through prevote or precommit. Once the transaction fails to pass the verification, the block will be sent back to the proposer for re-verification. Here we assume that the verification time of each round of the block obeys the exponential distribution with μ_1, and assumes that the block has k rounds of verification, so the entire verification stage obeys the k-order Erlang distribution.

The Maximum System Capacity: The maximum capacity of the Cosmos hub system is N.

Independence: All parameters included in this paper are independent of each other.

4.2   A Continuous-Time Markov Process

We regard the validator group as a service desk, service time includes block generation time and k-round block verification time. When transactions arrive as Poisson process and the transaction pool is limited, we establish a continuous-time Markov process for this Cosmos hub system, and the stable probability vector is solved by constructing the a series sub-rate matrix.

Assume that $\xi(t)$ and $\eta(t)$ represent the number of transactions in the system queue and the number of transactions in the block at time slot t, respectively. Then $(\xi(t), \eta(t))$ is a state of the queuing system at time t. Here $i = 0, 1, \cdots, N$, $j = 0, 1, 2, \cdots, b$ and $i + j \leq N$. Then

$$\Omega = \{(\xi, \eta) : \xi = 0, 1, \cdots, N; \eta = 0, 1, 2, \cdots, b\}$$

where $(\xi(t), \eta(t))$ is considered to be a continuous-time Markov process on Ω. Figure 3 shows the transfer relationship among the states.

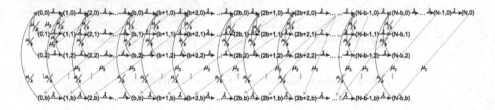

Fig. 3. State transition diagram.

The steady-state equations of cosmos hub system are obtained as follows.

- State $\{(0,0)\}$

$$- \lambda P(0,0) + \frac{\mu_1}{k}[P(0,1) + P(0,2) + \cdots + P(0,b)] = 0 \tag{1}$$

- State $\{(0,\eta), \eta = 1, 2, \cdots, b\}$

$$- (\lambda + \frac{\mu_1}{k})P(0,\eta) + \mu_2 P(\xi,0) = 0 \tag{2}$$

- State $\{(\xi,0), \xi = 1, 2, \cdots, N - b\}$

$$-(\lambda + \mu_2)P(\xi,0) + \lambda P(\xi - 1, 0) + \frac{\mu_1}{k}[P(\xi,1) + P(\xi,2) \\ + ... + P(\xi,b)] = 0 \tag{3}$$

- State $\{(\xi,b), \xi = 1, 2, \cdots, N - b - 1\}$

$$- (\lambda + \frac{\mu_1}{k})P(\xi,b) + \lambda P(\xi - 1, b) + \mu_2 P(b + \xi, 0) = 0 \tag{4}$$

- State $\{(N - b, b)\}$

$$- \frac{\mu_1}{k} P(N - b, b) + \lambda P(N - b - 1, b) + \mu_2 P(N, 0) = 0 \qquad (5)$$

- State $\{(N - b, \eta), \eta = 1, 2, \cdots, b - 1\}$

$$- \frac{\mu_1}{k} P(N - b, j) + \lambda P(N - b - 1, \eta) = 0 \qquad (6)$$

- State $\{(\xi, \eta), \xi = 1, 2, \cdots, N - b - 1; \eta = 1, 2, \cdots, b - 1\}$

$$-(\frac{\mu_1}{k} + \lambda) P(\xi, \eta) + \lambda P(\xi - 1, \eta) = 0 \qquad (7)$$

- State $\{(\xi, 0), \xi = N - b + 1, N - b + 2, \cdots, N - 1\}$

$$-(\mu_2 + \lambda) P(\xi, 0) + \lambda P(\xi - 1, 0) = 0 \qquad (8)$$

- State $\{(N, 0)\}$

$$- \mu_2 P(N, 0) + \lambda P(N - 1, 0) = 0 \qquad (9)$$

If the system fails to generate blocks, then transactions continue to accumulate in the queue. Here, we're particularly analyzing this situation, namely the state $\{(\xi, 0), \xi = N - b + 1, N - b + 2, \cdots, N - 1\}$.

We can obtain the following conclusion from Eqs. (8) and (9):

$$\begin{cases} P(N - b + 1, 0) = \frac{\lambda}{\lambda + \mu_2} P(N - b, 0) \\ P(N - b + 2, 0) = (\frac{\lambda}{\lambda + \mu_2})^2 P(N - b, 0) \\ \vdots \\ P(N - 1, 0) = (\frac{\lambda}{\lambda + \mu_2})^{b-1} P(N - b, 0) \\ P(N, 0) = \frac{\lambda^b}{(\lambda + \mu_2)^{b-1} \mu_2} P(N - b, 0) \end{cases} \qquad (10)$$

We plug Eq. (10) into Eqs. (4) and (5), then

$$\begin{cases} -(\frac{\mu_1}{k} + \lambda) P(\xi, b) + \lambda P(\xi - 1, b) + \mu_2 P(b + \xi, 0) = 0, \\ \xi = 1, 2, \cdots, N - 2b \\ (\frac{\mu_1}{k} + \lambda) P(\xi, b) + \lambda P(\xi - 1, b) + \mu_2(\frac{\lambda}{\lambda + \mu^2})^{\xi - (N - 2b)} P(N - b, 0) = 0, \\ \xi = N - 2b + 1, N - 2b + 2, \cdots, N - b - 1 \end{cases} \qquad (11)$$

$$- \frac{\mu_1}{k} P(N - b, b) + \lambda P(N - b - 1, b) + \frac{\lambda^b}{(\lambda + \mu_2)^{b-1}} P(N - b, 0) = 0 \qquad (12)$$

Combine Eqs. (1)–(3), (6)–(9) and (11), (12), we have a $(N - b + 1)$-order square matrix as minimum generator of this system:

$$Q = \begin{bmatrix} B_0 & A_0 & & & & & & & \\ B_1 & A_1 & A_0 & & & & & & \\ B_2 & & A_1 & A_0 & & & & & \\ \vdots & & & A_1 & A_0 & & & & \\ \vdots & & & & \ddots & \ddots & & & \\ B_b & & & & & A_1 & A_0 & & \\ & B_b & & & & & A_1 & A_0 & \\ & & B_b & & & & & \ddots & \ddots \\ & & & \ddots & & & & A_1 & A_0 \\ & & & & B_b & C_1 & C_2 & \cdots & C_{b-1} & A_M \end{bmatrix}$$

where $A_0, A_1, B_0, B_i (i = 1, 2, \cdots, b), C_j (j = 1, 2 \cdots, b-1), A_M$ are $(b+1)$-order square matrices, and

$$A_0 = \begin{bmatrix} \lambda & & & \\ & \lambda & & \\ & & \ddots & \\ & & & \lambda \end{bmatrix}, A_1 = \begin{bmatrix} -(\lambda + \mu_2) & & & \\ \frac{\mu_1}{k} & -(\lambda + \frac{\mu_1}{k}) & & \\ \vdots & & \ddots & \\ \frac{\mu_1}{k} & & & -(\lambda + \frac{\mu_1}{k}) \end{bmatrix},$$

$$B_0 = \begin{bmatrix} -\lambda & & & \\ \frac{\mu_1}{k} & -(\lambda + \frac{\mu_1}{k}) & & \\ \vdots & & \ddots & \\ \frac{\mu_1}{k} & & & -(\lambda + \frac{\mu_1}{k}) \end{bmatrix}, B_1 = \begin{bmatrix} 0 & \mu_2 & 0 & \cdots & 0 \\ & & & & \\ & & & & \\ & & & & \end{bmatrix}, B_2 = \begin{bmatrix} 0 & 0 & \mu_2 & \cdots & 0 \\ & & & & \\ & & & & \\ & & & & \end{bmatrix},$$

$\cdots,$

$$B_b = \begin{bmatrix} 0 & 0 & 0 & \cdots & \mu_2 \\ & & & & \\ & & & & \\ & & & & \end{bmatrix}, C_1 = \begin{bmatrix} 0 & \cdots & 0 & 0 & \mu_2(\frac{\lambda}{\lambda+\mu_2}) \\ & & & & \\ & & & & \\ & & & & \end{bmatrix}, C_2 = \begin{bmatrix} 0 & \cdots & 0 & 0 & \mu_2(\frac{\lambda}{\lambda+\mu_2})^2 \\ & & & & \\ & & & & \\ & & & & \end{bmatrix},$$

$\cdots,$

$$C_{b-1} = \begin{bmatrix} 0 & \cdots & 0 & 0 & \mu_2(\frac{\lambda}{\lambda+\mu_2})^{b-1} \\ & & & & \\ & & & & \\ & & & & \end{bmatrix}, A_M = \begin{bmatrix} -(\lambda + \mu_2) & 0 & \cdots & 0 & \frac{\lambda^b}{(\lambda+\mu_2)^{b-1}} \\ \frac{\mu_1}{k} & 0 & \cdots & 0 & 0 \\ \vdots & \vdots & & \vdots & \vdots \\ \frac{\mu_1}{k} & 0 & \cdots & 0 & 0 \end{bmatrix}$$

Suppose $\pi = (\pi_0, \pi_1, \pi_2, \cdots, \pi_{N-b})$ is the state probability vector based on the minimum generator, where $\pi_i = (\pi_{i0}, \pi_{i1}, \cdots, \pi_{ib}), i = 0, 1, 2, \cdots, N - b$ is a $b + 1$ dimensional row vector, then we have

$$\pi_0 B_0 + \pi_1 B_1 + \pi_2 B_2 + \cdots + \pi_b B_b = 0 \tag{13}$$

$$\pi_0 A_0 + \pi_1 A_1 + \pi_{b+1} B_b = 0 \tag{14}$$

$$\pi_{i-1}A_0 + \pi_i A_1 + \pi_{i+b}B_b = 0, i = 2, 3, \cdots, N - 2b \tag{15}$$

$$\pi_{i-1}A_0 + \pi_i A_1 + \pi_{N-b}C_{i-(N-2b)} = 0, \quad i = N - 2b + 1, N - 2b + 2, \cdots, N - b - 1 \tag{16}$$

$$\pi_{N-b-1}A_0 + \pi_{N-b}A_M = 0 \tag{17}$$

$$\pi e = 1 \tag{18}$$

The dimension of column vector e depends on the collocation matrix.

We use matrix analysis method to solve steady-state probability vector [21]. Here, the diagonal matrix A_0 is expressed as $A_0 = \lambda I$ (I is the $(b+1)$-order identity matrix). Let $R_{N-b} = I$, then

$$\pi_{N-b} = \pi_{N-b}R_{N-b} \tag{19}$$

From Eq. (17), we get

$$\pi_{N-b-1} = \pi_{N-b}(-\frac{1}{\lambda}A_M) = \pi_{N-b}R_{N-b-1} \tag{20}$$

Where $R_{N-b-1} = -\frac{1}{\lambda}A_M$ is a sub-rate matrix.
We put Eq. (20) into Eq. (16), then

$$\pi_{N-b-(i+1)} = \pi_{N-b}[-\frac{1}{\lambda}(R_{N-b-i}A_1 + C_{b-i})]$$
$$= \pi_{N-b}R_{N-b-(i+1)}, \tag{21}$$
$$i = 1, 2, \cdots, b - 1$$

where

$$R_{N-b-(i+1)} = -\frac{1}{\lambda}(R_{N-b-i}A_1 + C_{b-i}), i = 1, 2, \cdots, b - 1.$$

We plug Eq. (21) into Eq. (15), then

$$\pi_{N-b-(i+1)} = \pi_{N-b}[-\frac{1}{\lambda}(R_{N-b-i}A_1 + R_{N-i}B_b)]$$
$$= \pi_{N-b}R_{N-b-(i+1)}, \tag{22}$$
$$i = b, b + 1, \cdots, N - b - 1$$

where

$$R_{N-b-(i+1)} = -\frac{1}{\lambda}(R_{N-b-i}A_1 + R_{N-i}B_b), i = b, b + 1, \cdots, N - b - 1.$$

From Eq. (13), we get

$$\pi_0 = -\pi_{N-b}(R_1B_1 + R_2B_2 + \cdots + R_bB_b)B_0^{-1}$$
$$= \pi_{N-b}R_0, \tag{23}$$

where $R_0 = -(R_1B_1 + R_2B_2 + \cdots + R_bB_b)B_0^{-1}$. Figure 4 shows the solving process of $R_i, i = 0, 1, 2, \cdots, N - b$.

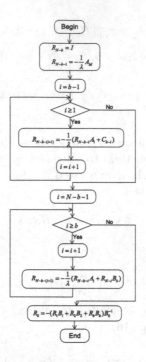

Fig. 4. R_i calculation flow chart.

Combine Eqs. (14) and (18), we get

$$\begin{cases} \pi_{N-b}(R_0A_0 + R_1A_1 + R_{b+1}B_b) = 0 \\ \pi_{N-b}(R_0 + R_1 + R_2 + \cdots + R_{N-b-1} + I)e = 1 \end{cases}. \tag{24}$$

π_{N-b} is substituted into the Eqs. (20)–(23) to solve the steady-state probability vector π.

Then we obtain the performance measures of consensus hub system, and analyze the influence of parameters on them. The conditions for a stable queue system are as follows:

$$\lim_{t \to +\infty} \xi(t) = \xi_q, \lim_{t \to +\infty} \eta(t) = \eta_b, \tag{25}$$

(a) Average number of transaction in queue

$$E(L_q) = \sum_{i=0}^{N-b} (i \sum_{j=0}^{b} \pi_{ij}) = \pi_{N-b}[R_1 + 2R_2 + \cdots + (N-b)R_{N-b}]e \tag{26}$$

(b) Average transaction execution time

$$E(T_{exe}) = \sum_{m=0}^{[\frac{N-b-l}{b}]} \sum_{l=0}^{b-1} \pi_{mb+l,0}(m+1)(\frac{k}{\mu_1} + \frac{1}{\mu_2})$$

$$+ \sum_{m=0}^{[\frac{N-b-l}{b}]} \sum_{l=0}^{b-1} \sum_{j=1}^{b} \pi_{mb+l,j}[\frac{k}{\mu_1} + (m+1)(\frac{k}{\mu_1} + \frac{1}{\mu_2})] \tag{27}$$

The proof is analogous to the literature [15], where $[\frac{N-b-l}{b}]$ is a integer function.

(c) Transaction rejection probability

$$P_{rjc} = \sum_{j=0}^{b} \pi_{N-b,j} = \pi_{N-b}e \tag{28}$$

(d) Average transaction response time

$$E(T_{resp}) = \frac{E(L_q)}{\lambda(1 - p_{rjc})} \tag{29}$$

(e) Throughput of system

$$E(TPS) = \lambda(1 - p_{rjc}) \tag{30}$$

5   Model Simulation and Evaluation

This section, we simulated the performance measures of Cosmos hub system by conducting experiments and testing necessary data. We provided several graphs of important measures about the parameter λ, N, and μ_1, μ_2.

5.1   Test Framework

In this section, $MATLABR2016a$ software platform is installed to study parameter's impact on performance measures by setting parameter ranges, so as to verify the accuracy of this model.

5.2   Performance Evaluation of Cosmos Hub System

(A) Impact of arrival rate λ on system performance

We set the variation range of λ to be 0 to 5000 txs/s, $\mu_1 = 4, \mu_2 = 1$ txs/s, the Cosmos hub system capacity $N = 500$. On average, each transaction performs one round of consensus verification, that is $k = 1$. Figure 5 shows the change trend in performance measures such as rejection probability and transaction response time, etc.

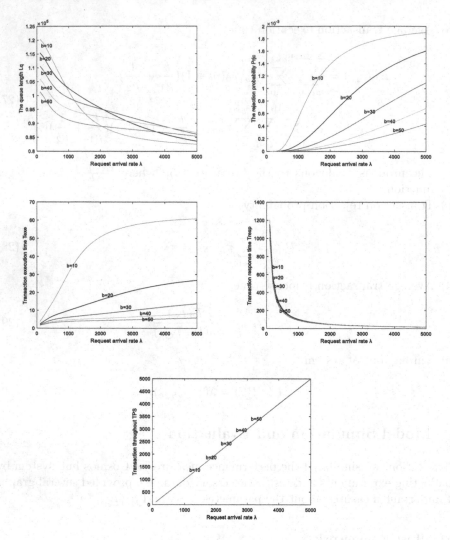

Fig. 5. Performance measures with λ

Figure 5 shows the trends of the five performance measures of the Cosmos hub system with respect to value of b and λ. When the value of b is determined, the larger the transaction arrival rate λ, the smaller the queue length L_q and the transaction response time T_{resp}, the larger is the rejection probability P_{rjc} and the transaction execution time T_{exe}, the transaction throughput TPS is proportional to the transaction arrival rate λ. When λ is determined, the queue length L_q decreases as the value of b increases, and the rejection probability P_{rjc} increases as the value of b increases. Execution time T_{exe} and system throughput TPS are independent of changes with block size b.

To sum up, when the value of λ is $\lambda \leq 1000$, we try to set a large block size. At this time, the queue length is small, and the consensus efficiency is also high. But when $\lambda \geq 1000$, the larger the block, the longer the queue length, so the system accumulation will increase, but the consensus efficiency is always high. Given several interrelated performance metrics, we cannot blindly pursue large block sizes when setting system parameters. An appropriate block size b ensures good system performance and small system builds.

(B) Influence of Cosmos hub system capacity (N)

We set the range of N to be 0 to 5000 transactions, $\mu_1 = 4, \mu_2 = 1$ txs/s. When the value of λ is $\lambda = 1000$ txs/s, and $k = 1$. Figure 6 shows the changes with the five performance measures.

Figure 6 shows the value of b is determined, and when the consensus system capacity is $N \geq 1000$, no matter the change of N, it has little effect on the rejection probability and throughput. When $N \leq 1000$, the system rejection probability P_{rjc} decreases with the increase of N, while the throughput increases with the increase of N. N has little effect on the transaction execution time T_{exe}, but its increase will lead to an increase in transaction response time. When N is determined, P_{rjc} decreases faster with the larger b, T_{exe} decreases with the increase of b, and the TPS growth rate also increases with the increase of b.

In summary, when the value of N increases, although the rejection probability gets closer to 0 and the transaction throughput (TPS) tends to stabilize (proportional to the transaction arrival rate λ), but the queue length and response time also increase. Therefore, an appropriately sized N will balance the performance of the entire system, rather than a larger N, the better the system performance.

(C) transaction consensus rate (μ_1) and consensus rounds (k)

The parameters μ_1, μ_2 represent a round transaction consensus rate and block generation rate. Their values are related to the number of ordering nodes and peer nodes. Consider the above test, let $\mu_1 = 4, \mu_2 = 1, N = 500, \lambda = 1000$, when the range of k varies from 1–20, the range of $\mu_{11} = \frac{\mu_1}{k}$ is 0.2–4. Figure 7 shows the trend of changes of five performance measures as the dependent variable μ_{11}.

From Fig. 7, we can see that when $\mu_{11} \leq 0.2$, the curve shakes violently, especially if the rejection probability is negative, obviously the system is wrong. When $\mu_{11} \geq 0.2$, the larger the μ_{11} is, the smaller the number of transaction consensus rounds k is, that is, the higher the transaction consensus efficiency is. At this time, when the block size b is fixed, the queue length, transaction response time and system throughput increase accordingly, while the rejection probability and transaction execution time decrease, indicating that the system performance is getting better and better. Compared to block size b, larger blocks also lead to better performance.

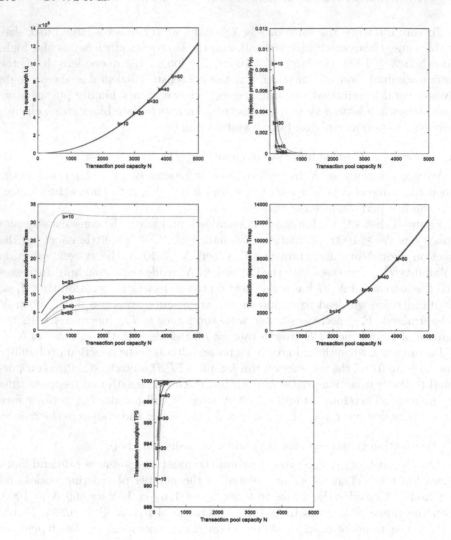

Fig. 6. Performance measures with N

To sum up, the variable μ_{11} is a reflection of the system settings. When the number of validator nodes is small, the system consensus efficiency is naturally high, but at the same time, there will be security problems. Therefore, when setting up the consensus system, choosing an appropriate number of nodes while taking into account both security and efficiency is also a problem that we need to consider.

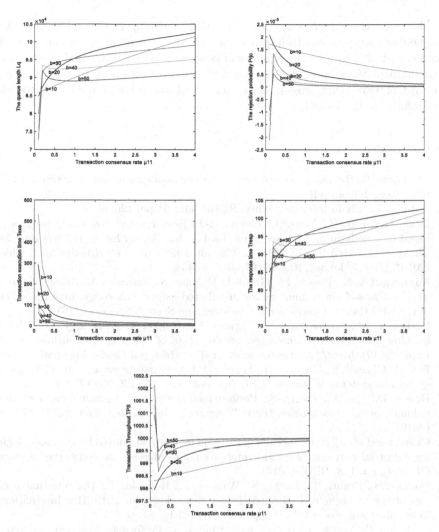

Fig. 7. Performance measures with μ_{11}

6 Conclusion

As a key technology in the development of blockchain field, the theory and performance of cross-chain technology is a main research topic. This paper first selects the representative cross-chain technology Cosmos to model the core cross-chain process. Secondly, we apply queuing theory to derive the performance evaluation measures of the Cosmos hub system. Finally, we simulated the model by testing the transaction consensus time and block generation rate of cross-chain transactions to verify the validity of the model. The model proposed and validated in this paper can still be used to evaluate the performance of other cross-chain technologies using similar patterns.

There are three future directions for this research: 1) Optimize the existing queuing theory model to improve the utilization of node group consensus in Cosmos Hub. 2) Improve the equipment configuration used to build the Cosmos cross-chain platform and identify the performance bottleneck of the relay system. 3) Compare other cross-chain systems with the relay model to expand the applicability of the model.

References

1. Nakamoto, S.: Bitcoin: a peer-to-peer electronic cash system, vol. 4 (2008). https://bitcoin.org/bitcoin.pdf
2. Buterin, V.: Chain interoperability. R3 Research Paper (2016)
3. Deng, L., Chen, H., Zeng, J., Zhang, L.-J.: Research on cross-chain technology based on sidechain and hash-locking. In: Liu, S., Tekinerdogan, B., Aoyama, M., Zhang, L.-J. (eds.) EDGE 2018. LNCS, vol. 10973, pp. 144–151. Springer, Cham (2018). https://doi.org/10.1007/978-3-319-94340-4_12
4. Kannengießer, N., Pfister, M., Greulich, M., Lins, S., Sunyaev, A.: Bridges between islands: Cross-chain technology for distributed ledger technology. In: Proceedings of the 53rd Hawaii International Conference on System Sciences (2020)
5. Borkowski, M., Frauenthaler, P., Sigwart, M., Hukkinen, T., Hladký, O., Schulte, S.: Cross-blockchain technologies: review, state of the art, and outlook. White Paper (2019). http://dsg.tuwien.ac.at/projects/tast/pub/tast-white-paper-4.pdf
6. Fan, C., Ghaemi, S., Khazaei, H., Musilek, P.: Performance evaluation of blockchain systems: a systematic survey. IEEE Access **8**, 126 927–126 950 (2020)
7. Huang, D., Ma, X., Zhang, S.: Performance analysis of the raft consensus algorithm for private blockchains. IEEE Trans. Syst. Man Cybern. Syst. **50**(1), 172–181 (2019)
8. Geyer, F., et al.: Performance perspective on private distributed ledger technologies for industrial networks. In: 2019 International Conference on Networked Systems (NetSys), pp. 1–8. IEEE (2019)
9. Geissler, S., Prantl, T., Lange, S., Wamser, F., Hossfeld, T.: Discrete-time analysis of the blockchain distributed ledger technology. In: 2019 31st International Teletraffic Congress (ITC 31), pp. 130–137. IEEE (2019)
10. Sukhwani, H., Wang, N., Trivedi, K.S., Rindos, A.: Performance modeling of hyperledger fabric (permissioned blockchain network). In: 2018 IEEE 17th International Symposium on Network Computing and Applications (NCA), pp. 1–8. IEEE (2018)
11. Yuan, P., Zheng, K., Xiong, X., Zhang, K., Lei, L.: Performance modeling and analysis of a hyperledger-based system using GSPN. Comput. Commun. **153**, 117–124 (2020)
12. Papadis, N., Borst, S., Walid, A., Grissa, M., Tassiulas, L.: Stochastic models and wide-area network measurements for blockchain design and analysis. In: IEEE INFOCOM 2018-IEEE Conference on Computer Communications, pp. 2546–2554. IEEE (2018)
13. Smetanin, S., Ometov, A., Komarov, M., Masek, P., Koucheryavy, Y.: Blockchain evaluation approaches: state-of-the-art and future perspective. Sensors **20**(12), 3358 (2020)
14. Kasahara, S., Kawahara, J.: Effect of bitcoin fee on transaction-confirmation process. J. Industr. Manage. Optim. **15**(1), 365 (2019)

15. Li, Q.-L., Ma, J.-Y., Chang, Y.-X.: Blockchain queue theory. In: Chen, X., Sen, A., Li, W.W., Thai, M.T. (eds.) CSoNet 2018. LNCS, vol. 11280, pp. 25–40. Springer, Cham (2018). https://doi.org/10.1007/978-3-030-04648-4_3

16. Jiang, L., Chang, X., Liu, Y., Mišić, J.V., Mišić, V.B.: Performance analysis of hyperledger fabric platform: a hierarchical model approach. Peer-to-Peer Netw. Appl. **13**(3), 1014–1025 (2020). https://doi.org/10.1007/s12083-019-00850-z

17. Memon, R.A., Li, J.P., Ahmed, J.: Simulation model for blockchain systems using queuing theory. Electronics **8**(2), 234 (2019)

18. Ricci, S., Ferreira, E., Menasche, D.S., Ziviani, A., Souza, J.E., Vieira, A.B.: Learning blockchain delays: a queueing theory approach. ACM SIGMETRICS Perform. Eval. Rev. **46**(3), 122–125 (2019)

19. Nakamoto, S.: Bitcoin: A peer-to-peer electronic cash system. Manubot, Technical report (2019)

20. Kwon, J., Buchman, E.: A network of distributed ledgers. Cosmos, dated, pp. 1–41 (2018)

21. Elhafsi, E.H., Molle, M.: On the solution to QBD processes with finite state space. Stochast. Anal. Appl. **25**(4), 763–779 (2007)

An Improved BP Neural Network Based on Adaptive Genetic Algorithm

Jiale Zhang, Lianshuan Shi[✉], Jiaxing Zhao, and Shuangyu Duan

School of Information Technology Engineering, Tianjin University of Technology and
Education, Tianjin 300222, China
shilianshuan@sina.com

Abstract. In order to improve the optimization effect of genetic algorithm on BP neural network, this paper proposes an improved BP neural network based on adaptive genetic algorithm. Firstly, the selection operation introduces the elite retention strategy. Secondly, adaptive operation is introduced into the crossover mutation operator, and the crossover mutation mode is optimized to adjust the population diversity, avoid the algorithm falling into the local optimal, and prevent the algorithm from precocious. Finally, the effectiveness of the proposed algorithm in reducing the time cost, improving the network fitting and improving the neural network's tendency to fall into the local optimal is verified by comparing with the two common algorithms.

Keywords: genetic algorithm · Adaptive · Algorithm optimization · BP neural network

1 Algorithm Introduction

Genetic algorithm (GA) was a computational model simulating Darwinian biological evolution [1]. By abstracting the biological evolution process, this iterative algorithm for global optimization search is obtained [2].

BP neural network is one of the most mature and widely used neural network models at present, with excellent self-learning ability and a very wide range of applications [3]. It still has some defects, for example, its learning convergence speed is slow [4], and the initial weight threshold selection has a great impact on the network training [5]. In view of these defects, this paper proposes an adaptive genetic algorithm to improve the BP neural network, improve the accuracy of the neural network and solve the problem that the neural network is prone to fall into the local optimal [6].

© ICST Institute for Computer Sciences, Social Informatics and Telecommunications Engineering 2023
Published by Springer Nature Switzerland AG 2023. All Rights Reserved
Y. Cao and X. Shao (Eds.): MONAMI 2022, LNICST 474, pp. 282–292, 2023.
https://doi.org/10.1007/978-3-031-32443-7_20

2   Algorithm Introduction

2.1   Genetic Algorithm Optimization

2.1.1   Initialize the Population

In this paper, the population size of 50 was determined by the fitting effect of different populations and neural network. The encoding method of this paper adopts real number encoding [7].

2.1.2   Fitness Function

Genetic algorithm is used to optimize BP neural network. After determining the topology of BP neural network, the chromosome length corresponding to the population individual can be obtained. The known training data can be used to train BP neural network. The sum of the absolute value of the error between the predicted result of the test sample and the expected output is taken as the fitness value of the individual.

2.1.3   Select Operations

The selection operation of genetic algorithm is to retain excellent individuals in the population to the next generation with a greater probability, and at the same time eliminate crossover individuals, so that the population can evolve in a more excellent direction [8]. Common selection methods include sorting selection, random selection without putting back, proportional selection. This paper introduces the elite retention strategy on the basis of proportional selection.

The basic idea of elite retention strategy is to preserve elite individuals, namely the best individuals, directly to the next generation without genetic manipulation. The introduction of elite retention strategy can ensure that excellent individuals will not be destroyed in the process of evolution, and the convergence ability of the population has been improved.

2.1.4   Adaptive Cross-Mutation

The main idea of crossover operator is to select two individuals in the population for local crossover to obtain new individuals and increase the diversity of the population [9]. It is an important part of genetic algorithm and its distinctive feature.

The main idea of mutation operator is to carry out local mutation of individual chromosomes, which is also an important part of genetic algorithm [10]. The main purposes of the algorithm are two: one is to make the algorithm have local search ability, the other is to keep the diversity of the population without destroying the good individuals of the population as much as possible.

Arithmetic crossover operator: now set two individuals X_t^m and X_t^n; arithmetically cross at t; then the two new individuals generated at after crossing are:

$$X_{t+1}^m = X_t^m - r * (X_t^m - X_t^n) \tag{1}$$

$$X_{t+1}^n = X_t^n - r * (X_t^m - X_t^n) \tag{2}$$

In formula 1 and 2, when parameter r is set to constant, it is uniform arithmetic crossing. When r is a variable, it is a non-uniform arithmetic crossover.

The mutation operation uses real variation:

$$X_{t+1} = X_t - u * rand \tag{3}$$

In the formula, u is a parameter, $rand$ is the corresponding to a random number.

In the evolution of population, the probability of crossover operator and mutation operator will greatly affect the result of the algorithm. In the crossover operation, if the crossover probability is too large, the good individuals of the population are easy to be destroyed. On the contrary, if the value is too small, it can not promote the diversity of the population well. In the mutation operation, too large mutation probability will make the algorithm similar to random search, making it lose the most distinctive characteristics of biological evolution of genetic algorithm [11], which cannot ensure the diversity of the population and obtain the optimal value.

Based on the above analysis, the crossover and mutation probabilities are optimized in this paper. On the basis of the original, evolutionary algebra and individual fitness value of the population are introduced, and a new adaptive crossover and mutation probability formula optimization algorithm is proposed. After adaptive adjustment, the population evolution effect can be adjusted in real time according to the fitness value and the current evolution algebra, which helps the algorithm to jump out of the local optimal.

The adaptive crossover probability formula is as follows:

$$P_c = \begin{cases} 0.8 - 0.3 * (f_{avg} - f_s)/(f_{max} - f_{min}), f_s \leq f_{avg} \\ 0.9 - 0.7 * g/G, f_s > f_{avg} \end{cases} \tag{4}$$

The adaptive mutation probability formula is as follows:

$$P_m = \begin{cases} 0.01 + 0.09 * (f_{avg} - f)/(f_{max} - f_{min}), (f \leq f_{avg}) \\ 0.08 + 0.02 * g/G, (f > f_{avg}) \end{cases} \tag{5}$$

Among them:

f_s is an individual with small fitness value in a cross parent;

f_{avg} is the average of the current population fitness value;

f_{max} is the maximum fitness value of individuals in the current population;

f_{min} is the minimum fitness value of individuals in the current population;

f is the fitness value of the mutated individual;

g is the current evolutionary algebra;

G is the total iteration number of the algorithm.

2.2 BP Neural Network

BP neural network is divided into the following parts. Firstly, the number of hidden layers of the neural network is determined, and the topology structure of the current neural network is determined jointly with the nodes of the input layer and output layer [12].

As shown in Fig. 1, in the topological structure of BP neural network, X_1, X_2 is the input value of the neural network, Y_1, Y_2 is the predicted value of the BP neural network, and is the weight of the BP neural network.

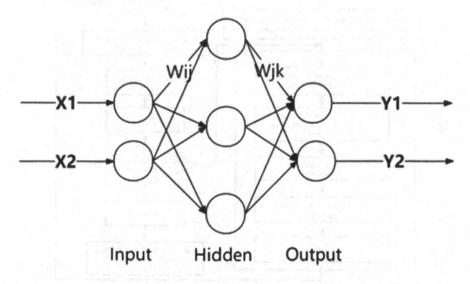

Fig. 1. Topology of BP neural network.

Secondly, the initial weights of the neural network input layer, output layer and hidden layer and the initial thresholds of hidden layer and output layer are determined. Finally, through training, the weight and threshold of the neural network can be dynamically updated through the error obtained by training. After repeated iterative evolution of the algorithm, the final neural network can be obtained, and finally the test data is used for evaluation.

2.3 Algorithm Process

Algorithm steps:

Step 1: According to the input and output of the system to determine the topology of the neural network;
Step two: parameter setting and fitness function selection;
Step 3: Initialize the population randomly;
Step 4: train the neural network, get the error and calculate the fitness value;

Step 5: Adaptive genetic algorithm iteration is carried out to get the final neural network;

Step 6: Test the final neural network, and evaluate the final neural network according to the predicted results and expected output.

The overall flow of the algorithm is shown in Fig. 2 below.

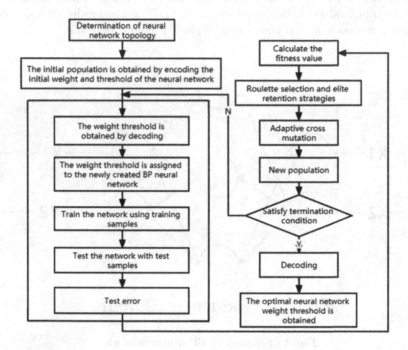

Fig. 2. Algorithm flow chart.

3   Experimental Analysis

In this paper, non - fitting linear function $y = x_1^2 + x_2^2$ is used to test the neural network; Experimental data: 4000 sets of data, among which 3900 sets of data were used for training network and 100 sets of data were used for neural network test; Population size: 50; Iterative algebra: 50.

3.1   Experimental Analysis

In this paper, non - fitting linear function is used to test the neural network; Experimental data: 4000 sets of data, among which 3900 sets of data were used for training network and 100 sets of data were used for neural network test; Population size: 50; Iterative algebra: 50.

3.2   BP Neural Network Simulation

Figure 3 shows BP neural network simulation optimized by standard particle swarm optimization algorithm.

Figure 4 shows the simulation of BP neural network optimized by simple genetic algorithm;

Figure 5 shows the BP neural network simulation optimized by adaptive genetic algorithm proposed in this paper.

In the diagram, the abscissa represents the test sample and the ordinate represents the output. Figure 6 shows the comparison of sample errors of the three algorithms in the 100 groups of test data.

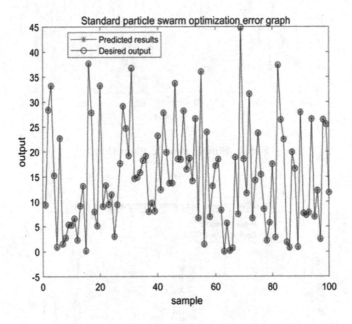

Fig. 3. Standard particle swarm optimization.

In the above figure, it can be clearly seen that the improved adaptive genetic algorithm proposed in this paper has obvious optimization effect on the neural network, the error is the smallest of the three algorithms, and its fitting function is also closer to the actual expected output.

It can be concluded that the improved adaptive genetic algorithm proposed in this paper has a great role in optimizing the accuracy of BP neural network.

3.3   Comparative Analysis

As shown in the figure above, Fig. 7 is the iterative evolution curve of the total error of the sample.

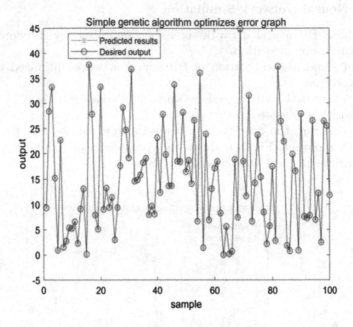

Fig. 4. Simple genetic algorithm.

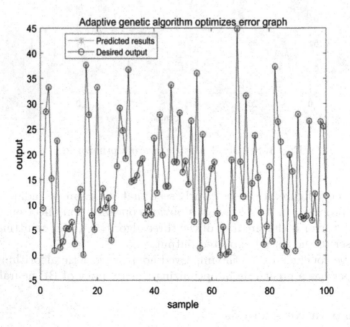

Fig. 5. Adaptive genetic algorithm.

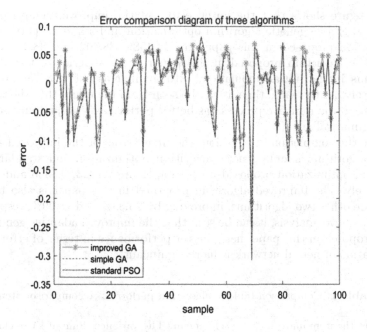

Fig. 6. Error comparison diagram of three algorithms.

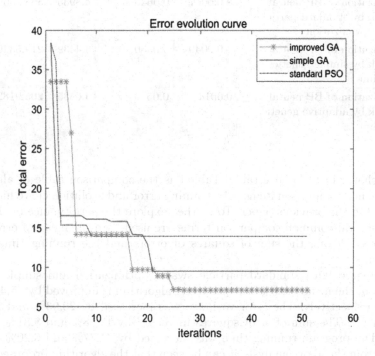

Fig. 7. Error evolution curve.

The figure shows that the initial errors of the improved adaptive genetic algorithm, simple genetic algorithm optimization and standard particle swarm optimization proposed in this paper are 33.4589, 38.402 and 38.4122, respectively. The algorithm proposed in this paper is far superior to the other two algorithms in the initial population, with an increase of 12.87% and 12.89% respectively. At the same time, it can be seen from the figure that the improved algorithm in the iterative process has better performance in jumping out of the local optimal value.

After the completion of iteration, the final errors of the improved adaptive genetic algorithm, simple genetic algorithm optimization and standard particle swarm optimization proposed in this paper are 7.1223, 9.5396 and 13.9649, respectively. The improved algorithm proposed in this paper is also far superior to the other two algorithms, improving by 25.33% and 48.99%, respectively. From the above analysis, it can be seen that the improved adaptive genetic algorithm proposed in this paper has a better performance in terms of error, and its optimization of neural network is more significant.

Table 1. Comparison table of algorithm performance comparison items

Compare the item and Algorithm	The mean	The variance	Sum of squares	The elapsed time
Optimization of BP neural network by standard particle swarm optimization	−0.0057	0.0645	4.8935	353.636903 s
Optimization of BP neural network by simple genetic algorithm	−0.0049	0.0580	4.4439	219.534010 s
Optimization of BP neural network by adaptive genetic algorithm	0.0014	0.0510	4.0535	205.918277 s

As shown in the above table, Table 1 is the comparison table of algorithm performance comparison items. The training error and evolution curve have been analyzed in the previous paper. To further explore the performance of the algorithm, several common comparison terms are used. Are the mean of errors, the variance of errors, the sum of squares of errors and the running time of the program.

Compared with standard particle swarm optimization and simple genetic algorithm, the mean error of the proposed algorithm is improved by 75.44% and 71.43% respectively. The error variance was increased by 20.93% and 12.07%, respectively. The sum of error squares increased by 17.18% and 8.81%, respectively. The program running time was increased by 41.77% and 6.20%, respectively. From the above analysis, it can be seen that the algorithm proposed in this paper has excellent performance in the four comparison terms, which proves that it has obvious advantages in the stability and accuracy of the neural network. In summary, the improved algorithm proposed in this paper reduces the time cost, reduces the network error, and improves the fitting of the neural network.

4 Conclusion

This paper presents a new adaptive genetic algorithm to improve the BP neural network. In the algorithm optimization part, the selection operator is optimized and the elite retention strategy is introduced. At the same time, adaptive operation is introduced in crossover and mutation operators to adjust the population diversity, so as to avoid the algorithm falling into local optimal and precocious algorithm.

Through the comparison experiment of the three groups of algorithms, the results show that the BP neural network optimized by adaptive genetic algorithm is obviously superior to the BP neural network optimized by simple genetic algorithm and standard particle swarm optimization. It has better fitting and effectively solves the shortcomings of the neural network which is easy to fall into the local optimal. The improved algorithm proposed in this paper is of great significance in the research and improvement of neural networks to improve the accuracy of neural network prediction.

References

1. Li, M., Xu, B., Kou, J.: Combination of genetic algorithm and neural network. Syst. Eng. Theory Pract. (02), 66–70+113 (1999)
2. Li, W., Song, D., Chen, B.: Artificial neural network based on genetic algorithm. Comput. Eng. Design (02), 316–318 (2006). https://doi.org/10.16208/j.issn1000-7024.2006.02.043
3. Meng, D., Fan, C., Wang, J.: Research on improvement of BP neural network based on chaotic genetic algorithm. Math. Theory Appl. **34**(01), 102–110 (2014)
4. Tian, X., Song, T., Liu, Y.: Optimization of structure and parameters of BP neural network based on genetic algorithm. Comput. Appl. Softw. (06), 69–71 (2004)
5. Zhai, Y., Li, H., Liu, H., Yuan, X.: Initial weights of neural network are optimized with genetic algorithm method. J. Jilin Univ. (Eng. Sci.) (02), 45–50 (2003). https://doi.org/10.13229/j.carolcarrollnkijdxbgxb2003.02.011
6. Wang, Z., Liu, Z., Gao, C., Lu, Y.: Application of genetic algorithm in BP network weight learning. J. Gansu Univ. Technol. (02), 20–22 (2001)
7. Li, P., Fan, D.: Research on improved genetic algorithm based on real coding. J. Astronaut. Meas. Technol. (06), 61–64 (2007)
8. Wu, W., Yue, T.: A review of selection operators in genetic algorithms. Fujian Comput. **28**(06), 43–44 (2012)
9. Deng, C.Y.: Crossover operator analysis of genetic algorithm. Agric. Netw. Inf. (05), 124–126 (2009)
10. Shen, C., Yue, T.: Review of mutation operator of genetic algorithm (GA). J. Horizon Sci. Technol. (23), 107–108+188 (2012). https://doi.org/10.19694/j.carolcarrollnkiissn2095-2457.2012.23.043

11. Xiong, S., Dong, L.: Adaptive genetic algorithm for labeled planar stereograms. J. Graph. **39**(06), 1105–1111 (2018)
12. Wang, J., Hu, Y., Zhang, X., Wu, B.: Based on GA - BP neural network to determine the water leakage of inevitable. J. Water Resour. Hydropower Technol. (Both Engl. Chin.) **52**(12), 201–211 (2021). https://doi.org/10.13928/j.carolcarrollnkiwrahe.2021.12.020

A Graph-Based Shortest Path Community Expansion Method

Wang Wenzhang and Zheng Xiaoyan[✉]

Tianjin University of Technology and Education, Tianjin 300222, China
zhengxy@tute.edu.cn

Abstract. With the advent of the era of big data, research on community discovery has become more and more popular. For the division of nodes in the network, the mainstream method is to calculate the fitness function of nodes and communities. This paper proposes a graph-based shortest path community expansion method (A Graph-Based Shortest Path Community Expansion Method, hereinafter referred to as SPCE algorithm). The algorithm mainly includes four steps: selecting seed nodes, expanding seed communities, finding overlapping nodes, and optimizing communities. In the process of community expansion, the SPCE algorithm does not use the current mainstream fitness function method for community expansion. Instead, it uses the characteristics of dense connections within communities and sparse connections between communities to expand using the shortest path method of graphs. After experiments in real networks and artificial networks, the SPCE algorithm can more accurately discover the community structure in the network.

Keywords: community discovery · shortest paths · community expansion · overlapping communities

1 Introduction

People are connecting more frequently and having tighter relationships as society develops and science and technology grow, and this intricate web of connections has given rise to a sophisticated social network. Protein interaction networks, email networks, gene association networks, metabolic networks, transportation networks, and many other networks are examples of networks that are comparable. Because of its complex structure, network development, diversity of connections and nodes, and multi-complexity fusion, this sort of network is referred to as

Supported by Tianjin Science and Technology Planning Project (Grant No. 64822KPXMRC00170), Science and Technology Think Tank Young Talent Program, China (Grant No. 64920220615ZZ07110153).

a complex network. Complex network research has long been popular in a wide range of disciplines. Complex networks frequently have community structure, and the network as a whole is made up of several communities. While connections between communities are scarce, those inside a community are intimately intertwined. To fully comprehend the structure and operation of a network, the appropriate social structure must be identified.

The biological field, metabolic network analysis, gene regulatory network analysis, master gene identification, etc., are currently the main applications of community discovery. In the new crown epidemic from the previous year, we can stop the epidemic's spread by strengthening protection, identifying medium- and high-risk areas, and disrupting the virus's transmission network. Community discovery is used in e-commerce to examine groups of individuals in order to carry out more precise ad placement, create a more trustworthy recommendation system, and actualize tailored interest suggestions. Additionally, community discovery may be used to investigate criminal activity, successfully attack criminal networks, and preserve social order.

2   Related Research

Among community discovery methods, it can be divided into global optimization and local optimization [1], where local optimization does not require the information of the entire network. Therefore, when the network size is larger, local optimization is more chosen. According to different strategies, local optimization can be mainly divided into four types: local expansion, faction filtering, label propagation, and local edge clustering [2].

Li et al. [3] proposed the CLFMw algorithm. Based on faction filtering, the LFM algorithm [4] is improved and combined with the CPM algorithm [5]. Start by finding the largest faction in the network for community expansion. After the max faction expansion is complete, lower factions re-expand until the min 2-faction. However, the small faction community may be expanded and annexed by the large faction community, resulting in an inaccurate division. Xie et al. [6]] proposed the CSLPA algorithm. First, the same BronKerbosch algorithm as the GCE algorithm [7] is used to find the K factions in the network. Then merge similar factions, treating each faction as a node. Start to iterate, the iterative process is the same as the SLPA algorithm [8]. The algorithm ends when the number of iterations is reached or the result no longer changes.

Although the faction approach can solve the problem that the community finds unstable results, it still has shortcomings. Not suitable for less dense networks. The results of the label transmission method are not stable and are strongly random. In contrast to the local expansion process, the seed nodes are selected by ranking, and communities of any size and density can be divided, and the community division results are stable. Therefore, the selection of seed nodes is very important. The selection of seed nodes can be divided into global ranking and local ranking.

Guo et al. [9] proposed the oclu-detect method, which calculates the node weight by the average connection strength and association density between the node and its adjacent nodes. The node with the largest weight is selected as the central node for community expansion. The second step is to calculate the membership degree of the node to the community and complete the dynamic division of the community according to the changing trend of the newly added data. Yang et al. [10] proposed a new method, which is mainly divided into three steps. In the first step, the connection strength between two adjacent nodes is calculated to convert the unweighted network into a weighted network. The second step is to generate the maximum spanning tree through the authorized network, find the core nodes in the network, and expand it. The third step is to optimize the community and merge overlapping communities.

For the method of selecting seeds by local ranking, Chen et al. [11] proposed the LMD algorithm, which uses the node with the largest local node degree as the central node to realize local community discovery. To become a central node, the degree of the node must be greater than or equal to that of other surrounding nodes, so only one node can become the central node in the local scope. Then expand the community to complete the community division. Wang et al. [12] proposed that the LCD-NJ algorithm needs to give an initial node and ensure that the initial node can be transferred to any core node in the local community within k steps. Through the PageRank algorithm, the nodes within the k steps of the initial node are ranked, and the core nodes are selected. Afterward, it expands outward through core nodes to complete social discovery.

This paper proposes a graph-based shortest path community expansion method (SPCE) and selects seed nodes through a combination of global and local methods. The node with the highest influence ranking is selected as the seed node, and its neighbor nodes are removed from the ranking list. After that, the seed node is expanded into a seed community, and the sum of the shortest path distances from the free node to the n nodes in the seed community is calculated. Add it to the seed community with the smallest distance to complete the community expansion. Then judge the overlapping nodes for the edge nodes. Finally, similar communities are merged to complete the division.

3   SPCE Algorithm

SPCE algorithm proposes new methods in three aspects: seed node selection, community expansion, and overlapping node detection. Specifically: (1) the SPCE algorithm adopts a combination of global and local methods in selecting seed nodes, avoiding the use of only global The problem is that the diversity of seed nodes cannot be guaranteed due to ranking. (2) A new shortest distance-based community expansion method is proposed by taking advantage of the characteristics of close connections within communities and sparse connections between communities. (3) In view of the large amount of calculation caused by the need to calculate the fitness between all nodes and all communities to find overlapping nodes using the fitness function, a new method for finding overlapping nodes is proposed, which only needs to calculate the edge nodes of the community, which can effectively reduce the amount of computation.

3.1   Algorithm Description

The algorithm is mainly divided into four steps: (1) seed node selection and seed community formation (2) seed community expansion (3) overlapping node discovery (4) community optimization. All node influence values are calculated in the first phase and are arranged in descending order of size. The node with the highest influence value in the list is chosen, and in order for it to serve as a seed node, its node degree must be higher than that of the majority of its neighbors. The seed node is then combined with its neighboring nodes to form a seed community. The free node is added to the closest seed community after calculating the shortest path between it and every other node in the seed community. Finding the community edge nodes' neighbors is the third phase. Calculate the similarity between the next node and the current community, and if it exceeds the threshold, join the community if it does not already belong. The merging of communities with a lot of similarities is the fourth step.

3.2   Seed Node Selection and Seed Community Formation

The selection of seed nodes is very important for the subsequent community expansion process, so the selection of seed nodes should be as close to the community center as possible. In a community network, the connections within a community tend to be tighter, which means there are more edges within the community. On the contrary, there are fewer edges between the community and the community, so the seed node of the community must have the characteristics of a high node degree. The influence value of a node is calculated by combining the node degree with the closeness of the node adjacent to the node. The formula for calculating the node influence value I(v) is as follows:

$$I(v) = k_v \times \sum_{u \in N(v)} (k_u \times J_{uv}) \tag{1}$$

The higher I(v), the higher the influence of node v in graph G, where kv is the degree of node v, and Juv is the Jaccard coefficient of nodes u, v, defined as follows:

$$Jaccard(u, v) = \frac{|N(u) \cap N(v)|}{|N(u) \cup N(v)|} \tag{2}$$

The larger the Jaccard coefficient, the higher the intimacy between the two nodes. The more similar the two nodes are. N(v) represents the set of adjacent nodes of node v, which is defined as follows:

$$N(v) = u : u \in V, (u, v) \in E \tag{3}$$

After calculating the node influence value, sort the nodes according to the node influence to get the ranking list (Inflist). Select the node n with the highest influence value and calculate that the influence of node n is greater than the

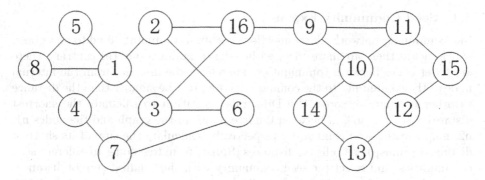

Fig. 1. Node distribution diagram

number L of all its adjacent nodes. When L is greater than the threshold, then n becomes the seed node. Remove node n and its neighbors from the ranking list (Inflist) to ensure that there is only one seed node in the local community. Continue to repeat this step until there are no nodes in the list. As shown in Fig. 1, the influence value of the nodes in the calculation graph is ranked, and the results are shown in Table 1. After selection, nodes 1 and 10 become seed nodes.

Table 1. Influence value table.

Node	Influence Value	Node	Influence Value
10	66.75	4	14.83
11	43.41	3	14.55
12	43.41	6	13.8
15	29.49	7	13
1	28.93	13	9.64
14	20.79	5	9.5
8	19.9	2	9.15
9	15.15	16	4.8

After obtaining the seed list (Seedlist), expand the seed node to obtain the seed community (Seedcommunity). According to formula (2), the neighbor node (Neigbornode) most similar to the seed node is calculated and extended to obtain the seed community. See formula (2) for calculating the similarity between the seed node and the adjacent node. As shown in Fig. 1, seed nodes 1 and 10 are expanded, and the two most similar nodes are selected to expand to become the seed community. Seed Community 1 (1, 5, 8) and Seed Community 2 (10, 11, 12) are available.

3.3   Seed Community Expansion

In a community network, the connections within a community tend to be tighter, which means there are more edges within the community. On the contrary, there are fewer edges between communities. Therefore, the distance from the internal node of the community to the community core must be smaller than the distance to other community cores. Use Dijkstra's algorithm to calculate the shortest distance sp1, sp2, sp3, ... between the free nodes in the graph and the nodes n1, n2, n3, ... in the seed community respectively. Calculate the sum of its shortest distances (Sumsp), get a list of distances (Splist) from free nodes to different seed communities, and select the seed community with the smallest sum of distances to join. Until all free nodes are divided, the community expansion is completed. Continuing to take Fig. 1 as an example, the results are shown in Table 2. Nodes 2, 3, 4, 6, and 7 are closer to seed community 1 and expand into community 1. Nodes 9, 13, 14, 15, and 16 are closer to seed community 2 and expand into community 2. Figure 1 is finally divided into two communities.

Table 2. Shortest distance table.

free node	Shortest distance from community 1	Shortest distance from community 2
2	5	10
3	5	16
4	4	16
6	8	13
7	7	16
9	11	4
13	17	5
14	17	4
15	17	3
16	8	7

3.4   Overlapping Node Discovery

In this step, overlapping nodes are primarily filtered. Find the nodes whose neighbor node (Neighbornode) and edge node (Sidenode) are members of separate communities. The similarity S between the community and its surrounding nodes can be calculated using formula (4). The node is included in the existing community if S exceeds the threshold. To finish the overlapping community discovery, iterate through each community. The following equation can be used to determine how similar a community and a node are:

$$S(C, v) = \frac{|N(C) \cap N(v)|}{|N(C) \cup N(v)|} \tag{4}$$

The larger S(C, v) is, the more likely the node v belongs to the community C. where N(C) represents the set of adjacent nodes of community C, which is defined as follows:

$$N(c) = \bigcup_{v \in c} N(v) \tag{5}$$

3.5 Community Optimization

Utilizing formula (6), the similarity S between the communities is determined as the final stage in community optimization. The two communities are joined if the resemblance is more than. Find out the outcome of the community division.

$$S(c_i, c_j) = \frac{|c_i \cap c_j|}{min(|c_i, c_j|)} \tag{6}$$

The larger S(Ci, Cj) is, the more similar the structures of the two communities Ci and Cj are. where Ci represents the nodes in the community and the adjacent nodes of the community.

4 Experiment

The experiment compares real data sets with fictional data sets of various scales in order to evaluate the performance of the algorithm. The testing environment consists of a laptop with an i7-10750H processor, a 6-core CPU, 16 GB of memory, and Windows 10 64-bit operating system. The algorithm code is implemented using Python 3.9.

4.1 Experimental Dataset

Real Dataset
The karate network Karate [13], the Dolphins network Dolphins [14], the American political book network Polbooks [15], the American college football network Football [16], and the Facebook network Facebook are selected. The details of the experimental dataset are shown in Table 3.

Table 3. Real network dataset.

network	number of nodes	number of sides
Karate	34	78
Dolphins	62	159
Polbooks	105	441
Football	115	616
Facebook	4039	88234

Artificial Dataset

Using the artificial simulation network generated by the LFR-benchmark bench-mark program [17], a total of 5 groups of different artificial simulation networks are generated. The specific network parameter settings are shown in Table 4.

Table 4. The LFR-benchmark benchmark network dataset.

network	number of nodes	mu	om	on
A	1000	0.1,0.3,0.5	0.1	3
B	5000	0.1–0.5	0.1	3
C	5000	0.3	0.1	2–6
D	5000	0.3	0.3	2–6
E	1000–20000	0.3	0.1	3

The rest of the parameters were set with the same settings: k = 20, Kmax = 50, Cmin = 20, and Cmax = 100.

where mu represents the network's complexity, and the higher its value, the more complicated the network is. The percentage of overlapping nodes in the network is represented by on. In om, overlapping nodes are members of n com-munities simultaneously.

4.2 Evaluation Standard

Overlapping Modularity EQ: Overlapping modularity [18] is an improvement from modularity and is often used as an evaluation criterion for judging the quality of overlapping community structures. The greater the modularity, the clearer the structure of the community. Therefore, the closer the value of EQ is to 1, the better the quality of the community is divided by the algorithm. Modular EQ is defined as follows:

$$EQ = \frac{1}{2m} \sum_{k=1}^{c} \sum_{i,j \in C_k} \frac{1}{O_i O_i} [A_{ij} - \frac{k_i k_j}{2m}] \tag{7}$$

Among them, m represents the total number of edges in the network, c rep-resents the number of divided communities, ki represents the degree of a node, Oi represents the number of communities to which a node belongs, and Aij rep-resents whether there is an edge between nodes I and j. If there is an edge, yes is indicated by 1, not by 0.

Normalized Mutual Information NMI: Normalized Mutual Information [19] uses entropy to measure the difference between a standard network and an algo-rithmically partitioned network. Therefore, it is suitable as an evaluation cri-terion for artificially generated network division. The closer the value of NMI is to 1, the better the community effect of the algorithm. Standardized mutual information NMI is defined as follows:

$$NMI = \frac{-2\sum_{i=1}^{C_A}\sum_{j=1}^{C_B} N_{ij}log(\frac{N_{ij}\times N}{N_i\times N_j})}{\sum_{i=1}^{C_A} N_i log(\frac{N_i}{N}) + \sum_{j=1}^{C_B} N_j log(\frac{N_j}{N})} \tag{8}$$

Among them, CA represents the standard community partition result, CB represents the community partition result obtained by the algorithm, the row of matrix N corresponds to the standard community partition result, and the column of matrix N corresponds to the community partition result obtained by the algorithm, and the sum of the i-th row is denoted as Ni, the sum of the j-th column is denoted as Nj.

4.3 Experimental Comparison

Real Network Comparison
By comparing with the other two algorithms, the experimental results are shown in Fig. 2. The SPCE algorithm only lags behind the dolphin network and the polbooks network and has good performance in other networks. The CPM algorithm cannot complete the division of the facebook network, so the EQ value is 0. The experimental results show that the SPCE algorithm can better discover the community structure no matter in the low-node network or the high-node network.

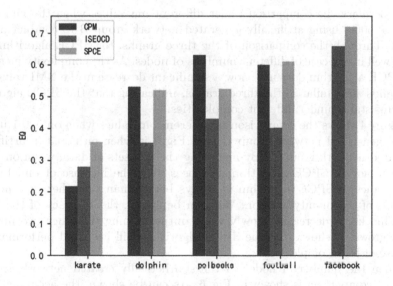

Fig. 2. Real network comparison

Artificial Network Comparison

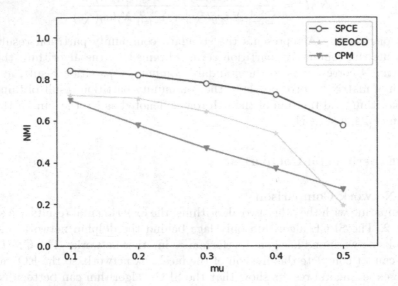

Fig. 3. Comparison of different mu values of 5000 nodes

Figure 3 shows the comparison under different mu values when the number of nodes is 5000, using artificially generated network group B to conduct experiments. Through the comparison of the three graphs, the SPCE algorithm performs well in the case of different numbers of nodes. As the complexity increases, the SPCE algorithm does not show a significant decrease in the NMI value, and the trends are similar in the three graphs, indicating that the SPCE algorithm performs stably under different complexities.

Figure 4 shows the comparison of different om values when on is 0.1 in artificially generated network group C, and Fig. 5 is when on is 0.3 in artificially generated network group D. By analyzing the two sets of data, when on is 0.1, the accuracy of SPCE algorithm decreases with the increase of om, but the performance of SPCE algorithm is always better than the other two methods in terms of community division. With on being 0.3, the accuracy of the SPCE algorithm keeps decreasing slowly while outperforming the other two methods as om grows. It shows that the SPCE algorithm still has good performance in the case of high complexity.

When the number of nodes in the synthetically created network group E varies, a comparison is shown in Fig. 6. As can be shown, the accuracy of the SPCE algorithm does not significantly decrease as the number of nodes rises. It demonstrates that even with a large number of nodes, the SPCE algorithm still operates effectively.

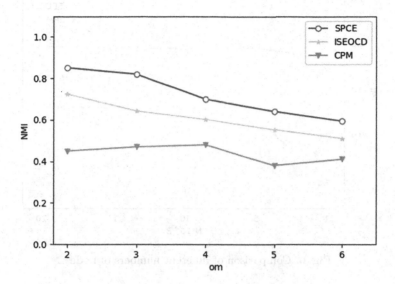

Fig. 4. Comparison of different om values at on = 0.1

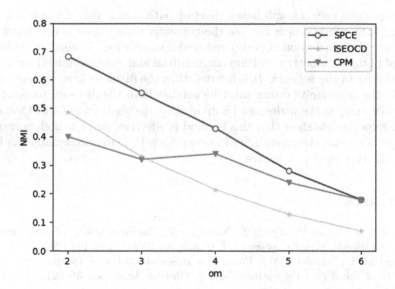

Fig. 5. Comparison of different om values at on = 0.3

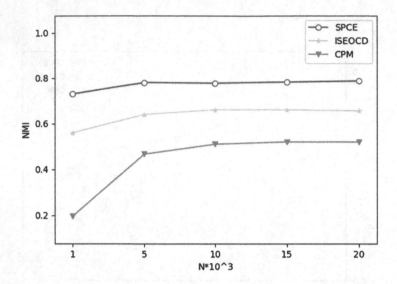

Fig. 6. Comparison of different numbers of nodes

5   Summarize

This paper proposes a graph-based shortest path community expansion method (SPCE). This method does not use the currently widely used fitness function to determine the attribution of nodes and seed communities. Instead, it utilizes the concept of tight connections within communities and sparse connections between communities in the network. It is inferred that the distance from the community node to the community center must be smaller than the distance to other community centers, so the nodes can be divided by the shortest path method of the graph. Experiments show that this method is effective, and has high accuracy in complex networks, strong stability in networks with many nodes, and can better divide the community structure.

References

1. Yancui, S., Yuan, W., Qing, Z., Xiankun, Z.: Research status of community discovery based on local expansion. J. Commun. **40**(01), 149–162 (2019)
2. Jianhua, L., Xiaofeng, W., Peng, W.: Research status of community discovery method based on local optimization. J. Chinese Acad. Sci. **30**(02): 238–247+180 (2015)
3. Jie, L., Xingwei, W., Jing, G., Chao, Y.: Local expansion group construction method for mobile communication networks. J. Northeast. Univ. (Nat. Sci. Ed.), **38**(12):1691–1695+1711 (2017)
4. Lancichinetti, A., Fortunato, S., Kertész, J.: Detecting the overlapping and hierarchical community structure in complex networks. New J. Phys. **11**(3), 033015–033015 (2009)

5. Lancichinetti, A., Fortunato, S.: Benchmarks for testing community detection algorithms on directed and weighted graphs with overlapping communities. Phys. Rev. E **80**(1), 016118 (2009)
6. Xie, H., Yan, Y.: Detecting an overlapping community structure by using clique-to-clique similarity based label propagation. J. Korean Phys. Soci. **75**(6), 436–442 (2019)
7. Lee, C., Reid, F., Mcdaid, A., et al.: Detecting highly overlapping community structure by greedy clique expansion (2010)
8. Xie, J., Szymanski, B.K., Liu, X.: SLPA: uncovering overlapping communities in social networks via a speaker-listener interaction dynamic process. In: 2011 IEEE 11th International Conference on Data Mining Workshops, pp. 344–349 (2011)
9. Lin, G., Wanli, Z., Tao, P.: Discovery of overlapping communities in social networks based on membership and analysis of dynamic cluster evolution. J. Electron. **44**(03), 587–594 (2016)
10. Yang, J.-X., Zhang, X.-D.: Finding overlapping communities using seed set. Physica A **467**, 96–106 (2017)
11. Chen, Q., Ting-Ting, W., Fang, M.: Detecting local community structures in complex networks based on local degree central nodes. Physica A **392**(3), 529–537 (2013)
12. Tao, W., Yang, L., Yaoyi, X.: A local community discovery algorithm based on core node jumping. J. Shanghai Jiaotong Univ. (Chin. Ed.) **49**(12), 1809–1816 (2015)
13. Zachary, W.W.: An information flow model for conflict and fission in small groups. J. Anthropol. Res. **33**(4), 452–473 (1977)
14. Lusseau, D., Schneider, K., Boisseau, O.J., Haase, P., Slooten, E., Dawson, S.M.: The bottlenose dolphin community of doubtful sound features a large proportion of long-lasting associations. Behav. Ecol. Sociobiol. **54**(4), 396–405 (2003)
15. Newman, M.E.J., Girvan, M.: Finding and evaluating community structure in networks. Phys. Rev. E Stat. Nonlinear Soft Matter Phys. **69**(2), 026113 2004
16. Girvan, M., Newman, M.E.J.: Community structure in social and biological networks. Proc. Nat. Acad. Sci. United States Am. **99**(12), 7821–7826 (2002)
17. Lancichinetti, A., Fortunato, S., Radicchi, F.: Benchmark graphs for testing community detection algorithms. Phys. Rev. E, Stat. Nonlinear, Soft Matter Phys. **78**(4), 046110 2008
18. Shen, H., et al.: Detect overlapping and hierarchical community structure in networks. Physica A: Stat. Mech. Appl. **388**(8), 1706–1712 (2009)
19. Danon, L., et al.: Comparing community structure identification. J. Stat. Mech. Theo. Exp. **2005**(09), P09008 (2005)

Secure Communication for 6TiSCH Wireless Networks Based on Hybrid ECC and AES Algorithms

Chengqi Hou, Wei Yang[✉], Zhiming Zhang, Qinghua Liu, and Jianmao Xiao

School of Software, Jiangxi Normal University, Nanchang, China
yw@jxnu.edu.cn

Abstract. The 6TiSCH protocol stack has been widely utilized in the industry to build highly reliable and energy efficiency wireless sensor networks (WSNs). The communication security between nodes mainly relies on the AES encryption algorithm, but the 6TiSCH protocol does not regulate the protection strategy for encryption keys in the network. Therefore, this paper proposes a hybrid ECC-AES data encryption scheme based on the 6TiSCH protocol stack. The Elliptic Curve Diffie Hellman (ECDH), Elliptic Curve Qu-Vanstone (ECQV) algorithms are used to negotiate the shared key for each two nodes in a WSN, and AES encryption with dynamic session keys are derived from the shared key during the nodes' communication phase. Meanwhile, since the ECC algorithm is used in the resource-constrained nodes, this paper considers the influence of the underlying elliptic curve operations on the computation speed of the shared key, and proposes a regular window algorithm to accelerate the scalar multiplication operation based on previous researches. To prove the scheme's viability, we conduct simulation experiments on the generation time of shared keys, and the experimental results prove that the encryption scheme under the regular window scalar multiplication has an impressive key generation speed.

Keywords: 6TiSCH Protocol · Security Communication · ECC Algorithm · AES Algorithm

1 Introduction

With the continuous development of communication technology and microelectronics, wireless sensor networks (WSNs) have been widely used in the fields of smart home, environmental monitoring and industrial control [1]. In order to achieve highly reliable, low-power data transmission between WSNs, the IEEE 802.15.4e [2] standard was released in 2012, which proposed a Time Slotted Channel Hopping (TSCH) technology. This technology coordinates the working state through precise time synchronization, and makes the communication channel for nodes change with the change in different communication time-slots, nodes that are non-working are in a dormant state. Only when there are data that need to be transmitted, the nodes turn on the RF module for

Y. Cao and X. Shao (Eds.): MONAMI 2022, LNICST 474, pp. 306–315, 2023.
https://doi.org/10.1007/978-3-031-32443-7_22

data transmission, as a way of reducing the energy consumption of sensor nodes and solving the idle listening problem [3] during the data communication phase. Based on this standard, in 2013, the Internet Engineering Task Force (IETF) started to develop a whole industrial IoT protocol stack – IETF 6TiSCH [4], aiming at low power consumption, high-reliability data and low latency transmission in industrial process control [5].

In the 6TiSCH protocol stack, the encryption and authentication operations for data security are implemented in the link layer using IEEE 802.15.4e protocol. The encryption algorithm in the protocol uses AES-CCM mode [6], which is a combination of Cipher Block Chaining Message Authentication Code (CBC-MAC) mode for authentication and Counter mode (CTR) mode for encryption. The hardware implementation of the AES algorithm [7] can finish encrypting and authenticating data in a short time. However, the keys in the AES algorithm generally come from the pre-set by the managers, and the whole network shares the same key, at this time, if there is a malicious node in the network that leaks the AES key of the whole network, it will expose the data transmission of the whole network nodes to danger.

Research on 6TiSCH WSNs has mainly focused on the resource scheduling of the network, while research on 6TiSCH network security is scarce. Sajjad [8] analyzed the security of the IEEE 802.15.4 protocol and pointed out that the protocol is susceptible to jamming-influenced DOS attacks at the MAC layer, and the IEEE 802.15.4 protocol itself does not specify the way for creating and exchanging keys during data encryption. To solve the DOS attacks caused by malicious nodes through jamming, the authors [9] proposed a dynamic scheme DISH with random replacement of time-slots and channels and proved that the scheme can effectively resist DOS attacks. However, the key negotiation and management problems in 6TiSCH networks are still a major threat that hinders secure transmission between nodes, and in [10], the authors hypothesize that when the keys are in the hands of malicious nodes, they will intercept and tamper with packets in inter-node data communication, and then attack the protocol stack through traffic dispersion attacks and overload attacks.

On the other hand, many researchers have focused on secure communication in WSNs using modified AES algorithms, for the reason that hardware-accelerated AES algorithms are suitable for implementation on restricted nodes with fast computation speed and less energy consumption, but in application scenarios such as industrial scenarios where high-security data transmission is required, AES is difficult to guarantee a sufficient degree of security. Sciancalepore et al. [11] proposed a security framework in IEEE 802.15.4 protocol with Diffie-Hellman (DH) protocol for key negotiation and AES algorithm for encryption. The article [12] proposed an encryption scheme in WSNs, where the scheme divides the plaintext into three parts for hybrid encryption, using AES, DES, and RSA algorithms for encryption respectively. Both articles use the high-energy RSA algorithm on restricted nodes, it will accelerate the energy consumption of nodes in the network. The paper [13] proposes a key extension algorithm based on the AES algorithm to increase the degree of confusion caused by the encryption process and complete hardware implementation of the improved algorithm, but the reconfiguration of the encryption steps of the AES algorithm itself could hardly to solve the problem of key leakage fundamentally.

To solve the key establishment problem between 6TiSCH network nodes, this paper proposes a hybrid encryption method of AES and ECC algorithms in the 6TiSCH sensor network, using elliptic curve encryption to establish keys on two nodes and encrypting the data by AES-CCM mode. The ECC algorithm is chosen because it has a shorter key length for the same level of security, 160 bit key length ECC algorithm can achieve the same level of security as the 1024 bit key length RSA algorithm [14]. Meanwhile, to accelerate the key generation time, this paper considers the underlying optimization algorithm of the ECC algorithm, and combines the work of Rivain [15] to propose a scalar multiplication algorithm with a regular window method to accelerate our proposed hybrid encryption algorithm.

This paper is organized as follows: Sect. 2 proposes a secure communication scheme based on a hybrid ECC-AES algorithm in the 6TiSCH WSN. Section 3 considers the scalar multiplication operation of the ECC algorithm, and a regular window algorithm is proposed to accelerate key generation time, in Sect. 4, the proposed scheme is simulated under different elliptic curve parameters, and Sect. 5 concludes the scheme and presents the future work.

2 Hybrid ECC-AES Encryption Scheme

In this section, we present a secure communication scheme with a hybrid ECC-AES algorithm. The scheme establishes a shared key for every two nodes in the sensor network by using the Elliptic Curve Diffie-Hellman (ECDH) algorithm, but the ECDH algorithm has the risk of being subject to man-in-the-middle (MITM) attacks. To resist MITM attacks, we generate an implicit certificate for each node when it joins the network using the ECQV algorithm [16]. The scheme divides the process of node communication into three phases, node joining phase, shared key establishment phase and dynamic key encryption phase, which are described in detail below. The main notations used in this paper are shown in Table 1.

First, taking a brief of the ECC algorithm, the ECC algorithm is defined on a finite field F_q, the general form of an elliptic curve is Weiertass equation: $y^2 = x^3 + ax + b$, $(4a^3 + 27b^3 \neq 0)$. The algorithm chooses a basis point G on the elliptic curve, it is feasible to select a positive integer to compute $k \cdot G$. This operation is called scalar multiplication, while it is computationally infeasible to find the integer k by the result $k \cdot G$ and the point G. This is the Elliptic Curve Discrete Logarithm Problem (ECDLP), which the security of the ECC algorithm is built on this.

2.1 Node Joining Phase

In this phase, to generate certificates for each edge node to join the WSN, the scheme adopts Certificate Authority (CA) in the joining phase, and the certificates do not use traditional X.509 certificates, because such certificates are too large in byte length and cause high energy consumption and transmission delay in the edge nodes during transmission, so this paper utilizes the ECQV protocol to generate implicit certificates to reduce such costs. During the join phase, the edge node obtains synchronization with the network through the beacon frame, gets the certificate through CA, and computes its public and private keys, only four information exchanges with the CA are required in the process. Throughout the communication process, it can be assumed that the parameters

Table 1. Symbols appearing in this paper

Symbol	Explanation
a, b	The two coefficients of the elliptic curve
F_q	Selected finite fields in the ECC algorithm
G	The selected base point, where $G = (x, y)$
n	The order of the base point G on the curve, $n \cdot G = 0$
r_A	Random number generated by node A
$Cert_A$	Certificate of node A
ASN	Time slot values in the network
K_{AB}	The shared key established by nodes A, B
$H()$	A hash function that compresses the given input into a 128bit bit output
d_A	The private key of node A
Q_A	The public key of node A
$addr_A$	64-bit MAC address of node A
ID_A	Identity information of node A in the network
$nonce_A$	The nonce value generated by node A based on the number of network time slots and its own MAC address

$\{F_q, a, b, G, n\}$ of the elliptic curve have been predetermined and stored in the edge node A and the CA. See Fig. 1 for the communication diagram of this phase.

1. The CA randomly selects $d_{CA} \in \{2, 3, \ldots, n-1\}$ as the private key of the CA in the initial stage, and calculates $Q_{CA} = d_{CA} \cdot G$ as the public key of the CA
2. CA will broadcast a beacon frame every certain time-slots, the frame includes network related information, and the node A expects to join the WSN will continuously listen to message communication in the network, once the beacon frame is received, the node will enter the computation state.
3. The edge node will randomly generate $r_A \in \{2, 3, \ldots, n-1\}$ and compute $R_A = r_A \cdot G$. The identity information ID_A of the node is generated based on the computed result $R_A = (x_A, y_A)$, $ID_A = H(x_A||addr_A)$. After the calculation is completed, the node sends an association request frame to CA, and the payload information in the frame includes $\{R_A, ID_A\}$.
4. After receiving the relevant information, the CA will calculate the certificate and part of the key information for the node according to the ECQV protocol.

$$P_A = R_A + r_{CA} \cdot G \tag{1}$$

$$cert_A = code(P_A, ID_A) \tag{2}$$

$$w = H(cert_A) \cdot r_{CA} + d_{CA}(mod n) \tag{3}$$

where r_{CA} is the random number generated by CA, and CA will send the result $\{P_A, cert_A, w\}$ as the payload in an association response frame to the edge node after the calculation step is completed.

5. The edge node receives the relevant information in the frame and calculates the public and private key of the node based on the relevant key information.

$$d_A = r_A \cdot H(cert_A) + w(mod\, n) \tag{4}$$

$$Q_A = d_A \cdot G \tag{5}$$

$$Q_A' = P_A \cdot H(cert_A) + Q_{CA} \tag{6}$$

The edge node checks whether the calculation result of Q_A is equal to Q_A', if so, it accomplishes the authentication to CA, proves that the association response frame is indeed sent by CA, and the node takes $\{d_A, Q_A\}$ as the key pair of the edge node, $cert_A$ as the certificate of the edge node, and pledge node sends the association confirm frame to CA, means that node joins the network successfully.

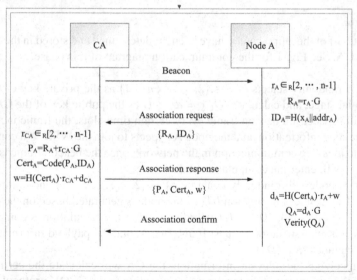

Fig. 1. Diagram of frames exchange between edge node A and CA during the join phase

2.2 Shared Key Establishment Phase

When a node A in the WSN wants to establish a connection with another node B, it enters the shared key generation phase, and the key establishment exploits the ECDH algorithm. To avoid MITM attacks, the scheme adds the authentication operation of the node before calculating the shared key, and the authentication operation utilizes the elliptic curve implicit certificate generated by CA. Also, in order to resist replay attacks, the scheme also adds the nonce value field in the authentication operation as a check against replay attacks. The communication diagram for this phase is shown in Fig. 2.

1. Node A in the network expects to establish communication connection with B, it will send an association request frame to node B. The payload of the frame contains $\{P_A, cert_A, Q_A, nonce_A, MIC_A\}$, where MIC_A is an authentication message to prevent replay attack, $MIC_A = auth(P_A, cert_A, Q_A, nonce_A)$.
2. After receiving the information in the frame, node B will first authenticate the MIC value, node B calculates $MIC'_A = auth(P_A, cert_A, Q_A, nonce_A)$, check whether MIC'_A and MIC_A are equal, if not, node B abort the session, otherwise, it calculates $Q'_A = P_A \cdot H(cert_A) + Q_{CA}$, check whether Q'_A is equal to Q_A, if so, then node B stores the relevant information of node A and replies the association response frame to node A with $\{P_B, cert_B, Q_B, nonce_B, MIC_B\}$ as the payload.
3. Node A receives the reply frame, calculates $MIC'_B = auth(P_B, cert_B, Q_B, nonce_B)$ and verifies whether MIC'_B is equal to MIC_B, if not, the session is aborted, otherwise, it continues to calculate $Q'_B = P_B \cdot H(cert_B) + Q_{CA}$ and checks whether Q'_B is equal to Q_B, if equal, then node B stores the relevant information of node A and sends association confirm frame, representing that node A,B authentication is completed and the calculation of shared key can be carried out.
4. Nodes A, B calculate the shared key K_{AB} starting from the time slots of association confirm frame transmission and reception respectively.

$$K_{AB} = r_A \cdot Q_B = r_B \cdot Q_A \tag{7}$$

2.3 Dynamic Key Encryption Phase

After two nodes complete the establishment of the shared key, the encryption and authentication of the data communication should be updated at a certain time to avoid the probability of key leakage during the node communication process, but re-computing the second phase when the key needs to be replaced will highly increase the energy consumption of the restricted nodes and the time delay of the communication process. Therefore, the shared key K_{AB} which established during the second phase can be stored in the node's memory space, and the session key can be updated by K_{AB} in each time-slot of the node's communication. The key update formula is as follows:

$$K_{AES-CBC} = H(x_k||addr_A||addr_B||ASN) \tag{8}$$

$$K_{AES-CTR} = H(y_k||addr_A||addr_B||ASN) \tag{9}$$

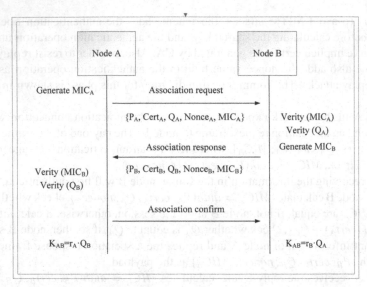

Fig. 2. Diagram of frames exchange between two 6TiSCH WSN nodes during the shared key establishment phase

It can be seen that only one hash operation is needed to update the session key, and the two communication nodes do not need to exchange any information, which achieves a fast key update with very little overhead, and the encryption process uses AES-CCM mode.

3 Consideration of ECC Optimization Algorithm

In the proposed dynamic shared key encryption scheme, since the usage of public key encryption algorithm, it is necessary to consider the overhead of the algorithm. The core operation in the ECC algorithm is the scalar multiplication $k \cdot G$, where k is a randomly large integer, and G is a base point on the elliptic curve. A large amount of research has been focused on acceleration of the scalar multiplication operation, such as the NAF window algorithm, Fixed-base comb algorithm, and other fast algorithms [17], but these algorithms usually have difficulty in achieving a regular computational flow during the scanning computation of k and are vulnerable to side-channel attacks such as Simple Power Attack (SPA). However, secure data transmission is extremely important in 6TiSCH industrial environments, so inspired by the work of Rivain [15], a regularized window method is proposed in this paper to defend against SPA attacks, and the pseudo-code implementation of the algorithm is shown below.

Regular window algorithm

INPUT: $G \in E(\mathbb{F}_P), k = (l_{d-1}, l_{d-2}, \ldots, l_0)_{2^\omega}$

OUTPUT: $Q = [k] \cdot G$

Compute $Q_i = i \cdot Q, i \in \{1, 2, \ldots, 2^\omega - 1\}$

$R_0 = Q_0, R_1 = Q_{l_{n-1}}$

for $i = l - 2$ to 0 do:

    $R_1 = 2^\omega \cdot R_1$

    $s = !! \, (l_i)$

    $R_s = R_s + Q_{l_i}$

end for

Return R_1

The algorithm uses unsigned bits representation, $k = \sum_{i=0}^{d-1} l_i \cdot 2^{i \cdot \omega}, l_i \in \{1, 2, \ldots, 2^\omega - 1\}, d = \lfloor \frac{n}{w} \rfloor$, this method avoids judging the positive and negative of l_i in the bit scanning. For the 0-bit scanning through k, which is the part of the Window NAF algorithm that does not need to be computed, but to avoid SPA attacks, the algorithm uses a virtual addition method to regular the computational flow. Virtual addition defines a virtual accumulator R_0. A virtual point addition operation with a similar amount of computation is performed on R_0 when bit 0 in k is scanned, but the virtual addition does not affect the final computation result.

4 Performance Analysis

In order to investigate the performance of exploiting the ECC algorithm to generate shared keys in our scheme, this section utilizes the open-source platform OpenWSN to simulate the implementation of our proposed hybrid ECC-AES encryption scheme on PC and conducts comparative experiments on the speed of nodes computing the key K_{AB} using the ECDH algorithm in the shared key generation phase. For the elliptic curve parameters of the scheme, three different elliptic curves secp160r1, secp192k1, and secp256k1 are experimentally selected, and the modular reduction operation adopts the Pseudo-Mersenne primes reduction algorithm [18]. The experiments select two regular scalar multiplication algorithms, the regular window method (window size $\omega = 4$) proposed in this paper and the common regular scalar multiplication algorithm Montgomery ladder [15], which under two elliptic curve coordinates (affine and projective) [19]. Simulation experiments are conducted to test the speed of shared key computation operation ($K_{AB} = r_A \cdot Q_B = r_B \cdot Q_A$) with different parameters mentioned above. Fifty repetitions of the experiments are performed for each parameter setting, and the results of the running times are recorded and plotted in Fig. 3.

The experimental results show the specific time required to compute the shared key K_{AB} for the scheme with different parameter settings after the authentication message is completed by two WSN nodes. It can be found that an appropriate increase of a part of RAM and ROM for the computation process (15 point-pairs need to be stored in the case of window size $w = 4$), through the underlying optimization algorithm, i.e. projective coordinate transformation and sliding window algorithm, can significantly

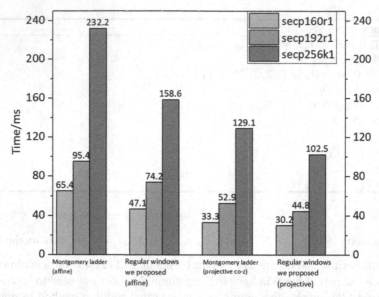

Fig. 3. Shared key calculation time ($K_{AB} = r_A \cdot Q_B = r_B \cdot Q_A$) under different elliptic curve parameters.

accelerate the key computation time of the nodes in the scheme. Since the window method requires pre-computation, this will bring a part of initialization time, but the percentage of this overhead will become smaller as the length of the elliptic curve key increases. Meanwhile, the window method is regularized in this paper, so it can resist most of the measured channel attacks.

5 Conclusion and Future Work

A hybrid ECC-AES encryption scheme is presented in this paper, and the scheme has proven to be highly robust in data communication between 6TiSCH WSN nodes. The scheme exploits the ECDH protocol to negotiate a shared key for two nodes in the network, the ECQV protocol to generate implicit certificates to resist man-in-the-middle attacks in the key generation phase, and add nonce values to the authentication process to prevent replay attacks, uses the underlying regular window method to avoid a certain degree of side-channel attacks. On the other hand, Simulation experiments are carried out on PC to calculate the shared key generate time in the scheme, it is proved that the scheme proposed in this paper is feasible in terms of calculation time.

Future work will focus on implementing the scheme proposed in this paper in a real wireless sensor network and proposing algorithms for generating group shared keys in the network.

Acknowledgments. This work is supported by the National Natural Science Foundation of China under Grant No.62002143 and the Natural Science Foundation of Jiangxi Province under Grant No. 20224BAB202011.

References

1. Gardašević, G., Katzis, K., Bajić, D., et al.: Emerging wireless sensor networks and Internet of Things technologies—foundations of smart healthcare. Sensors **20**(13), 3619 (2020)
2. 15.4e-2012: IEEE Standard for Local and Metropolitan Area Networks – Part 15.4: Low-Rate Wireless Personal Area Networks (LR-WPANs) Amendment 1: MAC Sublayer, Institute of Electrical and Electronics Engineers Std. (2012)
3. Vilajosana, X., et al.: Ietf 6tisch: a tutorial. IEEE Commun. Surv. Tutor. **22**(1), 595–615 (2019)
4. 6TiSCH Homepage: https://datatracker.ietf.org/wg/6tisch/charter/. Last accessed Oct 2018
5. Scanzio, S., et al.: Wireless sensor networks and TSCH: a compromise between reliability, power consumption, and latency. IEEE Access **8**, 167042–167058 (2020)
6. Vilajosana, X., Watteyne, T., Vučinić, M., et al.: 6TiSCH: industrial performance for IPv6 Internet-of-Things networks. Proc. IEEE **107**(6), 1153–1165 (2019)
7. Shahbazi, K., Ko, S.B.: Area-efficient nano-AES implementation for Internet-of-Things devices. IEEE Trans. Very Large Scale Integ. Syst. **29**(1), 136–148 (2020)
8. Sajjad, S.M., Yousaf, M.: Security analysis of IEEE 802.15. 4 MAC in the context of Internet of Things (IoT). In: 2014 Conference on Information Assurance and Cyber Security (CIACS), pp. 9–14. IEEE (2014)
9. Tiloca, M,. Guglielmo, D.D., Dini, G., et al.: Dish: Distributed shuffling against selective jamming attack in ieee 802.15. 4e tsch networks. ACM Trans. Sensor Netw. **15**(1), 1–28 (2018)
10. Carignani, G., Righetti, F., Vallati, C., et al.: Evaluation of feasibility and impact of attacks against the 6top protocol in 6tisch networks. In: 2020 IEEE 21st International Symposium on A World of Wireless, Mobile and Multimedia Networks (WoWMoM), pp. 68–77. IEEE (2020)
11. Sciancalepore, S., Piro, G., Vogli, E., et al.: On securing IEEE 802.15. 4 networks through a standard compliant framework. In: 2014 Euro Med Telco Conference (EMTC), pp. 1–6. IEEE (2014)
12. Pooja, C.R.K.: Triple phase hybrid cryptography technique in a wireless sensor network. Int. J. Comput. Appl. **44**(2), 148–153 (2022)
13. Lavanya, R., Karpagam, M.: Enhancing the security of AES through small scale confusion operations for data communication. Microprocess. Microsyst. **75**, 103041 (2020)
14. Bafandehkar, M., Yasin, S.M., Mahmod, R., et al.: Comparison of ECC and RSA algorithm in resource constrained devices. In: 2013 International Conference on IT Convergence and Security (ICITCS), pp. 1–3. IEEE (2013)
15. Rivain, M.: Fast and regular algorithms for scalar multiplication over elliptic curves. Cryptology ePrint Archive (2011)
16. Campagna, M.: SEC 4: Elliptic curve Qu-Vanstone implicit certificate scheme (ECQV). Standards for Efficient Cryptography, Version 1 (2013)
17. Brown, M., Hankerson, D., López, J., et al.: Software implementation of the NIST elliptic curves over prime fields. In: Cryptographers' Track at the RSA Conference, pp. 250–265. Springer, Berlin, Heidelberg (2001)
18. Gura, N., Patel, A., Wander, A., et al.: Comparing elliptic curve cryptography and RSA on 8 bit CPUs. In: International workshop on cryptographic hardware and embedded systems, pp. 119–132. Springer, Berlin, Heidelberg (2004)
19. Omondi, A.R.: Cryptography arithmetic. Springer International Publishing (2020)

Adaptive Monitoring Optimization Based on Deep-Q-Network for Energy Harvesting Wireless Sensor Networks

Xuecai Bao[1,2]([✉]), Peilun Bian[1,2], Wenqun Tan[1,2], Xiaohua Xu[2], and Jugen Nie[1,2]

[1] Jiangxi Province Key Laboratory of Water Information Cooperative Sensing and Intelligent Processing, Nanchang Institute of Technology, Nanchang, Jiangxi 330099, China
Lx97821@nit.edu.cn

[2] Jiangxi Provincial Technology Innovation Center for Ecological Water Engineering in Poyang Lake Basin, Jiangxi 330029, China

Abstract. In order to improve the energy efficiency of environmental monitoring for energy harvesting wireless sensor networks (EH-WSNs) in remote areas and achieve energy-neutral operation, an adaptive monitoring and energy management optimization method of EH-WSNs based on deep Q network (DQN) algorithm is proposed. In this paper, aiming at EH-WSNs with single-hop cluster structure, we first present a more realistic energy model established by combining different climate characteristics. Then, the optimization model of maximizing long-term monitoring utility is formulated based on harvested energy constraints. We use deep Q network (DQN) to learn random and dynamic solar energy harvesting process on solar-powered sensor nodes and optimize the monitored performance of EH-WSNs through the replay memory mechanism and freezing parameter mechanism. Finally, we present an adaptive monitoring optimization method based DQN to achieve the long-term utility. Through simulation verification and comparative analysis, in different rainy weather environments, the proposed optimization algorithm has greatly improved in terms of average monitoring reward, monitoring interruption rate and energy overflow rate. Moreover, it also indicates that the proposed algorithm has effective adaptation to the random and dynamic solar energy arrival.

Keywords: Energy Harvesting WSNs · Adaptive Monitoring · Deep Q Network · Long-term Utility

1 Introduction

Monitoring technology based on wireless sensor network (WSN) is one of the effective solutions to help supervise pollution emissions and promote the management of ecological environment [1, 2]. However, continuous monitoring often requires huge energy consumption and causes network congestion, such as high frequency monitoring or image monitoring. Although some congestion control and packet reordering algorithms provide the solution for network congestion [3, 4], traditional sensor network monitoring

Y. Cao and X. Shao (Eds.): MONAMI 2022, LNICST 474, pp. 316–330, 2023.
https://doi.org/10.1007/978-3-031-32443-7_23

system based on limited battery power still causes interruption of monitoring, especially in remote areas [1], where frequent battery replacement is too expensive and impractical. How to reduce the interruption of monitoring and improve the monitoring utility in remote areas is one of the important problems to be solved at present.

WSNs can use different types of energy sources, such as solar energy [5], wind energy [6] and so on. The energy from these external environments can be converted into electrical energy for the monitoring node by different energy conversion devices. Consequently, WSNs based on energy harvesting provide a solution for solving the energy management problem of monitoring in remote areas to a certain extent [7, 8].

In recent years, some traditional solutions based on energy harvesting technique have been applied to address the problem of sensor node lifetime [9–11]. Considering the large amount of energy consumption during cluster head selection stage and unequal harvested energy among nodes in EH-WSNs, Ren and Yao proposed an energy-efficient cluster head selection scheme [12]. Based on some traditional routing protocols such as LEACH, the scheme classified nodes with different functions and effectively scheduled them to deal with the energy management problem. Xiong focused on how to increase the network lifetime while satisfying the full target coverage in a novel hybrid EH-WSN, and then proposed a two-phase lifetime-enhancing method to meet these requirements [13]. To reduce transmission delay and improve network throughput, Bengheni deployed an enhanced energy management scheme in EH-WSNs to improve the overall performance of network [14], and it introduced an energy threshold policy to ensure a balance between the energy consumption and energy harvesting ability for each sensor node. Besides, Qiu started from the transmission strategy management in EH-WSNs, and used Lyapunov optimization theory to maximize the expected bits per packet transmission for source node in system [15].

However, solar energy has instability and random dynamic characteristics and cannot be controlled [16]. It is one of the major challenges for its energy management in EH-WSNs. Specially, it is very important to seek effective optimization strategies and realize efficient energy management of sensor networks for improving continuous environmental monitoring and prolonging network lifetime. Although many energy management methods were proposed to improve the network performance, most of them assumed that harvested energy was known in advance [17–20]. Therefore, in order to adapt the random and dynamic of solar energy, we propose a novel DQN-based adaptive monitoring optimization method for energy management in EH-WSNs. In the proposed method, we first present the dynamic energy model, consumed energy model and the network model of cluster structure. Then, we formulate the problem of adaptive monitoring in EH-WSNs. Considering the dynamic characteristic of energy and excessive energy state, the DQN algorithm is utilize to solve the problem and improve the utility of the whole network.

The rest of this paper is organized as follows. Section 2 and Sect. 3 present the model assumptions and optimization problem formulation, respectively. The detailed adaptive monitoring optimization for EH-WSNs based on solar energy harvesting is presented in Sect. 4. The simulation verification and analysis are presented in Sect. 5. Finally, conclusions are derived in Sect. 6.

2   System Model

In this section, we first present the EH-WSN model based on cluster structure, then the energy consumption model and energy harvesting model are described.

2.1   Network Model

At present, the topology of WSNs is generally divided into two types: single-hop cluster structure and multi-hop Mesh network. For environment image monitoring in remote areas, due to the relatively high bandwidth requirement, the cluster network topology with a lower delay is more suitable than the mesh network. Hence, we describe our network model as shown in Fig. 1.

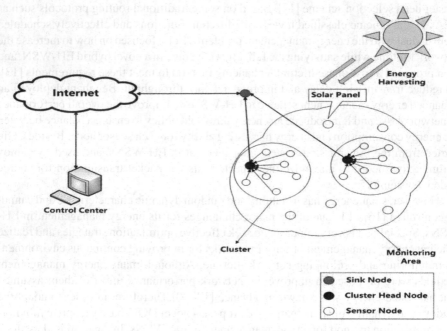

Fig. 1. Network model

2.2   Energy Consumption Model

In WSNs, the energy consumption of nodes is mainly composed of environmental monitoring, data transmission and data reception. Combined with two models of energy consumption [16, 20], the energy consumption models are defined as follows

$$E_{cons} = E_M + E_T + E_R \tag{1}$$

$$E_M = E_m * M s * T \tag{2}$$

$$E_T = E_{elec} * l + \xi_{amp} * l * d^2 \tag{3}$$

$$E_R = E_{elec} * l \tag{4}$$

where E_{cons} is the total consumption energy, E_M is the consumption energy of monitoring, E_T and E_R are the energy consumed by transmitting and receiving 1 bit data between two nodes with a distance of d, respectively. In (2), E_m is the energy consumed by once monitoring, which is a fixed value and M_s is the monitoring frequency of each time slot. Moreover, T refers to the total time slots of monitoring. It can be seen that the total energy consumption of environmental monitoring is basically proportional to the monitoring frequency. With the increase of monitoring frequency, the energy consumption of sensor nodes will also increase. In (3)–(4), E_{elec} denotes the energy dissipated per bit. d refers to the distance between sending node and receiving node and ξ_{amp} is the energy consumed by amplifier, which depends on the specification of sending amplifier. In this paper, we focus on the adaptive monitoring frequency optimization of sensor nodes and improve the total energy efficiency of monitoring.

2.3 Energy Harvesting Model

In this paper, we consider the solar energy as the harvested energy. For solar energy, solar panels are used to convert solar radiation into electrical energy to power the rechargeable battery in a node, and the battery provides energy for sensor node through energy management chip. Although solar energy is difficult to control, it is not completely unpredictable. Therefore, according to the model used in Lee and Zairi [16, 21], our model of solar energy harvesting process is defined as

$$E_H = \min\left\{ E_{bc}, \eta \int_{\tau}^{\tau+h} p(t)dt \right\} \tag{5}$$

where E_H is the total harvested energy, E_{bc} is the maximum capacity of battery in sensor node, η is the uncertainty factors affecting solar energy harvesting, such as climate and weather in the environment. τ and $\tau+h$ represent the duration of solar energy harvesting in a day, where h is the execution time of energy harvesting, and the energy harvesting can be considered to obey Poisson distribution according to Lee [15]. $p(t)$ is the probability density function of random process of solar energy harvesting in this period of time.

3 Problem Formulation

To improve the continuous monitoring and long-term survival of EH-WSNs in remote areas, we formulate the adaptive monitoring optimization based on the above system model to achieve trade-off between energy consumption and monitoring frequency, and the optimization problem can be described as maximizing the long-term utility of network through the adjustment of monitoring frequency for each time slot. The optimization problem is written as follows.

$$\max(\lim_{T\to\infty}\sum_{t=0}^{T}r_t(M_s)) \tag{6}$$

$$s.t.\ E_{res}(t+1) = \min\{E_H(t) + E_{res}(t) - E_{cons}(t), E_{bc}\} \tag{7}$$

$$E_H(t) \geqslant 0 \tag{8}$$

$$0 \leqslant E_{res}(t) \leqslant E_{bc} \tag{9}$$

$$0 \leqslant E_{cons}(t) \leqslant E_{res}(t) \tag{10}$$

The (6) denotes the optimization objection is to maximize cumulative environmental monitoring reward obtained over a period of time slots T, where $r_t(M_s)$ is the instant reward obtained through the optimized monitoring frequency M_s of sensor node in each time slot t under the premise of available residual energy. The (7)–(10) are the constrained conditions, where $E_H(t)$ is the harvested energy of nodes, $E_{res}(t)$ is the residual energy of nodes at current time slot t, $E_{cons}(t)$ is the energy consumed by nodes at time slot t, and E_{bc} is the total battery capacity of sensor nodes. In (7), the final value for the sum of $E_H(t)$ and $E_{res}(t)$ minus $E_{cons}(t)$ cannot exceed total recharge battery capacity of nodes.

Aiming at the optimization problem, traditional optimization methods are difficult to solve this complex optimization problem. The DQN algorithm, which combines the advantages of reinforcement learning and deep learning, can optimize the long-term utility and take multi-state dimension into consideration.

4 Adaptive Monitoring Optimization Method Based DQN

4.1 Algorithm Principle

In Q-learning algorithm, the Q value table is usually used to store the Q value obtained by taking different action a under each state s. However, this approach usually encounters dimension disaster problems in dealing with large or even continuous tasks. In order to better solve this problem, a function Q_N composed of parameters ω is introduced to approximate the Q value, namely value function approximation, as shown below.

$$Q_N(s, a; \omega) \approx Q(s, a) \tag{11}$$

where s and a are vector representations of state s and action a, respectively. And with the development of deep learning, neural network technology and the value function approximation show good compatibility. Therefore, the DQN algorithm comes into being through the combination of deep learning and Q-learning. Compared with Q-learning, the obvious feature of DQN algorithm is to convert Q-function into a neural network through the value function approximation.

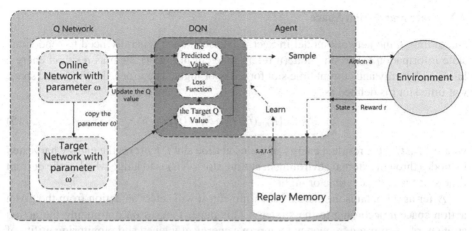

Fig. 2. DQN algorithm training process with replay memory and target network

Compared with Q-learning algorithm, DQN algorithm also has two new mechanisms, namely, replay memory and target network, as shown in Fig. 2.

To be specific, the first mechanism is to build replay memory to store the data obtained by interacting with the environment. When DQN algorithm is updated, it only needs to extract the previous experience data for learning. The second mechanism is to use the target network to freeze parameters ω. Specifically, the parameters ω are copied from the online network to target network at regular intervals by setting the appropriate update frequency. And in process of network training, only online network needs to be updated in real time. Therefore, when only the parameters of online network need to be adjusted, it becomes a regression problem. For two networks, the closer the target Q value is to the predicted Q value, the better the result is, so it is necessary to minimize its mean square error, which is defined as follows

$$L = (y - Q(s, a; \omega))^2 \tag{12}$$

where y and $Q(s, a; \omega)$ represent target Q value and predicted Q value respectively. Predicted Q value needs to be continuously updated by online network. The update process is similar to the Q-function update in Q-learning algorithm, and Q-function is updated as

$$Q_{t+1}(s_t, a_t) = Q_t(s_t, a_t) + \alpha\left[r_{t+1} + \gamma \max Q(s_{t+1}, a') - Q_t(s_t, a_t)\right] \tag{13}$$

Then parameters in target network are copied from online network, and the target Q value in target network can be obtain as

$$y = \begin{cases} r, & if\_ end\ is\ true \\ r + \gamma \max Q'(s', a'; \omega'), & if\_ end\ is false \end{cases} \tag{14}$$

where *if_end* is a sign to judge whether the algorithm ends.

4.2 State and Action Space

According to the network model in Sect. 2, sensor nodes generally need to send some state information to the sink node(it refers to agent in Fig. 4), such as residual energy, harvested energy and current time slot for a day or night. Therefore, the final state space s at time slot t is defined as

$$s = [E_{res}(t), E_H(t), N(t)] \tag{15}$$

where $E_{res}(t)$ is the residual energy of nodes at time slot t, $E_H(t)$ is the energy harvested by nodes through external environment at time slot t, $N(t)$ is to judge whether the current time slot t is in the daytime or night.

After agent obtains the state of environment, it will select an action from the given action space a according to the strategy. This paper focuses on optimizing the action strategy of monitoring frequency to improve energy efficiency and monitoring utility of EH-WSNs. Therefore, we set monitoring frequency $M_s(t)$ in each time slot as the action. Since continuous action cannot be processed, the action space needs to be discretized to reduce the convergence time of the algorithm. Therefore, the discretized action space can be written as follows.

$$a_D = [M_s(t)|d] \tag{16}$$

where d is the interval of discretization. The larger the interval of the discretization, the fewer actions contained in the action space. On the contrary, the smaller the interval, the more actions the action space can describe. Accordingly, assume that there is an action space set with A actions, namely $a_D = \{0, 1, 2, ..., n, ..., A-1\}$, 0 means that nodes enter sleep, and n means that nodes monitor n times in each time slot.

4.3 Reward Function

According to the description of the optimization model, the setting of reward function needs to consider two requirements: the first is to utilize the harvested energy of sensor nodes to improve long-term utility by increasing the number of monitoring times in each time slot as much as possible; the second is to avoid the situation that causes monitoring interruption of sensor nodes in many time slots due to insufficient residual energy.

Then, according to the energy model proposed in Sect. 2 and three-stage energy management strategy proposed in [6], we consider the differences of the energy harvested at different time period in different environments. Accordingly, we design the different reward functions for different state to optimize the action selection of nodes through the feedback of agent. In the designed reward function, harvested energy and different environments are added to help nodes to make better decisions. Moreover, we also make corresponding distinctions for the residual energy states in different intervals based on sigmoid curve and Mexican hat curve. Finally, we define reward functions r_c and r_s based on the different weather state W. The r_c and r_s represent the instant rewards obtained by agent in rainy and sunny days, respectively. The specific expressions are defined as follows

$$
r_c = \begin{cases}
c((1-s_3)(\frac{4}{(1+\exp(-ba))(1+\exp(ba))} - 1) + s_3(\frac{2}{1+\exp(-b\frac{s_1}{E_{bc}})} - 1)), a \neq 0, s_1 \in (0, \frac{E_{bc}}{6}] \\
c((1-s_3)(\frac{4}{(1+\exp(-ba))(1+\exp(ba))} - 1) + s_3(\frac{2}{1+\exp(-bs_2)} - 1)), a \neq 0, s_1 \in (\frac{E_{bc}}{6}, \frac{E_{bc}}{2}] \\
c((1-s_3)(\frac{4}{(1+\exp(-ba))(1+\exp(ba))} - 1) + s_3(\frac{2}{1+\exp(-b(s_2+\frac{s_1}{E_{bc}}))} - 1)), a \neq 0, s_1 \in (\frac{E_{bc}}{2}, E_{bc}] \\
-r_{\max}, a \neq 0, s_1 = 0 \\
0, a = 0
\end{cases}
\tag{17}
$$

$$
r_s = \begin{cases}
c((1-s_3)(\frac{4}{(1+\exp(-ba))(1+\exp(ba))} - 1) + s_2(\frac{2}{1+\exp(-bs_2)} - 1)), a \neq 0, s_1 \in (0, \frac{E_{bc}}{6}] \\
c((1-s_3)(\frac{4}{(1+\exp(-ba))(1+\exp(ba))} - 1) + s_2(\frac{2}{1+\exp(-b(s_1+a))} - 1)), a \neq 0, s_1 \in (\frac{E_{bc}}{6}, \frac{E_{bc}}{2}] \\
-r_{\max}, a \neq 0, s_1 = 0 \\
0, a = 0
\end{cases}
\tag{18}
$$

where a is the action, E_{bc} is the total battery capacity of nodes, s_1, s_2 and s_3 in (17) and (18) represent the first state $E_{res}(t)$, the second state $E_H(t)$ and the third state $N(t)$ in current time slot t, respectively. Moreover, $s_3 = 1$ means daytime and $s_3 = 0$ means night. Therefore, in the daytime, only the second half of formula is calculated, i.e., the sigmoid-like function. In the night, only the first half is calculated, i.e., the Mexican hat-like curve function. Furthermore, c and b represent the control of the amplitude and slope of the function, respectively. According to [6], c is set to 2 and b is set to 1 in (17) and (18). In rainy days, agent obtains different rewards based on the ratio of residual energy of nodes to total battery capacity and harvested energy. In sunny days, the rewards obtained by agent depend on harvested energy and action. At the same time, during the night, agent only obtains the reward value according to action. The larger the action taken, the smaller the reward received by agent. And the agent can avoid the excessive energy consumption of nodes through this negative feedback.

In addition, in order to further meet the energy storage constraints of nodes and avoid large-scale energy depletion of nodes, a penalty term $-r_{max}$ can help nodes constrain action decisions in different environments, where r_{max} is the maximum instant reward from current environment. This setting is to achieve that the instant rewards is imposed a heavy penalty when energy depletion of nodes happens. The specific description of the proposed DQN-based adaptive monitoring optimization algorithm for EH-WSNs is presented in **Algorithm 1**.

Next, the detail description of **Algorithm 1** is as follows. The initialization of a series of parameters and the corresponding setting is implemented in line 1–6. In line 7, the controller of sensor node sends the state to the agent, i.e., the deep Q network, and then the deep Q network feeds back the random or optimal action for current time slot t according to the ε-greedy policy, which is defined as

$$
a_t = \begin{cases}
\arg\max Q(s_t, a_t, \omega), & \text{if } p \geqslant \varepsilon \\
RandomAction, & \text{if } p < \varepsilon
\end{cases}
\tag{19}
$$

where *RandonAction* represents randomly selecting an action from the action space, ε is the greedy degree we set. The ε-greedy policy is utilized to balance the exploration and exploitation, i.e., to balance the reward maximization based on the knowledge already known with trying new actions to obtain unknown knowledge.

After obtaining the action, the system will transfer to the next state when an action is performed (line8), where the residual energy of nodes $E_{res}(t)$ will change with the energy consumed by the action selection of the current time slot, the second state $E_H(t)$ will change regularly according to the energy harvesting model proposed in Sect. 2.3 and the last state $N(t)$ also depends on the change of time.

Algorithm1: DQN-based Adaptive Monitoring Optimization Algorithm

---

1. **Initialization:** Initialize the online network Q with parameters ω, the target network Q' with parameters ω', the final episode M and the replay memory D

2. **while** episode $k \leq M$ **do**

3. Initialize the beginning state space s and current weather W.

4.   **For** $t = 1, 2 ..., T+1$ **do**

5.   Set environment as Env according to different weather characteristics.

6.   Choose a random probability p.

7.   Choose action a_t by using ε-greedy policy and execute it.

8.   Obtain the next state s_{t+1} based on the selected action and current environment.

9.   Calculate reward according to formula (18) and (19) , i.e. $r_t = \begin{cases} r_c \leftarrow Env(a_t), if\ W = 0 \\ r_s \leftarrow Env(a_t), if\ W = 1 \end{cases}$.

10.   Store the experience $\{s_t, a_t, r_t, s_{t+1}\}$ in replay memory D.

11.   Get a batch of samples $\{s_t, a_t, r_t, s_{t+1}\}$ from the replay memory D.

12.   Calculate $y = \begin{cases} r, if\ t\ terminates\ at\ step\ T+1 \\ r_t + \gamma \max Q'(s_{t+1}, a'; \omega'), otherwise \end{cases}$.

13.   Perform a gradient descent step by using $(y - Q(s_t, a_t; \omega))^2$ to update the parameters ω of online network.

14.   Return the value of parameters ω in the online network Q.

15.   Every N times update target network parameters ω'.

16.   episode $k= k+1$

17.   **End For**

18. **End while**

19. Output the target network Q'

Then the reward can be calculated according to the reward function (line 9). And it should be noted that when agent interacts with the environment, if the current weather is rainy, i.e., $W = 0$, the instant reward r_c can be obtained according to formula (17) above, and if the current weather is sunny, i.e., $W = 1$, the instant reward r_s can be obtained according to formula (18), both rewards depend on residual energy and harvested energy.

Inside the network, the replay memory stores agent's experience of each time slot (line 10). The parameters ω of online network are updated every time with samples from the replay memory (line 11–14), and finally the parameters ω' of target network are copied from the online network every N times (line 15).

5 Performance Evaluation

5.1 Simulation Settings

In our simulations, we used a GPU-based server with the software environment of Tensor-Flow 1.3.0 and Python 3.6. Thereafter, we investigate the performance of our proposed DQN-based adaptive monitoring optimization algorithm (Proposed DQN) compared with the Q-learning algorithm, random method and greedy algorithm [22] (Greedy).

Here, it should be noted that the rainy environment means that the number of rainy days is not less than that of sunny days during a period time. Simultaneously, we compare the performance of proposed algorithm with the other three methods and investigate the performance metrics related to average monitoring reward, monitoring interruption rate and energy overflow rate based on the same energy harvesting model. The detail parameter settings are summarized in Table 1.

Table 1. Parameter values used in the simulations

Parameter	Value	Description
Discount factor γ	0.9	Discount factor used for the DQN algorithm
Exploration ε	0.1	Chance of random action in the ε-greedy exploration
Learning rate α	0.0001	Learning rate used by AdamOptimizer
Total episode k	5000	How many episodes are used to train the network model
Replay memory size	1000	Size of the container for storing learning experiences
Target network update frequency N	10	Rate to update target Q network towards online Q network
Batch size	32	How many learning experience are used for each episode
Battery capacity E_{bc}	120	Maximum capacity of rechargeable battery for sensor node
Energy consumption units F_{oon}	0 to 4	Range of energy consumption units per time slot by monitoring
Harvested energy in sunny days E_H	0 to 9	Random range of harvested energy units per time slot in sunny days
Harvested energy in rainy days E_H	0 to 5	Random Range of harvested energy units per time slot in rainy days

In Table 1, we list the parameter values of harvested energy E_H in two different weathers and energy consumption units E_{cons} in different monitoring frequency. For action space a, we also set four actions, i.e., the node monitors 0 to 4 times in each time slot and consumes the corresponding amount of energy. Subsequently, since there is a certain gap for energy harvesting in different environments, we set two different ranges of values. In sunny days, due to the high solar radiation intensity, the range of harvested energy is set to 1 to 9 energy units; on the contrary, for the rainy days, the range is set to 1 to 5 energy units. If there is no light at night, the value of harvested energy is 0.

5.2 Results and Comparative Analysis

For environmental monitoring of EH-WSN in remote areas, the performance of the rainy environment is the most concerned about the optimization problem. Therefore, according to the simulation scenarios in above subsection, we center on the performance analysis of the proposed algorithm compared to other three algorithms under the rainy environment with two different ratio of rainy days to sunny days. Here, the rainy environment can better reflect the trade-off performance between monitoring frequency and energy consumption.

To verify the performance of proposed DQN-based algorithm, we present the results for rainy days accounted for 70%. The corresponding state-action result is shown in Fig. 3

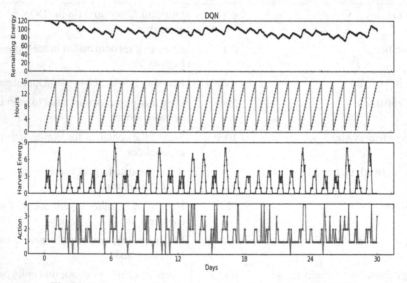

Fig.3. Node state-action diagram (rainy days account for 70%)

As shown in Fig. 3, we can see that the high probability of rainy days means the harvested energy is relatively lower in the whole 30 days. Compared with scenarios of rainy weather accounted for 50% in the previous subsection, the proposed DQN-based algorithm can also be adapted to the environmental characteristics and further improve

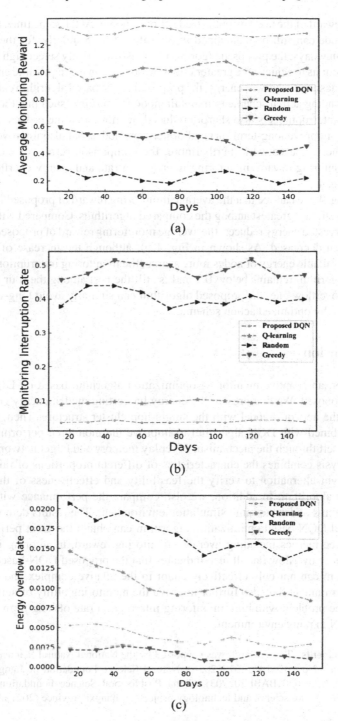

Fig. 4. Performance comparison of Four Algorithms (rainy days account for 70%)

long-term reward of the node by optimized action scheme. At the same time, the residual energy of node can still be maintained into a safe range. Similarly, for the 14th, 15th and 17th sunny days, the proposed algorithm can also adaptively select high monitoring frequency actions to achieve the greater utility. Moreover, in the night-time environment, although nodes cannot harvest energy, the proposed DQN-based algorithm can still select the corresponding action scheme to maintain node monitoring, such that the number of monitoring interruptions is also sharply reduced. It shows that the proposed algorithm can not only improve long-term survival of network nodes, but also improve long-term reward of the whole network. Furthermore, the comparison results of more relevant average monitoring reward, monitoring interruption rate and energy overflow rate are shown in Fig. 4.

From Fig. 4, we can see that the average monitoring reward of proposed DQN-based algorithm is still the greatest among the compared algorithms. Compared with Fig. 4(a), since the harvested energy reduces, the average monitoring reward of proposed algorithm has also been decreased. As shown in Fig. 4(b), although the increase of rainy days makes the available energy of nodes more scarce, the monitoring interruption rate of the proposed algorithm remains below 0.1 and is still the best among the four algorithms. In terms of overflow rate, the proposed algorithm can similarly avoid long-term energy overflow rate by optimized action scheme.

6 Conclusion

In this paper, an adaptive monitoring optimization algorithm based on DQN for EH-WSNs is proposed. We first present the energy harvesting model, energy consumption model and the network model with the single-hop cluster structure. Then, these models are combined with DQN algorithm to improve the monitored performance of the algorithm itself through the mechanism of replay memory and target network. The simulation analysis combines the characteristics of different proportions of rainy weather with day-night alternation to verify the feasibility and effectiveness of the proposed DQN-based algorithm. In addition, we also compare the performance with the other three algorithms under the same simulation environment. The results demonstrate that the proposed DQN-based optimization algorithm can obtain the great performance in terms of three metrics including average monitoring reward, monitoring interruption rate and energy overflow rate. It also indicates that the proposed DQN-based optimization algorithm can not only effectively adapt to the relative complex and changeable weather environment, but also further improve the monitoring utility of network nodes and solve the problem with high monitoring interruption rate of long-term monitoring for EH-WSN in rainy environment.

Acknowledgements. This research was supported by the National Natural Science Foundation of China (Grant No. 61961026, 61962036), Natural Science Foundation of Jiangxi Province, China (Grant No. 20202BABL202003), China Postdoctoral Science Foundation (Grant No. 2020M671556), Major science and technology projects in Jiangxi province (20213AAG01012).

References

1. Lombardo, L., Corbellini, S., Parvis, M., Elsayed, A., Angelini, E., Grassini, S.: Wireless sensor network for distributed environmental monitoring. IEEE Trans. Instrum. Meas. **67**(5), 1214–1222 (2017)
2. Muduli, L., Mishra, D.P., Jana, P.K.: Application of wireless sensor network for environmental monitoring in underground coal mines: a systematic review. J. Netw. Comput. Appl. **106**, 48–67 (2018)
3. Cao, Y., Ji, R., Ji, L., Lei, G., Wang, H., Shao, X.: I^2-MPTCP: a learning-driven latency-aware multipath transport scheme for industrial internet applications. IEEE Transactions on Industrial Informatics (2022)
4. Cao, Y., Ji, R., Huang, X., Lei, G., Shao, X., You, I.: Empirical Mode Decomposition-empowered Network Traffic Anomaly Detection for Secure Multipath TCP Communications, Mobile Networks and Applications (2022)
5. Antony, S.M., Indu, S., Pandey, R.: An efficient solar energy harvesting system for wireless sensor network nodes. J. Inf. Optim. Sci. **41**(1), 39–50 (2020)
6. Sun, W., Ding, Z., Qin, Z., Chu, F., Han, Q.: Wind energy harvesting based on fluttering double-flag type triboelectric nanogenerators. Nano Energy **70**, 104526 (2020)
7. Sharma, H., Haque, A., Jaffery, Z.A.: Modeling and optimisation of a solar energy harvesting system for wireless sensor network nodes. J. Sens. Actuator Netw. **7**(3), 40 (2018)
8. Sharma, H., Haque, A., Jaffery, Z.A.: Maximization of wireless sensor network lifetime using solar energy harvesting for smart agriculture monitoring. Ad Hoc Netw. **94**, 101966 (2019)
9. Sarang, S., Drieberg, M., Awang, A., Ahmad, R.: A QoS MAC protocol for prioritized data in energy harvesting wireless sensor networks. Comput. Netw. **144**, 141–153 (2018)
10. Lakshmi, P.S., Jibukumar, M.G., Neenu, V.S.: Network lifetime enhancement of multi-hop wireless sensor network by RF energy harvesting. In: Proceedings of the 2018 International Conference on Information Networking, pp. 738–743 (2018)
11. Nguyen, H.S., Ly, T.T.H., Nguyen, T.S., Huynh, V.V., Nguyen, T.L., Voznak, M.: Outage performance analysis and SWIPT optimization in energy-harvesting wireless sensor network deploying NOMA. Sensors **19**(3), 613 (2019)
12. Ren, Q., Yao, G.: An energy-efficient cluster head selection scheme for energy-harvesting wireless sensor networks. Sensors **20**(1), 187 (2020)
13. Xiong, Y., Chen, G., Lu, M., Wan, X., Wu, M., She, J.: A two-phase lifetime-enhancing method for hybrid energy-harvesting wireless sensor network. IEEE Sens. J. **20**(4), 1934–1946 (2019)
14. Bengheni, A., Didi, F., Bambrik, I.: EEM-EHWSN: enhanced energy management scheme in energy harvesting wireless sensor networks. Wireless Netw. **25**(6), 3029–3046 (2019)
15. Qiu, C., Hu, Y., Chen, Y., Zeng, B.: Lyapunov optimization for energy harvesting wireless sensor communications. IEEE Internet Things J. **5**(3), 1947–1956 (2018)
16. Lee, P., Eu, Z.A., Han, M., Tan, H.: Empirical modeling of a solar-powered energy harvesting wireless sensor node for time-slotted operation. In: Proceedings of the 2011 IEEE Wireless Communications and Networking Conference, pp. 179–184 (2011)
17. Fraternali, F., Balaji, B., Agarwal, Y., Gupta, R.K.: Aces: automatic configuration of energy harvesting sensors with reinforcement learning. ACM Trans. Sens. Netw. **16**(4), 1–31 (2020)
18. Tekin, N., Gungor, V.C.: The impact of error control schemes on lifetime of energy harvesting wireless sensor networks in industrial environments. Comput. Stand. Interfaces **70**, 103417 (2020)
19. Han, C., Zhang, S., Zhang, B., Zhou, J., Sun, L.: A distributed image compression scheme for energy harvesting wireless multimedia sensor networks. Sensors **20**(3), 667 (2020)
20. Raja, J., Mookhambika, N.: A novel energy harvesting with middle-order weighted probability (EHMoWP) for performance improvement in wireless sensor network (WSN). J. Ambient Intell. Humaniz. Comput. 1–12 (2021)

21. Zairi, S., Zouari, B., Niel, E., Dumitrescu, E.: Nodes self-scheduling approach for maximising wireless sensor network lifetime based on remaining energy. IET Wirel. Sens. Syst. **2**(1), 52–62 (2012)
22. Sahoo, J., Sahoo, B.: Solving target coverage problem in wireless sensor networks using greedy approach. In: Proceedings of the 2020 International Conference on Computer Science, Engineering and Applications, pp. 1–4 (2020)

Rabin Fingerprint-Based Provenance Compression Scheme for Wireless Sensor Network

Yu Yang⬛, Zhiming Zhang(✉)⬛, and Wei Yang⬛

Jiangxi Normal University, Nanchang 330022, China
zzm_9650@163.com

Abstract. Provenance is considered an effective mechanism to evaluate the reliability of data. To avoid the linear growth of provenances with the growth of the packet transmission path, this paper proposes a provenance compression scheme based on the Rabin fingerprint (RFP). In the RFP scheme, each node uses its identity ID as a seed to generate a fingerprint, the fingerprint is its provenance. When a node on the transmission path receives a packet, it performs a fingerprint connection operation between its provenance and the provenance stored in the packet to generate a new fixed-length fingerprint provenance, and the new provenance is updated to the package. When the base station receives the packet, it will recover the complete transmission path of the packet based on the provenance. Performance analysis and simulation results show that compared with existing provenance compression schemes, the provenance size of the RFP scheme not only does not increase as the path length becomes longer but also has great advantages in storage overhead and energy consumption.

Keywords: Wireless Sensor Network · Provenance · Rabin Fingerprint · Path Fingerprint

1 Introduction

The Wireless sensor network (WSN) is a distributed and self-organizing network [1]. According to the specific needs of users, many sensor nodes work together to monitor, collect and process environmental information, then transmit various environmental data to end-users through wireless channel transmission [2]. However, in sensitive fields such as health monitoring and military affairs, data is collected by sensor nodes and sent to servers [3]. Therefore, it is necessary to ensure the credibility of the sensor data collected by servers to provide reliable information to applications. Since provenance [4, 5] records the history of the packet transmission and the relevant operations on the packet [6, 7], it is possible to recover the complete path of packet transmission based on the provenance. Therefore, provenance is an effective mechanism for evaluating data credibility [8]. The simplest provenance scheme is to directly record the node ID [9] of all transmission nodes as provenance. Therefore, the size of provenance will increase linearly with the

© ICST Institute for Computer Sciences, Social Informatics and Telecommunications Engineering 2023
Published by Springer Nature Switzerland AG 2023. All Rights Reserved
Y. Cao and X. Shao (Eds.): MONAMI 2022, LNICST 474, pp. 331–344, 2023.
https://doi.org/10.1007/978-3-031-32443-7_24

growth of the packet transmission path. Still, the storage space, energy, and bandwidth of wireless sensor networks are limited, so it is necessary to compress the provenance for transmission.

In recent years, scholars have proposed effective schemes for provenance compression [10–15]. To reduce the size of provenance, the reference [10] proposed the probabilistic packet marking method, in which each node on the transmission path appends its information to the packet with a certain probability. But the shortcoming is that the base station needs to receive enough packets containing provenance information to recover the packet transmission path. To reduce the provenance size vigorously, the reference [12] proposed the method of the embedded bloom filter, which can effectively reduce the provenance size but has the problem of false positives. The reference [13] proposed an arithmetic coding-based provenance compression scheme, but as the network topology becomes complex, it increases the coding and decoding computation. The reference [14] proposed a digital dictionary-based provenance compression scheme, but if the network topology changes frequently, it will decrease the algorithm's efficiency. To improve the dictionary-based provenance method, which is sensitive to topology changes, reference [15] proposed a provenance compression scheme based on path index difference. However, when the network topology is complex, the efficiency of retrieving similar paths is not high. For most of the above schemes, the size of provenance increases with the path length.

This paper proposes a provenance compression scheme based on the Rabin fingerprint (RFP). The basic idea is that the base station first generates a tree with the base station as the root node from the entire wireless sensor network. Then calculates the path fingerprint of each path through the Rabin fingerprint algorithm and saves the path fingerprint and the corresponding path to the path fingerprint table. In the RFP scheme, each node uses its ID as the seed to calculate the Rabin fingerprint, and the fingerprint is its provenance. When a node on the transmission path receives a packet, it performs a fingerprint connection operation between its provenance and the provenance stored in the packet to generate a new fixed-length fingerprint provenance, and the new provenance is updated to the package. When the base station receives the packet sent by the node, it first extracts the provenance of the packet and then checks the path fingerprint table. If the path fingerprint is equal to the provenance, the path corresponding to the path fingerprint is the packet's complete transmission path. The performance analysis and experimental simulation show that compared with the existing schemes, the RF scheme has obvious advantages in terms of storage space and energy consumption as the path length increases.

2 Related Work

In recent years, scholars have proposed effective provenance compression schemes.

Chaudhari et al. [10] proposed the PPM (Probabilistic Packet Marking) method. When a packet passes through a node, each node will write its node ID into the packet with a certain probability. When the base station receives enough marked packets, it will obtain the ID of each node on the transmission path to recover the transmission path of the packet. Although the compression rate of this scheme is high, a large number of packets will overload the whole network, and problems such as a significant error rate in reconstructing the path will be associated.

Alam et al. [11] proposed the PPF (Probabilistic Provenance Flow) method, which uses the IDs of nodes to construct provenance. The IDs of each node were embedded into packets following different algorithms according to a certain probability. The compression effect of this method is better than PPM. However, similarly, the base station has to receive enough packets with marked information to reconstruct the transmission path of the packets.

Sultana et al. [12] proposed the IBF (in packet bloom filter) method. The core of this method is to embed a bloom filter in each packet and write the node's ID into the bloom filter using the Hash function. After receiving the packet, the base station extracts the provenance from the bloom filter and recovers the packet transmission path. However, this scheme has a false positive problem.

Hussain et al. [13] proposed a compression method based on arithmetic coding. This method assigns shorter code words to characters with a high probability of occurrence and otherwise allocates longer code words. The size of its provenance mainly depends on the probability of the packet passing through the node. The greater the probability is, the smaller the provenance is. Although it has a high compression rate, the encoding and decoding of provenance require a lot of computation. With the expansion of wireless sensor network scale and the complexity of network topology, excessive calculation will inevitably lead to the performance decline of the algorithm.

Wang et al. [14] proposed a dictionary-based compression scheme in which each node in the network has a dictionary sequence that stores the transmission paths of the packets. The base station only needs to query the path index value to get the complete transmission path. If the transmission path of packets does not change frequently, the dictionary usage will be high, and the algorithm will be more efficient. However, if the transmission path of packets changes frequently, the dictionary sequence will also change frequently, resulting in the inefficiency of the algorithm.

Xu et al. [15] proposed a provenance scheme based on the difference in path index. The scheme first builds the backbone path along the gradient direction, then de-duplicates the backbone path based on the method of Truncation Hamming Distance, and then builds the dictionary of the backbone path after de-duplication. When a new transmission path appears, the path most similar to it in the dictionary is retrieved, representing the new path as its index difference form. Although this scheme improves the problem that the dictionary-based provenance compression method is sensitive to network topology changes, it is inefficient to retrieve similar paths when the wireless sensor network is extensive in scale.

3   The System Model

3.1   Rabin Fingerprint

The Rabin fingerprint algorithm [16, 17] was proposed by Rabin, a professor at Harvard University in the United States. The basic ideas are as follows:

Assuming that $S(a_1, a_2, \cdots, a_n)$ is a binary string containing n binary bits, given an integer t over a finite field $GF(2^n)$, the corresponding (n-1) degree polynomial can be constructed from the string S:

$$S(t) = a_1 t^{n-1} + a_2 t^{n-2} + \cdots + a_n \tag{1}$$

Given an m-degree polynomial $R(t) = b_1 t^m + b_2 t^{m-1} + \cdots + b_m$, the Rabin fingerprint of the string S is calculated as follows:

$$RF(S) = S(t) \bmod R(t) \tag{2}$$

Let $M = R(t) = b_1 t^m + b_2 t^{m-1} + \cdots + b_m$, then the Rabin fingerprint of the string $S(a_1, a_2, \cdots, a_n)$ can be expressed as:

$$RF(a_1, a_2, \cdots, a_n) = a_1 t^{n-1} + a_2 t^{n-2} + \cdots + a_n \bmod M \tag{3}$$

The Rabin fingerprint connection calculation of nodes n_i and n_j is as follows:

$$RF(n_i n_j) = RF(n_i \| n_j) \bmod M = RF(RF(n_i) \| n_j) \bmod M$$
$$= \left[RF\left(RF(n_i) \times t^{l_j} \right) + RF(n_j) \right] \bmod M \tag{4}$$

where $\|$ denotes the connection operation, l_j denotes the string length of node n_j, and in this way, the Rabin fingerprint connection operation for nodes $n_1, n_2, \cdots, n_m$ is as follows:

$$RF(n_1 n_2 n_3 \cdots n_m) = RF(RF(n_1 n_2 n_3 \cdots n_{m-1}) \| n_m) \bmod M$$
$$= \left(RF\left(RF(n_1 n_2 n_3 \cdots n_{m-1}) \times t^{l_m} \right) + RF(n_m) \right) \bmod M \tag{5}$$

where $\|$ denotes the connection operation, l_m denotes the string length of node n_m.

3.2 The Network Model

The whole sensor network consists of n common nodes and a base station. G(N,L) denotes the topology of the wireless sensor network model, where N denotes the set of all nodes in the network, and L denotes the set of edges for all nodes in the network.

$N = \{n_i, i = 1, 2, \ldots, n\}, L = \{l_{ij}, i = 1, 2, \ldots, n; \ j = 1, 2, \ldots, n\}$.

Each node n_i is assigned a unique identification ID before deployment, and the ID is used as a seed to compute the Rabin fingerprint, which is the provenance that the node attaches to the packet. Once deployed, the nodes will no longer change their positions. All nodes are formed into a tree with the base station as the root, as shown in Fig. 1. If some nodes die due to energy exhaustion and the path of the wireless sensor network changes, the topology of the wireless sensor network will be automatically updated.

When the sensor node senses the data, it will send it to the base station. In the data transmission process, each node will attach its Rabin fingerprint as provenance to the packet and pass it to the next node. When the base station receives the packet, it will recover the complete transmission path of the data based on the provenance in the packet.

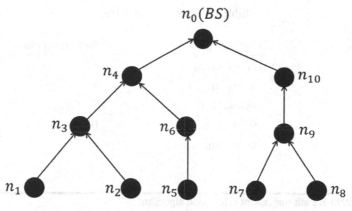

Fig. 1. Network tree topology.

4 Rabin Fingerprint-based Provenance Compression Scheme for Wireless Sensor Network

This paper proposes a Rabin fingerprint-based provenance compression scheme for wireless sensor networks (RFP). The RFP is divided into three steps: path fingerprint calculation by the base station, provenance coding, and provenance decoding.

4.1 Compute Path Fingerprint

When all nodes form a tree structure with the base station as the root node, the base station calculates the corresponding path fingerprint for each path according to algorithm 1. Assuming a path consists of nodes $n_1, n_2, \cdots, n_m$, the base station first calculates the fingerprint $RF(n_1)$, $RF(n_2)$, $\cdots$, $RF(n_m)$ of all nodes on the path according to the formula (3). The base station performs connection operation between $RF(n_1)$ and $RF(n_2)$ according to formula (4) to obtain the new fingerprint $RF(n_1 n_2)$. In this way, the path fingerprint $RF(n_1 n_2 \cdots n_m)$ of the path is finally calculated according to Formula (5).

In Fig. 1, assume that the ID of node n_1 is 1, the ID of node n_3 is 3 and the ID of node n_4 is 4. Set M = 11 and calculate the fingerprint $RF(n_1) = 1$, $RF(n_3) = 3$, $RF(n_4) = 4$ respectively according to Formula (3). Then $RF(n_1)$ and $RF(n_3)$ are connected according to Formula (4) to obtain the new fingerprint $RF(n_1 n_3) = 8$. Then $RF(n_1 n_3)$ and $RF(n_4)$ are connected according to Formula (5) to obtain the new fingerprint $RF(n_1 n_3 n_4) = 0$. Finally, the path fingerprint of the path $(n_1 n_3 n_4 n_0)$ is calculated as $RF(n_1 n_3 n_4 n_0) = 0$. In this way, the path fingerprints of other paths can be calculated according to algorithm 1, and finally, the path fingerprints corresponding to all paths can be stored in Table 1.

Table 1. Path fingerprint table.

Path coding	Complete path	Path fingerprint
1	(n_1, n_3, n_4, n_0)	0
2	(n_2, n_3, n_4, n_0)	3
3	(n_5, n_6, n_4, n_0)	5
4	(n_7, n_9, n_{10}, n_0)	10
5	(n_8, n_9, n_{10}, n_0)	2

Algorithm 1. Path fingerprint calculation algorithm

Input: A path with m nodes $n_1, n_2, \cdots, n_m$

Output: Path fingerprint $RF(n_1, n_2, \cdots, n_m)$

For(i=2;i≤m;i++) do

   $RF(n_1 n_2 \cdots n_i) = RF(RF(n_1 n_2 \cdots n_{i-1}) \| n_i)$

End for

Return $RF(n_1 n_2 \cdots n_m)$

4.2 Provenance Coding

(1) Source node provenance coding.

When a source node n_s wants to send sensor data to the base station, after generating the packet, it will create two fields on the packet to store the provenance. The format of the fields is shown in Table 2. The fingerprint field stores the path fingerprint of the current packet transmission path, and the length field denotes the path length. The source node n_s takes its ID as the seed and generates a fingerprint $RF(n_s)$ according to Formula (3). It then stores $RF(n_s)$ in the packets' fingerprint field and sets the field's value to 1. Finally, it sends the packet containing the provenance to the next node.

Table 2. Provenance of source node n_s.

fingerprint	length
$RF(n_s)$	1

(2) **Forwarding node provenance encoding.**

When a forwarding node n_i receives a packet from the previous node n_j, node n_i first extracts the original provenance fingerprint RF(Z) from the packet. It then uses its ID as the seed to calculate the fingerprint $RF(n_i)$. Then perform a fingerprint connection operation between $RF(n_i)$ and RF(Z) to obtain $RF(n_1n_2 \cdots n_i) = RF(RF(Z)\|n_i)$ mode M, take it as the new provenance, and update the fingerprint field. And then update the length field and set length = length + 1. Finally, send the updated packet to the next node. The provenance of forwarding node n_i is shown in Table 3:

Table 3. Provenance of forwarding node n_i.

Fingerprint	Length
$RF(n_1n_2 \cdots n_i)$	length + 1

4.3 Provenance Decoding

When the base station receives the packet sent by a node, it first extracts the provenance from the packet. It then checks Table 1 to find the path fingerprint equal to the provenance, the path corresponding to the path fingerprint is the packet's complete transmission path. The specific provenance decoding algorithm is shown in Algorithm 2, where k denotes the total number of paths in the path fingerprint table.

Algorithm 2. Provenance Decoding Algorithm

Input: A packet P(t)

Output: The set of complete paths corresponding to the packet TP(i)

Get RF(t) from P(t)

For(i=1;i≤k;i++) do

    If (RF(t)==RF(i)) then

        Return TP(i)

End if

End for

4.4 Example

To understand the RFP scheme more clearly, this section gives an example to illustrate how to encode and decode provenance in RFP scheme. In Fig. 1, assume that the identity

IDs of the nodes n_1, n_3, n_4 in the path (n_1, n_3, n_4, n_0) are 1, 3, 4. Set $M = 11$. If the source node n_1 wants to send the packet to the base station, it first uses its ID as the seed and calculates the fingerprint $RF(n_1) = 1$ according to formula (3). Then store $RF(n_1)$ in the fingerprint field of the packet, set the value of the length field is 1, and then send the packet to the next node n_3. Table 4 shows the provenance generated by source node n_1.

Table 4. Provenance of source node n_1.

Fingerprint	Length
$RF(n_1) = 1$	1

When node n_3 receives a packet from node n_1, it first extracts the provenance fingerprint $RF(n_1)$ from the packet, and then uses its ID as the seed to calculate the fingerprint $RF(n_3)$. Then perform a fingerprint connection operation between $RF(n_3)$ and $RF(n_1)$ to obtain $RF(n_1n_3) = 8$, take it as the new provenance and update the fingerprint field of the packet to 8. And then update the value of the length field to 2. Then send the updated packet to node n_4, and the provenance generated by the forwarding node n_3 is shown in Table 5. In this way, the provenance generated by the forwarding node n_4 is shown in Table 6.

Table 5. Provenance of forwarding node n_3.

Fingerprint	Length
$RF(n_1n_3) = 8$	2

Table 6. Provenance of forwarding node n_4.

Fingerprint	Length
$RF(n_1n_3n_4) = 0$	3

After the base station receives the packet sent by node n_4, to recover the complete transmission path of the packet, it first extracts the provenance $RF(n_1n_3n_4) = 0$ of the packet. It then checks Table 1 to find the path fingerprint equal to $RF(n_1n_3n_4)$. The path corresponding to fingerprint 0 is (n_1,n_3,n_4,n_0), so path (n_1,n_3,n_4,n_0) is the complete transmission path of this packet according to algorithm 2.

5 Performance Analysis

In this paper, we will compare RFP with BFP [12], OP [18], and MP (Message Authentication code-based provenance) from the aspects of storage overhead and energy consumption. BFP scheme is based on bloom filter, which writes provenance of nodes into bloom filter using Hash function. In the OP scheme, node performs an orthogonal code addition operation between its provenance and the original provenance of the packet to form new provenance and a new fixed-length message identification code chain. In the MP scheme, each node n_i appends its identity tag ID_i and message authentication code directly to the packet. Since this paper assumes that the base station's computing, storage, and communication capabilities are not limited, the storage overhead and energy consumption of the base station are not discussed here.

5.1 Storage Overhead Analysis

Suppose a transmission path passes through N nodes from the source node to the base station. In the BFP scheme, the storage overhead required for the provenance of a packet is $-N \times \ln(P_{fp})/(\ln 2)^2$ Bytes, where P_{fp} is the probability of false positivity of the bloom filter. In the MP scheme, the storage overhead required for the provenance of a packet is $N \times 6$ Bytes. In the OP scheme, the length of a node identity tag is 4 Bytes, and the storage overhead required for the provenance of a packet is 23 Bytes.

In the RFP scheme, the provenance of a data package consists of two fields. In other words, the provenance of a data package can be represented as fingerprint, length, where fingerprint denotes the path fingerprint value. According to the fingerprint connection operation property, the result is a fixed-length fingerprint value if multiple fingerprint values are connected. If a 4 Bytes ID generates a 4 Bytes fingerprint value, the fingerprint length is still 4 Bytes. And length indicates that the path length is 1 Byte. Therefore, in the RFP scheme, the storage overhead required for the provenance of a packet is 5 Bytes.

In conclusion, both BFP and MP schemes are related to the transmission path length. As the path length increases, the storage overhead increases. Although the storage overhead of the OP scheme is a fixed value independent of the path length, it is much higher than that of the RFP scheme. The storage overheads of the RFP scheme, BFP scheme, MP scheme, and OP scheme are shown in Table 7.

Table 7. Comparison of storage overhead.

Scheme	Storage Overhead/Bytes
BFP	$-N \times \ln(P_{fp})/(\ln 2)^2$
MP	$N \times 6$
OP	23
RFP	5

5.2 Energy Consumption Analysis

In the RFP scheme, the energy consumption of each node is mainly the receiving and sending of packets. Suppose a transmission path passes through N nodes from the source node to the base station. In the BFP and MP schemes, the storage overhead required for the provenance of a packet is $- N \times \ln(P_{fp})/(\ln 2)^2$ Bytes and $N \times 6$ Bytes, respectively. And the corresponding energy consumption increases proportionately to $- N \times \ln(P_{fp})/(\ln 2)^2$ and $N \times 6$ Bytes, respectively. In the OP scheme, the storage overhead of the provenance is a fixed value of 23 Bytes, but its energy consumption increases slowly as the transmission path increases. Compared with other schemes, the RFP scheme has a relatively small storage overhead of the provenance. Therefore, with the increase in path length, the energy consumption of the RFP scheme is much less than that of the other three schemes.

6 The Simulation Results

This paper simulates and evaluates the performance of RFP schemes in terms of average provenance size, energy consumption, and validation error rate. The simulation experiment environment is carried out on the OMNeT + + platform with 100 nodes randomly distributed at 500 m × 500 m square area. Before the node is deployed, each node is assigned a number from 0 to 99 as the unique identity ID, and the node numbered 0 is the base station. The communication range of each node is 150 m, the node will not move after deployment, and the base station is deployed in the center of the region. Randomly select some network nodes as data source nodes and others as intermediate forwarding nodes. The data source node sends a packet to the base station by multi-hop every 1 s. For each parameter, take the average of 100 simulations.

Figure 2 depicts the average provenance size of the RFP scheme, OP scheme, BFP scheme, and MP scheme under different path lengths. Assuming that the base station receives m packets sent by a source node, the average provenance size (APS) refers to the average length of the provenance for m packets. That is,

$$APS = \frac{\sum_{i=1}^{m} PR_i}{m} \tag{6}$$

where m denotes the number of packets received from a source node, and PR_i represents the length of the provenance for the ith packet. In the MP scheme, each node directly adds its ID to the packet as the provenance when forwarding the packet, so the average provenance size of the MP scheme increases linearly with the length of the transmission path. The average size of provenance in the BFP scheme is relatively flat compared with the MP scheme. Because in the BFP scheme, each node stores its provenance in the bloom filter of packets. Therefore, although the BFP scheme's provenance size is also related to the transmission path length, it is less obvious than in the MP scheme. In the OP scheme, when each node receives the packet, it makes an orthogonal operation between its provenance and the provenance in the packet to obtain a new provenance with a fixed-length value. Therefore, the average provenance size of the OP scheme is a constant value independent of the path length. In the RFP scheme, each node uses its ID as the seed to generate a fingerprint as provenance and performs a fingerprint connection calculation with the provenance fingerprint stored in packets to generate a new fixed-length fingerprint provenance. Therefore, the average provenance size of the RFP scheme is also a constant value. In the case of 100 nodes in the simulation experiment, no matter how the transmission path length increases, the average provenance size remains almost unchanged, accounting for about 5Bytes.

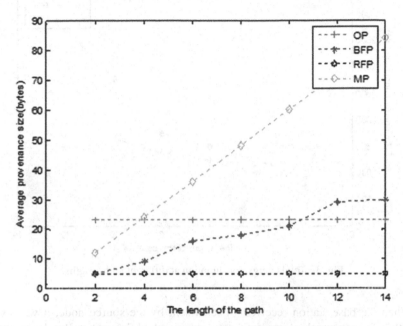

Fig. 2. Average provenance size under different path lengths.

In the RFP scheme, the energy consumption of each node is mainly on receiving and sending packets. So the total energy consumption (TEC) of all nodes in the network is,

$$TEC = \sum_{i=1}^{n} L*(M_i * e_r + N_i * e_s) \tag{7}$$

where n denotes the total number of nodes in the network, L represents the packet length, and M_i denotes the number of packets forwarded by node i. N_i represents the number of packets sent by node i, e_r represents the energy consumed for receiving 1bit data, and e_s represents the energy consumed for transmitting 1bit data. Figure 3 describes the total energy consumption of the RFP scheme, OP scheme, BFP scheme, and MP scheme under different path lengths. It can be seen that when the path length exceeds five hops, the total energy consumption of the OP scheme, BFP scheme, and MP scheme is greater than that of the RFP scheme. And with the increase in the path length, the energy-saving advantage of the RFP scheme is more obvious.

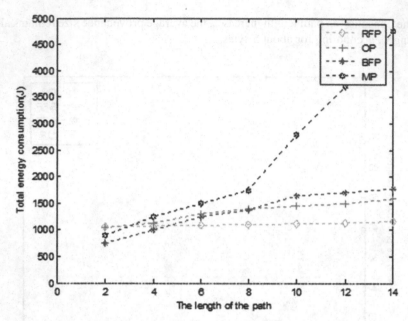

Fig. 3. Total energy consumption at different path lengths.

When the base station receives a packet sent by the source node, it will execute algorithm 2 to recover the complete transmission path of the packet. But due to changes in the network topology or packets that may be damaged in actual transmission, it will not recover the complete transmission path. Assuming that the base station receives a total of m packets, of which d have incorrect provenance, the validation error rate (VER) is,

$$\text{VER} = \frac{\text{d}}{\text{m}} \times 100\% \tag{8}$$

Figure 4 describes the verification error rates of the RFP scheme, the OP scheme, and the BFP scheme under different path lengths. As seen in Fig. 4, when the path length is less than eight hops, there is little difference in the verification error rate of the three schemes. However, when the path length is longer than eight hops, the verification error rate of the BFP scheme is significantly higher than that of the RFP and OP scheme because of the false positive problem of the bloom filter.

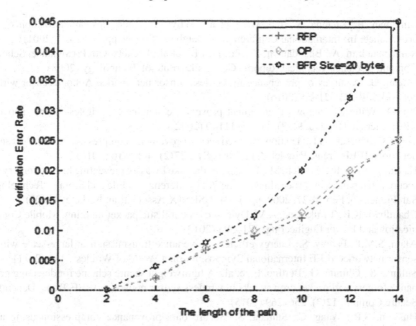

Fig. 4. Verification error rate under different path lengths.

7 Conclusion

This paper proposes an effective provenance compression scheme based on the Rabin fingerprint. In the RFP scheme, each node takes its identity ID as the seed to calculate the Rabin fingerprint as provenance. When a node n_i on the transmission path receives the packet, it performs a fingerprint connection operation with the provenance fingerprint stored in the packet to generate a new fixed-length fingerprint provenance. When the base station receives a packet sent by the node, it extracts its provenance fingerprint and then queries the path fingerprint table. If the fingerprint exists in the table, the base station can recover the complete transmission path of the packet. The RFP scheme only needs one packet to recover the transmission path, and the size of the provenance is independent of the length of the path. Performance analysis and simulation results show that compared with the existing provenance compression schemes, the RFP scheme has obvious advantages in storage overhead and energy consumption with increased path length.

References

1. Pottie, G.J., Kaiser, W.J.: Wireless Integrated Network Sensors(WINS): Principles and Practice. Commun. ACM **43**(5), 51–53 (2000)
2. Liu, V., Zhao, Y.: Wireless sensor networks for internet of things: a systematic review and classification. Info. Technol. J. **12**(16), 3581–3583 (2013)
3. Lal, S., Prathap, J.: An energy-efficient lightweight security protocol for optimal resource provenance in wireless sensor networks. Turkish J. Elec. Eng. Comp. Sci. **28**(6), 3208–3218 (2020)

4. Buneman, P., Khanna, S., Tan, W.C., et al.: Why and where: a characterization of data provenance. In: International Conference on Database Theory, pp. 316–330 (2001)
5. Ramachandran, A., Bhandankar, K., Tariq, M.B., et al.: Packets with Provenance. School of Computer Science Technical Reports, Georgia Institute of Technology (2008)
6. Dogan, G.: A survey of provenance in wireless sensor net- works. Adhoc&sensor wireless networks **30**(1/2), 21–35 (2016)
7. Xu, Q., Wang, C.: Stepwise refinement provenance scheme for wireless sensor networks. IEEE Internet Things J. **9**(13), 11126–11140 (2022)
8. Wang, C., Hussain, S.R.: Dictionary based secure provenance compression for wireless sensor networks. IEEE Trans. Parallel and Distrib. Sys. **27**(2), 405–416 (2016)
9. Hasan, R., Sion, R., Winslett, M.: The case of the fake Picasso: preventing history forgery with secure provenance. In: Proceedings of the 7th Conference on File and Storage Technologies, San Francisco, Feb 24-27, 2009, pp. 1–14. USENIX Association, Berkeley (2009)
10. Chaudhari, K.P., Turukmane, A.V.: Dynamic probabilistic packet marking. Mobile Communication and Power Engineering, 381–384 (2013)
11. Alam, S.M.I., Fahmy, S.: Energy-efficient provenance transmission in large-scale wireless sensor networks. IEEE International Symposium on a World of Wireless, 1–6 (2011)
12. Sultana, S., Ghinita, G., Bertino, E., et al.: A lightweight secure scheme for detecting provenance forgery and packet drop attacks in wireless sensor networks. IEEE Trans. Dependable Secure Comput. **12**(3), 256–269 (2015)
13. Hussain, S.R., Wang, C., Sultana, S.: Secure data provenance compression using arithmetic coding in wireless sensor networks. In: Performance Computing & Communications Conference, pp. 1–10 (2014)
14. Wang, C., Hussain, S., Bertino, E.: Dictionary based secure provenance compression for wireless sensor networks. IEEE Trans. Parallel Distrib. Syst. **27**(2), 405–418 (2015)
15. Xu, Q., Zhang, X., Wang, C.: Provenance compression using packet-path-index differences in wireless sensor networks. In: International Conference on Mobile Ad-Hoc and Sensor Networks (MSN), pp. 200–205 (2019)
16. Sun, J., Chen, H., et al.: Redundant network traffic elimination with GPU accelerated rabin fingerprinting. IEEE Trans. Parallel Distrib. Syst. **27**(7), 2130–2142 (2016)
17. Lu, P., Randall, O., McDonald, E.: An empirical study of rabin fingerprinting parameters. In: IEEE International Conference on Big Data (Big Data), pp. 3686–3691 (2019)
18. Zhang, Z., Deng, J.: A secure and effective method for provenance in Wireless Sensor Networks. Computer science and exploration **13**(4), 608–619 (2019)

Research on the Restoration Perception Evaluation of Historical Blocks Along the Inner Mongolia Section of the Middle East Railway Based on Network Text Big Data

Zhiqiang Wang[1], Siwei Zhang[1(✉)], Xiaomin Zhang[2], Shuang Xu[1], and Jianxun Zhang[2]

[1] Key Laboratory of Green Building at Universities of Inner Mongolia Autonomous Region, College of architecture, Inner Mongolia University of Technology, Baotou 300072, Inner Mongolia, China
1085067016@qq.com
[2] Architecture School, Tianjin University, Tianjin 300072, China

Abstract. Under the information technology, cloud computing technology is gradually emerging. Using big data technology to analyze and process data through cloud computing can further mine information resources and give full play to the value of data resources. Using massive multi-source data as the basis for evaluation, solving the problem of difficulty in the evaluation of the restoration of historical blocks is the key to promoting the research on the restoration of historical blocks. Introduce the concept of restorative environment in the study of historical blocks along the Inner Mongolia section of the Middle East Railway, and select 51,696 online text data from 6 mainstream Chinese online media platforms Ctrip, Tuniu, Fliggy, Tongcheng, Mofang and Weibo as data sources. Through big data processing and analysis, an IPA model is established, and the characteristics of the model are used to evaluate the restoration perception of multiple historical blocks in Inner Mongolia along the Middle East Railway, and propose improvement strategies to explore the impact of the spatial perception restoration of historical blocks along the Inner Mongolia section of the Middle East Railway from the perspective of tourists' experience perception On this basis, the restoration design inspiration of the historic district is proposed.

Keywords: Big data analytics technology · Smart City · historic district · restorative environment · middle east railway

© ICST Institute for Computer Sciences, Social Informatics and Telecommunications Engineering 2023
Published by Springer Nature Switzerland AG 2023. All Rights Reserved
Y. Cao and X. Shao (Eds.): MONAMI 2022, LNICST 474, pp. 345–361, 2023.
https://doi.org/10.1007/978-3-031-32443-7_25

1   Introduction

At present, the rapid development of information and communication technology and the rapid construction of smart cities, the application of big data to urban research has become a major strategy for urbanization development, and the status of big data in urban research is becoming more and more important. It has functions such as visualization and big data prediction, and affects the innovation of smart city planning concepts and methods. At present, researchers have used big data to conduct a lot of research and discussion on cities, mainly by using social network data such as Twitter, Facebook and Sina Weibo, including geographic location, individual activity information, individual emotional texts, etc. to mine and analyze the foundation. In the past, the internal connection between cities is judged by studying the network activities between cities [6], big data has received a lot of attention in the fields of urban transportation, urban functional area planning, etc., but the research on the utilization of characteristic functional areas and urban infrastructure is still relatively Weak, it is difficult to meet the needs of urban residents, enterprises and the government []. Therefore, it is necessary to use big data analysis techniques to explore a complete urban research framework based on big data so as to realize the wisdom of urban research. Existing studies have proved the restorative effect of historical blocks on the human body [7,10]. Carmen Hidalgo et al. [4] consider that more attractive urban spaces are usually "historical and cultural" places. In the evaluation of the restoration perception of historical blocks, early scholars used questionnaire methods to collect sample data, and combined their own professional knowledge to evaluate historical blocks. Among them, scholars in the fields of landscape architecture, urban planning, architecture, etc. The restorability has been studied in depth. Their research results provide a theoretical basis and empirical evidence for the restorative environmental cognitive mechanism of urban space. For example, Mohamed Elsadek et al. [1] surveyed 364 urban space participants and found that the restoration effect and vitality of the landscape ramp in the walking block were improved, and the trees around the city streets were used as resources to relieve stress and promote the health of urban residents. Ernest Bielinis [5] et al. conducted a controlled experiment on a questionnaire survey of 75 Polish young people and found that the green space environment of the block has a positive effect on the physical and psychological relaxation of the subjects compared with the living in the apartment residential area in the block space. As mentioned above, most of the existing studies conducted questionnaire surveys in a limited population, and the sample size and questionnaire response rate were generally low. In addition, questionnaire surveys will inevitably produce problems such as the high aggregation of sampled data and the limited test population, which may affect the reliability of the results and the scalability of the design strategy. In the Internet age, online platforms allow tourists to express their true feelings and opinions. Compared with questionnaire surveys, the latter can more intuitively and thoroughly understand the perceptions of each tourist's innermost city destinations. Mobile Internet With the rapid development of the Internet of Things, the use of online media has increased dramatically worldwide. Every day, tens of millions of users generate tens of millions of data on online platforms such as Ctrip, Fliggy, and Tuniu. Researchers mine these data to help reveal user behavior patterns and social phenomena without violating moral constraints. In addition, network media data is not limited by sample size, time and space, and has the advantage of eliminating non-response bias [3]. In existing studies, previous studies have confirmed the value of these data in restorative environmental research. For example, Stephanie Wilkie et al. [9] use Twitter with 5,624 data texts in this document serve as data support to verify the restorative environmental characteristics of the urban green space landscape. Using Attention Recovery Theory (ART) as a framework for content analysis of tweets. Four characteristics of attention recovery are explored: distance, fascination, compatibility, and abundance. The study found that tweets most often refer to obsession or compatibility, but less than 5% of tweets indicate distance, and restorative environmental characteristics are analyzed through text data. In view of the advantages of these research methods and the existing research foundation, this study uses the text data of China's six mainstream online media platforms to analyze the restorative influencing factors and important characteristics of its historical districts through the data.

At the same time, considering that restorability is a psychological content that is difficult to measure through quantitative methods, this article needs to introduce a bottom-up qualitative research method. Grounded Theory [2] is a qualitative research method based on empirical data. It extracts initial concepts through subjective perception or evaluation, clusters them through coding analysis, and obtains the final result after screening and optimization. Good applicability. Therefore, this article first obtains the factors that affect spatial resilience through grounded theory; then conducts statistical analysis of network text data, establishes a data model to explore the universality and difference of the factors' impact on spatial resilience, and finally derives the spatial resilience design based on the influencing factors Enlightenment.

2   Materials and Methods

2.1   Study Area

The study area was selected as the historical district along the Inner Mongolia section of the Middle East Railway (Fig. 1). The total length of the Middle East Railway is 2489.20 km. The Inner Mongolia section of the main trunk line starts from Manzhouli and passes through Hailar, Zhalai Nuoer, Yakeshi, Boketu, Zhalantun, etc., which contains a complete historical block area along the railway line. The historical buildings of the Middle East Railway include the church in Manzhouli, the Tsarist Russia prison exhibition hall b, the expert building and its water tower a, the woodcut in the north area, the history museum d in Zhalai Nuoer, the old railway station e, the coal pit f, and the railway station in Yakeshi n. Water tower o, the century-old machine garage i in the blog picture, the former site of the police station g, the former site of the Czarist Russian Route Guard headquarters h, the historic buildings on Shuiyuan Street, the office of the centennial section chief, the former site of the 8172 Army, and the site of Zhalantun Suspension Bridge Park j, the former residence site of Tsarist Russian executives k, the Six Nations Hotel i, the Puppet Hinggan East Provincial Historical Exhibition Hall m, the Middle East Railway History Research Society, etc. The historical block contains a large number of cultural relics protection units, historical buildings and traditional buildings, and block space It is also unique, which makes this multicultural historical district extremely advantageous.

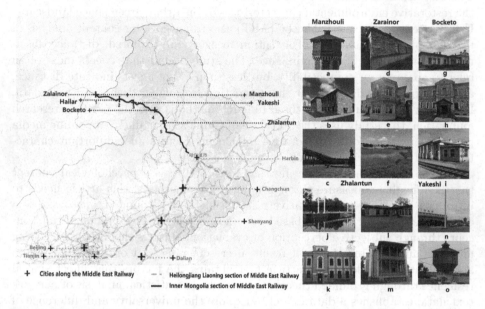

Fig. 1. Historic District along the Inner Mongolia Section of the Middle East Railway

2.2   Materials and Methods

The main process of this research includes: (1) Collecting and sorting out the network text data related to the historical blocks of the Inner Mongolia section of the Middle East Railway; (2) Based on the grounded theory, the basic elements of the historical block space are obtained from the text data clustering category; (3) Determine the spatial restorative perception elements of historical blocks through data text analysis; (4) Explore the universality and difference of the impact of the elements on the spatial restorability; (5)Finally, the IPO model is used to evaluate the relative importance of each influencing factor to analyze; (6) Analyze and interpret the results. Finally, according to the influencing factors, the enlightenment of spatial restoration design is derived, and the workflow is shown in Fig. 2.

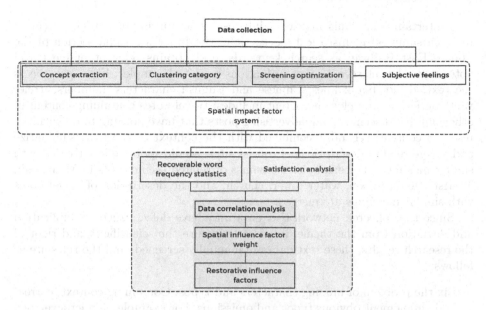

Fig. 2. Data processing and analysis process.

2.3 Data Acquisition and Preprocessing

Data Acquisition. Select Qunar.com, Ctrip.com, Weibo, Tongcheng.com, Mofang, Fliggy Travel and other software to crawl the travel notes and travel evaluation text content of historical districts along the Middle East Railway Inner Mongolia. In the relevant content of travel notes and evaluations, relevant travel notes and evaluations are retrieved, and pure pictures without text and pure scenic introductory text are removed, and the final travel notes and evaluations are obtained. These travel notes describe the travel experience and impressions of tourists in the tourist destination, Mainly including text and pictures, only extract the text content, and copy all the text content to the csv file for content analysis. Statistics on the search results, an example is shown in the following Table 1:

Collect information about the "historical districts along the Inner Mongolia section of the Inner Mongolia section of the Middle East Railway" in the travel notes and evaluation columns of the six major online travel network platforms, and set the three elements of the visitor's net name, release time, and content for each review of each travel note. After the information is collected successfully, it will be exported and summarized in the form of "Travel Notes of Historic Districts along the Middle East Railway Inner Mongolia.xlsx" or "Evaluation of Historic Districts along the Middle East Railway Inner Mongolia.xlsx".

By using tools to capture webpage data and accurately identify various webpage elements in batches according to the collection needs of the corresponding topics, the online travel notes published by users of major domestic websites include information such as travel, food, accommodation, sightseeing, shopping, and entertainment. This article mainly uses relevant important nodes (main research samples) of historical blocks along the Inner Mongolia section of the Middle East Railway as search keywords, and obtains relevant online travel notes and relevant scenic spots evaluations as initial samples. First, preprocess the text: delete blank lines, Chinese and English characters, numbers, irrelevant content, etc. Irrelevant content includes: travel notes containing content of other unrelated scenic spots; advertising posts that have nothing to do with the research content; secondly, combined with the context of the text, summarize and merge related descriptions of tourist sites, scenic spots, and activities with similar meanings. For example: the names of related scenic spots in Manzhouli, Tsarist Russia prison, water tower, church, and the description of travel notes with similar meanings are merged.

Since the collected network text data may have defects such as duplication and deviation from the theme, in order to ensure the scientificity and rigor of the research results, these text data are manually screened, and the rules are as follows:

- Fix the problem of missing characters and typos. Combining context, correct and supplement obvious typos and omissions. For example, "underdeveloped shopping" is revised to "underdeveloped shopping", and "full of people in the mountains" is revised to "full of", etc.
- Delete meaningless content. Visitors are less constrained when sharing the evaluation of online travel notes, so the content is relatively free and free. After reading the text, it is found that some of the content does not revolve around the main historical block, mainly including: a. The text is not correct and the topic b. It has nothing to do with the research theme or content. Advertisements c. Tourist destinations are miscellaneous and d. The content is irrelevant and blank and other meaningless content. After carefully reading the texts one by one, 143 repetitive and invalid travel notes were eliminated, 294 posts were evaluated, and 51,696 valid evaluations were finally obtained.

Code Analysis. First, open coding: decompose the original sentence, code and label the extracted keyword sentences, and generate the initial concept samples and categories of the influential elements. Import 51696 sample transcripts into Nvivo11 software for encoding. After labeling and conceptualization, the initial concepts are mined, and elements that are not related to space are eliminated. The initial concepts are clustered into 6 main categories based on similarity, causality, etc., and then The main categories are connected together through the canonical model to form the core category. The initial concept, main category, and core category together constitute the spatial impact factor system. The system includes 6 core categories: scale, traffic accessibility, activity support, natural characteristics, cultural heritage, and emotional elements, which are divided into 13 s-level subcategories and 30 third-level subcategories (Fig. 3).

2.4   Extraction of Important Factors Based on Data Analysis

The grounded theory has preliminarily determined the spatial influence elements, but the content of the data article is vague and complicated. In order to obtain the degree of influence of the restoration of each element more accurately, further analysis and processing of the text data is required. On the one hand, it analyzes the proportion of word frequency statistics, establishes the standard of restorative lexicon, classifies the three-level category text to obtain 30 txt format text files, and sequentially measures the four categories of rich, compatible, distant, and charming texts. The factor is the framework for restorative word frequency statistics, and the percentage of vocabulary frequency in the total vocabulary is used as the restorative value. On the other hand, sentiment analysis is performed on the text and the sentiment score of high-frequency vocabulary is used as the satisfaction value. Establish an IPA model and use the characteristics of the model to evaluate the degree of influence of the above elements on the restoration of different perception elements in the historic district (Figs. 4 and 5).

Data Analysis Strategy. The spatial resilience measurement uses the Chinese version of the Healing Environment Scale compiled by Ye Liuhong in 2010 as a framework for network text statistics. The percentage of the restorative high-frequency vocabulary in the total high-frequency words is taken as the resilience value of the high-frequency words, including 4 A measurement factor [9], the statistical results are shown in Table 3. Spatial element satisfaction uses ROST CM software to do sentiment analysis, and then refer to the University of Michigan SRC index compilation method [10], the difference between the number of words in positive emotions and the number of words in negative emotions is A, and the number of words in positive emotions is sum The sum of the number of words in negative emotions is B, and the satisfaction of high-frequency words is $X(X = A/B)$; Analyze the evaluation of restorative perception elements in the historical districts of the Middle East Railway, and select the Middle East from March 2020 to March 2021 Crawling of travel post data related to the historical blocks in the Inner Mongolia section of the railway. It mainly includes: 12,675 Feizhu websites, 1995 Mofang websites, 4967 Qunar websites, 5,415 Tongcheng websites, 1508 Xiecheng websites, 25136 Weibo posts, with a total of 51696 comments of 2398912 words.

Text Data Analysis. Integrate all the collected comment information into one document, perform word segmentation and word frequency statistics In the ROST CM6.0 software, and manually filter out irrelevant words. First, use the 30 indicators of the three-level category as the standard for text data Comment statistics, summarized into 30 text files corresponding to the indicators, and classify the three-level category text to obtain 30 txt format text files. In turn, perform word frequency statistics on the category text with the four measurement factors of rich, compatible, distant, and charming. Taking the vocabulary

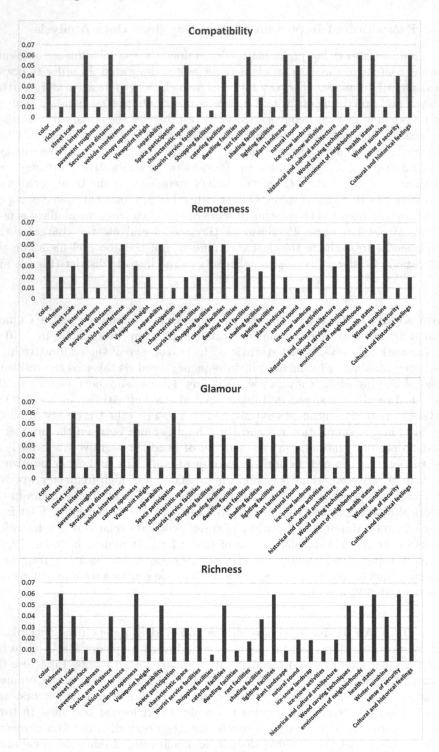

Fig. 3. Statistics of importance proportion.

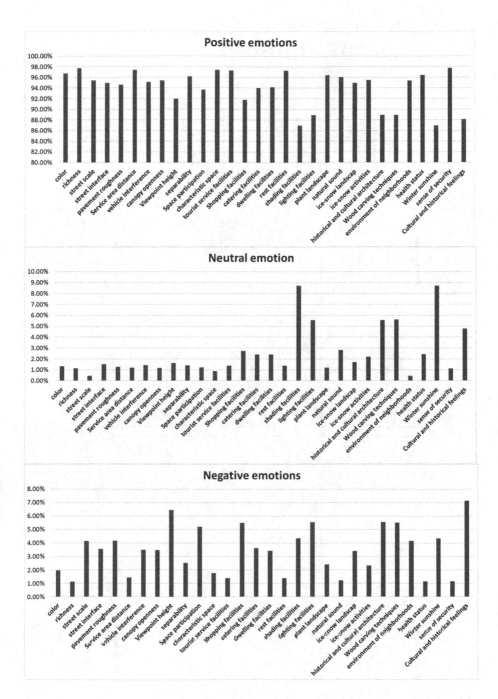

Fig. 4. Statistics of satisfaction ratio.

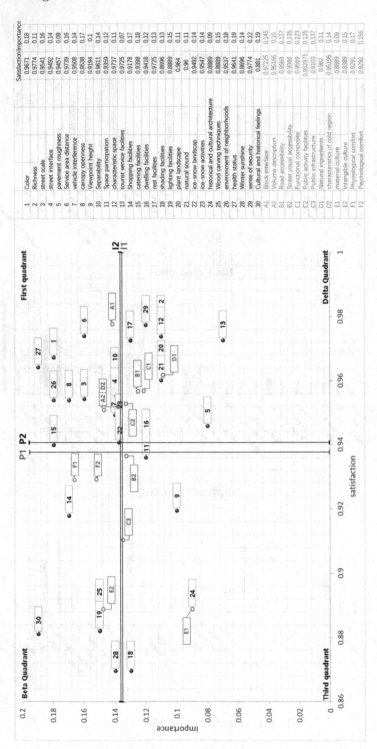

Fig. 5. IPA model.

frequency as the percentage of the total word segmentation vocabulary as the importance value, and dividing the extracted high-frequency vocabulary into six categories: scale, traffic accessibility, activity support, natural feature vocabulary, cultural heritage vocabulary, and emotional element. Statistics, the results are shown in (Table 2). Collection of travel notes and comments related to the historical districts along the Inner Mongolia section of the Middle East Railway through the Internet, sorted and summarized tables according to frequency. The word with the highest frequency symbolizes the most attractive features of the historical district, while the lower frequency indicates that tourists are not interested in it and need to be rectified accordingly. Based on the statistical results, the historical district can be effectively located on the basis of restorative characteristics (See Fig. 3).

IPA Model Analysis. The IPA model [8] is the "importance-performance" analysis method jointly proposed by Martilla and James. The analysis principle is that the degree of customer satisfaction with the product or service is related to the company's emphasis on the attributes of the product or service, so as to continuously improve the improvement of the product or service quality.

Taking the importance of high-frequency words as the X-axis and the satisfaction of high-frequency words as the Y-axis, an IPA model was established, and the model results (Table 4) are used to analyze the pros and cons of the historical block update and restoration evaluation.

3 Research Results and Analysis

After statistical analysis of the data obtained by SPSS2.0, the average value of the importance of the secondary category is 1.36, and the average value of the satisfaction is 0.936, that is, $I1 = 1.36$ and $P1 = 0.936$, forming a vertical intersection of the X-axis and the Y-axis Point, establish the IPA model, the model is divided into four quadrants (Fig. 6).

The average value of the three-level category importance is 0.1359, and the average value of satisfaction is 0.9375, that is, $I2 = 0.1359$ and $P2 = 0.9375$, which form the vertical intersection of the X-axis and the Y-axis, and establish the IPA model. The model is divided into four quadrants.

The first quadrant is the continued maintenance area. The second-level category indicators include block interface, volume description, and cold area characteristics. The third-level category indicators include color, street scale, street interface, vehicle interference, visual openness, There are 9 options, physical environment of the block, and sanitary conditions. According to the characteristics of the IPA model, the satisfaction and importance of these indicators are higher than the average, and they play an important role in the development of the historical districts along the Inner Mongolia section of the Middle East Railway. They are the potential for the development of historical districts, so these indicators need to be maintained and improved on the basis of maintaining the status quo.

Table 1. Summary of important notations

Root Category	Sum W.F.	Subcategory	Word Frequency	Child Category	Word Num.	Faraway	Charming	abundant	Compatibility	W.F.
A Scale	0.59	A1 Street	0.29	Color	4060	162	203	203	162	0.18
				Diversity	27672	553	553	1660	276	0.11
		A2 Size	0.3	Street Size	28074	842	1684	1122	842	0.16
				Street Front	5149	308	51	51	308	0.14
B Traffic Accessibility	0.65	B1 Accessible	0.38	Street Smooth	6516	65	325	65	65	0.08
				Service Distance	12310	492	246	492	738	0.16
				Vehicle Interference	29293	1464	878	878	878	0.14
		B2 Street Visual Accessible	0.27	Horizon Level	33024	990	1651	1981	990	0.17
				Viewpoint Height	4191	83	125	125	83	0.1
C Activity Support	1.32	C1 Function Composite	0.37	Choosability	5499	274	54	274	164	0.14
				Spatial Participation	13254	132	795	397	265	0.12
				Personalized Space	4459	189	44	133	222	0.11
				Tourist Service Facilities	5415	108	54	162	54	0.07
		C2 Public Facilities	0.54	Shopping Facilities	857	42	34	34	34	0.17
				Catering Facilities	2388	119	95	119	95	0.18
				Residence Facilities	5959	238	178	59	238	0.12
				Rest Facilities	276	8	5	5	16	0.13
		C2 Public Infrastructure	0.41	Sunshade Facilities	158	4	6	6	3	0.13
				Lighting Facilities	1958	78	78	117	19	0.15
D Natural Feature	0.5	D1 Natural Ingredients	0.22	Plants Landscape	26078	521	521	260	1564	0.11
				Natural Sounds	3832	38	114	76	191	0.11
		D2 Cold Region Characteristics	0.28	Snow-ice Landscape	573	11	22	11	34	0.14
				Snow-ice Activities	1434	86	71	14	28	0.14
Cultural Inheritance	0.24	E1 Material Culture	0.09	Historical Buildings	2113	63	21	42	63	0.09
		E2 Non-Material Cultural	0.15	Woodcut Construction Techniques	822	41	32	41	8	0.15
F Emotional Factors	0.82	F1 Physical Comfort	0.51	Block Physical Environment	1508	60	45	75	90	0.18
				Sanitary Conditions	3913	195	78	234	234	0.19
				Winter Sunshine	4602	276	138	184	46	0.14
		F2 Psychological Comfort	0.31	Security Sense	1500	15	15	90	60	0.12
				Historical Culture Sense	5946	118	297	356	356	0.19

Table 2. Summary of important notations

item	positive emotion	neutral emotion	negative emotion	item	positive emotion	neutral emotion	negative emotion
color	96.71%	1.32%	1.97%	dwelling facilities	94.18%	2.40%	3.42%
richness	97.74%	1.13%	1.13%	rest facilities	97.25%	1.37%	1.37%
street scale	95.41%	0.46%	4.13%	shading facilities	86.96%	8.70%	4.35%
street interface	94.92%	1.52%	3.55%	lighting facilities	88.89%	5.56%	5.56%
pavement roughness	94.57%	1.27%	4.17%	plant landscape	96.40%	1%	2.40%
Service area distance	97.39%	1.19%	1.43%	natural sound	96.00%	2.80%	1%
vehicle interference	95.08%	1.43%	3.48%	ice-snow landscape	94.92%	1.69%	3.39%
canopy openness	95.38%	1.16%	3.47%	ice-snow activities	95.47%	2.20%	2.33%
Viewpoint height	91.94%	1.61%	6.45%	historical and cultural architecture	88.89%	5.56%	5.56%
separability	96.11%	1.39%	3%	Wood carving techniques	88.89%	5.61%	5.50%
Space participation	93.59%	1%	5.20%	environment of neighborhoods	95.37%	0.46%	4.17%
characteristic space	97.37%	0.88%	1.75%	health status	96.41%	2.44%	1.15%
tourist service facilities	97.25%	1.37%	1.37%	Winter sunshine	86.96%	8.70%	4.35%
Shopping facilities	91.78%	2.74%	5.48%	sense of security	97.74%	1.12%	1.14%
catering facilities	93.98%	2.41%	3.61%	Cultural and historical feelings	88.10%	4.76%	7.14%

The second quadrant is the over-supply area. The second-level category indicators include intangible culture, psychological comfort, and physical comfort. The third-level category indicators include cultural and historical sense, shopping facilities, catering facilities, lighting facilities, and woodcarving craftsmanship. There are a total of six winter sunshine. According to the characteristics of the IPA model, it shows that the satisfaction of these high-frequency words is higher than the average, and the importance is lower than the average. The praise of historical blocks is far greater than the estimated value, and more in-depth values of such indicators should be tapped.

The third quadrant is the area with lower priority. The second-level category indicators include E2 intangible culture, street visual accessibility, and public infrastructure. The third-level category indicators include viewpoint height, spatial participation, shading facilities, There are a total of four historical and cultural buildings. According to the characteristics of the IPA model, people's attention to these indicators is not high, and long-term plans need to be formulated to gradually improve people's awareness of the intangible culture of historical blocks, the visual accessibility of historical blocks, and historical blocks. A sense of identity in public facilities.

The fourth quadrant is to strengthen the improvement of key areas. The second-level category indicators include street and pavement accessibility, functional composite, public activity facilities, and natural components. The third-level category indicators include richness, road surface smoothness, and personalized space. There are nine tourist service facilities, rest facilities, plant landscape, natural sound, and sense of security. According to the characteristics of the IPA model, it reflects that people have a high degree of attention to these words and low satisfaction, and need to improve the road to reach; increase the block Functions; increase and upgrade public facilities; increase natural landscape elements to improve space quality.

Table 3. Summary of important notations

1st category	2nd category	Average value of satisfaction	importance value	3rd category	satisfaction value	importance value
A Scale form	A1 block interface	0.97225	0.145	color	0.9671	0.18
				complexity	0.9774	0.11
	A2 volume description	0.95165	0.15	street scale	0.9541	0.16
				street interface	0.9492	0.14
B Traffic accessibility	B1 Street pavement accessibility	0.9568	0.127	road surface roughness	0.9457	0.08
				service area distance	0.9739	0.16
				vehicle interference	0.9508	0.14
	B2 Street visual accessibility	0.9366	0.135	visual openness	0.9538	0.17
				viewpoint height	0.9194	0.1
C Activity support	C1 Function composite	0.9569	0.123	optionality	0.9611	0.14
				spatial participation	0.9359	0.12
				personalized space	0.9737	0.11
				tourist service facilities	0.9725	0.07
	C2 Public event facilities	0.952975	0.135	shopping facilities	0.9178	0.17
				dining facilities	0.9398	0.18
				residential facilities	0.9418	0.12
	C3 Public infrastructure	0.9103	0.137	rest facilities	0.9725	0.13
				shading facilities	0.8696	0.13
				lighting facilities	0.8889	0.15
D Natural characteristics	D1 natural ingredients	0.962	0.11	plant landscape	0.9640	0.11
				natural sound	0.9600	0.11
	D2 regional characteristics of cold regions	0.95195	0.14	ice-snow landscape	0.9492	0.14
				ice-snow activities	0.9547	0.14
E Cultural heritage	E1 material culture	0.8889	0.09	historical and cultural buildings	0.8889	0.09
	E2 intangible Culture	0.8889	0.15	woodcut craftsmanship	0.8889	0.15
				block physical environment	0.9537	0.18
F Emotional element	F1 physical comfort	0.9292	0.17	health condition	0.9641	0.19
				winter sunshine	0.8969	0.14
	F2 psychological comfort	0.9292	0.155	sense of security	0.9774	0.12
				sense of cultural history	0.8810	0.19

3.1   Natural Restoration Design Based on Natural Components

For spaces that already have green resources or have the conditions to create a virtual green environment: green plants, natural sounds, seasonal landscapes and other natural components should be used as the core elements to trigger restoration. The element information in this part reflects that people have a high degree of attention to it, but low satisfaction, so it is necessary to focus on solving the problems in this area. Specific measures should focus on improving the quality of the landscape sketches, and the introduction of ice and snow sculptures to activate the restoration function of the winter space to make up for the restoration defects caused by the scarcity of vegetation species and the short green vision cycle.

In the outdoor environment, add a node space with suitable virtual reality and a certain green view rate of the opening to block unfavorable weather and noise interference, and provide a place for tourists to interact with the outdoor nature. Secondly, optimize the landscape facilities, promote the interaction between the individual and the space, increase participation, ensure the individual's physical comfort and security, and extend the experience time. Finally, for natural landscape space, on the basis of improving path accessibility, more attention should be paid to visual accessibility, so as to maximize its recovery ability.

3.2   Artificial Restoration Design Based on Activity Attraction

For spaces with entertainment, public exhibitions, etc. as their main functions, the activities carried by the body can be completed without the use of directional attention. When an individual engages in such activities, the brain is quickly occupied by rich information, and the stressful event is temporarily forgotten, so that non-directed attention is activated. Therefore, maximizing support for multiple activities is the key to the restoration of this type of space.

First of all, it is necessary to ensure the adequacy and perfection of activity facilities, and control the density of people flow to avoid the psychological discomfort caused by the overcrowding. Secondly, establish a complete outdoor climate shelter system to create a relatively suitable physical environment for individual travel and outdoor activities in winter, and enhance the accessibility of indoor activity spaces. In addition, ice and snow sports facilities can be introduced to create an activity experience with characteristics of cold regions.

3.3   Supportive Recovery Design Based on Multiple Choices

For the space with sightseeing and rest as its main functions, the activities carried by it are the main source of attention recovery. As far as the same activity is concerned, different individuals will differentiate their needs according to their preferences. The support and respect for individual needs can improve the compatibility between the user and the activity to a certain extent, that is, reduce the "unwillingness" in the brain. Do it" idea. Therefore, refining the main functions, mining sub-functions that support multiple choices, assigning sub-functions to unit functional components, and incorporating the form of unit space into the overall space are the main strategies for this type of space restorative design. At the same time, it can appropriately embellish the environmental features that can cause directional attention to temporarily rest, such as potted plants, artistic murals, light and shadow changes, etc., to provide the brain with mental content that is different from learning and work, and promote recovery.

3.4   Aesthetic Restoration Design Based on Perception Experience

Spaces in historical blocks with deep cultural connotations or strong artistic atmosphere, such as exhibition halls, historical museums, historical ancient buildings, etc., not only contain entertainment activities, but also have aesthetic spatial content, and the form is limited by functions, and the architectural aesthetics Value can be more easily displayed and displayed. Therefore, this kind of space should focus on strengthening the aesthetic experience, and on the basis of the beauty of the form, give the space a humane connotation that can be interpreted, expand the breadth of the individual brain's interpretation of the space, and establish the emotional connection between the individual and the environment. Specifically, it can be through deepening the existing historical and cultural background, or creating symbolic sign language, or through the logical connection of sequences to achieve the function of space "narration", depicting a scene and telling a story; it can also be through exhibits or interior The decoration renders the sense of future technology and triggers psychological content different from the current environment.

4   Conclusion

The Inner Mongolia section along the Middle East Railway is a well-known scenic spot with local characteristics, with a profound cultural heritage and numerous attractions. However, the evaluation and optimization strategies for the recovery perception of the block are always inaccurate. This article starts with the subjective feelings of tourists, aims to improve the attention recovery function of historical districts, and uses grounded theory as the basis to explore relevant influencing factors using network text analysis. The research finally drew 30 spatial impact evaluation elements, and deduced the degree of influence of spatial elements in the space of historical districts. The data statistics are large and the analysis results are more accurate. From this, the "Evaluation of Historic Districts Along the Middle East Railway Inner Mongolia" is derived. Restoration evaluation and satisfaction score. Based on this data analysis, the IPO score of the historic district of the Middle East Railway is carried out, and finally the restoration influence factor system of the historic district space is established, and the restoration design enlightenment is proposed to expand the influence and attraction of the historic district force. The research results can be used to guide the design of historic districts, to achieve the goal of improving tourists' life pleasure and mental health, and to facilitate the perception and evaluation of the restorative environment of historic districts. The research method based on network data analysis in this paper can provide a good reference for restorative perception evaluation of other historical blocks.

Acknowledgement. Inner Mongolia Natural Science Foundation Project (Project Approval Number: 2021LHBS05002); Inner Mongolia University of Technology Scientific Research Project (Project Approval Number: ZZ202014/BS2020018); Inner Mongolia Autonomous Region Key Technology Research Project.

References

1. Elsadek, M., Liu, B., Lian, Z., Xie, J.: The influence of urban roadside trees and their physical environment on stress relief measures: a field experiment in Shanghai. Urban For. Urban Green. **42**, 51–60 (2019)
2. Glaser, B.G., Strauss, A.L., Strutzel, E.: The discovery of grounded theory; strategies for qualitative research. Nurs. Res. **17**(4), 364 (1968)
3. Hausmann, A., et al.: Social media data can be used to understand tourists' preferences for nature-based experiences in protected areas. Conserv. Lett. **11**(1), e12343 (2018)
4. Hidalgo, M.C., Berto, R., Galindo, M.P., Getrevi, A.: Identifying attractive and unattractive urban places: categories, restorativeness and aesthetic attributes. Medio Ambiente Comportamiento Humano **7**(2), 115–133 (2006)
5. Janeczko, E., et al.: When urban environment is restorative: the effect of walking in suburbs and forests on psychological and physiological relaxation of young polish adults. Forests **11**(5), 591 (2020)
6. Kang, C., Yi, Z., Ma, X., Yu, L.: Inferring properties and revealing geographical impacts of intercity mobile communication network of china using a subnet data set. Int. J. Geogr. Inf. Sci. **27**(3), 1–18 (2012)
7. Kaplan, S., Bardwell, L.V., Slakter, D.B.: The museum as a restorative environment. Environ. Behav. **25**(6), 725–742 (1993)
8. Song, Z.B., Ying-Min, A.N., Zheng, P.: An IPA analysis of tourism destination image—a case study of Xi'an residents' perception on the tourism destination image of Hainan, China. Tour. Tribune **21**, 26–32 (2006)
9. Wilkie, S., Thompson, E., Cranner, P., Ginty, K.: Attention restoration theory as a framework for analysis of tweets about urban green space: a case study. Landsc. Res. **45**(6), 777–788 (2020)
10. Xu, L., Meng, R., Chen, Z.: Fascinating streets: the impact of building facades and green view. Landsc. Archit. **10**, 33 (2017)

Network Communications
and Computing

A Survey of QUIC-Based Network Traffic Identification

Xiaolin Gui[✉], Yuanlong Cao, Longjun Huang, Yong Luo, and Jianmao Xiao

School of Software, Jiangxi Normal University, Nanchang, China
{xlgui,ylcao,luoyong1020,jm_xiao}@jxnu.edu.cn

Abstract. With the QUIC (Quick UDP Internet Connection) protocol recognized by the Internet Engineering Task Force as the core protocol of HTTP/3, network traffic based on the QUIC protocol (also known as "QUIC traffic") will become one of the primary traffics on the Internet. Network administrators use QUIC traffic identification as the foundation for network management. Numerous studies on QUIC traffic identification and application are already underway with the goal of assisting network operators, and pertinent results are beginning to emerge. We evaluate the topic of QUIC traffic identification to help future researchers rapidly grasp the research frontier of QUIC traffic identification and to summarize the present research and understand the obstacles in the field.

Keywords: QUIC · HTTP/3 · Network traffic identification

1 Introduction

1.1 Backgroud

At present, network traffic encryption is mainly implemented by adding an SSL/TLS (Secure Sockets Layer/Transport Layer Security) layer on top of the TCP (Transport Control Protocol) protocol at the transport layer. To increase communication effectiveness, Google suggested the QUIC (Quick UDP Internet Connection) protocol [1]. To ensure reliable communication, the protocol incorporates multiplexing, traffic encryption, congestion control, and forward error correction. Additionally, it avoids the requirement for numerous handshakes and key negotiations in the TCP protocol by employing the UDP protocol at the lowest layer. Since then, other academic academics have examined the QUIC protocol, assessed its effectiveness, and verified its benefits [2–5]. The application of the QUIC protocol has also been monitored and supported by the industry. Web browsers represented by Chrome, Firefox, and Safari have successively announced their support for the QUIC protocol. Internet companies represented by Google and Akamai have successively deployed QUIC applications on the server side. The IETF (Internet Engineering Task Force) recognized the QUIC protocol as a global standard for HTTP/3 in May 2021. With the promotion of academia, industry, and the International Organization for Standardization, it is foreseeable that network encrypted traffic based on the

© ICST Institute for Computer Sciences, Social Informatics and Telecommunications Engineering 2023
Published by Springer Nature Switzerland AG 2023. All Rights Reserved
Y. Cao and X. Shao (Eds.): MONAMI 2022, LNICST 474, pp. 365–372, 2023.
https://doi.org/10.1007/978-3-031-32443-7_26

QUIC protocol (also known as "QUIC traffic") will become one of the main traffics on the future Internet. Therefore, there is an urgent need for network operators to identify QUIC traffic in order to effectively manage the network. To this end, many researchers have started research on QUIC traffic identification and have achieved some results. This article aims to review these results and discuss possible future research directions.

2   Overview of QUIC-Based Network Traffic

2.1   QUIC-Based Network Traffic Datasets

As the QUIC protocol is not yet commonly used, datasets available for QUIC traffic identification are relatively scarce. At present, the widely used public QUIC traffic datasets are released by the team led by Professor Xin Liu at the University of California, USA. The datasets were captured in the lab at the University of California, Davis, and include 5 Google services: Google Drive, Youtube, Google Docs, Google Search, and Google Music [6]. The datasets were acquired on several systems with different configurations, including Windows 7, 8, 10, and Ubuntu 16.4, using Selenium WebDriver and AutoIT tools to write scripts to mimic human behavior when surfing the Internet. During the preprocessing of this dataset, all non-QUIC traffic is removed, and all flows in this dataset are marked, suitable for validating some of the methods in this project. In addition, the researchers constructed some private datasets according to their own research needs.

2.2   Categories of QUIC-Based Network Traffic Identification

QUIC traffic identification refers to the output form of the identification result. The identification level is determined by the requirements of network operators. QUIC traffic can be gradually refined from attributes such as protocol, application, and service to realize protocol identification, application identification, and abnormal traffic identification. We summarize the varied kinds of identification as follows:

1) Protocol identification. It is to distinguish QUIC traffic from hybrid network traffic. In the future, the traffic based on the QUIC protocol on the Internet will coexist with the traffic based on the traditional protocol for a long time. How to identify the QUIC traffic and reveal its characteristics is a problem that needs to be studied.
2) Application identification. It is to identify the application to which the traffic belongs, such as WeChat, BitTorrent, or YouTube. These applications can be further refined; for example, WeChat can be divided into text short messages, voice short messages, voice calls, video calls, and file transfer.
3) Service identification. It is to identify the type of service to which QUIC traffic belongs, such as web browsing, streaming media, instant messaging, and cloud storage.
4) Abnormal traffic identification. It is to identify malicious traffic such as DDoS, botnet, and APT.

3 Review of Recent QUIC-Based Traffic Research

Due to the multiplexing, traffic encryption, congestion control, forward error correction, and 0RTT (0 Round Trip Time) connection establishment of the QUIC protocol, there are fewer feature dimensions extracted from QUIC traffic than from traditional protocols. The characteristics extracted from QUIC traffic mainly include time series dimension information, statistical information, and byte stream information. At present, there are few works that take QUIC traffic as the research object, and the existing research can be divided into four categories: (1) Protocol identification [7]; (2) Application identification [8, 9]; (3) Service identification [6, 10]; (4) Abnormal traffic identification [11, 12]. Details will be given below.

3.1 Protocol Identification

There are varying data encapsulation formats as well as interaction processes for different communication protocols. Therefore, we need to understand the interaction process of different protocols, and find out the characteristics and laws that can be used to distinguish different applications in the interaction process. And then, it is possible to summarize the best feature attributes of each application protocol in network traffic [7]. And finally, these features lay the foundation for improving the granularity and accuracy of overall flow identification. Protocol identification can be at different levels in communication, such as identification of QUIC and non-QUIC protocols, identification of encrypted protocols, etc. Among them, the identification of QUIC and non-QUIC protocols is relatively simple and can be distinguished by the fingerprint feature of the packet header. The identification of encryption protocols is the key and most difficult content of protocol identification. The interaction process of encryption protocols can be roughly divided into two stages: (1) the first stage is to establish a secure connection, including a handshake, authentication, and key exchange. During this process, both parties negotiate supported encryption algorithms, mutual authentication, and key generation; (2) the second stage uses the key generated in the first stage to encrypt and transmit data. At present, the three mainstream encryption protocols are IPSec, SSH, and SSL.

3.2 Application and Service Identification

Traditional machine learning methods are widely used in the field of traffic identification. For QUIC, a new type of traffic, researchers also try to use traditional machine learning methods to identify QUIC traffic. The authors in [9] proposed a method to extract the characteristics of combined application data units from network traffic and used a variety of traditional machine learning methods to evaluate the quality of video streams based on the QUIC protocol, and obtained good results. This method could solve the difficult problem of video stream quality assessment caused by QUIC stream multiplexing. However, this method could not be used for other QUIC application network flows and could not be effectively applied to the application-level classification of QUIC traffic.

With the application of deep learning in various situations, more and more researchers try to use deep learning methods for QUIC traffic identification. The authors in [10] proposed a method that uses a convolutional neural network (CNN) to integrate feature extraction and classification and applies it to five services based on Google's QUIC protocol. This kind of method integrates feature extraction and classification by using CNN, and these methods always have high accuracy in private datasets. However, the method mentioned in [10] classifies a single QUIC stream ten times, which in turn consumes a lot of CPU time and memory space, and at the same time extracts fewer feature dimensions. In [6], the authors propose a semi-supervised CNN to classify QUIC traffic. Specifically, the authors use a large amount of unlabeled encrypted traffic data for initial training of the CNN and then use a small number of labeled QUIC encrypted traffic data sets for secondary training of the model. It is suitable for the case when there are only a few labeled samples. This method can avoid the problem that a large amount of labeled data is required for model training. However, the generalization performance is poor, and the classification accuracy on some datasets cannot meet the requirements of practical applications.

At present, although there are few works on QUIC traffic classification, in the field of non-QUIC traffic research, there have been many research results in recent years, such as using traditional machine learning algorithms to classify encrypted network traffic [13, 14], malicious traffic detection [15], using deep learning to classify encrypted traffic such as VPN and HTTPS, etc. [16–19]. These results have important reference significance for the research on QUIC traffic classification.

3.3 Abnormal Traffic Identification

Website fingerprinting attackers can infer the website visited by network users from network traffic. And website fingerprinting attacks (WFP) can be implemented through multi-classification tasks. In [11], the authors studied the safety of the three protocols, that is, QUIC, gQUIC, and HTTPS/2, to resist WFP from the perspective of traffic analysis. The authors collect network traffic through a controlled environment consisting of three Web servers running Ubuntu 18.04. In addition, the author selected the official landing pages of the top 100 schools from the Times World University Rankings. The main Web pages of these websites were downloaded and stored on three hosting servers. Each server uses Docker to isolate resources from these websites. To compare the effectiveness of different protocols against fingerprinting attacks, the authors used five machine learning models for testing, namely random forest, decision tree, k-nearest neighbor, naive bayes, and support vector machines, and used 10-fold cross-validation to obtain experiment results. According to the experiments, the following conclusions can be drawn: (1) At the beginning of the connection, the gQUIC and QUIC protocols are more vulnerable to the threat of WFP than HTTPS/2, but if considering the full-traffic situation, the performances of the three protocols are similar. (2) When considering the full traffic of both parties in communication, most of the characteristics of the three protocols can be converted to each other. While the traffic characteristics of the three protocols are quite different if only considering the traffic at the beginning of the connection. (3) When tested with only 40 packets and some simple features, the attack accuracy of gQUIC reaches 95.4%, QUIC is 95.5%, and HTTPS/2 is only 60.7%. Since the QUIC protocol includes the function of network padding, the authors in [12] studied the effectiveness of network layer padding in preventing website fingerprinting attacks. To this end, the author prepared two datasets, the hybrid datasets and the QUIC datasets.

The authors found that in a mixed dataset with only 4% of QUIC traffic, the classifier was biased towards TLS-specific features. Therefore, the author constructed a dataset with QUIC traffic accounting for 70%. In this paper, the random forest model is used for classification, and the results show that the network layer padding is almost ineffective against network fingerprinting attacks. In addition, the author also proposes the idea of padding data at the application layer to counteract website fingerprinting attacks. To sum up, although the QUIC protocol has been improved in many aspects, it does not have a big advantage in resisting website fingerprinting attacks. And in some scenarios, it is even weaker than HTTPS/2.

4 Evaluation

At present, the evaluation of traffic identification and classification is mainly based on the use of accuracy-related indicators. This indicator is relatively simple. To meet the network traffic analysis requirements, there are many new evaluation indicators proposed. The following introduces several common evaluation indicators currently used in QUIC traffic identification and classification.

(1) Accuracy

The percentage of the total number of samples that are correctly predicted. The details of the parameters are described in Eq. (1).

$$Accuracy = \frac{TP + TN}{TP + TN + FP + FN} \tag{1}$$

The accuracy indicator has a disadvantage, that is, the data samples are not balanced, and this indicator cannot evaluate the performance of the model. Suppose a test set has 99 positive samples and 1 negative sample. The probability that the model predicts all samples as positive will be 99%.

(2) Precision.

Precision is an evaluation index for prediction results. Among the results predicted by the model as positive samples, the percentage of true positive samples can be calculated in Eq. (2).

$$precision = \frac{TP}{TP + FP} \tag{2}$$

The meaning of the precision is how many of the results were predicted as positive samples.

(3) Recall

Recall is an evaluation index for the original sample. Among the actual positive samples, the percentage of predicted positive samples can be described in Eq. (3).

$$recall = \frac{TP}{TP + FN} \tag{3}$$

5 Discussion

With the growth of QUIC traffic on the Internet, identifying the type of traffic carried by the QUIC protocol and effectively managing and controlling it has become a problem that network operators are about to face. Compared with the current protocol of the transport layer, the QUIC protocol integrates more functions, and its QUIC packet organization and traffic characteristics are quite different from the current transport layer protocol. Therefore, the existing encrypted traffic classification methods cannot be directly used for QUIC traffic classification. In order to cope with the management and service of the future network calmly, it is urgent to research the classification of QUIC traffic. We believe that there may be the following three challenges in the field of QUIC traffic classification.

(1) How to build a classification model for QUIC traffic?
    The QUIC protocol has the functions of multiplexing, traffic encryption, congestion control, and forward error correction and data transmission using the UDP protocol. These functional characteristics create the unique traffic characteristics of the QUIC protocol, which can be used for traffic classification. QUIC traffic classification can be subdivided into multiple levels, such as: protocol classification, application classification, user behavior classification, and so on. For these different levels of classification requirements, it is necessary to understand the corresponding QUIC traffic characteristics and build a suitable model to classify QUIC traffic.
(2) How to solve the stability of the QUIC traffic classification model?
    The training data set in the field of network traffic classification generally has an unbalanced distribution of traffic data. Generally speaking, the classification result always has the problem of majority bias if you train the unbalanced data set directly. That is, it is easy to misreport the category of the traffic with a small number of samples. Therefore, it is necessary to consider how to keep the classification accuracy stable when building a QUIC traffic classification model.
(3) How to enhance the scalability of the QUIC traffic classification model?

In the face of complex and changeable network environments, the scalability of the QUIC traffic classification model is important for network operators. That is, the classification model can quickly identify new types of traffic based on the existing classification functions. Therefore, this kind of model needs a new structure to meet the requirements. Therefore, it is necessary to study the scalability method for the QUIC traffic classification model.

Acknowledgment. This work was supported by the Natural Science Foundation of Jiangxi Province under Grant No. 20192ACBL21031.

References

1. Langley, A., et al.: The quic transport protocol: Design and internet-scale deployment. In: Proceedings of the conference of the ACM special interest group on data communication, 183–196 (2017)
2. McMillan Kenneth, L., Zuck Lenore, D.: Formal specification and testing of QUIC. In: Proceedings of the ACM Special Interest Group on Data Communication, pp. 227–240 (2019)
3. De Coninck, Q., et al.: Pluginizing quic. In: Proceedings of the ACM Special Interest Group on Data Communication, pp. 59–74 (2019)
4. Shreedhar, T., Panda, R., Podanev, S., Bajpai, V.: Evaluating quic performance over web, cloud storage and video workloads. IEEE Transactions on Network and Service Management, 1–16 (2021)
5. Chiariotti, F., Deshpande, A.A., Giordani, M., Antonakoglou, K., Mahmoodi, T., Zanella, A.: QUIC-EST: a QUIC-enabled scheduling and transmission scheme to maximize VoI with correlated data flows. IEEE Commun. Mag. **59**(4), 30–36 (2021)
6. Shahbaz, R., Xin, L.: How to achieve high classification accuracy with just a few labels: a semi-supervised approach using sampled packets (2018). arXiv preprint arXiv:1812.09761
7. Zhao, J., Jing, X., Yan, Z., et al.: Network traffic classification for data fusion: a survey. Information Fusion **72**, 22–47 (2021)
8. Van, T., Anh, T.H., Souihi, S., Mellouk, A.: A novel quic traffic classifier based on convolutional neural networks. In: 2018 IEEE global communications conference (GLOBECOM). IEEE, pp. 1–6 (2018)
9. Hua, W., Guang, C., Xiaoyan, H.: Inferring adu combinations from encrypted quic stream. In: Proceedings of the 14th International Conference on Future Internet Technologies, pp. 1–6 (2019)
10. Peng, Y., He, M., Wang, Y.: A federated semi-supervised learning approach for network traffic classification (2021). arXiv preprint arXiv:2107.03933
11. Zhan, P., Wang, L., Tang, Y.: Website fingerprinting on early QUIC traffic. Comput. Netw. **200**, 108538 (2021)
12. Barman, L., Siby, S., Wood, C., et al.: This is not the padding you are looking for! On the ineffectiveness of QUIC PADDING against website fingerprinting (2022). arXiv preprint arXiv:2203.07806
13. Giuseppe, A., Giampaolo, B., Domenico, C., Antonio, M., Valerio, P., Antonio, P.: Characterization and prediction of mobile-app traffic using Markov modeling. IEEE Trans. Netw. Serv. Manage. **18**(1), 907–925 (2021)
14. Shi, D.: Multi class SVM algorithm with active learning for network traffic classification. Expert Syst. Appl. **176**, 114885 (2021)
15. Chang, L., Longtao, H., Gang, X., Zigang, C., Zhen, L.: Fs-net: A flow sequence network for encrypted traffic classification. In: IEEE INFOCOM 2019-IEEE Conference On Computer Communications, pp. 1171–1179. IEEE (2019)
16. Cong, D., Zhang Chen, L., Zhigang, L.B., Bo, J.: CETAnalytics: comprehensive effective traffic information analytics for encrypted traffic classification. Comput. Netw. **176**, 107258 (2020)
17. Giuseppe, A., Domenico, C., Antonio, M., Antonio, P.: DISTILLER: encrypted traffic classification via multimodal multitask deep learning. J. Netw. Comput. Appl. **183**, 102985 (2021)

18. Lin, X., Xiong, G., Gou, G., Li, Z., Shi, J., Yu, J.: ET-BERT: a contextualized datagram representation with pre-training transformers for encrypted traffic classification (2022). arXiv preprint arXiv:2202.06335
19. Cao, Y., Ji, R., Ji, L., Lei, G., Wang, H., Shao, X.: l2-MPTCP: A Learning-driven Latency-aware Multipath Transport Scheme for Industrial Internet Applications. IEEE Trans. Industr. Inf. (2022). https://doi.org/10.1109/TII.2022.3151093
20. Cao, Y., Ji, R., Huang, X., Lei, G., Shao, X., You, I.: Empirical mode decomposition-empowered network traffic anomaly detection for secure multipath TCP communications. Mobile Networks and Applications (2022). https://doi.org/10.1007/s11036-022-02005-6

A Survey of Multipath Transport Mechanism in Data Center Networks

Ruiwen Ji[✉][iD], Lejun Ji[iD], Keyang Gu[iD], Junyi Wu[iD], and Gang Lei[iD]

School of Software, Jiangxi Normal University, Nanchang 330022, China
jiruiwen@jxnu.edu.cn

Abstract. With the profound revolution in the data center industry and the increasing size of data center networks (DCNs), researchers have been focusing on achieving efficient and fast transport of traffic within the data center. In addition, the number of devices equipped with multiple interfaces is increasing, which allows multiple paths to be used simultaneously. Multipath transmission mechanisms can significantly improve the performance of data transmission in DCNs. However, some issues remain when MPTCP is deployed in DCNs. We have investigated multipath transport mechanisms in data center networks. First, the Multipath TCP (MPTCP) protocol is briefly described. Then, a study of routing algorithms, congestion control, and energy-saving techniques for applying MPTCP in DCNs are summarized separately. Finally, we propose the future direction of the multipath transmission mechanism in DCNs.

Keywords: data center networks · multipath TCP · software defined network

1 Introduction

The fourth industrial revolution driven by digital technology as the core is bringing profound changes to human production and life. As a physical base for carrying various digital technology applications, data centers are gradually highlighting their industrial empowerment value [1]. Major countries around the world are actively guiding the development of the data center industry. The data center market is growing in size and traffic convergence within data center networks (DCNs) is also increasing. If the DCNs experience network congestion, there may occur problems such as communication delays, long query times, and degraded service quality, causing a series of significant losses [2,3]. To avoid traffic surges that strain data centers and affect the quality of service, achieving efficient and fast transmission of traffic within DCNs has become a hot research topic today.

This work was supported by the National Natural Science Foundation of China (NSFC) under Grant No. 61962026, and by the Postgraduate Innovation Fund of Jiangxi Provincial Department of Education under Grant YC2021-S258.

Y. Cao and X. Shao (Eds.): MONAMI 2022, LNICST 474, pp. 373–385, 2023.
https://doi.org/10.1007/978-3-031-32443-7_27

As different kinds of network access technologies flourish, the next-generation network will be a heterogeneous network with multiple access networks coexisting in wired, wireless, and cellular networks [4]. With the accelerated deployment of IPv6, multiple addresses of hosts will become more popular. The servers in DCNs are basically multi-homed hosts, and there are usually multiple available paths between two hosts. However, traditional TCP can only select one path at random, which wastes a lot of network resources. Designed as an extension to TCP, Multipath TCP (MPTCP) [5] takes advantage of multiple subflows on different paths to enable high throughput and dynamic traffic migration. There are many solutions based on MPTCP [6–9] that have shown particular advantages for viable deployment, low latency and high throughput in DCNs. In brief, MPTCP can achieve load balancing by creating multiple subflows to distribute data to multiple paths within the network [10]. Figure 1 shows an MPTCP communication scenario under DCNs where two multi-homed hosts (Host A and Host B) can establish connections over three paths, meaning that multiple paths can be used to exchange data between the hosts simultaneously. This kind of multipath solution increases throughput and builds higher resistance to network failures [11].

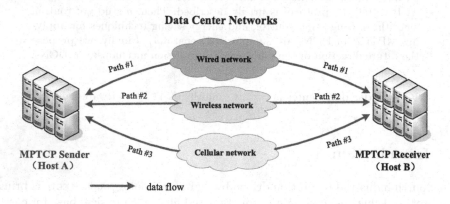

Fig. 1. MPTCP communication scenarios in DCNs.

However, some problems still exist when MPTCP is deployed in DCNs. For instance, due to the multi-versus-one model and the abundance of short pulses in DCNs, all traffics are prone to collision on shared links and on the same output port. Because the buffers of ToRs are usually too small to handle bursts, MPTCP incast problems inevitably occur during transmission [12], causing bottleneck collapse and dramatic throughput degradation. In addition, it is shown that in modern DCNs, MPTCP is effective over long traffic but not over short traffic [6]. Massive timeout retransmissions usually cause short traffic to arrive late. Which significantly reduces the transmission efficiency of a large number of delay-sensitive short flows in DCNs. These network topologies with multipath characteristics can generate large resource wastage when the network load is low.

Since the energy consumption of current DCNs devices and components is less affected by load variation, they consume essentially similar energy at low loads as at full loads [13], and the more underutilized devices can significantly pull down the efficiency of the network. The huge energy consumption of DCNs leads to high electricity costs, constrains the expansion of DCNs, and exacerbates the damage and impact on the environment [14]. Therefore, the performance and energy consumption issues of multipath transmission in DCNs have aroused widespread concern in academia and industry.

This paper surveys the research on multipath transport mechanisms in DCNs, and proposes future development directions and challenges. The survey is organized as follows. Section 2 introduces the MPTCP overview. Section 3 reviews MPTCP technologies in DCNs. Section 4 discusses the directions for future research. And we summarize in Sect. 5.

2   MPTCP Overview

With the continuous development of communication technology, modern communication terminals generally have multiple network interfaces. However, traditional TCP can only utilize a single interface for communication during one data transmission. To fully utilize the network resources among multi-homed hosts, in 2013, the International Internet Engineering Task Force (IETF) proposed the MPTCP [4], and standardized the protocol stack design, architecture, congestion control, application interfaces, and usage scenarios, etc. The MPTCP enables multi-homed terminals to access multiple networks simultaneously and fit multiple link bandwidths to achieve multi-path data transmission, so as to increase data transfer rates and maximize network resource utilization.

As shown in Fig. 2, the MPTCP layer is located below the application layer and above the TCP layer in the protocol stack [15], providing a standard TCP interface for the application layer to hide multipaths while multiple TCP subflows need to be managed. With functions such as path management [16], packet scheduling [17] and congestion control [18], MPTCP is currently the most researched and widely used transport layer multipath transport technology. MPTCP has attracted a lot of attention in the DCN field due to the following advantages.

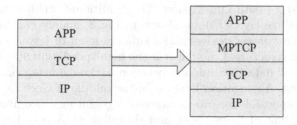

Fig. 2. MPTCP protocol stack.

The main advantages of the MPTCP protocol are as follows.

- **Improve throughput.** Traditional TCP only supports single-path data transmission between communicating pairs. MPTCP can take full advantage of multiple hosts equipped with multiple network interfaces to create multiple TCP subflows to transmit data in parallel between communicating pairs, fully aggregating the bandwidth on different physical links and improving throughput.
- **Enhance robustness.** In the event of poor link communication quality or disconnection, traditional TCP must disconnect the current connection and establish a new TCP connection on another link to re-transmit the data. For MPTCP, when a subflow fails, MPTCP management can quickly and seamlessly switch services to other available subflows, maintaining continuous data transmission and improving resilience to dynamic network environments.
- **Congestion Balance.** MPTCP assigns data to different subflows for transmission based on the subflow status and transfers the more congested subflows to the idle subflows through the congestion control mechanism to achieve load balancing of the entire network and improve the resource utilization of the network.
- **Traditional TCP compatibility.** MPTCP is an extension of traditional TCP. When the communication counterpart supports the MPTCP, it is preferred to use the MPTCP for data transmission to take advantage of multipath; when the communication counterpart does not support the MPTCP, it can also directly degrade to the traditional TCP to continue the single-path transmission.
- **Other Compatibility.** The MPTCP addresses compatibility issues including with the application layer, network middleware, and other users in the network, and ensures the security of data transmission in the face of attacks [19].

3 Status of Research on Multipath Transport Mechanisms in DCNs

3.1 Data Center Networks

The data center acts as an infrastructure service provisioning role to deliver, compute, and store data information. The traditional architecture of DCNs is organized into three layers [20], as shown in Fig. 3, mainly consisting of a large number of Layer 2 access devices and a small number of Layer 3 devices with a tree-like layered structure. Core Layer is the high-speed switching backbone that enables optimized data transmission between backbone networks through high-speed forwarding. Aggregation Layer is in the middle of Core Layer and Access Layer, and is responsible for processing and aggregating all communication data flows in the uplink of Core Layer and downlink of Access Layer, as well as providing firewall and intrusion detection services. Access Layer, also known

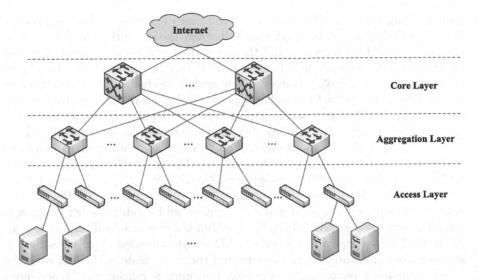

Fig. 3. The topology of traditional DCNs.

as Edge Layer, is mainly responsible for the access of network devices such as servers.

In recent years, with the rapid growth of data center traffic and the application requirements of virtualization technology, DCNs bandwidth and performance are facing great challenges. The traditional network architecture is no longer suitable for the development of the new generation of data centers, so researchers have designed a variety of network architectures, such as fat-tree [21] and VL2 [22] with switches as the core, and Dcell [23] with servers as the core.

In DCNs, the flows with high bandwidth demand are called long flows (also called elephant flows), which are mainly generated by data backups, and the flows with less bandwidth demand but more sensitive to latency are called short flows (also called rat flows), which are mainly generated by online searches [24]. These two types of traffic in the data center are distributed in a heavy-tailed manner. 90% of the volume of the network is rat streams, which accounts for less than 10% of the whole network's traffic. The other less than 10% of the number of elephant streams accounts for more than 80% of the total network traffic.

3.2 Routing Algorithms for Multipath Transmission in DCNs

Due to the popularity of multipath DCNs topologies, researchers have proposed many routing algorithms to solve the load balancing problem of DCNs. The equal-cost multipath routing (ECMP) algorithm [25] is the main routing algorithm used in DCNs to solve load balancing problems, which first numbers multiple equivalent paths, then hashes the packet header fields, and finally maps the data flow to the corresponding path. However, the ECMP algorithm may map multiple long flows onto the same link, resulting in link congestion and packet loss. The ECMP algorithm performs well when the network load is light, but as the network load increases and the network fluctuations increase, the load on the network becomes unbalanced. ECMP has two obvious disadvantages, (i) ECMP does not have a congestion awareness mechanism, and continues to assign forwarding tasks to already congested links, resulting in increased congestion; (ii) ECMP does not distinguish between elephant flows and rat flows, and this indiscriminate forwarding strategy is obviously no longer applicable to today's DCNs. RPS [26] maps every packet randomly to all available paths to optimise the resources of the multipath, but this approach can easily lead to packet reordering. To prevent packet reranking, CAPS [27] handles short flows and propagates them to all paths. For avoiding drastic reordering, Hermes [28] only reorders packets to good paths in a timely and careful manner when it is advantageous to do so. The DLB [29] algorithm is a dynamic load balancing algorithm for fat-tree topology networks, DLB adopts the idea of greedy strategy, starting from the sending end and selecting the other node of the link with the largest remaining bandwidth as the next hop until it reaches the highest-level switch that the flow needs to reach. However, the path obtained by the DLB algorithm is only locally optimal, which may cause congestion of some locally optimal paths. He, K. *et al.* [30, 31] improved network elasticity by making subflows not pass overlapping links in DCNs. However, the routing scheme only considers the current single connection and completely ignores the other connections in the network, and cannot do anything about the collisions between the subflows of different connections.

MPTCP transmits data in subflows, making full use of multipath resources. A number of works have emerged to improve the performance of MPTCP in DCNs. Raiciu, C. *et al.* [32] demonstrate that multipath transmission control protocols, while fully utilizing bandwidth and increasing throughput, increase finish times for short flows. Cao, Y. *et al.* [33] Achieve high data transmission performance by dynamically constructing disjoint paths for each MPTCP flow to take advantage of the path diversity of DCNs. However, MPTCP seeks to realise enough link usage by depleting buffers, resulting in sizeable queuing delays and packet loss. This affects the performance of the short, latency-sensitive traffic. Therefore, XMP [34] controls switch buffer occupancy using the ECN mechanism to lessen the influence of long flows against short flows. MMPTCP [6] differs long and short flows based on the amount of bytes, as well as applying different transmission policies.

As a network innovation architecture, Software Defined Network (SDN) realizes the decoupling of control plane and data plane under the traditional network architecture, as shown in Fig. 4. In theory, SDN can explore, allocate, and manage network resources for each MPTCP connection in a fair, efficient, and fast manner. In the DCNs based on SDN, Duan, J. *et al.* [35] designed a responsive MPTCP path management system, which consists of two modules: one is the centralized control module, which is responsible for the intelligent computing function of subflow routes; the other is the monitoring module, which proactively tunes the number of subflows depending on the network requirements. Hussein, A. *et al.* [36] designed an enhanced MPTCP architecture using SDN technology to achieve the target of maximising DCNs' throughput. However, collisions between different subflows of the same connection will affect transmission efficiency. Zannettou, S. *et al.* [37] designed a disjoint allocation strategy for MPTCP subflows. By parsing the MPTCP packet header information, the SDN controller assigns different subflows of the same connection to non-overlapping paths, thus making full use of network bandwidth. However, these methods ignore the quality difference between paths, which leads to serious packet disorder and a sharp decline in transmission performance. Kukreja, N. *et al.* [38] proposed the design of an MPTCP path manager based on SDN. With an intensive analysis of different scheduling algorithms, they discussed the impact of delay differences on the general performance of MPTCP and effectively mitigated the performance degradation caused by path quality differences.

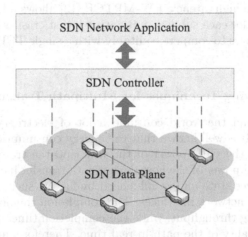

Fig. 4. SDN Architecture.

3.3 Congestion Control for Multipath Transmission in DCNs

More and more studies have shown that multipath transport technology would become the critical technology for DCNs. However, MPTCP has a problem with incast crashes, and its throughput drops drastically when the receiver makes data requests on multiple servers at the same time. Researchers have proposed many congestion control mechanisms to prevent MPTCP's incremental crash problem and thus improve MPTCP's performance in DCNs.

Kheirkhah, M. *et al.* [6] analysed the obstacles to deploying MPTCP in DCNs. The authors proposed a multipath congestion control scheme that can adaptively switch between multi-run and single-run traffic. Ye, J. *et al.* [39] proposed an enhanced MPTCP protocol that can adjust the congestion control mechanism under different numbers of subflows. Kimura, B. *et al.* [40] proposed an algorithm to adjust the send operations of all subflows in a collocated way to accomplish diverse goals such as friendliness, improved throughput and congestion balancing. However, this method does not reduce the number of lost packets. QCBF [41] is a multi-homed fat-tree topology MPTCP transport control method based on ToR cluster buffer assignment, which effectively eliminates the MPTCP incremental problem. DCMPTCP [8] controls the creation of subflows to alleviate congestion in data center communication mode. MMPTCP [6] randomly disperses short flow packets to allow for high aggregated throughput to balance the traffic load across multiple paths. FUSO [42] modifies the retransmission mechanism of MPTCP subflows. In cases where the sender suspects that a packet is lost, it will rapidly retransmit the lost packet using other congestion windows with small loads, cutting down on the total completion time of the subflow. MPTCP_OPN [44] adapts the number of parallel subflows based on real-time network conditions and moves traffic away from crowded paths flexibly to alleviate high latency. EW-MPTCP [12] allows additional congestion control operations for each subflow, mitigating incast crashes by permitting several MPTCP subflows to compete equitably with a single TCP flow at a common bottleneck.

3.4   Energy-Saving Techniques for Multipath Transmission in DCNs

Data centers around the world consume a lot of electricity, generating huge carbon emissions. It is well known that the energy consumption of data communications relies on the CPU power of the host and the traffic finish time. The instantaneous CPU power of the host during data transfer increases significantly compared to the free state and is influenced by factors such as the sending rate and the number of network interfaces. The completion time of elephant streams falls with increasing throughput, while the completion time of rat streams relies strongly on the quality of the path in real time. Therefore, energy optimisation for data transmission must take all these factors into account.

The reduction in completion time for long flows and the energy consumption using MPTCP compared to single-path TCP more than offset the increase in host CPU power. Researchers have proposed a variety of data center network energy-saving algorithms. Zhao, J. *et al.* [45] devised an energy-efficient approach for data centers, MPTCP-D. It reduces energy consumption by minimising traffic fulfilment time and closes the congestion window for additional subflows, guaranteeing that only one subflow remains on the overlapping path. Raiciu, C. *et al.* [32] demonstrated that MPTCP can improve data center utilisation at different network sizes and topologies. Khalili, R. *et al.* [46] studied the problem of optimal resource assignment between vast numbers of synchronous MPTCP flows. Interference of different MPTCP subflows on a common link raises the cost of traffic management overhead and increases energy consumption. If packet loss occurs, current approaches still need to wait for a retransmission mechanism to make a decision [47], which is less efficient for short delay-sensitive traffic. Gupta,

M. *et al.* [48] proposed that during periods of low activity, changing routes aggregates traffic onto fewer routes, causing idle devices to sleep. Vasić, N.*et al.* [49] proposed EATE to reduce energy consumption by combining sleep, rate adaptation, and routing coordination. Lin, M. *et al.* [50] studied data center energy proportional management to match energy consumption to server workloads.

4   Future Directions and Challenges

With the deployment of IPv6, the scale of multiple hosts in DCNs will be further expanded. At present, the research on multipath transmission mechanisms in DCNs mainly focuses on routing algorithms, congestion control, and energy-saving technology, which shows the advantages of multipath transmission technology. However, future research will face many challenges.

- **Design a multipath transmission strategy for hybrid flows in DCNs.** Many existing transport schemes first distinguish between elephant and rat flows in DCNs, and then perform path selection and data scheduling, respectively. However, there is currently no precise method for traffic detection and differentiation, and if an error is detected, it will seriously affect the data transmission performance. Future research should combine transmission control strategies with different traffic patterns, comprehensively consider switch caching, real-time link congestion, etc., design hybrid streaming transmission strategies for DCNs, and make balanced use of network resources.
- **Design the deployment scheme of large-scale SDN in DCNs.** As a new network architecture [51], the core idea of SDN is numerical control separation. The controller can create flexible network forwarding policies based on complex and variable service scenarios, providing a new mindset for data center traffic load balancing. MPTCP synchronous traffic arrivals can easily cause switch buffer overflows. Future work should address MPTCP load issues on SDN controllers, for example, by using multiple controllers to alleviate performance bottlenecks.
- **Study the energy consumption model of multipath transmission in DCNs.** With the expansion of the data center scale and business, energy consumption is a direct reflection of the cost. To the research community, the power consumption of MPTCP for DCNs remains largely unknown. In the future, energy-saving schemes should be studied to realize that the energy consumption of a data center is proportional to the workload level under the active state, and maximize the load balance and energy-saving effect by means of game theory.
- **Study the robustness optimization scheme of multipath transmission in DCNs.** Traffic bursts can be fatal to data center applications and can lead to serious performance degradation. If a critical transmission path in DCNs encounters random failures or external network attacks, the transmission performance of the path deteriorates, affecting the overall performance of the multipath transmission. At present, there are few studies on the security

of multipath transmission in DCNs. Therefore, future research can combine dynamic system modeling theory with complex network analysis methods to establish DCNs multipath transmission system robustness analysis model.

5   Conclusion

The multipath transmission mechanism will improve the transmission performance of DCNs. In recent years, great progress has been made in improving MPTCP performance in DCNs. This paper presents a current survey of the multipath transmission mechanism in DCNs. In order to analyse this field, we discuss the study of routing algorithms, congestion control, and energy-saving techniques for applying MPTCP in DCNs. In addition, we also put forward the development trend of the multipath transmission mechanisms in DCNs and the key problems to be solved to help researchers carry out further research.

References

1. Zhang, T., Lei, Y., Zhang, Q., Zou, S., Huang, J., Li, F.: Fine-grained load balancing with traffic-aware rerouting in datacenter networks. J. Cloud Comput. **10**(37), 1–20 (2021)
2. Xu, C., Wang, K., Sun, Y., Guo, S., Zomaya, A.Y.: Redundancy avoidance for big data in data centers: a conventional neural network approach. IEEE Trans. Netw. Sci. Eng. **7**(1), 104–114 (2020)
3. Huang, J., Li, S., Han, R., Wang, J.: Receiver-driven fair congestion control for TCP outcast in data center networks. J. Netw. Comput. Appl. **131**, 75–88 (2019)
4. Cao, Y., Ji, R., Ji, L., Lei, G., Wang, H., Shao, X.: l^2-MPTCP: a learning-driven latency-aware multipath transport scheme for industrial internet applications. IEEE Trans. Industr. Inf. (2022). https://doi.org/10.1109/TII.2022.3151093
5. Ford, A., Raiciu, C., Handley, M., Bonaventure, O.: TCP Extensions for Multipath Operation with Multiple Addresses. RFC 6824, IETF (2013)
6. Kheirkhah, M., Wakeman, I., Parisis, G.: Multipath transport and packet spraying for efficient data delivery in data centers. Comput. Netw. **162**, 1–15 (2019)
7. Kheirkhah, M., Lee, M.: A solution to MPTCP's inefficiencies under the incast problem for data center networks. Comput. Commun. **161**, 238–247 (2020)
8. Dong, E., Fu, X., Xu, M., Yang, Y.: DCMPTCP: host-based load balancing for datacenters. In: 2018 IEEE 38th International Conference on Distributed Computing Systems (ICDCS), pp. 622–633. IEEE, Piscataway (2018)
9. Duan, J., Wang, Z., Wu, C.: Responsive multipath TCP in SDN-based datacenters. In: 2015 IEEE International Conference on Communications (ICC), pp. 5296–5301. IEEE, Piscataway (2015)
10. Mahmud, I., Lubna, T., Song, Y.-J., Cho, Y.-Z.: Coupled multipath BBR (C-MPBBR): a efficient congestion control algorithm for multipath TCP. IEEE Access **8**, 165497–165511 (2020)
11. Cao, Y., Ji, R., Huang, X., et al.: Empirical mode decomposition-empowered network traffic anomaly detection for secure multipath TCP communications. Mob. Netw. Appl. **27**, 1–10 (2022)
12. Li, M., Lukyanenko, A., Tarkoma, S., Ylä-Jääski, A.: MPTCP incast in data center networks. China Commun. **11**(4), 25–37 (2014)

13. Heller, B., Seetharaman, S., Mahadevan, P., et al.: ElasticTree: saving energy in data center networks. In: the 2010 USENIX Conference on Networked Systems Design & Implementation, pp. 249–264. USENIX Association, USA (2010)

14. Bhattacharya, T., Qin, X.: Modeling energy efficiency of future green data centers. In: 2020 11th International Green and Sustainable Computing Workshops (IGSC), pp. 1–3 (2020)

15. Ford, A., Raiciu, C., Handley, M., Barre, S., Iyengar, J.: Architectural guidelines for multipath TCP development. RFC 6182 (2011)

16. Chung, J., Han, D., Kim J., Kim, C.: Machine learning based path management for mobile devices over MPTCP. In: 2017 IEEE International Conference on Big Data and Smart Computing (BigComp), pp. 206–209. IEEE, Piscataway (2017)

17. Hwang, J., Yoo, J.: Packet scheduling for multipath TCP. In: 2015 Seventh International Conference on Ubiquitous and Future Networks, pp. 177–179. IEEE, Piscataway (2015)

18. Wei, W., Xue, K., Han, J., Wei, D., Hong, P.: Shared Bottleneck-based congestion control and packet scheduling for multipath TCP. IEEE/ACM Trans. Network. **28**(2), 653–666 (2020)

19. Nguyen, V.D., Ro, S.: Performance evaluation of MPTCP over shared bottleneck link. J. Korean Inst. Commun. Inf. Sci. **40**(1), 70–77 (2015)

20. Chen, K., Singla, A., Singh, A., et al.: OSA: an optical switching architecture for data center networks with unprecedented flexibility. In: the USENIX Symposium on Networked Systems Design and Implementation (NSDI), pp. 498–511. IEEE, Piscataway (2014)

21. Al-Fares, M., Loukissas, A., Vahdat, A.: A scalable, commodity data center network architecture. ACM SIGCOMM Comput. Commun. Rev. **38**(4), 63–74 (2008)

22. Greenberg, A., Hamilton, J.R., Jain, N., et al.: VL2: a scalable and flexible data center network. In: the Special Interest Group on Data Communication (SIGCOMM), pp. 51–62. Association for Computing Machinery, New York, NY, USA (2009)

23. Guo, C., Wu, H., Tan, K., Shi, L., Zhang, Y., Lu, S.: DCell: a scalable and fault-tolerant network structure for data centers. In: the ACM SIGCOMM 2008 Conference on Data Communication (SIGCOMM 2008), pp. 75–86. Association for Computing Machinery, New York, NY, USA (2008)

24. Benson, T., Akella, A., Maltz, D.A.: Network traffic characteristics of data centers in the wild. In: the 10th ACM SIGCOMM Conference on Internet Measurement, pp. 267–280. Association for Computing Machinery, New York, NY, USA (2010)

25. Hopps, C.: Analysis of an equal-cost multi-path algorithm, RFC2992 (2000). https://doi.org/10.17487/RFC2992. Accessed 01 Nov 2000

26. He, K., Rozner, E., Agarwal, K., Felter, W., Carter, J., Akella, A.: Presto: edge-based load balancing for fast datacenter networks. In: the Conference on Special Interest Group on Data Communication SIGCOMM 2015. Association for Computing Machinery, New York, NY, USA (2015)

27. Hu, J., Huang, J., Lv, W., Zhou, Y., Wang, J., He, T.: CAPS: coding based adaptive packet spraying to reduce flow completion time in data center. IEEE/ACM Trans. Network. **27**(6), 2338–2353 (2019)

28. Zhang, H., Zhang, J., Bai, W., Chen, K., Chowdhury, M.: Resilient datacenter load balancing in the wild. In: The Conference of the ACM Special Interest Group on Data Communication SIGCOMM' 17. Association for Computing Machinery, pp. 253–266. NY, USA, New York (2017)

29. Yu, L., Deng, P.: Open flow based load balancing for fat-tree networks with multi-path support. In: IEEE International Conference on Communications (ICC). IEEE, Piscataway (2013)
30. He, K., Rozner, E., Agarwal, K., Felter, W., Carter, J., Akella, A.: Presto: edge-based load balancing for fast datacenter networks. In: the Conference on Special Interest Group on Data Communication SIGCOMM' 15, pp. 75–86. Association for Computing Machinery, New York, NY, USA (2015)
31. Sandri, M., Silva, A., Rocha, L.A., Verdi, F.L.: On the benefits of using multipath TCP and openflow in shared bottlenecks. In: 2015 IEEE 29th International Conference on Advanced Information Networking and Applications, pp. 9–16. IEEE, Piscataway (2015)
32. Raiciu, C., Barre, S., Pluntke, C., et al.: Improving datacenter performance and robustness with multipath TCP. ACM SIGCOMM Comput. Commun. Rev. **41**(4), 266–277 (2011)
33. Cao, Y., Xu, M.: Dual-NAT: dynamic multipath flow scheduling for data center networks. In: 2013 21st IEEE International Conference on Network Protocols (ICNP), pp. 1–2. IEEE, Piscataway (2013)
34. Cao, Y., Xu, M., Fu, X., Dong, E.: Explicit multipath congestion control for data center networks. In: the Ninth ACM Conference on Emerging Networking Experiments and Technologies - CoNEXT' 13, pp. 73–84. Association for Computing Machinery, New York, NY, USA (2013)
35. Duan, J., Wang, Z., Wu, C.: Responsive multipath TCP in SDN-based datacenters. In: 2015 IEEE International Conference on Communications (ICC), pp. 5296–5301. IEEE, Piscataway (2015)
36. Hussein, A., Elhajj, I.H., Chehab, A., et al.: SDN for MPTCP: an enhanced architecture for large data transfers in datacenters. In: IEEE International Conference on Communications, pp. 1–7. IEEE, Piscataway (2017)
37. Zannettou, S., Sirivianos M., Papadopoulos, F.: Exploiting path diversity in data-centers using MPTCP-aware SDN. In: 2016 IEEE Symposium on Computers and Communication (ISCC), pp. 539–546. IEEE, Piscataway (2016)
38. Kukreja, N., Maier, G., Alvizu R., Pattavina, A.: SDN based automated testbed for evaluating multipath TCP. In: 2016 IEEE International Conference on Communications Workshops (ICC), pp. 718–723. IEEE, Piscataway (2016)
39. Ye, J., Feng, L., Xie, Z., Huang, J., Li, X.: Fine-grained congestion control for MultiPath TCP in data center networks. IEEE Access **7**, 31782–31790 (2019)
40. Kimura, B., Loureiro, A.: MPTCP linux kernel congestion controls. Technical report (2018)
41. Pang, S., Yao, J., Wang, X., Ding, T., Zhang, L.: Transmission control of MPTCP Incast based on buffer balance factor allocation in data center networks. IEEE Access **7**, 183428–183434 (2019)
42. Guo, C., Lu, Y., Yuan, M., et al.: Fast and cautious: leveraging multi-path diversity for transport loss recovery in data centers. In: USENIX Annual Technical Conference, pp. 29–42. USENIX Association, USA (2016)
43. Liu, S., Huang, J., Jiang, W., Wang, J.: Reducing traffic burstiness for MPTCP in data center networks. J. Netw. Comput. Appl. **192**, 1–12 (2021)
44. Huang, J., Li, W., Li, Q., Zhang, T., Dong, P., Wang, J.: Tuning high flow concurrency for MPTCP in data center networks. J. Cloud Comput. Adv. Syst. Appl. **9**(13), 1–15 (2020)
45. Zhao, J., Liu, J., Wang, H., Xu, C., Gong, W., Xu, C.: Measurement, analysis, and enhancement of multipath TCP energy efficiency for datacenters. IEEE/ACM Trans. Network. **28**(1), 57–70 (2020)

46. Khalili, R., Gast, N., Popovic, M., Upadhyay, U., Boudec, J.: MPTCP is not Pareto-optimal: performance issues and a possible solution. In: the 8th International Conference on Emerging Networking Experiments and Technologies (CoNEXT 2012), pp. 1–12. Association for Computing Machinery, New York, NY, USA (2012)
47. Ferlin, S., Alay, Ö., Dreibholz, T., Hayes, D.A., Welzl, M.: Revisiting congestion control for multipath TCP with shared bottleneck detection. In: the 35th Annual IEEE International Conference on Computer Communications, pp. 1–9. IEEE, Piscataway (2016)
48. Gupta, M., Singh, S.: Greening of the internet. In: Conference on Applications. Technologies, Architectures, and Protocols for Computer Communications, pp. 19–26. Association for Computing Machinery, New York, NY, USA (2003)
49. Vasić, N., Kostić, D.: Energy-aware traffic engineering. In: the 1st International Conference on Energy-Efficient Computing and Networking (e-Energy 2010), pp. 169–178. Association for Computing Machinery, New York, NY, USA (2010)
50. Lin, M., Wierman, A., Andrew, L.L., Thereska, E.: Dynamic right-sizing for power-proportional data centers. IEEE/ACM Trans. Network. 21(5), 1378–1391 (2013)
51. Hu, F., Hao, Q., Bao, K.: A survey on software-defined network and Openflow: from concept to implementation. Commun. Surv. Tutorials 16(4), 2181–2206 (2014)

AgBFPN: Attention Guided Bidirectional Feature Pyramid Network for Object Detection

Lanjie Jiang[1,2], Xiang Zhang[1,2(✉)], Ruijing Yang[1,2], and Yudie Liu[1,2]

[1] University of Electronic Science and Technology of China, Chengdu 611731, Sichuan, China
{202052012112,202022012111,202152011924}@std.uestc.edu.cn
[2] Yangtze Delta Region Institute (Quzhou), University of Electronic Science and Technology of China, Quzhou 324000, Zhejiang, China
uestchero@uestc.edu.cn

Abstract. Object detection is increasingly in demand in IoT service applications. Deep learning based object detection algorithms are now in fashion. As the most popular multi-scale object detection network at present, Feature Pyramid Network achieves feature augmentation by fusing features of neighboring layers. It is widely used in the most advanced object detectors to detect objects of different scales. In this paper, we propose a new attention mechanism guided bidirectional feature pyramid architecture named AgBFPN to enhance the transfer of semantic and spatial information between each feature map. We design Channel Attention Guided Fusion(CAGF) Module and Spatial Attention Guided Fusion(SAGF) Module to enhance feature fusion. The CAGF mitigates the loss of information induced by channel reduction and better transfers the semantic information from high-level to low-level features. The SAGF passes the rich spatial information of shallow features into deep features. Our experiments show that AgBFPN achieves higher Average Precision for multi-scale object detection.

Keywords: Deep learning · Object detection · Feature pyramid network · Attentional mechanisms

1 Introduction

With the rapid expansion of IoT, there is an increasing demand for object detection in IoT application scenarios such as intelligent transportation and public

Supported by National Science Foundation of China (U19A2052, U1733111), National Key R&D Program of China (2021YFB1600500), Chengdu Science and Technology Project (2021-JB00-00025-GX), Key R&D Program of Sichuan Province (2020YFG0478), the Municipal Government of Quzhou under Grant Number 2021D012.

Y. Cao and X. Shao (Eds.): MONAMI 2022, LNICST 474, pp. 386–397, 2023.
https://doi.org/10.1007/978-3-031-32443-7_28

safety. Object detection algorithms based on the deep convolutional network have already achieved significant advancements in recent years. The object scale is the important factor related to the performance of object detection. Some detailed information about small objects is contained in shallow features. With deeper layers, the geometric details may vanish entirely (oversized receptive field), making it hard to detect small objects using deep features. Deeper feature maps can provide semantic information about large objects. Thus, object detection with a wide range of object scale changes is still a challenging problem [1].

Deep features in convolutional neural networks have a large receptive field and rich semantic information but lose geometric detail information. In contrast, shallow features have rich detail information with small receptive fields, but lack of semantic information. Multi-scale learning combines deep semantic information and shallow representation information, which is an effective strategy to improve the performance of object detection [2–4]. FPN [4] is the frequently utilized multi-scale object detection network at present. It passes down the high-level feature information and supplements the low-level semantics to solve the multi-scale problem in object detection.

We think about two issues that may exist in feature pyramid network. The first is before feature fusion, different level features will go through a convolutional layer with a convolution kernel of size 1×1 to reduce feature channels, and excessive channel attenuation will bring about unavoidable information loss. In addition, in the top-down pathway, the top-level pyramid does not get supplementary information, so the reduction of channels will lose information instead.

Based on these issues, we design the Channel Attention Guided Fusion (CAGF) Module, which introduced the attention mechanism. The features of high-level layers with sufficient classification details can be applied as attention to guide the low-level features. It transfers different scale semantic features from top to bottom, so that can obtain high-resolution and strong semantic features, which is beneficial to the detection of multi-scale objects. Furthermore, we add a new bottom-up spatial perception pathway by Spatial Attention Guided Fusion (SAGF) Module to pass the rich spatial information of shallow features into deep features. Combined Channel Attention Guided Fusion Module and Spatial Attention Guided Fusion, our AgBFPN architecture archives effective accuracy improvements on PASCAL VOC2007 [5] and MS COCO [6].

Based on these issues, the main contributions of our paper are as follows:

- Firstly, we design the Channel Attention Guided Fusion (CAGF) Module, which introduces the attention mechanism. The deep features have sufficient classification information to guide the shallow features. It conveys semantic feature information from top to bottom at various scales, which helps multi-scale object detection.
- Furthermore, we add a new bottom-up spatial perception pathway by Spatial Attention Guided Fusion (SAGF) Module to pass the rich spatial information of shallow features into deep features.

– Combined Channel Attention Guided Fusion Module and Spatial Attention Guided Fusion, our AgBFPN architecture archives effective accuracy improvements on PASCAL VOC2007 [5] and MS COCO [6].

2   Related Work

Early multi-scale detection has two ideas. One is to utilize different convolution kernel sizes to acquire various scale information through different sizes of the receptive field, and the other is to use image pyramids to detect different scale objects by inputting images at various scales. However, these two methods are computationally expensive and suffer from a limited range of receptive fields. Later, multi-scale detection is gradually developed to execute object detection based on the feature pyramid, using feature maps of various stages to build a feature pyramid network to detect multi-scale objects. Since FPN [4] was proposed, multiple versions have been iterated successively [9–12], from no fusion to top-down unidirectional fusion, and then gradually to bidirectional fusion as in Fig. 1.

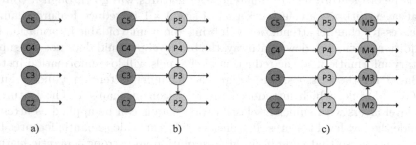

Fig. 1. Evolution of Feature Pyramid Networks: a) No fusion; (b) Top-down unidirectional fusion; and (c) Simple bidirectional fusion

2.1   No Fusion

Most classical object detection networks use the last layer of deep neural networks to make predictions. However, it is going to be hard to detect small objects in the last feature map due to the loss of spatial and detailed feature information. SSD [2] is one of the typical representatives of no fusion using multi-scale features. It uses shallower feature maps to detect smaller objects and Deeper feature maps to detect larger objects.

2.2   Top-Down Unidirectional Fusion

The current object detection model's main fusion mode is top-down unidirectional fusion FPN [4]. It introduces a top-down network architecture to enhance features with feature fusion from neighboring layers. Based on FPN [4], Liang [8] proposes a deep feature pyramid network, which enhances the semantic features of small objects by using feature pyramids with lateral connections. Libra R-CNN [9] fuses and refines multi-scale feature elements with a balanced feature pyramid. AugFPN [10] proposes a series of FPN enhancement methods.

2.3   Bidirectional Fusion

Only top-to-bottom feature maps are fused by FPN [4]. Secondary fusion from bottom to top has been proposed for the first time by PANet [13]. Based on traditional feature pyramid networks, PANet [13] increases the shallow information to the deep layer just by adding a bottom-up fusion pathway. Since the proposal of PANet [13] proves the effectiveness of bidirectional fusion, several relevant researches try more complex bidirectional fusion, such as NAS-FPN [14], ASFF [15] and BiFPN [16]. NAS-FPN [14] employs neural architecture search to learn all cross-scale connections for better fusion. For simple and fast feature fusion, BiFPN [16] proposes a weighted bidirectional feature pyramid network.

3   Proposed Methods

We describe our attention guided bidirectional Feature Pyramid Network architecture in this section. By introducing an attention mechanism, it fully utilizes semantic information from deep features and spatial information from shallow features to optimize the fusion of feature information at different scales. In AgBFPN, two main components are proposed: a Channel Attention Guided Fusion (CAGF) Module and a Spatial Attention Guided Fusion (SAGF) Module. We will describe them in detail below.

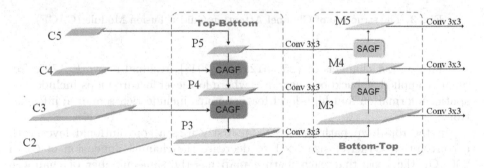

Fig. 2. An overview of our Attention guided Bidirectional Feature Pyramid Network(AgBFPN)

3.1 Overall

Figure 2 depicts the overall framework of AgBFPN. Following the config-uration of FPN [4], the outputs of the backbone features are indicated as $\{C2, C3, C4, C5\}$ to build a feature pyramid, which corresponds to the $\{4, 8, 16, 32\}$ strides. We separate $C2$ from the four-level input features entering the feature pyramid network because the $C2$ would take up more computational resources. We keep $\{C3, C4, C5\}$ to build the feature pyramid. In FPN, horizon-tal connections are required to reduce the number of channels of each feature layer to the same 256. Different from this, we retain the number of input chan-nels and complete the top-down semantic information transfer between different features through the CAGF. $\{P3, P4, P5\}$ are the features generated by the top-down path of the feature pyramid. We build a spatial perception bottom-top pathway with the SAGF that successively transfers the spatial information from low-level features to high-level features. $\{M3, M4, M5\}$ are the features generated by the spatial perception bottom-top pathway.

3.2 Channel Attention Guided Fusion Module

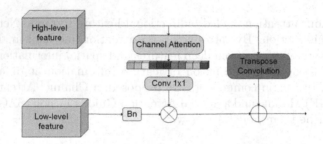

Fig. 3. The structure of Channel Attention Guided Fusion Module (CAGF)

With output channels of $\{256, 512, 1024, 2048\}$, residual network [17] is fre-quently applied as backbone network, where low-level feature maps include rich spatial information and high-level feature maps include rich semantic informa-tion.

In the top-down pathway, FPN [4] firstly uses a convolutional layer with a convolution kernel of size 1×1 to decrease the channel dimension of C_i to 256. On the basis that each feature map has the same number of channels, FPN [4] uses nearest neighbor interpolation to upsample and then fuse them by adding to transfer the features from the upper layer to the bottom. This approach reduces the number of channels of the top-level feature $C5$ from 2048 to 256 before fusion, which will result in severe loss of channel information. For this purpose, we introduce a method to fuse the features of neighboring layers without changing the number of channels.

We design Channel Attention Guided Fusion Module (CAGF) inspired by PAN [18]. The channel attention mechanism is introduced in CAGF, as illustrated in Fig. 3. Each channel mapping of high-level layer features can be seen as the response to a specific class. Obtaining the interdependence between different channel mappings can effectively enhance the characterization of feature maps for specific semantics. High-level layer features have adequate classifieds, that can be directed as the attention to direct the low-level.

The basic idea is that high-level features are weighted by predicting a channel weight mask and then weighting the low-level features. In specific, high-level feature map channel weight masks are predicted using a channel attention module [19].

This mask is then multiplied by the low-level feature map after the batch normalization layer to obtain a weighted feature map. At last, the high-level feature maps upsampled by transposed convolution are fused to the weighted low-level feature map and passed layer by layer.

3.3   Spatial Attention Guided Fusion Module

The top-down pathway complements the semantics from high-level features for high-resolution low-level features. But the features of the top-level pyramid lose information due to the reduction of channels in the top-level feature map. So we build a bottom-up spatial awareness path, aiming to supplement high-level features with spatial and detailed information from low-level to help multi-scale object detection.

After the top-down pathway, the result passes through a 3×3 convolution to mitigate the upsample aliasing effect. At this point, each layer of the feature map has the same number of 256 channels. For the deepest feature $C5$, the number of channels is reduced from 2048 to 256 without additional information, so there is a loss of information instead.

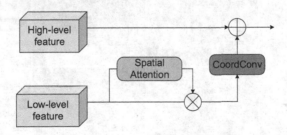

Fig. 4. The structure of Spatial Attention Guided Fusion Module (SAGF)

As Fig. 4 shows, we construct a spatial attention guided fusion module (SAGF) in the spatial perception pathway, which introduces a spatial attention mechanism in SAGF. The high-resolution low-level features have enough detailed spatial information to complement the high-level features.

To obtain the spatial attention map, low-level features are first passed through the spatial attention module. Then, applying the spatial attention map to the original feature map completes the spatial information calibration. After that, we downsample the low-level features using CoordConv [20], which adds two coordinate channels to enable the convolutional downsampling process to sense the feature map's spatial information. The downsampled low-level features are additively fused with the high-level features so that the high-level features fuse the spatial information from the low-level features.

Fig. 5. Result comparison: (a) is the original image; (b) is the result of RetinaNet with FPN; (c) is the result of RetinaNet with AgBFPN (ours).

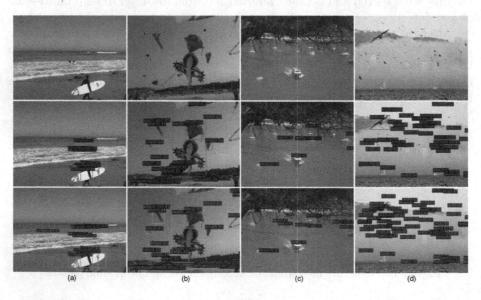

Fig. 6. Qualitative result comparison. The first row is the original image, the second row is the result of RetinaNet with FPN and the third row is the result of RetinaNet with AgBFPN (ours).

4   Experiments

4.1   Dataset and Evaluation Metric

We conduct experiments on the PASCAL VOC2007 [5] and MS COCO2017 [6] detection datasets. PASCAL VOC2007 [5] has 9,963 images with 20 classes, 50% of which are used for training/validation and 50% for testing. MS COCO2017 [6] has 80 classes and provides train2017 containing 115k images, val2017 containing 5k images, and test2017 containing 20k images.

For PASCAL VOC2007 [5], we report Mean Average Precision(mAP) on the basis that the IOU threshold is selected as 0.5. For MS COCO2017 [6], all reported results adhere to the standard COCO-style Mean Average Precision (mAP) metrics at multiple IoU thresholds from 0.5 to 0.95 with a 0.05 interval.

Table 1. Comparison of object detection performance on COCO test-dev. The asterisk (*) indicates that the results were re-implemented with MMDetection v2.0.

Baseline	Neck	Dataset	Schedule	AP	AP_{50}	AP_{75}	AP_S	AP_M	AP_L
RetinaNet* [21]	FPN	COCO	1x	34.6	52.7	36.7	19.3	37.8	45.3
RetinaNet* [21]	PAFPN [13]	COCO	1x	36.0	55.5	38.4	20.1	39.9	47.0
RetinaNet* [21]	FPN	mini	2x	24.6	39.9	25.8	12.6	28.4	33.9
Faster RCNN* [7]	FPN	mini	1x	24.2	45.4	23.8	12.5	30.5	32.6
FCOS* [23]	FPN	mini	1x	18.3	31.3	18.8	12.5	20.2	23.8
RetinaNet	**AgBFPN**	COCO	1x	37.1	56.6	39.2	22.2	40.9	47.5
RetinaNet	**AgBFPN**	mini	1x	21.4	36.0	22.9	12.6	25.7	30.5
RetinaNet	**AgBFPN**	mini	2x	26.4	42.7	26.7	15.9	31.7	36.1
FCOS	**AgBFPN**	mini	1x	20.2	33.7	21.5	14.2	24.6	27.5
Faster RCNN	**AgBFPN**	mini	1x	27.0	48.6	27.3	15.5	31.7	34.9

Table 2. Comparison of object detection performance on VOC test-dev. The asterisk (*) indicates that the results were re-implemented with MMDetection v2.0.

Baseline	Neck	Dataset	Schedule	AP
RetinaNet* [21]	FPN	VOC	1x	72.4
RetinaNet* [21]	PAFPN [13]	VOC	1x	72.7
RetinaNet* [21]	NASFPN [14]	VOC	1x	73.1
RetinaNet	**AgBFPN**	VOC	1x	74.7

4.2   Implementation Details and Main Results

Each of our experiments is based on MMDetection v2.0 [22]. By default, we train the networks for 12 epochs using NVIDIA 3060 TI (2 images per GPU). For the training process, the 1x schedule represents 12 epochs and the 2x schedule represents 24 epochs. The initial learning rate is 0.001. It respectively decreases by 0.1 at 9 and 12 epochs in the 1x schedule, corresponding to the 17 and 23 epochs in the 2x schedule.

Figure 5 compares the outcomes between the FPN and our AgBFPN. As can be observed, our AgBFPN is more sensitive to multi-scale object detection. More contrast can be seen in Fig. 6.

We assess AgBFPN on the COCO test-dev subset to validate the effectiveness of our approach for performance enhancement. To facilitate the verification, we randomly extracted part of the data of the MS COCO2017 detection dataset as miniCOCO (the same ratio of train/val/test to COCO) for part of the experiments.

To guarantee the designed network's generalization capabilities, we train the model on training data, validate on validation data, and lastly test with the optimal parameters on test data.

We exhibit re-implemented results of the corresponding baselines for fair comparisons. By swapping out FPN for AgBFPN, RetinaNet using ResNet-50 as the backbone achieves 37.1 AP on COCO test-dev, 2.5 points above the baseline, as demonstrated in Table 1. The same network achieves 74.7 AP on VOC test-dev, 2.3 points above the baseline, as demonstrated in Table 2.

4.3   Ablation Experiments

we also test the impact of each proposed AgBFPN component with RetinaNet [21] baseline on PASCAL VOC2007 [5] in Table 3. The training procedure runs on 1x schedule (12 epochs). For fair comparisons, ablation experiments are conducted under the same conditions.

Table 3. Effect of each component on VOC test-dev.

baseline	CAGF	SAGF	AP
✓			72.4
✓	✓		73.4
✓		✓	73.3
✓	✓	✓	**74.7**

Table 4. Ablation studies of Channel Attention Guided Fusion Module on VOC test-dev.

baseline	SE	CAM	BN	AP
✓				72.4
✓	✓			72.7
✓	✓		✓	73.2
✓		✓		72.6
✓		✓	✓	**73.4**

Channel Attention Guided Fusion Module. CAGF introduces channel attention to optimize feature fusion of adjacent feature layers in the top-down pathway and CAGF boosts performance by 1.0 AP.

We conduct ablation experiments in this module to examine the impact of different attentional mechanisms. In addition, to better integrate semantic information from higher levels, we verified the effectiveness of adding a Bn layer before the fusion of low-level features shown in Table 4.

We speed up network convergence by adding a Batch Normalization [24] layer. To avoid the gradient from vanishing or exploding and speed up training, Batch Normalization can address the issue that the middle layer's data distribution changes during the training process.

Spatial Attention Guided Fusion Module. Then we add SAGF on RetinaNet with the CAGF. According to Table 3, the combined module increases AP by 2.3 points above the corresponding baseline. Adding the SAGF module raises the AP by 1.3 points above the CAGF-only baseline. We also do ablation tests to assess CoordConv's effect compared with the traditional 3×3 convolution downsample layer in Table 5.

Table 5. Ablation studies of Spatial Attention Guided Fusion Module on VOC test-dev.

baseline w/ CAGF	Conv	CoordConv	AP
✓			73.4
✓	✓		73.3
✓		✓	**74.7**

5   Conclusion

In this paper, we propose a novel Attention guided Bidirectional Feature Pyramid Network (AgBFPN) for object detection to further improve the performance of multi-scale learning. To better convey the semantic information in the deep feature maps, we design a Channel Attention Guided Fusion Module. The module uses the higher-level feature maps to guide the lower-level feature maps during the top-down pathway in the feature pyramid network. Moreover, we build a Spatial Perception Bottom-up Pathway with Spatial Attention Guided Fusion Module to effectively transfer the spatial information in the underlying feature maps. According to the results of our experiment, the proposed methods can improve the performance of object detection algorithms based on the FPN framework on MS COCO2017 and PASCAL VOC2007 object detection benchmark. AgBFPN improves RetinaNet by 2.3 points AP on PASCAL VOC2007 and 2.5 points AP on MS COCO2017 when using ResNet50 as the backbone.

References

1. Zou, Z., Shi, Z., Guo, Y., Ye, J.: Object detection in 20 years: a survey. arXiv preprint arXiv:1905.05055 (2019)
2. Liu, W., et al.: SSD: single shot multibox detector. In: Leibe, B., Matas, J., Sebe, N., Welling, M. (eds.) ECCV 2016. LNCS, vol. 9905, pp. 21–37. Springer, Cham (2016). https://doi.org/10.1007/978-3-319-46448-0_2
3. Cao, G., Xie, X., Yang, W., Liao, Q., Shi, G., Wu, J.: Feature-fused SSD: fast detection for small objects. In: Ninth International Conference on Graphic and Image Processing, vol. 10615, pp. 381–388 (2018)
4. Lin, T.Y., Dollár, P., Girshick, R., He, K., Hariharan, B., Belongie, S.: Feature pyramid networks for object detection. In: Proceedings of the IEEE Conference on Computer Vision and Pattern Recognition, pp. 2117–2125 (2017)
5. Everingham, M., Gool, L.V., Williams, C.K.I., Winn, J., Zisserman, A.: The PASCAL Visual Object Classes Challenge 2007 (VOC2007) Results (2007). https://www.pascal-network.org/challenges/VOC/voc2007/workshop/index.html
6. Lin, T.-Y.: Microsoft COCO: common objects in context. In: Fleet, D., Pajdla, T., Schiele, B., Tuytelaars, T. (eds.) ECCV 2014. LNCS, vol. 8693, pp. 740–755. Springer, Cham (2014). https://doi.org/10.1007/978-3-319-10602-1_48
7. Ren, S., He, K., Girshick, R., Sun, J.: Faster r-cnn: towards real-time object detection with region proposal networks. In: Advances in Neural Information Processing Systems, vol. 28 (2015)
8. Liang, Z., Shao, J., Zhang, D., Gao, L.: Small object detection using deep feature pyramid networks. In: Hong, R., Cheng, W.-H., Yamasaki, T., Wang, M., Ngo, C.-W. (eds.) PCM 2018. LNCS, vol. 11166, pp. 554–564. Springer, Cham (2018). https://doi.org/10.1007/978-3-030-00764-5_51
9. Pang, J., Chen, K., Shi, J., Feng, H., Ouyang, W., Lin, D.: Libra R-CNN: towards balanced learning for object detection. In: Proceedings of the IEEE/CVF Conference on Computer Vision and Pattern Recognition, pp. 821–830 (2019)
10. Guo, C., Fan, B., Zhang, Q., Xiang, S., Pan, C.: Augfpn: improving multi-scale feature learning for object detection. In: Proceedings of the IEEE/CVF Conference on Computer Vision and Pattern Recognition, pp. 12595–12604 (2020)
11. Luo, Y., et al.: CE-FPN: enhancing channel information for object detection. Multimed. Tools Appl. 1–20 (2022). https://doi.org/10.1007/s11042-022-11940-1
12. Zhao, H., Shi, J., Qi, X., Wang, X., Jia, J.: Pyramid scene parsing network. In: Proceedings of the IEEE Conference on Computer Vision and Pattern Recognition, pp. 2881–2890 (2017)

13. Liu, S., Qi, L., Qin, H., Shi, J., Jia, J.: Path aggregation network for instance segmentation. In: Proceedings of the IEEE Conference on Computer Vision and Pattern Recognition, pp. 8759–8768 (2018)
14. Ghiasi, G., Lin, T.Y., Le, Q.V. : NAS-FPN: learning scalable feature pyramid architecture for object detection. In: Proceedings of the IEEE/CVF Conference on Computer Vision and Pattern Recognition, pp. 7036–7045 (2019)
15. Liu, S., Huang, D., Wang, Y.: Learning spatial fusion for single-shot object detection. arXiv preprint arXiv:1911.09516 (2019)
16. Tan, M., Pang, R., Le, Q.V.: Efficientdet: scalable and efficient object detection. In: Proceedings of the IEEE/CVF Conference on Computer Vision and Pattern Recognition, pp. 10781–10790 (2020)
17. He, K., Zhang, X., Ren, S., Sun, J.: Deep residual learning for image recognition. In: Proceedings of the IEEE Conference on Computer Vision and Pattern Recognition, pp. 770–778 (2016)
18. Li, H., Xiong, P., An, J., Wang, L.: Pyramid attention network for semantic segmentation. arXiv preprint arXiv:1805.10180 (2018)
19. Woo, S., Park, J., Lee, J.Y., Kweon, I.S.: CBAM: convolutional block attention module. In: Proceedings of the European Conference on Computer Vision, pp. 3–19 (2018)
20. Liu, R., et al.: An intriguing failing of convolutional neural networks and the coordconv solution. In: Advances in Neural Information Processing Systems, vol. 31 (2018)
21. Lin, T.Y., Goyal, P., Girshick, R., He, K., Dollár, P.: Focal loss for dense object detection. In: Proceedings of the IEEE International Conference on Computer Vision, pp. 2980–2988 (2017)
22. Chen, K., et al.: MMDetection: open MMlab detection toolbox and benchmark. arXiv preprint arXiv:1906.07155 (2019)
23. Tian, Z., Shen, C., Chen, H., He, T.: FCOS: fully convolutional one-stage object detection. In: Proceedings of the IEEE/CVF International Conference on Computer Vision, pp. 9627–9636 (2019)
24. Ioffe, S., Szegedy, C.: Batch normalization: accelerating deep network training by reducing internal covariate shift. In: International Conference on Machine Learning, pp. 448–456 (2015)

Research on Attack Signal Feature Extraction Method of Multipath TCP Transmission System Based on Wavelet Energy Entropy

Lejun Ji, Gang Lei(✉), Ruiwen Ji, Junyi Wu, and Keyang Gu

School of Software, Jiangxi Normal University, Nanchang 330022, China
leigang@jxnu.edu.cn

Abstract. Multipath transmission technology provides a strong theoretical support for the realization of parallel multi-channel data transmission for multi-host mobile terminal devices, and is an ideal scheme for high performance and high quality data transmission in wireless network environment. MPTCP is one of the representative achievements, and its security and robustness have aroused wide concern and discussion among researchers at home and abroad. In view of the characteristics of non-stationary signals transmitted by MPTCP, this paper combines wavelet transform analysis method and information entropy theory, and uses wavelet energy entropy to achieve the method of feature extraction of attack signals. Finally, the simulation analysis is carried out and good experimental results are obtained. The following conclusions are drawn: according to the law of wavelet energy entropy changing with wavelet decomposition scale, the attack signal is different from the normal signal. Based on this feature, attack signals in MPTCP transmission system can be well detected, which provides a new thinking and new means for anomaly detection and online monitoring of MPTCP transmission system.

Keywords: Multipath TCP · Wavelet transform · Wavelet energy entropy · Feature extraction · Robustness

1 Introduction

With the booming development of mobile Internet technology and the increasing popularity of multi-host mobile smart terminal devices, multipath transmission

This work was supported by the National Natural Science Foundation of China (NSFC) under Grant No. 61962026, and by the Postgraduate Innovation Fund of Jiangxi Provincial Department of Education under Grant YC2021-S258.

technology has been widely studied and discussed, and its application fields and practical values are being constantly broadened and explored. Compared with the traditional single-path transmission mode, multipath transmission technology can organically integrate various wireless access technologies (WiFi, 4G, Bluetooth, etc.) and better aggregate a variety of heterogeneous wireless network resources, thus effectively improving the performance of application data transmission and transmission quality of service [1]. Among them, the most representative MPTCP (Multipath TCP) can meet the requirements of network application data transmission with high bandwidth, high rate, and low delay, and maximize the utilization of network resources. Therefore, MPTCP will become the core transmission protocol of the Internet in the future [2]. However, facing the increasingly complex and critical cyber security situation, the security and robustness of MPTCP transmission system has become a hot topic for national and international research scholars.

In the real network environment, the robustness of multipath transmission system mainly includes structural robustness and performance robustness. However, the complex and changeable intentional network attack will have a serious impact on the structural and performance robustness of MPTCP transmission system, and then affect the transmission performance of the transmission system and user service quality [3]. However, the research of multipath transmission theory and algorithm based on MPTCP is mainly focused on path management and data scheduling, while the research of network security and robustness is relatively lacking [4–6]. Among the only relevant studies, the research on security-related issues can be roughly divided into abnormal attack traffic detection and robustness modeling and optimization. Therefore, the characteristics of abnormal attack traffic signals can be extracted timely and effectively to accurately distinguish normal signals from attack signals, which will play a decisive role in the rapid detection of attack signals in MPTCP transmission system.

Among the existing signal analysis methods, the wavelet analysis method is a time-frequency multi-resolution analysis method proposed by the French scientist J. Morlet in the early 1980s [7]. This method overcomes the disadvantage that the STFT (Short-Time Fourier Transform) window size does not vary with frequency, and evolves on this basis, which provides a possibility for studying time series better [8]. It is an ideal tool for time-frequency analysis and processing of non-stationary signals because it can intuitively reveal the various cycles of variation hidden in the time series, fully reflect the trend of the system on different time scales, and further estimate the future development trend of the system. Wavelet analysis theory has been widely used in signal analysis and detection, image recognition, computer classification and processing, medical imaging and diagnosis [9], numerical analysis [10] and other scientific fields [11].

In this paper, the wavelet transform analysis method is applied in MPTCP transmission system to realize multi-resolution analysis and time-division and frequency localization fine expression of MPTCP non-stationary signals, so as to extract component sequences of different frequency ranges. Meanwhile, this paper uses wavelet energy entropy to design and implement attack feature extraction method suitable for MPTCP transmission system, and studies the numerical characteristics of attack signal different from normal signal. Finally, this paper conducts simulation experiment analysis based on NS2 (Network Simulator version 2) platform [12] to verify the rationality and effectiveness of the design method. The experimental results show that wavelet energy entropy can be used as the classification feature of normal signals and attack signals in MPTCP transmission system, which lays a theoretical foundation for anomaly detection in multipath transmission system, and further improves the robustness and security of MPTCP multipath transmission system.

The organization of the remaining chapters is as follows. In Sect. 2, we mainly introduce the wavelet transform analysis method, information entropy and wavelet energy entropy related theoretical knowledge, including the basic concept and working principle. In Sect. 3, we introduce in detail the research thinking and design process of attack signal feature extraction method of MPTCP transmission system. In Sect. 4, we elaborate on the construction of MPTCP transmission system simulation environment and the results of experimental operation, and finally draw experimental conclusions. In Sect. 5, we give a brief summary of the paper and look into the future work and challenges to be faced.

2   Wavelet Transform and Wavelet Energy Entropy

2.1   Wavelet Transform

Wavelet transform is a time-frequency domain multi-resolution function analysis method based on FT (Fourier Transform), which attracts more and more attention. At first, the wavelet transform analysis method was used to analyze the local characteristics of seismic signals, but now it has been gradually applied in nonlinear scientific research fields such as data compression, speech analysis and processing, fault detection and signal analysis [13]. In this method, the infinite trig function basis of FT is replaced by the attenuation wavelet basis of finite length, which overcomes and breaks through the limitation of FT, and has good localization properties in both time domain and frequency domain, and solves the problem of resolution contradiction between time domain and frequency domain [14].

The basic principle of wavelet transform is a process of multi-scale decomposition (transformation) or reconstruction (inverse transformation) of time-varying signals through the expansion and translation operation of wavelet to form wavelet basis (wavelet function), analyze the general picture or details of signals, and realize the analysis of local characteristics of different time scales and space of signals [15]. Its main feature is that certain aspects of the problem are sufficiently highlighted through transformations, culminating in temporal segmentation at high frequencies and frequency segmentation at low frequencies, so that any detail of the signal can be attended to and the time-frequency variation characteristics of the time series can be analysed through wavelet coefficients.

The selection of wavelet function is the premise of wavelet analysis. It refers to a class of functions that are oscillatory and can rapidly decay to zero, namely, the wavelet function $\psi(t) \in L^2(R)$ and satisfy:

$$\int_{-\infty}^{+\infty} \psi(t)\, dt = 0 \tag{1}$$

After a series of scaling and translation operations, it can form the general form of the wavelet function [16],

$$\psi_{a,b}(t) = |a|^{-\frac{1}{2}} \psi\left(\frac{t-b}{a}\right), a, b \in R, a \neq 0 \tag{2}$$

where, $\psi_{a,b}(t)$ is basic wavelet; a is the scaling scale, reflecting the period length of wavelet; b is the translation parameter, the translation in reaction time. For the same signal or time series, if different wavelet functions are selected, the results will often be different, sometimes even very different. The most common wavelet transform forms are CWT (Continuous Wavelet Transform) and DWT (Discrete Wavelet Transform) [17].

For any given finite signal $f(t) \in L^2(R)$, its continuous wavelet transform form is

$$W_f(a,b) = |a|^{-\frac{1}{2}} \int_R f(t)\, \overline{\psi}\left(\frac{t-b}{a}\right) dt \tag{3}$$

where, $W_f(a,b)$ is the CWT coefficient, $\overline{\psi}\left(\frac{x-b}{a}\right)$ and is the complex conjugate function of $\psi\left(\frac{x-b}{a}\right)$. For discrete time series signals, suppose the function $f(k\Delta t)$ ($k = 1, 2, \cdots N$; Δt is the sampling interval), then the discrete wavelet transform form is [18]

$$W_f(a,b) = |a|^{-\frac{1}{2}} \Delta t \sum_{k=1}^{N} f(k\Delta t)\, \overline{\psi}\left(\frac{k\Delta t - b}{a}\right) \tag{4}$$

At this point, $W_f(a,b)$ is the DWT coefficient.

2.2 Information Entropy

In the 1940s, C. E. Shannon proposed the basic concept of information entropy by referring to the concept of thermodynamics, and gave the mathematical expression of information entropy. In information theory, information entropy describes the uncertainty of each possible event of information source, and represents the average amount of information provided by each symbol and the average uncertainty of information source [19,20]. Information entropy can generally be used as a quantitative statistical indicator of the information content of a system, and can also be used to estimate the complexity of random signals.

For a system with an uncertain state, if a random variable X is used to characterize the state of the system, the probability of x_j is $p_j = p\{X = x_j\}, j =$

$1, \cdots, L$, and $\sum_{j=1}^{L} p_j = 1$, the information obtained from a certain result of X can be represented by $I_j = \log(1/p_j)$, so the information entropy of X is [21]

$$H(X) = -\sum_{j=1}^{L} p_j \log(p_j) \tag{5}$$

where, when $p_j = 0$, $p_j \log(p_j) = 0$. It is easy to see from the form of expression that information entropy has the basic properties of monotonicity, non-negativity and accumulation.

2.3   Wavelet Energy Entropy

Wavelet transform has good ability of time-frequency localization analysis. Multi-scale analysis brings the construction and implementation of wavelet function into a unified framework and has corresponding practical fast algorithm. Therefore, wavelet energy entropy of signal can be obtained by combining wavelet transform analysis method with information entropy theory.

Let $E = E_1, E_2, \cdots, E_m$ be the wavelet energy entropy of the signal $x(t)$ at the m scale. In a given time window, the power E_j of each component is added up to equal the total power of the signal. Suppose $p_j = E_j/E$, then the corresponding wavelet energy entropy is defined as [22]

$$WEE = -\sum_{j=1} p_j \log(p_j) \tag{6}$$

3   Attack Signal Feature Extraction Method of MPTCP Transmission System

Based on previous theoretical research, according to the characteristics of MPTCP transmission system multipath parallel transmission, wavelet transform analysis method, information entropy theory knowledge, in MPTCP transmission system, wavelet entropy correlation technology is used to design feature extraction method suitable for multipath transmission system attack signal. This method can realize online monitoring and anomaly detection of transmission system and provide a new solution to anomaly detection in multipath transmission system. The general steps of the attack signal feature extraction method are shown in Fig. 1.

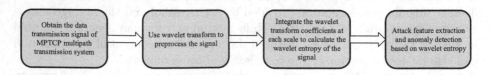

Fig. 1. Schematic diagram of MPTCP attack signal feature extraction method.

According to the schematic diagram of the above operation process, this feature extraction method can roughly include signal preprocessing, wavelet energy entropy calculation, attack signal feature extraction and anomaly detection.

3.1 Signal Preprocessing

From a macroscopic point of view, the large-scale network traffic in MPTCP transmission system almost shows all the characteristics of signals [23]. Therefore, we can regard MPTCP network transmission data flow as signal, and further analyze the characteristics of MPTCP transmission data flow, such as change trend, change amplitude and change period, by using signal processing method. Under normal circumstances, the collected signals can not be directly extracted from the features, often need to be preprocessed. Therefore, this paper uses wavelet transform analysis method to denoise and scale decompose the original signal.

The wavelet denoising method in this paper uses threshold denoising method [24]. Its basic principle is to set a threshold value for the wavelet coefficients on the decomposition scale, and it is considered that the wavelet coefficients smaller than the threshold value are caused by noise, and the wavelet coefficients larger than the threshold value are caused by signals. Then, the wavelet coefficients corresponding to the noises on these decomposition scales are thresholding to zero, and the wavelet coefficients corresponding to the signals on these decomposition scales are retained [25]. Finally, the thresholding signal is reconstructed, so the reconstructed signal is denoising signal based on wavelet transform, and the next step of feature extraction can be carried out.

In general, two problems need to be considered to extract signal features by wavelet decomposition: the selection of wavelet basis function and the determination of decomposition layers. If there are too few layers, it is difficult to extract fault details of signals, while if there are too many layers, the calculation is complicated, feature extraction dimension is high, and transmission and storage costs are high [26]. At present, we use different wavelet functions and decomposition layers to decompose and reconstruct the transmitted signal, and determine the best wavelet basis function and decomposition scale by comparing with the original signal.

3.2 Calculation of Wavelet Energy Entropy

After wavelet transform, the original signal is mapped to the time-scale plane, and the signal changes can be observed at multiple scales (different resolutions) at any time interval. Because a large number of wavelet decomposition coefficients reflect the results of wavelet transform multi-resolution analysis, these coefficients contain a large amount of characteristic information about the transmission system or the signal itself [27]. Assuming that each scale is a signal source, the wavelet coefficients at each scale are equivalent to the information sent by a signal source. Therefore, in this paper, these wavelet transform coefficients are fused and processed effectively, and the universal characteristics of signals in MPTCP multipath transmission system are characterized by calculating the wavelet energy entropy of signals.

3.3 Attack Feature Extraction and Anomaly Detection

For non-stationary signals, a good time-frequency analysis method can detect the unstable change of signal frequency with time, and then extract the important features of the signal. In this paper, according to the calculated wavelet energy entropy, through the comparison of experimental results to achieve the accurate differentiation of normal signals and attack signals, more intuitive, effective and convenient to carry out information extraction, signal detection and feature recognition of various transmission signals in the MPTCP transmission system.

4   Experimental Simulation Analysis

In order to verify the rationality and effectiveness of the attack signal feature extraction method of the MPTCP transmission system, this paper simulates the MPTCP multipath transmission system based on NS2 experimental platform. In addition, this document uses LDDoS (Lowrate Distributed Denial Service) attacks [28] as an example to simulate a network attack on a multipathing transmission system. Finally, the reliability of wavelet energy entropy as attack feature classification is verified by comparing the results of wavelet energy entropy without attack and with attack, so as to realize feature extraction and anomaly detection of network attack signals in MPTCP multipath transmission system.

4.1   Simulation Environment Construction

In this paper, the MPTCP multipath transmission system is built on the NS2 simulation experimental platform based on TCL (Tool Command Language) programming, and the end-to-end multipath parallel transmission communication between communication devices is simulated. At the same time, in order to simulate the network attack of MPTCP multipath transmission system, this paper deploys ten dummy computers to send LDDoS attack data stream to a router at the same time, and ensures the best attack effect.

As shown in Fig. 2, in the simulated MPTCP multipath transmission system, the Sender (server) and the Receiver (multi-host mobile terminal device) are realizing parallel multipath data transmission through three different communication modes (Path A, Path B and Path C), and ten puppet machines ($Attack_0, Attack_1, \cdots, Attack_9$) are simultaneously attacking the router R_0. In this case, the MPTCP multipath transmission system includes normal data flow and LDDoS attack data flow. Table 1 shows the settings of basic parameters such as the bandwidth, transmission delay, and path management algorithm of each transmission path in the MPTCP multipath transmission system. The total data transmission time is 300 s. Except that the network parameters of LDDoS

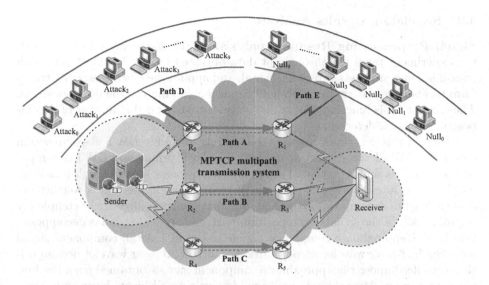

Fig. 2. MPTCP multipath transmission system network topology.

Table 1. MPTCP multipath transmission system network parameter settings.

Path	Bandwidth	Transfer delay	Path management algorithm
Path A	10 Mb	50 ms	DropTail
Path B	10 Mb	50 ms	DropTail
Path C	10 Mb	50 ms	DropTail
Path D	1 Mb	50 ms	DropTail
Path E	1 Mb	50 ms	DropTail

attack are different, the network topology parameters in the case of no attack are the same as those in the case of attack.

As for the simulation implementation of LDDoS attack in MPTCP multipath transmission system, this experiment realizes constant bit rate data transmission based on CBR type data packets, and each packet size is 200 bytes. We set the attack period of LDDoS attack as 200 ms, the attack duration as 600 ms and the attack rate as 1 Mbps. The specific parameter settings can be represented by the following expression [29]. P indicates the attack period, T indicates the attack duration, and V indicates the attack rate. In order to achieve better attack effect, this paper sets up ten dummy computers to launch network attacks of different durations on the transmission system on the nodes whose operation time is 50 s, 120 s and 200 s respectively.

$$LDDoS\left(P,T,V\right) = \left(200\,\text{ms}, 600\,\text{ms}, 1\,\text{Mbps}\right) \tag{7}$$

4.2   Simulation Results Analysis

Signal Preprocessing Results Analysis. In the signal preprocessing part, the experiment takes the throughput data obtained by the MPTCP multipath transmission system as the original signal, and applies the discrete wavelet transform technology to carry out threshold denoising and multi-scale decomposition. The wavelet basis function adopts db6 wavelet basis, and the number of decomposition layers is determined to be 6.

Discrete wavelet transform method mainly includes DWT decomposition method and DWT reconstruction method. The basic principle of DWT decomposition method is similar to that of signal filtering by using a pair of high-pass filter and low-pass filter. The basic principle of reconstruction method is roughly the same as that of decomposition method, but the operation direction is completely opposite [30]. In the signal decomposition part, the original signal is decomposed into level 1 approximate component signal and level 1 detail component signal after the first layer wavelet decomposition. The second layer wavelet decomposition is to decompose the approximate component signals obtained from the first layer, and so on. After the original signal is decomposed by six-layer multi-scale discrete wavelet transform, the specific decomposition results are shown in Fig. 3 and 4.

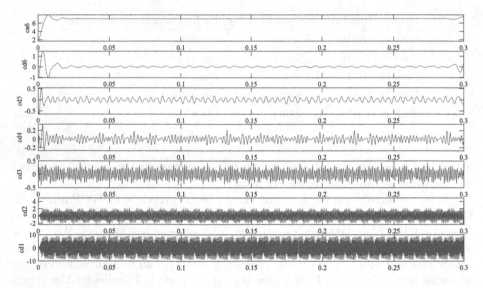

Fig. 3. Multi-scale detail component signal and level 6 approximate component signal without attack.

As shown in the Fig. 3 and 4, $cd1, cd2, \cdots, cd6$ respectively represent the detail component signals obtained by discrete wavelet multi-scale decomposition, and $ca6$ represent the level 6 approximate component signals obtained by discrete wavelet multi-scale decomposition. The multi-scale detail component

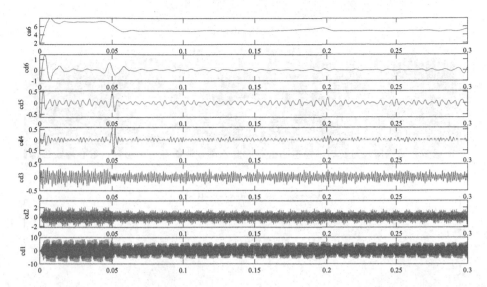

Fig. 4. Multi-scale detail component signal and level 6 approximate component signal under attack.

signal represents the high frequency information of the original signal, which is assumed to be the "noise" information of the original signal and continuously filtered out in the decomposition process. The multi-scale approximate component signal represents the low-frequency information of the original signal, and the level 6 approximate component signal is the decomposed signal obtained by the final wavelet decomposition. Figure 5 and 6 show the comparison of original signal and decomposed signal without attack and with attack.

As shown in the Fig. 5 and 6, whether in the case of no attack or with attack, the original signal with complex changes and frequent jitter is constantly removed from the influence of high-frequency noise during the decomposition process of discrete wavelet transform, and finally the decomposed signal with obvious change trend and easy for intuitive analysis is obtained. Thus, the characteristics of the original signal can be observed on a broad time scale, which really embodies the advantages of multi-scale time-frequency analysis of wavelet transform.

Wavelet Energy Entropy Comparative Analysis. The wavelet coefficients at each scale obtained from the above discrete wavelet multi-scale decomposition include various characteristic analyses of the transmission system or the signal itself. Based on Shannon information entropy theory, the wavelet energy entropy of the multi-scale signal is calculated and its change curve is drawn. Figure 7 shows the comparison of multi-scale wavelet energy entropy changes under the two conditions. As shown in the Fig. 7, the blue curve represents the change of wavelet energy entropy with the increase of scale in the case of no attack, and

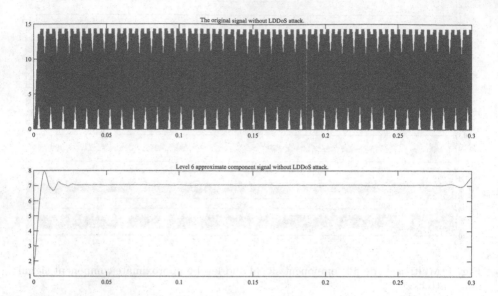

Fig. 5. Original signal and decomposition signal without attack.

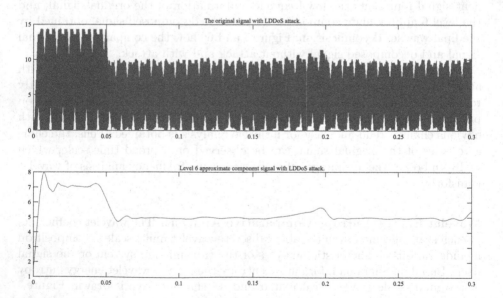

Fig. 6. Original signal and decomposition signal under attack.

the red curve represents the change of wavelet energy entropy with the increase of scale in the case of attack.

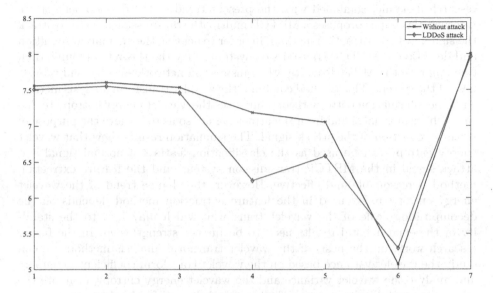

Fig. 7. Comparison diagram of multi-scale wavelet energy entropy change.

According to the working principle of wavelet energy entropy, the wavelet energy entropy value of multi-scale signal without attack is 7.5605, 7.6072, 7.5368, 7.1882, 7.0518, 5.0716, 8.0005 respectively. The wavelet energy entropy of multi-scale signal with attack is 7.5092, 7.5536, 7.4593, 6.2430, 6.5813, 5.2960 and 7.9596, respectively. In this paper, the mean value and variance of wavelet energy entropy are calculated to observe the overall trend of wavelet energy entropy under the two conditions. By calculation, the mean value of wavelet energy entropy without attack is 7.1452, and the variance is 0.9302. In the case of attack, the mean value of wavelet energy entropy is 6.9431 and the variance is 0.8878.

Through comparative analysis, it is found that the mean value of wavelet energy entropy in the case of attack is smaller than that in the case of no attack, and the variation range of wavelet energy entropy in the case of attack is smaller than that in the case of no attack. It can be found that attack abnormal signals can reduce the mean and amplitude of wavelet energy entropy of MPTCP multipath transmission signals, indicating that MPTCP transmission signals have worse similarity and higher complexity in the case of attack. Therefore, wavelet energy entropy can be used as the classification feature of normal signals and attack signals in the MPTCP multipath transmission system, and can be used as the indicator basis for abnormal detection of attack signals.

5 Conclusions and Future Works

In this paper, on the basis of the research status at home and abroad and the research dynamic, combined with the present trend of the development of the Internet, this paper proposes a MPTCP multipath transmission system to attack the signal feature extraction method, in order to achieve the anomaly recognition and detection of MPTCP transmission system to lay the theoretical foundation, thus improve the MPTCP multipath transmission network security and robustness of the system. This method combines the wavelet transform analysis method with the information entropy theory, and uses the wavelet energy entropy to distinguish the normal signal from the attack signal, so as to achieve the purpose of feature extraction of the attack signal. The simulation results show that wavelet energy entropy can be used as the classification feature of normal signal and attack signal in the MPTCP transmission system, and the feature extraction method is reasonable and effective. However, the change trend of the wavelet energy entropy index used in the feature extraction method depends on the decomposition scale of the wavelet transform, which may lead to the stability of the experimental results need to be further strengthened. In the future research work, on the basis of the wavelet transform analysis method, we can study the wavelet variance based on the wavelet transform coefficients, compare and analyze the wavelet variance and the wavelet energy entropy, compare the advantages and disadvantages of the two methods, and further improve research on feature extraction method of attack signal in the MPTCP multipath transmission system.

References

1. Cao, Y., Liu, Q., Zuo, Y., Ke, F., Wang, H., Huang, M.: Receiver-centric buffer blocking-aware multipath data distribution in MPTCP-based heterogeneous wireless networks. KSII Trans. Internet Inf. Syst. **10**(10), 4642–4660 (2017)
2. Nguyen, K., Kibria, M., Ishizu, K., Kojima, F., Sekiya, H.: An approach to reinforce multipath TCP with path-aware information. Sensors **19**(3), 476 (2019)
3. Cao, Y., Ji, R., Ji, L., Shao, X., Lei, G., Wang, H.: MPTCP-meLearning: a multi-expert learning-based MPTCP extension to enhance multipathing robustness against network attacks. IEICE Trans. Inf. Syst. **E104D**(11), 1795–1804 (2021)
4. Zhu, M., et al.: BELIA: bandwidth estimate-based link increase algorithm for MPTCP. IET Netw. **6**(5), 94–101 (2017)
5. Cao, Y., Ji, R., Ji, L., Lei, G., Wang, H., Shao, X.: l^2-MPTCP: a learning-driven latency-aware multipath transport scheme for industrial internet applications. IEEE Trans. Industr. Inform. **18**, 8456–8466 (2022)
6. Cao, Y., Ji, R., Huang, X., Lei, G., Shao, X., You, I.: Empirical mode decomposition-empowered network traffic anomaly detection for secure multipath TCP communications. Mob. Netw. Appl. (2022)
7. Li, B., Chen, X.: Wavelet-based numerical analysis: a review and classification. Finite Elem. Anal. Des. **81**, 14–31 (2014)
8. Ling, T., Liu, H., Gong, S., Huang, F.: Construction and application of a new biorthogonal wavelet basis for a quantitative analysis of GPR signals. J. Appl. Geophys. **170**, 103837 (2019)

9. Hu, R., Monebhurrun, V., Himeno, R., Yokota, H., Costen, F.: An adaptive least angle regression method for uncertainty quantification in FDTD computation. IEEE Trans. Antennas Propag. **66**(12), 7188–7197 (2018)
10. Hu, R., Monebhurrun, V., Himeno, R., Yokota, H., Costen, F.: A general framework for building surrogate models for uncertainty quantification in computational electromagnetics. IEEE Trans. Antennas Propag. **70**(2), 1402–1414 (2021)
11. Li, Q., Tong, X.: Application of wavelet analysis method in radar echo signal detection. In: Han, S., Ye, L., Meng, W. (eds.) AICON 2019. LNICST, vol. 286, pp. 327–333. Springer, Cham (2019). https://doi.org/10.1007/978-3-030-22968-9_28
12. Wu, M., Shanmugam, S., Welsch, C., Yi, M.: Palmitoylation of hepatitis C Virus NS2 regulates its subcellular localization and NS2-NS3 autocleavage. J. Virol. **94**(1) (2020)
13. Hu, R., Liu, Y., Gu, K., Min, X., Zhai, G.: Toward a no-reference quality metric for camera-captured images. IEEE Trans. Cybern. (2021)
14. Kumar, T., Mandal, U.: Wavelet transform associated with linear canonical Hankel transform. Math. Methods Appl. Sci. **42**(9), 3167–3178 (2019)
15. Abuhamdia, T., Taheri, S., Burns, J.: Laplace wavelet transform theory and applications. J. Vib. Control **24**(9), 1600–1620 (2018)
16. Ramya laxmi, K., Pallavi, S., Ramya, N.: A hybrid approach of wavelet transform using lifting scheme and discrete wavelet transform technique for image processing. In: Satapathy, S.C., Raju, K.S., Shyamala, K., Krishna, D.R., Favorskaya, M.N. (eds.) Advances in Decision Sciences, Image Processing, Security and Computer Vision. LAIS, vol. 3, pp. 643–651. Springer, Cham (2020). https://doi.org/10.1007/978-3-030-24322-7_76
17. Pandey, C., Phukan, P.: Continuous and discrete wavelet transforms associated with Hermite transform. Int. J. Anal. Appl. **18**(4), 531–549 (2020)
18. Shin, D.K., Moon, Y.S.: Super-resolution image reconstruction using wavelet based patch and discrete wavelet transform. J. Signal Process. Syst. **81**, 71–81 (2015)
19. Li, Z., Qu, L., Zhang, G., Xie, N.: Attribute selection for heterogeneous data based on information entropy. Int. J. Gen. Syst. **50**(5), 548–566 (2021)
20. Gao, J., Liu, F., Zhang, J., Hu, J., Cao, Y.: Information entropy as a basic building block of complexity theory. Entropy **15**(9), 3396–3418 (2014)
21. Salazar, S.J.C., Laguna, H.G., Dahiya, B., Sagar, R.P.: Correction to: Shannon information entropy sum of the confined hydrogenic atom under the influence of an electric field. Eur. Phys. J. D **75**(255), 127 (2021)
22. Chen, Y., Zhang, Y., Lu, H.M., Chen, X., Li, J., Wang, S.: Wavelet energy entropy and linear regression classifier for detecting abnormal breasts. Multimed. Tools Appl. **77**, 3813–3832 (2018)
23. Tychkov, A.Y., Alimuradov, A.K., Churakov, P.P.: Erratum to: adaptive signal processing method for speech organ diagnostics. Meas. Tech. **59**, 684 (2016)
24. Wu, G., He, Y.: Application of wavelet threshold denoising model to infrared spectral signal processing. Spectrosc. Spectr. Anal. **29**(12), 3246–3249 (2009)
25. Zhang, X., Zou, Z., Guo, H., Yin, J.: Wavelet denoising Method with a novel wavelet threshold function applied in enoising ship maneuvering test data. Indian J. Geo-Marine Sci. **46**(9), 1780–1787 (2017)
26. Khatter, A., Reddy, N., Thakur, A.: Wavelet decomposition based authentication scheme for dental CBCT images. In: Kolhe, M.L., Tiwari, S., Trivedi, M.C., Mishra, K.K. (eds.) Advances in Data and Information Sciences. LNNS, vol. 94, pp. 567–576. Springer, Singapore (2020). https://doi.org/10.1007/978-981-15-0694-9_53

27. Patil, D.D., Singh, R.P.: ECG classification using wavelet transform and wavelet network classifier. In: Dash, S.S., Naidu, P.C.B., Bayindir, R., Das, S. (eds.) Artificial Intelligence and Evolutionary Computations in Engineering Systems. AISC, vol. 668, pp. 289–303. Springer, Singapore (2018). https://doi.org/10.1007/978-981-10-7868-2_29
28. Lei, G., Ji, L., Ji, R., Cao, Y., Yang, W., Wang, H.: Can wavelet transform detect LDDoS abnormal traffic in multipath TCP transmission system? Secur. Commun. Netw. **2021**, 1–8 (2021)
29. Lei, G., Ji, L., Ji, R., Cao, Y., Shao, X., Huang, X.: Extracting low-rate DDoS attack characteristics: the case of multipath TCP-based communication networks. Wireless Commun. Mob. Comput. **2021**, 1–10 (2021)
30. Dutt, R., Balouria, A., Acharyya, A.: Discrete wavelet transform based methodology for radar pulse deinterleaving. CSI Trans. ICT **7**, 141–147 (2019)

Anomaly Detection with Ensemble Empirical Mode Decomposition for Secure QUIC Communications: A Simple Use Case

Keyang Gu[1]([✉])[iD], Junyi Wu[1][iD], Fan Jiang[1][iD], Ruiwen Ji[1][iD], Lejun Ji[1][iD], and Tao Lei[2]

[1] Jiangxi Normal University, Nanchang 330022, China
gukeyang@jxnu.edu.cn
[2] University College London, London, England
lei.tao.21@ucl.ac.uk

Abstract. QUIC (Quick UDP Internet Connections) proposed by Google is a new secure general-purpose network transport protocol. Compared with TCP and TLS, QUIC combines the advantages of many other protocols and is a new multiplexing and secure transmission protocol. However, with the development of network technology and the gradual expansion of network scale, the network environment has become increasingly complex, and network security has become increasingly severe. QUIC network monitoring faces enormous challenges. Based on the self-similarity of QUIC traffic, an anomaly detection method for QUIC traffic based on Ensemble Empirical Mode Decomposition (EEMD) is proposed in this paper. By decomposing the network traffic, several Intrinsic Mode Functions (IMFs) and a residual trend term are obtained, and then several IMF components with low frequency and low noise are selected for reconstruction. Calculate the Hurst value of the reconstructed signal and judge whether the QUIC network has been attacked by comparing the change of the Hurst value before and after adding abnormal traffic. The simulation experiment verifies the effectiveness and accuracy of the method.

Keywords: QUIC · Ensemble Empirical Mode Decomposition · Anomaly detection · Hurst parameters

1 Introduction

Nowadays, with the continuous development of network technology and the rapid increase of Internet traffic, people are increasingly dependent on the Internet.

© ICST Institute for Computer Sciences, Social Informatics and Telecommunications Engineering 2023
Y. Cao and X. Shao (Eds.): MONAMI 2022, LNICST 474, pp. 413–422, 2023.
https://doi.org/10.1007/978-3-031-32443-7_30

Therefore, researchers are exploring and improving new network protocols and seeking to develop new technologies. So Google developed the QUIC protocol (Quick UDP Internet Connections) [1] in 2013. QUIC is a protocol used at the transport layer. Unlike other traditional protocols, the UDP protocol is used instead of the TCP protocol. By transferring the reliability of TCP from the transport layer to the application layer, QUIC enables faster development and even allows multiple variants of the protocol [2].

Google published QUIC-related papers at the SIGCOMM conference in 2017, which has aroused significant repercussions in the industry. Nowadays, more than 50% of Chrome browser traffic and 75% of Facebook traffic use QUIC for transmission. But since QUIC is a new protocol, only a few studies have focused on examining its security. DeConinck et al. [3] and Viernickel et al. [4] introduced the concept of multipath into QUIC so that a QUIC connection can use multiple underlying network links simultaneously. Han Y et al. [5] proposed an enhanced BBR Congestion Control Algorithm (eBCC). Chiariotti et al. [6] combined the congestion control and multi-stream properties of the QUIC transport protocol with an appropriate scheduling algorithm to maximize the value of the information at the receiving end. Shi X et al. [7] proposed a priority-based multipath QUIC stream scheduling mechanism to avoid the blocking problem between multipath QUIC streams. Shi X et al. [8] designed an MPQUIC scheduler by prioritizing the streams that make up the critical rendering path, which can effectively speed up the first rendering time in page loading. There is a severe lack of research on QUIC traffic security.

Statistical analysis of network traffic to detect network anomalies is the focus of research in abnormal traffic detection. In recent years, Leland et al. [9] analyzed different networks and found that network traffic has statistical self-similarity. Numerous studies have shown that normal network traffic has self-similarity [10,11], and abnormal traffic will impact the network's self-similarity. By observing and summarizing network traffic behavior, Barford et al. [12] stipulated that the similarity of statistical features at the network flow level was used to classify network anomalies into three categories: network operation anomalies, network attack anomalies, and sudden congestion anomalies. Pei J et al. [13] proposed a network traffic anomaly detection method based on long-term and short-term memory network self-encoding. Pan Y et al. [14] proposed a custom user abnormal behavior detection model based on a deep neural network. The fine-grained analysis and customized user behavior management settings can be used to achieve anomaly detection in specific network environments. Hu Z et al. [15] proposed various processing methods for network traffic indicators for further evaluation of network information security.

Based on the self-similarity of QUIC traffic, this paper adopts an Ensemble Empirical Mode Decomposition (EEMD) method to detect abnormal traffic. Compared with the problems existing in the traditional network traffic anomaly detection, such as poor adaptive ability, low efficiency, and high energy consumption, this method detects whether an attack occurs by observing the change of the Hurst parameter, which has the advantages of less computation and less resource consumption.

2   Related Technology Introduction

2.1   QUIC Protocol

The QUIC protocol was first designed and proposed by Google as a network protocol applied to the transport layer. It is based on the UDP protocol drafted by the IETF working group. Figure 1 is a structural diagram of the QUIC protocol. The OSI reference architecture shows that the QUIC protocol is above the network layer and involves the transport, session, presentation, and application layers. As shown in the figure, the protocol used at the transport layer is the UDP protocol instead of the TCP protocol, precisely because the QUIC protocol is designed to bypass the TCP protocol.

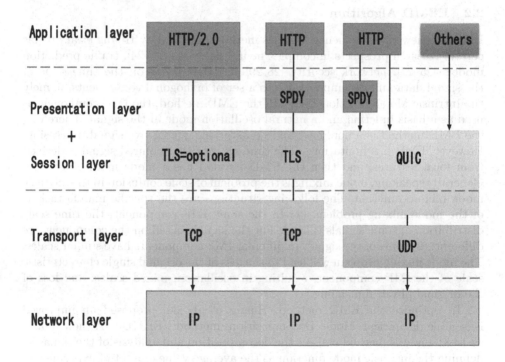

Fig. 1. QUIC protocol stack

QUIC uses the TLS1.3 method implemented in the session layer and presentation layer to encrypt effectively, which enhances the security of the protocol to a certain extent [16]. At the same time, HTTP/3 at the application layer only needs to parse the HTTP protocol so that the QUIC protocol can complete functions such as HTTP/3 multiplexing and link selection, scheduling, and management [2]. Based on the characteristics of UDP, the QUIC protocol does not require ordered packet delivery, which cleverly avoids the HOL blocking problem [17]. QUIC replaces the traditional IP quadruple by adding the connection

ID parameter to all data packets, thereby achieving a zero round-trip time (0-RTT) between the two terminals that have established a connection, reducing the connection cost [18].

At present, multipath transmission protocols such as Multi-path TCP (MPTCP) have excellent deployment resistance, and most of the research is in path management and data scheduling [19,20]. Therefore, Multi-path QUIC (MPQUIC) supporting parallel data transfer has gradually become a new research hotspot. MPQUIC can realize mobile ultra-high-definition video data transmission in 5G signal coverage holes and weak coverage scenarios, which has great practical significance for the development of the new generation of mobile ultra-high-definition video applications [21].

2.2 EEMD Algorithm

EMD is a new time-frequency analysis method proposed by Huang et al.. It has certain research prospects in complex neural networks [22–24], traffic prediction models [25–27], network security [28,29]. EMD is based on the time scale of the signal data and decomposes it into a set of orthogonal components, namely the Intrinsic Mode Function(IMF). In the EMD method, the IMF component is used as a basis function and a natural oscillation mode in the signal. Therefore, the EMD method is a nonlinear and non-stationary adaptive signal processing. However, EMD has limitations. The time scale of the acquired signal is derived from local features, and then the EMD method has a mode mixing problem. Generally speaking, mode mixing is the problem of scale confusion in the intrinsic mode mixing function. The following situations are the specific manifestations of the mode mixing problem: (1) In the same IMF component, the time scale distribution of some signals is large, but the signals based on the component are different; (2) some of the signals in different IMF components have similar scales. The mode mixing problem will lead to the loss of the original single characteristic scale of the IMF component, resulting in oscillation, mixed scales, and loss of the original physical meaning.

To optimize the EMD method, Huang et al. [30] proposed an improved Ensemble Empirical Mode Decomposition method (EEMD). A new noise-assisted analysis method realizes the decomposition and analysis of the signal by defining the intrinsic mode function as the average value of a set of experiments. Each experiment adds a finite amplitude white noise to the decomposed signal result. This method is based on the statistical analysis of white noise characteristics [31,32], which shows that adding auxiliary white noise based on the EMD method can effectively form a particular adaptive binary filter bank. In addition, Flandrin et al. [33] show that white noise is helpful for the EMD method for signal data analysis. The above studies have promoted the generation of the EEMD method to some extent.

The content of the EEMD method is to add white noise to the original signal and then decompose the original signal after adding white noise. The decomposition operation is repeated to obtain the data of multiple decompositions.

Finally, the results of these data are summarized by the formula, and the average value is obtained. The white noise added to the original signal can fill the space of the entire time frequency uniformly by using components of different time scales, thus forming a uniform white noise background. The signal is automatically projected when a new signal uses this background as a reference scale. Because each time the signal with added white noise is decomposed, it will get more detailed results, but in a single experiment, different noises are taken in each experiment, reducing sufficient trajectories in the ensemble average. The ensemble mean is the only correct answer because as more and more trials are added to the ensemble, the only persistently stable part is the signal data. Specific steps are as follows:

1) First, obtain an original signal data $A(t)$, and then add white noise $c_i(t)$ conforming to the normal distribution of the data. The formula is as follows:

$$A_i(t) = A(t) + c_i(t) \tag{1}$$

2) The generated new signal data $A_i(t)$ is decomposed by the EEMD method, thereby obtaining multiple IMF components $imf_{i,j}(t)$. i represents adding i times of white noise, and j represents the jth IMF component.

3) Repeat the operations of steps 1 and 2 of the cycle for N times. You need to add a different white noise that conforms to the normal distribution each time. Form these M IMF components into a set.

$$imf_{i,1}(t), imf_{i,2}(t), ...imf_{i,M}(t), i = 1, 2, 3...N \tag{2}$$

4) After multiple cyclic operations, multiple IMF components are obtained, and an average procedure is performed on these IMF components to get a new IMF, which is expressed as $IMF_i(t)$. The formula is as follows:

$$IMF_i(t) = \frac{1}{M} \sum_{i=1}^{M} imf_{i,j}, i = 1, 2, ...N \tag{3}$$

3   Experiment Analysis

This paper conducts network simulation experiments in the network simulator NS-3 equipped with the QUIC environment to generate the sample sequences required for the experiments. The original data obtained are decomposed and reconstructed by the EEMD method. The amplitude ratio coefficient of adding white noise is preset as 0.2, and the overall average number of times is 100.

Figure 2 shows the jitter of the normal QUIC network, and Fig. 3 shows the jitter of the QUIC network after the attack. From the comparison, it can be seen that after adding attack traffic, the QUIC network jitter fluctuates violently and obviously. The experiment also compared the jitter reconstruction graph and Hurst parameters before and after adding attack traffic. Figure 4 shows the reconstructed QUIC network jitter before and after the attack. By comparison, it

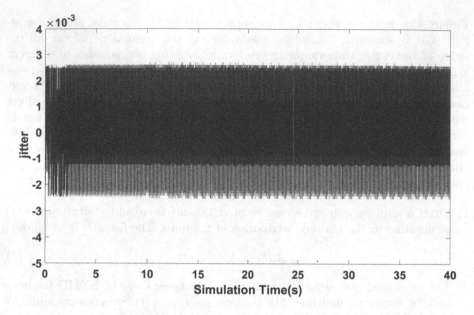

Fig. 2. Jitter in normal QUIC network

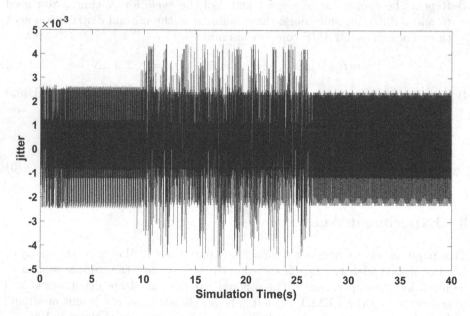

Fig. 3. Jitter in attacked QUIC network

can be seen that the addition of the attack traffic will cause the jitter to oscillate significantly, indicating that the QUIC network has been affected by the attack traffic.

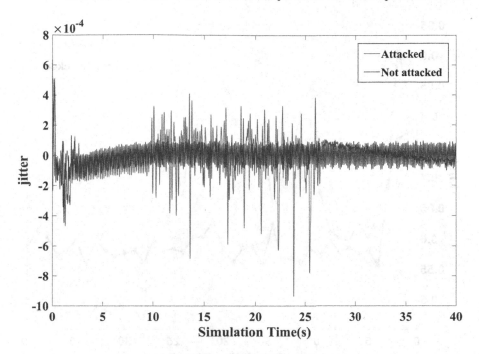

Fig. 4. Reconstruction graph of jitter in the QUIC network before and after the attack

Studies have shown that normal network traffic has self-similarity and Long-Range Dependence (LRD), and abnormal traffic will impact the self-similarity of the network. The Hurst parameter is an important parameter to describe long-range dependence. The higher the Hurst parameter, the higher the degree of self-similarity and the stronger the burst degree of network traffic. In the experiment based on QUIC traffic anomaly detection, the Hurst value before and after the attack is compared to determine whether the QUIC network generates abnormal traffic. The comparison results are shown in Fig. 5.

It can be seen from the comparison results that the Hurst value maintained a stable fluctuation before the attack traffic was added. When the attack traffic is added in the 9s, the Hurst value fluctuates violently, which disappears until the attack stops in the 29s and maintains a relatively stable fluctuation. The comparison results also show that abnormal traffic attacks can destroy or affect the self-similarity of normal network traffic. Therefore, this paper proposes an anomaly detection method for QUIC traffic based on Ensemble Empirical Mode Decomposition (EEMD) to detect abnormal traffic accurately and has a significant detection effect.

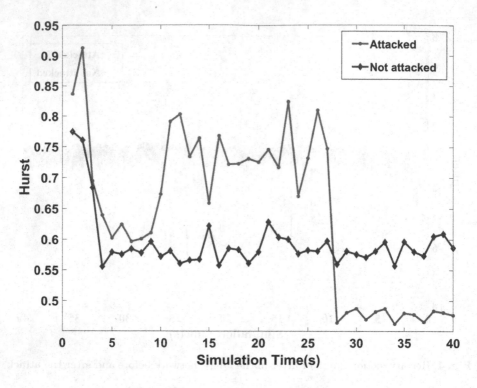

Fig. 5. Hurst parameter comparison chart

Conclusion

This paper uses an EEMD-based method to detect traffic anomalies in the QUIC network. This method overcomes the mode mixing problem in the decomposition process. The complex signal containing noise is decomposed into several relatively stable IMF components and a residual trend term, and then reconstructing the IMF component, and the high-frequency noise is removed to achieve effective denoising of the original signal. This method has good adaptability. The reconstructed signal can maintain many original data characteristics and reduce the experimental data's computational complexity. In the simulation experiment, the Hurst parameter is used as the judgment basis to test the self-similarity of the QUIC traffic to detect abnormal traffic in the QUIC network. The simulation results show that abnormal traffic will significantly affect the Hurst value, and continuous attacks will make the Hurst parameter vibrate intensely. In addition, based on the observation of the change of the Hurst parameter, the occurrence of the attack can also be judged, which has a good detection effect. Future work must consider other feature extraction and noise reduction methods to analyze the intrinsic mode components, search for the accurate criteria of attack occurrence, and study new detection mechanisms.

Acknowledgment. This work was supported by the National Natural Science Foundation of China (NSFC) under Grant No. 61962026.

References

1. Iyengar, J., Thomson, M.: QUIC: A UDP-based multiplexed and secure transport. Internet Engineering Task Force, Internet-Draft draft-ietf-quic-transport-27 (2020)
2. Nithya, B., Prakash. L.M., Kishore, J.N., Akash, M.N.: Performance analysis of pluggable congestion control in QUIC protocol. In: AIP Conference Proceedings, p. 02003. AIP Publishing LLC (2022)
3. De Quentin, C., Bonaventure, O.: Multipath QUIC: design and evaluation. In: Proceedings of the 13th International Conference on Emerging Networking Experiments and Technologies, pp. 160–166 (2017)
4. Viernickel, T., Froemmgen, A., Rizk, A., Koldehofe, B., Steinmetz, R.: Multipath QUIC: a deployable multipath transport protocol. In: 2018 IEEE International Conference on Communications (ICC), pp. 1–7. IEEE (2018)
5. Han, Y., Zuo, M., Yuan, H., Zhong, Y., Yuan, Z., Bi, T.: A QoS-based fairness-aware BBR congestion control algorithm using QUIC. Wirele. Commun. Mob. Comput. (2022)
6. Chiariotti, F., Deshpande, A.A., Giordani, M., Antonakoglou, K., Mahmoodi, T., Zanella, A.: QUIC-EST: a QUIC-enabled scheduling and transmission scheme to maximize VoI with correlated data flows. IEEE Commun. Mag. **59**(4), 30–36 (2021)
7. Shi, X., Wang, L., Zhang, F., Zhou, B., Liu, Z.: PStream: priority-based stream scheduling for heterogeneous paths in multipath-QUIC. In: 29th International Conference on Computer Communications and Networks, pp. 1–8. IEEE (2020)
8. Shi, X., Zhang, F., Liu, Z.: PriorityBucket: a multipath-QUIC scheduler on accelerating first rendering time in page loading. In: Proceedings of the Eleventh ACM International Conference on Future Energy Systems, pp. 572–577 (2020)
9. Leland, W.E., Taqqu, M.S., Willinger, W., Wilson, D.V.: On the self-similar nature of Ethernet traffic (extended version). IEEE/ACM Trans. Netw. **2**(1), 1–15 (1994)
10. Giorgi, G., Narduzzi, C.: A study of measurement-based traffic models for network diagnostics. IEEE Trans. Instrum. Meas. **57**(8), 1642–1650 (2008)
11. Lemeshko, O., Mersni, A., Nevzorova, O.: Analysis of influence of network architecture nonuniformity and traffic self-similarity properties to load balancing and average end-to-end delay. In: Radivilova, T., Ageyev, D., Kryvinska, N. (eds.) Data-Centric Business and Applications. LNDECT, vol. 48, pp. 767–787. Springer, Cham (2021). https://doi.org/10.1007/978-3-030-43070-2_33
12. Barford, P., Plonka, D.: Characteristics of network traffic flow anomalies. In: Proceedings of the 1st ACM SIGCOMM Workshop on Internet Measurement, pp. 69–73 (2001)
13. Pei, J., Zhong, K., Jan, M.A., Li, J.: Personalized federated learning framework for network traffic anomaly detection. Comput. Netw. **200**, 108006 (2022)
14. Pan, Y.: Network security and user abnormal behavior detection by using deep neural network. Internet Technol. Lett. **4**(3), e260 (2021)
15. Hu, Z., et al.: Statistical techniques for detecting cyberattacks on computer networks based on an analysis of abnormal traffic behavior. Int. J. Comput. Netw. Inf. Sec. **12**, 1 (2020)
16. Kumari, N., Mohapatra, A.K.: A comprehensive and critical analysis of TLS 1.3. J. Inf. Optim. Sci., 1–15 (2022)

17. Morawski, M., Karbowańczyk, M.: Multipath QUIC – directions of the improvements. In: Xiang, W., Han, F., Phan, T.K. (eds.) BROADNETS 2021. LNICST, vol. 413, pp. 193–207. Springer, Cham (2022). https://doi.org/10.1007/978-3-030-93479-8_13

18. Sharma, A., Kamthania, D.: QUIC protocol based monitoring probes for network devices monitor and alerts. In: Singh, U., Abraham, A., Kaklauskas, A., Hong, T.-P. (eds.) Smart Sensor Networks. SBD, vol. 92, pp. 127–150. Springer, Cham (2022). https://doi.org/10.1007/978-3-030-77214-7_6

19. Wu, B., Li, H., Wu, Q., Jiang, Z., Liu, J.: TMPTCP: a lightweight trust extension for multipath-TCP. In: 2020 International Conference on Networking and Network Applications, pp. 342–347. IEEE (2020)

20. Cao, Y., Ji, R., Ji, L., Lei, G., Wang, H., Shao, X.: l^2-MPTCP: a learning-driven latency-aware multipath transport scheme for industrial internet applications. IEEE Trans. Ind. Inf. **18**, 8456–8466 (2022)

21. Zheng, Z., et al.: Xlink: Qoe-driven multi-path QUIC transport in large-scale video services. In: Proceedings of the 2021 ACM SIGCOMM 2021 Conference 2021, pp. 418–432 (2021)

22. Xu, R., Joshi, J., Li, C.: NN-EMD: efficiently training neural networks using encrypted multi-sourced datasets. IEEE Trans. Dependable Sec. Comput. **19**, 2807–2820 (2021)

23. Du, S., Xu, Z., Lv, J.: An EMD-and GRU-based hybrid network traffic prediction model with data reconstruction. In: 2021 IEEE International Conference on Communications Workshops (ICC Workshops), pp. 1–7. IEEE (2021)

24. Malik, H., Alotaibi, M.A., Almutairi, A.: A new hybrid model combining EMD and neural network for multi-step ahead load forecasting. J. Intell. Fuzzy Syst. **42**(2), 1099–1114 (2022)

25. Tian, M., Sun, C., Wu, S.: An EMD and ARMA-based network traffic prediction approach in SDN-based internet of vehicles. Wirel. Netw., 1–3 (2021)

26. Tian, Z., Song, P.: A novel network traffic combination prediction model. Int. J. Commun. Syst. **35**(7), e5097 (2022)

27. Zhang, L., et al.: LNTP: an end-to-end online prediction model for network traffic. IEEE Netw. **35**(1), 226–233 (2020)

28. Cao, Y., Ji, R., Huang, X., Lei, G., Shao, X., You, I.: Empirical mode decomposition-empowered network traffic anomaly detection for secure multipath TCP communications. Mob. Netw. Appl. **27**, 2254–2263 (2022)

29. Tao, X., Peng, Y., Zhao, F., Wang, S.F., Liu, Z.: An improved parallel network traffic anomaly detection method based on bagging and GRU. In: Yu, D., Dressler, F., Yu, J. (eds.) WASA 2020. LNCS, vol. 12384, pp. 420–431. Springer, Cham (2020). https://doi.org/10.1007/978-3-030-59016-1_35

30. Wu, Z., Huang, N.E.: Ensemble empirical mode decomposition: a noise-assisted data analysis method. Adv. Adapt. Data Anal. **1**(01), 1–41 (2009)

31. Flandrin, P., Rilling, G., Goncalves, P.: Empirical mode decomposition as a filter bank. IEEE Sign. Process. Lett. **11**(2), 112–114 (2004)

32. Wu, Z., Huang, N.E.: A study of the characteristics of white noise using the empirical mode decomposition method. In: Proceedings of the Royal Society of London, pp. 1597–1611 (2004)

33. Flandrin, P., Gonçalves, P., Rilling, G.: EMD equivalent filter banks, from interpretation to applications. In: Hilbert-Huang Transform and its Applications, pp. 57–74 (2005)

An Extended TODIM Method for Multi-criteria Decision Making Under q-Rung Orthopair Fuzzy Environment

Shanshan Qiu[1,2,3], Qinmin[1,2], Qinghua Liu[1], Yanru Chen[4], Zhen Jin[5], and Xiaofang Deng[1,3(✉)]

[1] Software School, Jiangxi Normal University, Nanchang 330027, People's Republic of China
dxf@gzmtu.edu.cn
[2] Management Science and Engineering Research Center, Jiangxi Normal University, Nanchang 330027, People's Republic of China
[3] School of Information and Communication Engineering, Guangzhou Maritime University, Guangzhou 510725, People's Republic of China
[4] Foreign Languages College, Jiangxi Normal University, Nanchang 330022, People's Republic of China
[5] Department of Fundamental and Social Science, Guangzhou Maritime University, Guangzhou 510725, People's Republic of China

Abstract. Multi-criteria fuzzy decision making theory is one of the important tools to solve modern decision making problems. Facing complex and changeable decision making problems in real life, decision makers evaluate and quantify various decisions based on expert index system. They evaluate and rank options through a series of methods to produce scientific and reasonable results. The purpose of this paper is to propose a new q-rung orthopair fuzzy number (q-ROFN) ranking method based on the analysis of the existing q-ROFN ranking methods, and apply this new proposal in the TOMID decision making method.

Keywords: q-rung orthopair fuzzy number · Multi-criteria decision making (MCDM) · Ranking function

1 Introduction

Decision making is essential to people's daily lives, Such as the choice of clothing, food, lifestyle and even major national decisions. How do people make decisions? Ancients often relied on their previous experience to make decisions, but in current society, Decisions are made based on various considerations. In this case, even for a simple decision, needs a comprehensive consideration, and all these considerations constitute the criteria for making certain decision. Due to the complexity of real-world problems and the limitations of the cognitive level of experts, evaluating quasi is not completely objective, there is widespread uncertainty and hesitation when considering problems. In 1965, Zadeh [1] proposed the theory of Fuzzy set (Fuzzy set, FS), the membership degree

Y. Cao and X. Shao (Eds.): MONAMI 2022, LNICST 474, pp. 423–436, 2023.
https://doi.org/10.1007/978-3-031-32443-7_31

$\mu(x)$ indicates the degree of support for an attribute of x. This is used to quantify the options and help make decisions. In 1970, Bellman and Zadeh [2] introduced fuzzy set theory into multi-criteria decision making, they proposed the concepts and models of fuzzy decision making analysis and used this theory to solve the problem of uncertainty in practical decision making. However, the single membership μ of the fuzzy set can only represent the content of "if it is non-black $(1 - \mu(x))$ then it be white $(\mu(x))$", so it cannot describe a neutrality state. Due to this limitation, in 1983, the Bulgarian scholar Atanassov [3] proposed the concept of Intuitionistic Fuzzy Set (Intuitionistic Fuzzy Set, IFS). In contrast to the fuzzy set with a single scale measurement, Atanassov introduces the notion of non-membership degree $v(x)$ and the hesitation degree, and defined that an IFS must meet the sum of membership, non-membership, and hesitation degree $\pi(x)$ is less than or equal to 1. Thus, the IFS can simultaneously express support (membership degree) $\mu(x)$, , against (non-membership degree) $v(x)$, , and no support or against (hesitation degree) $\pi(x)$. To enrich the expression form of the criterion, Atanassov [4] proposed the concept of Interval-valued intuition fuzzy sets (Interval-valued intuition fuzzy sets, IVIFS). It means we can represent membership and non-membership in the form of interval values. The introduction of this concept increases the validity of decision making and attracts attention from many experts and scholars [5, 6] who apply it to teaching practice [7], smart medical [8], financial investment [9], evaluation system [10] and other fields [11]. But this expression form also has some limitations in the range of representation of the data. To expand the range of expression of intuitionistic fuzzy numbers, Yager [12] introduced the concept of Pythagorean fuzzy set (Pythagorean fuzzy set, PFS), and defined that the sum of the square of membership degree and non-membership is less than or equal to 1. Yager extended the triangular region of the intuitive fuzzy set to the sector region of the Pythagoras fuzzy set. The proposal of this concept provided an extended direction for the study of fuzzy sets. Yager [13] proposed a series of operators including weighted average operators, weighted geometry operators, weighted power average operators, weighted power geometric operators, and ordered weighted average operators of PF, to solve MCDM problems. Gou et al. [14] defined the PF functions, and further investigated the continuity, derivability, and differentiability of the PF functions, and enriched the PFS theory. Peng and Yang [15] defined some new operating methods of Pythagoras fuzzy clustering operators, and discussed their boundedness, idempotent, and monotonicity, etc. With the abundance of PF related operators, the MCDM related with PF was widely awakened by experts. Zhang and Xu [16] proposed new ranking methods that expand the TOPSIS decision making method to solve the MCDM problem by computing the distance to the positive and negative ideal solutions. Zhang [17] innovated the idea of relative progress and proposed a ranking method of the Pythagorean fuzzy numbers and the Interval-valued Pythagorean fuzzy numbers (Interval-valued Pythagorean fuzzy numbers, IVPFNs). Ho et al. [18] proposed a Pearson-based association measure method to obtain the ranking results by scoring the interval-valued Pythagoras fuzzy numbers. And Qiu [19] proposed a new ranking method about Interval-valued Pythagoras fuzzy ranking methods. These methods enrich the fuzzy decision making theory, broaden the application scope of fuzzy decision making, and greatly enhance the vitality of fuzzy decision making.

Although the PF fuzzy set extends the triangular region of the intuitive fuzzy set to the sector region. The Pythagoras fuzzy set still has some limitations. For example, the number $(0.8, 0.7)$ goes beyond the scope of the Pythagorean fuzzy set, $0.8^2 + 0.7^2 > 1$. Therefore, in 2017, Yager [20] proposed the concept of Orthopair Fuzzy Set (Orthopair Fuzzy Set, OFS) and Interval-Valued Orthopair Fuzzy Set (Interval-Valued Orthopair Fuzzy Set, IVOFS). The q-rung orthopair fuzzy set extended the range of membership and non-membership to square regions of edge length 1, thus it greatly expanded the scope of the research. Yager [20] proposed the concept of q-rung Orthopair Fuzzy Set (q-rung Orthopair Fuzzy Set, or q-ROFS), which was a generalization of the fuzzy set. When $q = 1$, it represents the intuitive fuzzy set; when $q = 2$, it indicates the Pythagorean fuzzy set; When $q \geqslant 3$, it can indicate the $(0.8, 0.7)$ and more fuzzy numbers. So far, some scholars have conducted some theoretical studies on q-ROFS [21–23].

To provide practical decision making schemes, experts and scholars have conducted specific studies on the ranking problem of q-ROFNS. Yager [20] proposed a score function based on membership and non-membership, but since it was difficult for this method to distinguish the degree of merits and demerits of two q-ROFNs in some cases, Yager proposed a further precise function in [24], Post-supplementary sequencing method. This method overcame the problem of failing to distinguish certain fuzzy numbers in [20], but there are still deficiencies in the judgment of the advantages and disadvantages of fuzzy numbers. Thus, Liu and Wang [25] proposed a score function for the sum of informative quantities. Peng [26] improved Yager's ranking method, To avoid the loss of information, Peng et al. aggregated the hesitation value information and proposed new scoring functions and ranking methods, but this method Could not compare two fuzzy numbers with the same membership and non-membership values. And this problem also exists in [27]. In order to solve the above problem, Mi [28] defined a score function for q-ROF environments, Peng [29] added the hesitation degree to the operation and Wang [30] proposed a new ranking method to rank q-ROFNs with high accuracy, in which they solved this problem to different degrees. However, the change in q-values in the q-ROFNS environment, when calculated by these three methods, will cause the completely opposite results. These methods still need to be perfected. Therefore, more research is necessary in the q-ROFNS ranking problem.

In terms of expanding decision making methods, Garg [31] combined the AHP and TOPSIS fuzzy decision making theory to present a new solution to the interval value q-ROFS fuzzy decision problem. But in terms of q-ROF fuzzy decision making issues, the current study only extends it to the TOPSIS method, and the problem with the TOPSIS method is its failure to reflect the proximity of each solution to the ideal solution. TODIM reflects experts' different preferences for earnings and loss. It constructs the advantage matrix of pairwise comparison in which the attribute advantages of each candidate are combined to be the basis of further ranking of these candidates. As we can see, TODIM decision method provides a ranking method based on prospect theory. This ranking method makes the decision more rational. This prospect theory considers that the judgment of decision making experts may have certain limitations at the rational level, and this consideration reduces the risk caused by experts misjudgment and then, more and more experts and scholars started studying the TODIM approach [32–35].

Through a review of the above studies, we found that the ranking function for q-ROF environments have partial drawbacks and decision making methods which suitable for q-ROF environments are yet to be developed. This paper will focus on the relevant ranking method and the distance formula of the q-ROFNs. The main contributions of this article are as follows:

1) proposed a new q-ROFNs ranking method and based on the analysis of the existing q-ROFNs ranking method;
2) Defined a new distance measure for q-ROFNs;
3) The TODIM method is extended to q-ROFNs environment by combing traditional TODIM with the proposed ranking method and the distance formula.

The rest of the paper is organized as follows: Sect. 2 mainly reviews the basic concepts of q-ROFS and introduces some existing research foundations; Sect. 3 presents a new q-ROFNS-based scoring function and ranking method for information reliability; Sect. 4 presents new distance formulas based on q-ROFNs; Sect. 5 generalizes the TODIM approach to q-ROF decision making environments.

2 Preliminary

This section introduces some relevant definitions and computational rules of q-ROFS, and introduces a traditional distance formula. These basic theories lay the theoretical basis for the study of q-ROFS.

Definition 1. [20] Let X be an ordinary set, then a q-ROFS A defined on X is given by

$$A = \langle x, \mu_A(x), \nu_A(x) | x \in X \rangle \tag{1}$$

where $\mu_A(x)$ and $\nu_A(x)$ are the membership and non-membership degrees, respectively, and $0 \leqslant \mu_A(x) \leqslant 1, 0 \leqslant \nu_A(x) \leqslant 1$ and $0 \leqslant \mu_A(x)^q + \nu_A(x)^q \leqslant 1$. And $\pi_A(x)$ is the hesitancy degree, $0 \leqslant \pi_A(x) \leqslant 1$ and $\pi_A(x) = (1 - (\mu_A(x)^q + \nu_A(x)^q))^{1/q}$.

Definition 2. [25] Given three q-ROFNs $A = (\mu, \nu), A_1 = (\mu_1, \nu_1)$ and $A_2 = (\mu_2, \nu_2)$, and they satisfy the following operational rules.

1. $A_1 \oplus A_2 = \left((\mu_1^q + \mu_2^q - \mu_1^q \mu_2^q)^{1/q}, \nu_1 \nu_2 \right)$
2. $A_1 \otimes A_2 = \left(\mu_1 \mu_2, (\nu_1^q + \nu_2^q - \nu_1^q \nu_2^q)^{1/q} \right)$
3. $\lambda A = \left((1 - (1 - \mu^q)^\lambda)^{1/q}, \nu^q \right)$
4. $A^\lambda = \left(\mu^\lambda, (1 - (1 - \nu^q)^\lambda)^{1/q} \right)$

Where, λ is a positive real number.

Definition 3. [36] Let $A(\mu_A, v_A)$ and $B(\mu_B, v_B)$ be any two q-ROFNs, And their hesitancy degree are $\pi_A(x) = (1 - (\mu_A(x)^q + v_A(x)^q))^{1/q}$ and $\pi_B(x) = (1 - (\mu_B(x)^q + v_B(x)^q))^{1/q}$ respectively, then the hamming distance measure of two q-ROFNs A and B is defined as follows.

$$d(A, B) = \frac{1}{2}\left(\left|\mu_A(x)^q - \mu_B(x)^q\right| + \left|v_A(x)^q - v_B(x)^q\right| + \left|\pi_A(x)^q - \pi_B(x)^q\right|\right) \quad (2)$$

These definitions are augmented based on the original Pythagoras fuzzy set. By doing so, the fuzzy set theory and its application are being enriched. Meanwhile, this augmented distance formula transforms abstract data comparisons into metrics on vectors. Both of them provide a theoretical basis for the study of fuzzy decision-making.

3   A New Ranking Method for q-rung Orthopair Fuzzy Numbers

Based on the above study analysis, we learn that the existing scoring function still has some problems in dealing with the q-rung orthopair fuzzy ordering problem of order q-ROFNS. For example, 1) Some score functions contradict common sense, thus the accuracy is not high; 2) Some scoring functions are exactly the opposite of all other methods, thus reliability is insufficient; 3) Some scoring functions do not adapt to the change of q value in q-ROFN and its stability needs to be improved. As we can see, there are still some problems needs to be overcome. So, to address the above problems, we propose new scoring functions and ranking method.

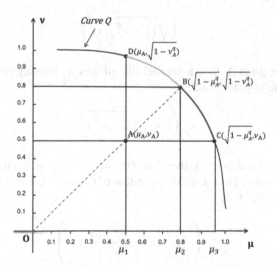

Fig. 1. Geometric illustration of the proposed ranking method

As shown in Fig. 1, The values of the q-rung orthopair fuzzy number of order q is presented on the right axis of the plane. Curve Q indicates the q-ROFNs with a hesitation degree of 0, and the value of q-ROFNs is $\mu^q + v^q - 1 \leqslant 0$. For any two points

$A = (\mu_A, \nu_A)$ and $F = (\mu_F, \nu_F)$ in the range of values, take point A as an example. It contains information of membership degree μ_A (μ axis) and ν_A (ν axis). This information is expanded to project the curve Q in the μ-axis direction to obtain point C, and point D is obtained by making the projection of curve Q in the axis direction of ν. In this way, this information is expanded to obtain the length of arc BD, arc BC, and arc CD. The advantage of this practice is that we can obtain more effective information by reasonably mining the potential value of existing data. By obtaining the length of line segment through arc differential equation, the comparison of abstract fuzzy number can be transformed into visual length comparison, which improves the readability and understandability of fuzzy number comparison. Membership (μ-axis) and non-membership (ν-axis) represent different meanings respectively. The greater the degree of membership (or non-membership), the better the value. Following this principle, this method fully extracts the information of q-order orthogonal fuzzy numbers, and makes some improvements (μ) and ($1/\nu$) Adjustment in direction, and according to this condition, reasonable comparison and ranking methods are proposed to obtain the score value $S(A)$ of point A. Similarly, we can obtain the score value $S(F)$ of point F. The final ranking is obtained by comparing the sizes of $S(A)$ and $S(A)$.

Take point A as an example, the specific calculation steps and calculation methods are shown below.

As Fig. 1 shows, Q is a curve $\mu^q + \nu^q - 1 = 0$, $A = (\mu_A, \nu_A)$ is a q-ROFN, μ_A is membership degree of A, ν_A is non-membership degree of A.

1) Over point A draw a parallel line of axis X which meets curve Q at point C. The coordinate of point C is,

$$\left(\sqrt[q]{\left(1 - \nu_A^q\right)}, \nu_A \right) \tag{3}$$

2) Similarly, over point A draw a parallel line of axis X, meeting curve Q at point D. The coordinate of point D is,

$$\left(\mu_A, \sqrt[q]{\left(1 - \mu_A^q\right)} \right) \tag{4}$$

3) Connect point O and point A, then line OA means $L : \nu = \nu_A/\mu_A \times \mu$ (A straight line over the origin). Draw the extension line of OA and meet curve Q at point B, the coordinate of point B is,

$$\left(\frac{\mu_A}{\sqrt[q]{\mu_A^q + \nu_A^q}}, \frac{\nu_A}{\sqrt[q]{\mu_A^q + \nu_A^q}} \right) \tag{5}$$

When point A is located on curve Q, the hesitancy degree of q-ROFN A is 0. Then there is no intersection point B, C, D. Therefore, the distance of point A from curve Q is 0. Point A has the highest degree of information reliability, and the larger of μ_A, the better the q-ROFN A.

When point A is not on the curve Q, according to the principle of arc length, the farther point A is from curve Q, the lower the reliability and the longer the arc length CD. Based on this, we use arc-length CD as a measure to represent the information reliability of q-ROFN A.

$$L_{CD} = L_{BC} + L_{BD} \tag{6}$$

where, L_{CD} is the length of arc CD, L_{BD} is the length of arc BD, L_{BC} is the length of arc BC. Use the arc differential formula,

$$L_{BD} = \int_{\mu_s}^{\mu_v} \sqrt{1 + (f'(\mu))^2} d\mu \tag{7}$$

$$L_{BC} = \int_{\mu_c}^{\mu_s} \sqrt{1 + (f'(\mu))^2} d\mu \tag{8}$$

where, $f'(\mu)$ indicates the log μ for the derivative, and $\int_{\mu_B}^{\mu_D} X$, $\int_{\mu_C}^{\mu_B} X$ express the Integrals of arcBD and arcBC in the direction. The equation $L = \int_{x_2}^{x_1} \sqrt{1 + (f'(x))^2} dx$ is the arc differential equation.

And, the smaller of non-membership degree, the better the q-ROFN is. Considering this factor, we proposed a new score function.

Definition 4. A new ranking method is proposed.

$$S = \frac{\mu + 1}{\frac{v^* L_{CD}}{L} + 1} \tag{9}$$

where L is the total length of the curve Q. For two q-ROFNs $q_1(\mu_{q_1}, v_{q_1})$, $q_2(\mu_{q_2}, v_{q_2})$, the ranking methods are as follows.

$$\begin{aligned}
&IF\ S(q_1) > S(q_2),\ THEN\ q_1 \succ q_2 \\
&IF\ S(q_1) < S(q_2),\ THEN\ q_1 \prec q_2 \\
&IF\ S(q_1) = S(q_2),\ THEN\ q_1\ q_2
\end{aligned} \tag{10}$$

4   A New Distance Measure for q-rung Orthopair Fuzzy Numbers

The study of the existing distance formulas is based on the general fuzzy numbers, while the q-ROFNs expand the expression range of the data infinitely, and the existing distance formulas have some limitations to both the accuracy of the data and the completeness of the information. Therefore, it is very necessary to propose a distance formula adapted to q-ROFNs environment.

Definition 5. Because of the development of fuzzy numbers, previous experts and scholars have extended the expression of q-ROFNs. To fit the expression of the q-ROFNs, we also extend the distance formula to order q. The proposed distance formula is as follows.

$$d(q_1, q_2) = \sqrt[q]{\frac{1}{2}\left(\left|\sqrt[q]{\mu_{q_1}^q} - \mu_{q_2}^q\right| + \left|\sqrt[q]{v_{q_1}^q} - v_{q_2}^q \ominus\right| + \left|\sqrt[q]{\pi_{q_1}^q} - \pi_{q_2}^q \ominus\right|\right)} \tag{11}$$

The proposed distance formula satisfies the following three basic theorems,

Let $A_1 = (\mu_1, \nu_1)$ and $A_2 = (\mu_2, \nu_2)$ be two q-ROFNs, then

Property 1 $d(A_1, A_2) = d(A_2, A_1)$

Property 2 $d(A_1, A_2) = 0$ only if $A_1 = A_2$

Property 3 $0 \leqslant d(A_1, A_2) \leqslant 1$

Proof. For two q-ROFNs $A_1 = (\mu_{A_1}, \nu_{A_1})$ and $A_2 = (\mu_{A_2}, \nu_{A_2})$. $\mu_{A_1}, \mu_{A_2}, \nu_{A_1}, \nu_{A_2} \in$ [0, 1][0, 1], and $0 \leqslant \mu_{A_1}^q + \nu_{A_1}^q \leqslant 1, 0 \leqslant \mu_{A_2}^q + \nu_{A_2}^q \leqslant 1$. Then,

$$d(A_1, A_2) = \sqrt[q]{\frac{1}{2}\left(\left|\sqrt[q]{\mu_{A_1}^q - \mu_{A_2}^q}\right| + \left|\sqrt[q]{\nu_{A_1}^q - \nu_{A_2}^q}\right| + \left|\sqrt[q]{\pi_{A_1}^q - \pi_{A_2}^q}\right|\right)} = \sqrt[q]{\frac{1}{2}\left(\left|\sqrt[q]{\mu_{A_2}^q - \mu_{A_1}^q}\right| + \left|\sqrt[q]{\nu_{A_2}^q - \nu_{A_1}^q}\right| + \left|\sqrt[q]{\pi_{A_2}^q - \pi_{A_1}^q}\right|\right)} = 0$$

Let $d(A_1, A_2) = \sqrt[q]{\frac{1}{2}\left(\left|\sqrt[q]{\mu_{A_1}^q - \mu_{A_2}^q}\right| + \left|\sqrt[q]{\nu_{A_1}^q - \nu_{A_2}^q}\right| + \left|\sqrt[q]{\pi_{A_1}^q - \pi_{A_2}^q}\right|\right)} = 0$, it must

be $\left|\sqrt[q]{\mu_{A_1}^q - \mu_{A_2}^q}\right| = \left|\sqrt[q]{\nu_{A_1}^q - \nu_{A_2}^q}\right| = \left|\sqrt[q]{\pi_{A_1}^q - \pi_{A_2}^q}\right| = 0$, only when $\mu_{A_1} = \mu_{A_2}, \nu_{A_4} = \nu_{A_2}, \pi_{A_4} = \pi_{A_2}$ then the equations will only be established.

$$d(A_1, A_2) = \sqrt[q]{\frac{1}{2}\left(\left|\sqrt[q]{\mu_{A_1}^q - \mu_{A_2}^q}\right| + \left|\sqrt[q]{\nu_{A_1}^q - \nu_{A_2}^q}\right| + \left|\sqrt[q]{\pi_{A_1}^q - \pi_{A_2}^q}\right|\right)}$$

$$= \sqrt[q]{\frac{1}{2}\left(\left|\sqrt[q]{\mu_{A_1}^q - \mu_{A_2}^q}\right| + \left|\sqrt[q]{\nu_{A_1}^q - \nu_{A_2}^q}\right| + \left|\sqrt[q]{\left(1 - \mu_{A_1}^q - \nu_{A_1}^q\right) - \left(1 - \mu_{A_2}^q - \nu_{A_2}^q\right)}\right|\right)}$$

$$= \sqrt[q]{\frac{1}{2}\left(\left|\sqrt[q]{\mu_{A_1}^q - \mu_{A_2}^q}\right| + \left|\sqrt[q]{\nu_{A_1}^q - \nu_{A_2}^q}\right| + \left|\sqrt[q]{\left(\mu_{A_2}^q - \nu_{A_1}^q\right) + \left(\mu_{A_2}^q - \nu_{A_1}^q\right)}\right|\right)}$$

$$\leqslant \sqrt[q]{\frac{1}{2}\left(\left|\sqrt[q]{\mu_{A_1}^q}\right| + \left|\sqrt[q]{\nu_{A_1}^q}\right| + \left|\sqrt[q]{\mu_{A_2}^q + \nu_{A_2}^q}\right|\right)} \leqslant \sqrt[q]{\frac{q}{2}\left(\mu_{A_1}^q + \nu_{A_1}^q + \mu_{A_2}^q + \nu_{A_2}^q\right)} \leqslant 1$$

And it is obviously that $d(A_1, A_2) \geqslant 0$.

The distance formula proposed in this paper expands the data table widely based on the traditional distance, and it makes full use of precision of the data and the completeness of the information, So the calculation of the orthogonal fuzzy number distances of the two q orders can be more accurate.

5   The Extended TODIM Method Under q-rung Orthopair Fuzzy Environment

The TODIM method is the method proposed by Gomes [37]. It does not need to determine the reference point and it fully considers expert mindset. This method ranks candidates by calculating their relative advantages. The approach is defined as follows.

Let candidate set $A = \{A_1, A_2, \cdots, A_m\}$ as a collection of m options; C is a collection of n evaluation criteria. It is presented as $C = \{C_1, C_2, \cdots, C_n\}$ v. And the evaluation of the criteria weight vectors is s$\omega = \{\omega_1, \omega_2, \cdots, \omega_n\}^T$, where $\sum_{j=1}^{n} \omega_j = 1, 0 \leqslant \omega_j \leqslant 1$. we define $\omega_{jr} = \omega_j/\omega_r$ as the relative weight of the criterion C_j to C_r, and $\omega_r = \max\{\omega_j | j = 1, 2, \cdots, n\}$.

The evaluation value of candidate A on criteria C is expressed by $a_{ij} = (\mu_A, \nu_A)$, $(i = 1, 2, \cdots, m; j = 1, 2, \cdots, n)$. Where $0 \leqslant \mu_A^q \leqslant 1, 0 \leqslant \nu_A^q \leqslant 1, 0 \leqslant \mu_A^q + \nu_A^q \leqslant 1$. Then the classical TODIM approach involves the following steps.

Step 1. Construct the decision making matrix $X = \left[a_{ij}\right]_{m \times n}$.

Step 2. Consider experts' psychological behavior (i.e., the reference dependence and loss aversion). Calculate the relative dominance degree $\phi_j = (A_i, A_r)$ of scheme A_i to scheme A_r under each criterion C_j.

$$
\phi_j(A_i, A_r) = \begin{cases} \sqrt{\omega_{jr} * \left(a_{ij} - a_{rj}\right)/\sum_{j=1}^{n} \omega_{jr}} & IF\ a_{ij} - a_{rj} > 0 \\ 0 & IF\ a_{ij} - a_{rj} = 0 \\ -\frac{1}{\theta}\sqrt{\left(\sum_{j=1}^{n} \omega_{jr}\right) * \left(a_{ij} - a_{rj}\right)/\omega_{jr}} & IF\ a_{ij} - a_{rj} < 0 \end{cases} \quad (12)
$$

In the above dominance degree formula, θ is an attenuation factor of losses with a range of $0 < \theta < \sum_{j=1}^{n} \omega_j/\omega_r$ [38]. The smaller the value θ, the higher the experts' aversion to loss.

Step 3. According to the Dominance Degree Matrix, the Overall Dominance $\phi_j = (A_i, A_r)$ of the Scheme A_i for A_r Can Be Calculated.

$$
\phi(A_i, A_r) = \sum_{j=1}^{n} \phi_j(A_i, A_r), j \in N, r \in N \quad (13)
$$

Step 4. Comprehensively calculate the overall advantage of candidate A_i and other candidates $\Phi(A_i)$, and rank the candidates according to the size of $\Phi(A_i)$.

$$
\Phi(A_i) = \frac{\left(\sum_{r=1}^{n} \phi(A_i, A_r) - \min\left\{\sum_{r=1}^{n} \phi(A_i, A_r)\right\}\right)}{\max\left\{\sum_{r=1}^{n} \phi(A_i, A_r)\right\} - \min\left\{\sum_{r=1}^{n} \phi(A_i, A_r)\right\}} \quad (14)
$$

To accommodate the complexity of the data when solving practical problems, the proposed method extends every link of the TODIM decision making method process to order q. Firstly, it proposes a ranking comparison of q-rung orthopair fuzzy numbers of order q, then it proposes distance formulas that can accommodate the q-ROFS. Based on this, this paper integrates this approach with the traditional TODIM methods, and it proposes an extended TODIM decision making method based on q-rung orthopair fuzzy decision making of q-ROFS.

Step 1. Based on the decision making scheme, the main evaluation criteria, decision making experts evaluate different candidates A according to criterion C. Then we get the decision making matrix $X_q = \left[a_{ij}\right]_{m \times n}$, $a_{ij} = (\mu_A, \nu_A)(i = 1, 2, \cdots, m; j = 1, 2, \cdots, n)$. It is defined as follows.

$$
X_q = \left(a_{ij}\right)_{m \times n} = \begin{array}{c} \\ A_1 \\ A_2 \\ \vdots \\ A_m \end{array} \overset{\textstyle C_1\ C_2\ \cdots\ C_n}{\left[\begin{array}{cccc} a_{11} & a_{12} & \cdots & a_{1n} \\ a_{21} & a_{22} & \cdots & a_{2n} \\ \vdots & \vdots & \ddots & \vdots \\ a_{m1} & a_{m2} & \cdots & a_{mn} \end{array}\right]} \quad (15)
$$

Step 2. The relative weights of C_j were calculated based on the different weight values for each evaluation criterion.

$$\omega_{jr} = \omega_j / \omega_r, j, r = 1, 2 \ldots \ldots n \tag{16}$$

Where ω_j is the weight of the criterion C_j, $\omega_r = \max\{\omega_j \ominus j = 1, 2, \cdots, n\}$, and $0 \leqslant \omega_r \leqslant 1$

Step 3. Standardize the evaluation criteria and assign scores to each data metric using the proposed score function, then get the score matrix $S_q = \left[S_{ij}\right]_{m \times n}$, S_{ij} is a score value.

$$S_q = \left(s_{ij}\right)_{m \times n} = \begin{array}{c} \\ A_1 \\ A_2 \\ \vdots \\ A_m \end{array} \overset{\displaystyle C_1\ C_2 \cdots C_n}{\left[\begin{array}{cccc} s_{11} & s_{12} & \cdots & s_{1n} \\ s_{21} & s_{22} & \cdots & s_{2n} \\ \vdots & \vdots & \ddots & \vdots \\ s_{m1} & s_{m2} & \cdots & s_{mn} \end{array}\right]} \tag{17}$$

Step 4. Calculate the dominance degree under each criterion, and use the scoring matrix to make judgment and get a dominance degree matrix.

$$\phi_j(A_i, A_r) = \begin{cases} \sqrt{\omega_{jr} * d\left(a_{ij} - a_{rj}\right) / \sum_{j=1}^{n} \omega_{jr}} & \text{IF } s_{ij} - s_{rj} > 0 \\ 0 & \text{IF } s_{ij} - s_{rj} = 0 \\ -\frac{1}{\theta}\sqrt{\left(\sum_{j=1}^{n} \omega_{jr}\right) * d\left(a_{ij} - a_{rj}\right) / \omega_{jr}} & \text{IF } s_{ij} - s_{rj} < 0 \end{cases} \tag{18}$$

Consider the two matrices, X_q and S_q. If $s_{ij} > s_{rj}$, then the dominance degree of $\phi_j = (A_i, A_r)$ will be represented as $\sqrt{\omega_{jr} \times d\left(a_{ij}, a_{rj}\right) / \sum_{j=1}^{n} \omega_{jr}}$, where $d\left(a_{ij}, a_{rj}\right)$ is the distance formula for the expansion mentioned above. And if $s_{ij} = s_{rj}$, the dominance degree between a_{ij} and a_{rj} is zero.

From this, derive a dominance matrix of the jth criterion. And it is shown as follows.

$$\phi_j = \left[\phi_j(A_i, A_r)\right]_{(m \times m)} = \begin{array}{c} \\ A_1 \\ A_2 \\ \vdots \\ A_m \end{array} \overset{\displaystyle A_1 \; A_2 \; \cdots \; A_n}{\begin{bmatrix} 0 & \phi_j(A_1, A_2) & \dots & \phi_j(A_1, A_m) \\ \phi_j(A_2, A_1) & 0 & \dots & \phi_j(A_2, A_m) \\ \vdots & \vdots & \ddots & \vdots \\ \phi_j(A_n, A_1) & \phi_j(A_n, A_2) & \dots & 0 \end{bmatrix}} \tag{19}$$

Step 5. Calculate the overall dominance $\varphi(A_i)$ of each candidate A_i over the candidate A_i, the calculation method is as follows.

$$\varphi(A_i, A_t) = \sum_{j=1}^{m} \phi_j(A_i, A_t), i = 1, 2 \ldots m \tag{20}$$

The overall dominance matrix is obtained as follows.

$$\varphi = \left[\varphi(A_i, A_t)\right]_{(m \times m)} = \begin{array}{c} \\ A_1 \\ A_2 \\ \vdots \\ A_m \end{array} \overset{\displaystyle A_1 \; A_2 \; \cdots \; A_n}{\begin{bmatrix} 0 & \varphi_j(A_1, A_2) & \dots & \varphi_j(A_1, A_m) \\ \varphi_j(A_2, A_1) & 0 & \dots & \varphi_j(A_2, A_m) \\ \vdots & \vdots & \ddots & \vdots \\ \varphi_j(A_n, A_1) & \varphi_j(A_n, A_2) & \dots & 0 \end{bmatrix}} \tag{21}$$

Step 6. The Final Decision Making Value.

$$\Gamma(A_i) = \frac{\left(\sum_{r=1}^{n} \varphi(A_i, A_t) - \min\left\{\sum_{r=1}^{n} \varphi(A_i, A_t)\right\}\right)}{\max\left\{\sum_{r=1}^{n} \varphi(A_i, A_t)\right\} - \min\left\{\sum_{r=1}^{n} \varphi(A_i, A_t)\right\}} \tag{22}$$

To clearly illustrate the idea of the proposed method, we make a flow chart as shown in Fig. 2.

Compared to the traditional TODIM decision making method, the proposed method in this paper firstly innovates the score function in calculating the relative dominance degree, and it uses the geometric significance and connection between fuzzy numbers to propose a ranking method based on information reliability to compare the advantages and disadvantages of two fuzzy numbers; Secondly, this paper proposes a distance formula more adapted to the q-rung orthogonal fuzzy environments, and uses this distance formula to calculate the relative advantage matrix to increase the objectivity of the method; Finally, this paper extends the traditional TODIM decision method to the q-rung orthogonal fuzzy environment, and proposes the extended q-rung orthogonal fuzzy TODIM decision method by combining the proposed ranking method and the distance formula, and applies it to the decision making method.

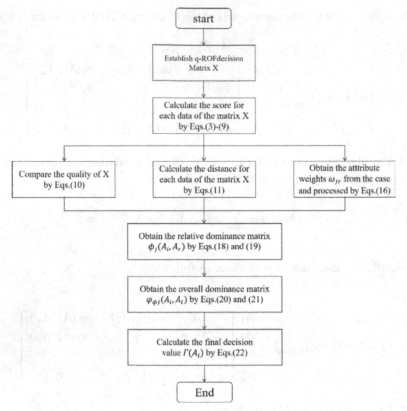

Fig. 2. Flow chart of decision making process

6 Conclusions

Based on the analysis of previous q-ROFNs ranking method, this paper proposes a new q-ROFNs ranking method by eliminating some drawbacks of the former. Besides, this paper proposes a new distance formula for q-ROFNs, and applies it to the decision making method.

References

1. Zadeh, L.A.: Fuzzy sets. Inf. Control **8**(3), 338–353 (1965)
2. Bellman, R.E., Zadeh, L.A.: Decision-making in a fuzzy environment. Manag. Sci. **17**(4), B-141–B−164 (1970). https://doi.org/10.1287/mnsc.17.4.B141
3. Atanassov, K.T.: Intuitionistic fuzzy sets. Fuzzy Sets Syst. **20**(1), 87–96 (1986)
4. Atanassov, K.T., Gargov, G.: Interval valued intuitionistic fuzzy sets. Fuzzy Sets Syst. **31**(3), 343–349 (1989)
5. Atanassov, K.T.: Operators over interval valued intuitionistic fuzzy sets. Fuzzy Sets Syst. **64**(2), 159–174 (1994)
6. Xie, J., Liu, S.: Cartesian product over interval valued intuitionistic fuzzy sets. J. Syst. Eng. Electron. **28**(6), 1152–1161 (2017)

7. Zhang, Z.H., et al.: Some average index models on interval valued intuitionistic fuzzy sets and their application to practical teaching evaluation in university. In: International Conference on Advanced Educational Technology and Information Engineering, pp. 84–91 (2015)
8. Büyüközkan, G., Göçer, F.: Smart medical device selection based on interval valued intuitionistic fuzzy VIKOR. In: Kacprzyk, J., Szmidt, E., Zadrożny, S., Atanassov, K.T., Krawczak, M. (eds.) IWIFSGN/EUSFLAT -2017. AISC, vol. 641, pp. 306–317. Springer, Cham (2018). https://doi.org/10.1007/978-3-319-66830-7_28
9. Zhang, Z., et al.: Incentive-punitive risk function with interval valued intuitionistic fuzzy information for outsourced software project risk assessment. J. Intell. Fuzzy Syst. 32(5), 3749–3760 (2017)
10. Sennaroglu, B., Mutlu, M., Tuzkaya, G.: An interval valued intuitionistic fuzzy promethee approach for hospital service quality evaluation. In: Zeng, X., et al. (eds.) Uncertainty Modelling In Knowledge Engineering and Decision Making, vol. 10, pp. 588–594 (2016)
11. Garg, H., Kumar, K.: A novel possibility measure to interval-valued intuitionistic fuzzy set using connection number of set pair analysis and its applications. Neural Comput. Appl. 32(8), 3337–3348 (2019). https://doi.org/10.1007/s00521-019-04291-w
12. Yager, R.R., Abbasov, A.M.: Pythagorean membership grades, complex numbers, and decision making. Int. J. Intell. Syst. 28(5), 436–452 (2013)
13. Yager, R.R.: Pythagorean membership grades in multicriteria decision making. IEEE Trans. Fuzzy Syst. 22(4), 958–965 (2014)
14. Gou, X., Xu, Z., Ren, P.: The properties of continuous pythagorean fuzzy information. Int. J. Intell. Syst. 31(5), 401–424 (2016)
15. Peng, X., Yang, Y.: Some results for pythagorean fuzzy sets. Int. J. Intell. Syst. 30(11), 1133–1160 (2015)
16. Liang, D., Xu, Z.: The new extension of TOPSIS method for multiple criteria decision making with hesitant Pythagorean fuzzy sets. Appl. Soft Comput. 60, 167–179 (2017)
17. Zhang, X.: Multicriteria Pythagorean fuzzy decision analysis: A hierarchical QUALIFLEX approach with the closeness index-based ranking methods. Inf. Sci. 330, 104–124 (2016)
18. Ho, L.-H., Lin, Y.-L., Chen, T.-Y.: A Pearson-like correlation-based TOPSIS method with interval-valued Pythagorean fuzzy uncertainty and its application to multiple criteria decision analysis of stroke rehabilitation treatments. Neural Comput. Appl. 32(12), 8265–8295 (2019). https://doi.org/10.1007/s00521-019-04304-8
19. Qiu, S., Fu, D., Deng, X.: A multicriteria selection framework for wireless communication infrastructure with interval-valued pythagorean fuzzy assessment. Wirel. Commun. Mob. Comput. 2021, 9913737 (2021)
20. Yager, R.R.: Generalized Orthopair Fuzzy Sets. IEEE Trans. Fuzzy Syst. 25(5), 1222–1230 (2017)
21. Liu, Z., Wang, X., Li, L., Zhao, X., Liu, P.: Q-rung orthopair fuzzy multiple attribute group decision-making method based on normalized bidirectional projection model and generalized knowledge-based entropy measure. J. Ambient. Intell. Humaniz. Comput. 12(2), 2715–2730 (2020). https://doi.org/10.1007/s12652-020-02433-w
22. Pinar, A., Boran, F.E.: A q-rung orthopair fuzzy multi-criteria group decision making method for supplier selection based on a novel distance measure. Int. J. Mach. Learn. Cybern. 11(8), 1749–1780 (2020). https://doi.org/10.1007/s13042-020-01070-1
23. Garg, H.: A novel trigonometric operation-based q-rung orthopair fuzzy aggregation operator and its fundamental properties. Neural Comput. Appl. 32(18), 15077–15099 (2020)
24. Wei, G., Gao, H., Wei, Y.: Some q-rung orthopair fuzzy Heronian mean operators in multiple attribute decision making. Int. J. Intell. Syst. 33(7), 1426–1458 (2018)
25. Liu, P., Wang, P.: Some q-rung orthopair fuzzy aggregation operators and their applications to multiple-attribute decision making. Int. J. Intell. Syst. 33(2), 259–280 (2018)

26. Peng, X., Dai, J., Garg, H.: Exponential operation and aggregation operator for q-rung orthopair fuzzy set and their decision-making method with a new score function. Int. J. Intell. Syst. **33**(11), 2255–2282 (2018)

27. Peng, X., Dai, J.: Research on the assessment of classroom teaching quality with q-rung orthopair fuzzy information based on multiparametric similarity measure and combinative distance-based assessment. Int. J. Intell. Syst. **34**(7), 1588–1630 (2019)

28. Mi, X., et al.: Hospitality brand management by a score-based q-rung ortho pair fuzzy VIKOR method integrated with the best worst method. Econ. Res.-Ekonomska istraživanja. **32**(1), 3266–3295 (2019)

29. Peng, X., Krishankumar, R., Ravichandran, K.S.: Generalized orthopair fuzzy weighted distance-based approximation (WDBA) algorithm in emergency decision-making. Int. J. Intell. Syst. **34**(10), 2364–2402 (2019)

30. Wang, J., et al.: A novel approach to multi-attribute group decision-making based on q-rung orthopair fuzzy power dual Muirhead mean operators and novel score function. J. Intell. Fuzzy Syst. **39**(1), 561–580 (2020)

31. Garg, H., Ali, Z., Mahmood, T.: Algorithms for complex interval-valued q-rung orthopair fuzzy sets in decision making based on aggregation operators, AHP, and TOPSIS. Expert Syst. **38**, e12609 (2020)

32. Ren, P., Xu, Z., Gou, X.: Pythagorean fuzzy TODIM approach to multi-criteria decision making. Appl. Soft Comput. **42**, 246–259 (2016)

33. Chen, L., Luo, N., Gou, X.: A novel q-rung orthopair fuzzy TODIM approach for multi-criteria group decision making based on Shapley value and relative entropy. J. Intell. Fuzzy Syst. **40**(1), 235–250 (2021)

34. Prakash, K., et al.: Lifetime prolongation of a wireless charging sensor network using a mobile robot via linear Diophantine fuzzy graph environment. Complex Intell. Syst. **8**(3), 2419–2434 (2022). https://doi.org/10.1007/s40747-022-00653-5

35. Garg, K., Chauhan, N., Agrawal, R.: Optimized resource allocation for fog network using neuro-fuzzy offloading approach. Arabian J. Sci. Eng. **47**(8), 10333–10346 (2022). https://doi.org/10.1007/s13369-022-06563-5

36. Liu, P., Liu, W.: Multiple-attribute group decision-making method of linguistic q-rung orthopair fuzzy power Muirhead mean operators based on entropy weight. Int. J. Intell. Syst. **34**(8), 1755–1794 (2019)

37. Gomes, L.F.A.M., Lima, M.M.P.P.: TODIM: basics and application to multicriteria ranking of projects with environmental impacts. Found. Comput. Decis. Sci. **16**(4), 113–127 (1992)

38. Lahdelma, R., Salminen, P.: Prospect theory and stochastic multicriteria acceptability analysis (SMAA). Omega **37**(5), 961–971 (2009)

Author Index

Printed in the United States
by Baker & Taylor Publisher Services